"This book is an excellent source for vi
accommodations in the area's small comm...
off-the-beaten-track resorts and lodges . . . a great book to κ...
—Outdoor Retailer

" . . . a top-notch trail guide opus. Directions to the trailhead are
explicit, the maps are simple and clear, the index is good,
and the trail descriptions are excellent, detailed beyond
any other trail guide you are likely to find."
—Sierra Club *Bonanza*

"Morey makes the High Sierra appealing and accessible, combining
marvelous dayhikes with comfortable lodging."
—Library Research Associates

". . . this book is a good read in itself."
—*Sierra Heritage*

"I loved the detail of the description . . . an excellent guide for hiking trips."
—Sierra Club *Loma Prietan*

"With this book you need no longer quail before the soaring massif of
the Sierra Nevada range. It tells you everything you need to know."
—*Books of the Southwest*

". . . a top-notch trail guide."
—Sierra Club *Toiyabe Trails*

Cathedral Peak, Trip 76

Hot Showers, Soft Beds, & Dayhikes in the Sierra

WALKS & STROLLS
NEAR LODGINGS

Kathy Morey

 WILDERNESS PRESS ... *on the trail since 1967*
BERKELEY, CA

Hot Showers, Soft Beds, & Dayhikes in the Sierra: Walks & Strolls near Lodgings

1st EDITION October 1996
2nd EDITION October 2002
3rd EDITION July 2008
   2nd printing 2010

Front cover photos copyright © 2008 by Kathy Morey
Interior photos and maps, except where noted, by the author
Cover design, book design, and layout: Lisa Pletka
Book editor: Laura Shauger

ISBN 978-0-89997-435-4

Manufactured in the United States of America

Published by: **Wilderness Press**
               1345 8th Street
               Berkeley, CA 94710
               (800) 443-7227; FAX (510) 558-1696
               info@wildernesspress.com
               www.wildernesspress.com
Visit our website for a complete listing of our books and for ordering information.
Distributed by Publishers Group West

Cover photos (clockwise from upper left):
Crystal Crag over Tarn (Trip 22); view eastward up Yosemite Valley over the Merced
River to North Dome (left) and Half Dome (Trip 79); Lower Yosemite falls; Sierra Crest
from Bishop in the Owens Valley; the second crossing of McGee Creek (Trip 15); giant
sequoias in the Mariposa Grove (Trip 61)

SAFETY NOTICE: Although Wilderness Press and the author have made every attempt
to ensure that the information in this book is accurate at press time, they are not responsible for any loss, damage, injury, or inconvenience that may occur to anyone while using
this book. You are responsible for your own safety and health while in the wilderness.
The fact that a trail is described in this book does not mean that it will be safe for you.
Be aware that trail conditions can change from day to day. Always check local conditions
and know your own limitations.

Sierra Nevada Overview

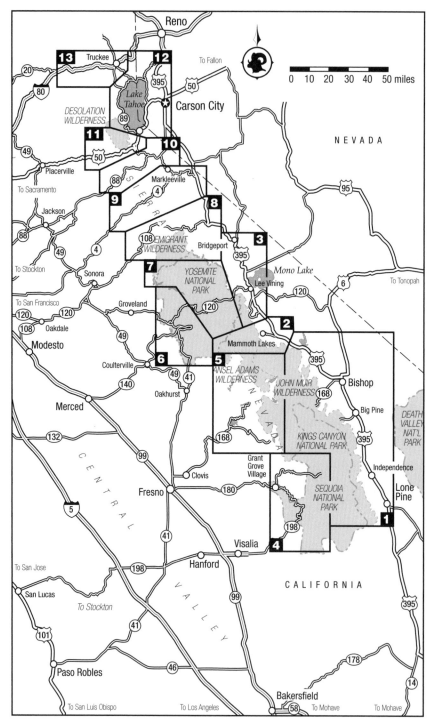

Contents

Eastern Sierra

Western Sierra

Northern Sierra

Summary of the Trips' Best Features

Below is a summary of the highlights of all 112 hikes. Trip type and difficulty level are explained on pp. 12–13. The distance in miles is the total to and from the first interim destination, if any, followed by the total to and from the last destination. The best features covers lakes, flora, waterfalls, views, and fall color. "Lakes" means that a lake, or several lakes, is the hike's best feature. "Flora" means that the hike features a fine, but seasonal display of flowers, except for the hikes where the "Flora" column contains a tree icon, which indicates that a hike visits giant sequoias (*that's* flora!). "Falls" means the hike features waterfalls and either reaches them or has a great view of a waterfall. "View" means that a hike has superb, long-ranging views. "Color" means that a hike features a fine, but seasonal, fall-color display. If you're looking for different kinds of interesting features, see Appendix A: Top Picks (page 316).

Trip Number and Title	Trip Type	Distance in Miles	Difficulty Level	Best Features				
				Lakes	Flora	Falls	Views	Fall Color
1 Chicken Spring Lake	O&B	3–9	E–S	X			X	
2 Lone Pine Lake	O&B	5.5	M	X		X		X
3 Kearsarge Trail Lakes	O&B	3.3–6.6	M–S	X		X		
4 Big Pine Lakes	O&B	0.5–9.5	E–S	X		X		
5 Treasure Lakes	O&B	6	S	X			X	
6 Chocolate Lakes Loop	Semi	4.5–7.5	M–S	X			X	
7 Bishop Lake	O&B	4.5–8.6	M–S	X			X	
8 Lake Sabrina and Blue, Donkey, Emerald, and Dingleberry Lakes	O&B	6–9.6	S	X				
9 Grass and Lamarck Lakes	O&B	3.5–7.5	M–S	X				X
10 Loch Leven and Piute Lake	O&B	6.6–9	S	X	X	X	X	X
11 Francis and Dorothy Lakes	O&B	5.5–8.5	M–S	X	X			
12 Hilton Lakes	O&B	8.6–10	S	X				
13 Little Lakes Valley	O&B	1–6.5	E–S	X	X		X	
14 Ruby Lake	O&B	1–4.5	E–S	X			X	
15 McGee Canyon to Grass Lake	O&B	6–10	M–S	X	X			X
16 Convict Lake	Semi	3	E	X				
17 Sherwin and Valentine Lakes	O&B	4–9.5	M–S	X				
18 Heart Lake	O&B	2	E	X			X	
19 Duck Pass	O&B	2.6–9.3	E–S	X			X	
20 Emerald and Skelton Lakes	Loop	1.5–3.25	E–M	X				
21 Barrett and T J Lakes	O&B	1–1.5	E	X				
22 Crystal Lake and Crest	O&B	2.75–6	E–S	X		X	X	

Trip Number and Title	Trip Type	Distance in Miles	Difficulty Level	Best Features				
				Lakes	Flora	Falls	Views	Fall Color
23 McCloud Lake and Red Cones	Semi	1–7.6	E–S	X	X		X	
24 San Joaquin Ridge	O&B	4.5	M		X		X	
25 Olaine and Shadow Lakes	O&B	3–7	M–S	X		X		
26 Minaret Falls	O&B	1–3.5	M			X		
27 Johnston Lake	O&B	1–5	M	X		X		
28 Rainbow and Lower Falls	O&B	2–3	E–M			X		
29 Fern and Yost Lakes	O&B	3–5.6	M–S	X			X	
30 Agnew and Gem Lakes	O&B	5–7	S	X		X	X	
31 Parker Lake	O&B	3	M	X		X		X
32 Walker and Sardine Lakes	O&B	0.3–7	M–S	X			X	X
33 Walker Lake	O&B	4–6	MS	X				X
34 Gibbs Lake	O&B	6.5	S	X				X
35 May Lundy Mine and Oneida Lake	O&B	5.75–6.6	S	X				X
36 Lundy Canyon	O&B	1.3–5	E–M	X		X		
37 Virginia Lakes	O&B	0.6–6	E–S	X			X	
38 Green, East, and West Lakes	O&B	6–9.3	M–S	X	X		X	
39 Barney Lake	O&B	6	S	X	X		X	X
40 Eagle or Lower Mosquito Lake	O&B	7 or 7.6	S	X		X	X	
41 Lower Monarch Lake	O&B	9	S	X			X	
42 Giant Forest Sequoia Loop	Semi	2.6–6.7	M–S		🌲			
43 Panther Gap	O&B	5	M		X		X	
44 Heather Lake	Semi	8	S	X			X	
45 Tokopah Falls	O&B	3.5	M			X		
46 Little Baldy	O&B	3.3	M				X	
47 Weaver Lake	O&B	3.75	M	X				
48 Big Baldy	O&B	4	M				X	
49 Buena Vista Peak	O&B	1.6	E				X	
50 Redwood Mountain	Loop	4–6	M–S		🌲		X	
51 Park Ridge Loop	Loop	0.3–4.25	E–M				X	
52 Cedar Grove Overlook	Loop	5.6–7	S				X	
53 Roaring River Falls and Zumwalt Meadows	Semi	0.5–4	E–M			X		
54 Mist Falls	O&B	7.3	S			X	X	
55 Dinkey Lakes	Semi	5–6.5	M–S	X			X	X

Trip Number and Title	Trip Type	Distance in Miles	Difficulty Level	Best Features				
				Lakes	Flora	Falls	Views	Fall Color
56 Rancheria Falls	O&B	1.3	E		X			
57 Twin Lakes	O&B	4–6.25	M–S	X	X		X	
58 Dutch Lake	O&B	6.25	S	X				
59 Doris and Tule Lakes	O&B	1.5–3	E–M	X				
60 Along Lake Edison	O&B	9	S	X			X	X
61 Mariposa Grove	Semi	1.3–5.3	E–M		♠			
62 Chilnualna Falls	O&B	8–8.5	S			X	X	
63 Sentinel Dome and Taft Point	Loop	2–4.5	E–M			X	X	
64 To Yosemite Valley via Falls	Shuttle	7.75	S			X	X	
65 Four Mile Trail	Shuttle	5.3	M			X	X	X
66 Vernal and Nevada Falls	Semi	1.5–6	M–S			X	X	
67 Tueeulala and Wapama Falls	O&B	3–4	E–M			X		
68 Bennettville Site and Lakes	O&B	1.5–3.75	E–M	X			X	X
69 Gardisky Lake	O&B	2	M	X			X	
70 20 Lakes Basin	Loop	2.5–7.5	E–S					
71 Gaylor Lakes and Great Sierra Mine Ruins	O&B	2–4	M–S	X			X	
72 Summit and Spillway Lakes	O&B	7–8.5	S	X			X	
73 Dog Lake and Dog Dome	Semi	2.5–3.6	E–M	X			X	
74 Tuolumne Meadows Loop	Loop	4.6	M		X		X	
75 Elizabeth Lake	O&B	4	M	X				X
76 Cathedral Lakes	O&B	6.6–7	S	X			X	
77 Lower Sunrise Lake	O&B	6.5	S	X	X		X	
78 May Lake	O&B	2	E	X			X	
79 North Dome	O&B	8	S				X	
80 Lukens Lake	O&B	4	M	X	X			
81 Harden Lake	O&B	4	M	X				
82 Leavitt Meadow Loop	Semi	5.3–6	M–S	X			X	X
83 Relief Reservoir Overlook	O&B	6.25	S	X			X	X
84 Boulder Creek and Lake	O&B	4.6–8.6	M–S	X				X
85 Sword Lake	O&B	4.75	M	X				
86 Camp Lake	O&B	5	E		X			
87 Noble Lake	O&B	3.5–7.6	M–S			X		X

Trip Number and Title	Trip Type	Distance in Miles	Difficulty Level	Best Features				
				Lakes	Flora	Falls	Views	Fall Color
88 Heiser and Bull Run Lakes	O&B	4–9	M–S	X				
89 Duck Lake	Semi	3.3	M	X				
90 Three Lakes Loop	Loop	4.6	E–M	X				
91 Dardanelles and Round Lakes	O&B	1–9	E–S	X	X			
92 Lily Pad and Upper Sunset Lakes	O&B	3.75–4.5	M	X	X			
93 Blue Lakes to Granite Lake	O&B	3.5	M	X				
94 Frog and Winnemucca Lakes	O&B	2–4	E–M	X	X		X	
95 Meiss and Round Lakes	O&B	2–9.5	E–S	X	X		X	
96 Woods Lake Loop	Loop	2.6–4	M	X	X		X	
97 Emigrant Lake	O&B	7.75	S	X				
98 Lake Margaret	O&B	4.6	M	X				
99 Silver Lake to Granite and Hidden Lakes	O&B	2–6	E–M	X			X	
100 Shealor Lake	O&B	2.5	M	X			X	
101 Tamarack and Triangle Lakes	Semi	7–9.3	S	X			X	
102 Bloodsucker Lake	O&B	4	M	X	X			
103 Grouse and Hemlock Lakes	O&B	4.6–6	M–S	X				
104 Twin and Island Lakes	O&B	5.5–7	M–S	X			X	
105 Grass Lake	O&B	4.5	M	X				
106 Gilmore, Half Moon, or Susie Lake	O&B	8.5–10	S	X				
107 Granite, Velma, or Dicks Lake	O&B	1–10	E–S	X			X	
108 Waterfall below Eagle Lake and Eagle, Velma, or Dicks Lake	O&B	0.2–10	E–S	X		X	X	
109 Meeks Creek Lakes	O&B	8.5–10	S	X	X			X
110 Five Lakes Basin	O&B	4	M	X				
111 Long Lake	O&B	1.3	E	X				
112 Loch Leven and Salmon Lakes	O&B	5.5–9.5	M–S	X				

Preface to the Third Edition

Welcome to the third edition of this book! I've made many changes to help make the book more compact and more useful. I've weeded out some of the less interesting trips and shortened a few of the remaining trips by deleting some of the less interesting or overly demanding final destinations. In addition, I've added one new trip, out of the Pinecrest area, which I had previously overlooked, on State Route 108 to delightful Camp Lake. If you go, I hope you'll enjoy it as much as I did.

Regarding lodgings, I have eliminated the lengthy descriptions of each lodging in favor of more-compact and easier-to-use tables of lodgings and towns and agencies at the beginning of each chapter. The overwhelming majority of lodgings, towns, and agencies have websites that can give you far more up-to-date information than I can in a book, so these tables refer you to websites, as well as to address and telephone numbers, depending on what information is available for a particular lodge. A few lodgings still aren't on the Web, but if I've listed them in previous editions, I've "grandfathered" them in, anyway. In the appendices, there's a new, alphabetical index to lodgings listing their general locations and the chapter(s) each lodging appears in.

The book, as explained in the introduction, has been reorganized somewhat. It continues to be organized into South (East and then West) and then North (by highway). However, the East side has been divided into three parts (Lone Pine to Convict Lake, Mammoth Lakes, and June Lake to Bridgeport), and the west side has also been divided into three parts (Sequoia and Kings Canyon National Parks, Between the Parks, and Yosemite National Park).

I've also made many minor changes, one of which is substituting decimals for regular fractions: 0.5 for ½, 0.3 for ⅓, 0.25 for ¼, 0.1 for ¹⁄₁₀, 0.6 for ⅔, and 0.75 for ¾. Please understand that all distances remain best-guess approximations; they are *not* precise to tenths and hundredths of a mile. The best-season icons have been replaced with a simple time of year of listing so that it's immediately clear. Of course, the best time to visit shifts slightly each year depending on the preceding winter.

In connection with making the changes described above, I updated the language of all the hikes and their corresponding maps. The credit for a number of these good ideas goes not to me but to my gifted and incredibly patient editor, Laura Shauger. My thanks go also to Roslyn Bullas, the managing editor of Wilderness Press, with whom I initially discussed and agreed upon many of these helpful changes. Any errors, however, are all mine—doggone it.

Introduction

Hikes from lodgings throughout California's Sierra Nevada mountain range is a huge subject. Geologists estimate that the entire range is, as the crow flies, 430 miles long and 50–80 miles wide. It runs from southeast to northwest in eastern California and barely dips its toes into western Nevada. Millions come to enjoy the Sierra Nevada every year. Some backpack, some car camp, and some stay in lodgings. This book introduces those hikers who prefer to stay in lodgings to lodgings and trailheads they may not have known about and helps those who want to stay in lodgings but haven't done so yet. It will help them learn where to stay, where to hike, and what to expect from the lodgings as well as from the trails. Exploring mountain trails while staying in lodgings is a wonderful way to experience the glorious Sierra Nevada!

The range reaches its greatest elevation on its east side—that's where its crest is. There, the range rises very abruptly from the Owens Valley at 4000 feet to its crest ranging from 11,000 to 14,491 feet on Mt. Whitney, the highest peak in the contiguous 48 states. On the range's east side, good roads climb from U.S. Highway 395 in Owens Valley 2 to 24 miles to trailheads ranging from 7600 to 10,230 feet. On its west, the range rises very slowly from California's Central Valley, near sea level, through rolling foothills and up long, gentle, wooded slopes toward the crest. From the west and in the southern Sierra, good roads wind into the southern Sierra for as much as 80 miles to high trailheads, but don't cross the crest. The high road point is a non-crest pass, Kaiser Pass at 9200 feet. In the northern Sierra, good to adequate roads cross crest passes from the east side to the west side. Yosemite National Park's Tioga Pass at 9945 feet is the highest and southernmost pass crossed by those roads. All these roads determine how hikers get to lodgings and trailheads: in the southern Sierra by roads branching into but not across the Sierra and in the northern Sierra by roads that cross the range.

History, Geology, and Biology

This book is hefty enough without including as much as I'd like to about the Sierra's history, geology, and biology. Of course, as relevant to each area or hike, there are brief discussions of the area's history and the geology, wildlife, and wildflowers seen along the hike.

Here's a *very* brief human history of the general area: Native Americans explored the Sierra extensively, especially while hunting and gathering in the summer. However, they did not live in the range year-round (without modern amenities, the range is too barren, harsh, and cold for year-round habitation). The low-elevation Yosemite Valley is an exception; there were once permanent Native American villages there.

The range is full of prehistoric sites, most still waiting to be studied. Sharp-eyed hikers may find rings of stones that once anchored temporary dwellings, obsidian chips indicating tool-makers' work sites, and deep hollows in horizontal granite surfaces, hollows in which people ground acorns for flour. These sites aren't hard to find: Since their makers were people like us, the sites are where we, too, would have liked to put our tents, chipped our tools, and chatted in the shade as we ground our flour. Theirs were the original human trails throughout the range. (Please enjoy but never disturb such sites or remove artifacts like chips and arrowheads.)

California's earliest-known European visitors, the Spanish, had little interest in the high range far to the east as they laid out their Pacific Coast chain of missions along the King's Highway (*El Camino Real*) in the 18th century. Beginning in the 19th century, English-speaking mountain men and explorers came, seeking furs and knowledge and often following Native American trails. Settlers seeking farms in California's Central Valley considered the range an obstacle and a deadly hazard—think of the Donner Party.

With the discovery of gold in 1848 in the western Sierra foothills came the Gold Rush and more settlers, all carving trails across the range to the western foothills and the Central Valley. So California's biggest and richest cities of the 19th century grew up on the state's west side (think of San Francisco and Sacramento). The highways that now cross the north end of the range are like an echo of these migrations, in a few places closely following the old emigrant trails. Miners who sought riches in the range's minerals and livestock owners who wanted summer pastures for their herds and flocks tramped throughout the range, using old trails and making new ones.

Meanwhile, the state-chartered California Geological Survey in the 1860s, led by Josiah Whitney, provided the first scientific description of the range. The vivid writings of one of the survey's members, Clarence King, inspired many an adventurer to seek the Sierra's high peaks and remote valleys.

As the gold played out on the west side, miners filtered east and south in search of more gold—or any other valuable minerals. The Sierra is pocked with old mineshafts and dotted with the ruins of mining operations.

It wasn't long before people came to appreciate the range's huge recreational potential. Trout were unknown in the range except in the far south, on the Kern Plateau, home of the famed golden trout, so trout were planted in most of the range's thousands of lakes to lure anglers. Stock-packers offered their services to visitors, and other entrepreneurs offered hotels and restaurants. (Exploring the range while staying in lodgings has a long and honorable history!)

Maps

This book includes its own, simplified trail maps, but many visitors will enjoy having additional maps that allow them to gain a better understanding of an area's features and placement in the mountain range. For trail and topographic maps of the Sierra Nevada, check offerings from Wilderness Press (www.wildernesspress.com or 1-800-443-7227), the Forest Service (www.fs.fed.us) and the national parks (www.nps.gov), the United States Geological Survey (USGS, www.usgs.gov), and major outdoors stores like REI.

The most popular maps for hiking are the very detailed 7.5′ series of USGS topographic maps ("topos"), which show distances at a scale of about 2 inches per mile and elevation contours at intervals of 40 (rarely 80) feet apart. A few are metric (20-meter contour intervals). These maps are the most finely detailed that are readily available, but they are not perfect and certainly are not updated frequently.

Also popular are the maps of individual wilderness areas, published by the government agencies in charge. Although coarser in detail than the 7.5′ maps, these still have plenty of detail (especially for dayhikes), include elevation contours, and are usually updated fairly often.

Another possibility is a commercial map, like Wilderness Press's maps based on selected USGS 15′ topos (the hugely popular series that preceded the 7.5′ series). Fifteen-minute topos are, as you'd expect, half as finely detailed as the 7.5′ maps; and it takes four 7.5′ maps to replace a single 15′ topo. For example, the typical contour interval of a 15′ map is 80 feet as opposed to an interval of 40 feet for the 7.5′ maps.

Other commercial maps include the National Geographic series of national park maps and the Tom Harrison area maps. These are updated much more frequently than the USGS topos, and some include useful features like the distances between points. However, none is as finely detailed as a USGS 7.5′ topo.

When choosing maps, you might also consider software like National Geographic's TOPO!, which provides a database of scanned USGS maps—five levels of increasing detail, down to the popular 7.5′ series at Level 5 and allows users to do things like print out the maps, draw chosen routes on them, make elevation profiles of those routes, calculate route lengths, and get very exact position data for any point you specify—very helpful for global positioning system (GPS) navigation.

All the maps, compasses, and GPS units in the world can't keep you safely on course if you don't know how to use them together. Take a hands-on, in-the-field course in navigating with these aids. Groups like the Sierra Club and the Yosemite Association offer these courses; they're great fun, too!

Criteria for Area Inclusion

This book covers the most scenic part of the Sierra Nevada, which meets the following criteria: lies wholly within California; east of State Routes 41, 49, and 99; west of U.S. Highway 395; north of a line roughly connecting Visalia on the west with Lone Pine on the east; and south of Interstate 80. The area covered also lies above 6000 feet, with the exception of the great valleys of the national parks—Kings Canyon, Wawona, Yosemite Valley, and Hetch Hetchy Valley.

In accordance with these considerations, the hikes in this book are divided into regional chapters as follows:

Southern Sierra: East Side: Lone Pine to Convict Lake, Mammoth Lakes, and June Lake to Bridgeport

Southern Sierra: West Side: Sequoia and Kings Canyon National Parks, including Mineral King, Generals Highway, Giant Sequoia National Monument in Sequoia National Forest, and Kings Canyon proper; Between the Parks; and the Valleys of Yosemite National Park

Northern Sierra: State Route 120: The Yosemite High Country; State Route 108: Sonora Pass Country; State Route 4: Ebbetts Pass Country; State Routes 88 and 89:

Wildflower Country; U.S. Highway 50: South of Tahoe; State Route 89 Around Lake Tahoe; and Interstate 80: Donner Summit Country

Within each region, the hikes are organized from south to north or east to west, depending on the orientation of the major roads serving the region. As is evident on the map at the top of the next page, these regions overlap somewhat.

Criteria for Hike Inclusion

To be included in this book, a hike must lie within the area covered (above). In addition, hikes must be no longer than 10 miles long or less—preferably shorter. Most hikes identify interim destinations so you can adjust the hike's length to suit yourself. In a very few cases, the farthest destination identified for a hike pushes that 10-mile limit a little. Hikes must also have no more than 2600 feet of elevation gain—preferably less; have few, if any, long, very steep stretches—preferably none; go to a worthwhile final destination—a fantastic viewpoint, a beautiful lake, a thundering waterfall, or a grove of giant sequoias; and be on official, maintained trail. Brief excursions onto well-trod use trails are okay if they go to destinations visible from the main trail. There's no real cross-country travel or bushwhacking in this book. Hikes must be within an hour's drive (roughly, 30 miles) of at least one lodging or one town that qualifies for this book. This criterion includes these considerations: the quality of the driving experience, including road conditions; the traffic to be encountered; and the area's sensitivity to an increase in traffic. There are no outrageously long, difficult drives—though a few come close. No drives require four-wheel-drive (4WD), but it may be nice to have that as an option for a very few drives. A few drives do require a high-clearance vehicle.

Criteria for Lodgings Inclusion

To qualify for inclusion in this book, a lodging, community, or agency must be, in my judgment, within 30 miles or an hour's drive of hikes (that is, trailheads) included in this book. For example, a community may be within 30 miles of the entrance to Yosemite Valley, but if it is more than 30 miles from the nearest Yosemite trailhead included in this book, it's not eligible. I also require that a lodging not give me the creeps. I further prefer that a lodging have an adequate presence on the World Wide Web, such as its own, well-maintained web site. However, some well-established lodgings that I've included in previous editions still do not have web sites. If such a lodging is still in business, I've continued to include it.

Individual Lodgings

A lodging that's truly outside a town or village and in the mountains rates special mention. Some lodgings are just on a community's fringes, and since deciding where to classify them was a judgment call, don't overlook lodgings served through communities and agencies. Previous editions of this book described individual lodgings exhaustively, but details can change. This edition, therefore, refers hikers to the company's website, since that is the best place to find the latest information, if the site is maintained properly. In this edition, individual lodgings are tabulated alphabetically at the beginning of each chapter in the following format:

Individual Lodgings

Name	Nearest Community	Type	Facilities	Price Range	Contact Information	Website and Email Address
Echo Chalet	Kyburz	Mountain	Cabins	$–$$$	9900 Echo Lakes Road Echo Lake, CA 95721 *Summer* (phone): 530-659-7207 *Winter* (fax): 530-620-7207	www.echochalet.com echochalet-since1939@ earthlink.net
Kyburz Resort Motel	Kyburz	Other	Rooms	$–$$	P.O. Box 27 Kyburz, CA 95720 Phone: 530-293-3382	http://kyburzresort motel.com
Strawberry Lodge	Kyburz	Other	Rooms, cabins	$–$$$	17510 Highway 50 Kyburz, CA 95720 Phone: 530-659-7200	http://strawberry lodge.com info@strawberrylodge .com

All of these columns are self-explanatory, except "Type," "Facilities," and "Price Range." For the "Type" category, the label "Mountain" means that a given lodging is actually in the mountains (preferably above 6000 feet), removed from the hustle and bustle of a busy community (but they may be technically within a community's official boundaries), and not on a busy road. A lodging labeled "Other" fails to meet one or two of the criteria given for "Mountain." For example, many lodgings that are otherwise very desirable are unfortunately set next to busy, noisy roads.

Facilities vary from a bunk in a dormitory to luxurious condos with everything. Within this category, "Dormitories" are rooms, usually limited to the same sex, with multiple beds and shared bathrooms. "Rooms" have one or more beds and may or may not have a private bath. They may be in a central lodge building (like a hotel), or they may be arranged as in a motel. "Tent cabins" are sleeping-only cabins. Part of the structure is made of canvas, like a tent. Occupants of tent cabins share central bath facilities. "Cabins" range from simple sleeping-only cabins to luxurious, multi-room buildings with complete kitchens and baths. "Trailers" means just that: the accommodation is a travel trailer fixed to its site. These usually have modest kitchens and baths. "Condos" are condominiums, with all that that usually means: full kitchens, baths, TVs, VCRs or DVD players, etc.

For "Price Range," the rates per night are as follows budget ($), under $100; moderate ($$), $100–200; and expensive ($$$), more than $200. For some lodgings, weekly and monthly rates, as well as special packages, may be available. For year-round lodgings, these rate ranges are provided for spring through fall only. Be careful, though, because rates alone can be misleading! A room with two beds may be moderate, but if two people share the room and split the cost, it might be budget for each of them. A cabin that sleeps six may be expensive (say, $480 per night), but if six people split the cost, it's only $80 per person per night—a budget rate. So the rate for your visit depends on how many people are chipping in to pay for the accommodation. A per-week or per-month rental rate will surely provide a significant price break over a per-night rental cost. Keep in mind that when you go may affect the rate—some lodgings charge higher rates for holiday periods and weekends.

Towns and Agencies

Towns (also referred to as communities) and agencies are listed alphabetically at the beginning of each chapter in the following table format. Unless otherwise noted, all telephone numbers in area codes beginning with an eight are toll-free.

Towns and Agencies

Name	Nearest Community	Type	Contact Information	Website and Email Address
El Dorado County Visitors Authority (includes Kyburz)	Placerville	Chamber of Commerce	542 Main Street Placerville, CA 95667 Phone: 530-621-5885 or 800-457-6279	www.visiteldorado.com tourism@eldoradocounty.org
Lake Tahoe Visitor Information (VirtualTahoe)	South Lake Tahoe	Agency	P.O. Box 7172 #173 Stateline, NV 89449-7172 Phone: 800-210-3459, 800-371-2620, or 530-544-5050	www.virtualtahoe.com contactus@virtualtahoe.com
South Lake Tahoe Chamber of Commerce	South Lake Tahoe	Chamber of Commerce	3066 Lake Tahoe Blvd. South Lake Tahoe, CA 96150 Phone: 530-541-5255	www.tahoeinfo.com sltcc@sierra.net

For these lodgings "Type" is "Community" or "Agency." "Community" refers to a town or village with lodgings, and the reference is generally to the community's Chamber of Commerce or Visitors Bureau, which can offer visitors lodging information. Lodgings in this category are more apt to provide urbanlike amenities (proximity to shopping, TVs, DVD players, etc.) than the Mountain or Other lodgings listed in the previous table. "Agency" means a commercial operation, like a real estate agency, that represents a number of lodgings in the area. Lodgings represented may be of any kind (e.g., motel, condo, mountain cabins, upscale hotel). An agency typically represents only some, not all, of the available lodgings and should have the latest information on those. This book uses Agencies only when a Visitors Bureau or Chamber of Commerce apparently isn't available for an area. "Price Range" is unnecessary because lodgings in this category are available at a range of prices.

Auto-Club Lodging Information

National auto clubs usually have publications that provide information on lodgings. These publications are typically free to members. If you belong to an auto club that provides this service, take advantage of it. Note, however, that some of the more rustic mountain lodgings in this book don't meet auto-club criteria for reasons I think are less important than the joy of being in the mountains.

Sneak Preview

Dedicated websites and brochures emphasize a lodging's good points and gloss over its rough spots. Former guests are apt to be less tactful. There are online sites where real people give their unvarnished opinions of real accommodations they've stayed in. For example, one such site is www.TripAdvisor.com. It's worth checking such sites to see if real people say that an accommodation is all its brochure claims it is.

Above Relief Reservoir

Get Ready to Hike!

This section contains suggestions that I hope will make your hikes safer and more enjoyable, and perhaps will better protect you and the environment. Remember that no book can substitute for or provide five things: physical fitness, preparedness, experience, caution, and common sense. Don't leave the trailhead without them.

Minimum Equipment

Wear or carry at least these items:

- Sunglasses.

- Coach's whistle: A hiker can blow a whistle for help longer and louder than s/he can shout.

- Appropriate footwear, preferably hiking boots.

- Strong sunblock that hikers should apply before setting out.

- Insect repellent for those whom the bugs annoy. DEET remains the best insect repellent available and is safe for most people but shouldn't be used on children under 2 months old (for use on children, see the American Academy of Pediatrics's website, www.aap.org/family/wnv-jun03.htm). Be sure the concentration of DEET is at least 30% (per *Backpacker* magazine tests). DEET is controversial and can have some unpleasant side effects; avoid putting it directly on your skin. Some repellents made with natural plant extracts can be effective as well.

- Extra food, including at least a few high-energy, concentrated-nutrition snack bars.

- Water: Since no open source of water in the U.S. is safe to drink untreated, fill your water bottles and hydration packs at lodgings. The recommended minimum is 1 pint for easy hikes, 1–2 quarts for moderate hikes, and 2 quarts for strenuous hikes.

- Lightweight "space blanket": a couple of ounces of metallized mylar film to wrap around your body to stay warm.

- Extra clothing for keeping warm when the temperature drops, when it rains, or when it gets windy: Sierra weather can become very nasty very abruptly. Be prepared with extra, appropriate clothing, especially a warm cap, when it does so. For more information, see "Hypothermia" on p. 10.

- If you wear glasses or contact lenses, take extra lenses.

- If you require any special medications, carry a small supply, especially emergency medication like an inhaler.
- Map and a compass if you can use it or a map and a Global Positioning System (GPS) unit with extra batteries.
- Flashlight with an extra bulb and batteries.
- A small trowel or some other means to dig a hole 6–8 inches deep in order to bury solid body wastes. Don't bury or burn tissue—pack it out.
- Pocket knife.
- First-aid kit, preferably backed up by first-aid training.
- Waterproof matches or a lighter and something to keep a flame going (such as a candle) only when necessary to save a life.

Hiking Partners

The standard advice is never to hike alone, but thousands of people do, including me. If you do, it is recommended that you be overprepared; be prepared to bivouac; know and respect your limits; carry and know how to navigate with a map and compass or a map and a GPS unit; know first aid; stick to major, well-marked trails; and always leave your itinerary with a friend or relative who can be trusted to notice if you are overdue and to call the authorities. Be sure to call the friend or relative when you return safely to avoid making them worry unnecessarily and to avoid an unnecessary call to the authorities if someone believes you're missing. Finally, learn to hike by taking classes from reputable organizations and by hiking in the Sierra with others before hiking alone.

Sanitation

Preferably, take care of body wastes at lodgings or at trailhead toilets. Otherwise, eliminate body wastes at least 100 feet from any body of water and any trail or potential campsite. Bury solid wastes in a hole 6–8 inches deep. Carry out any garbage, toilet tissue, facial tissue, sanitary napkins, tampons, and disposable diapers; don't burn or bury them.

Hunting Season

Hunting is legal in the Sierra's national forests, though not in national parks, typically from a little after Labor Day until some time in December (check for exact dates). Be visible during hunting season by wearing bright colors; an inexpensive cap-and-vest set in fluorescent orange or red will do the trick. Arrows and bullets know no boundaries, and illegal hunting has occurred in national parks.

Other Hazards

Rattlesnakes are found in the Sierra, though they are rarely seen above 7000 feet. If you hear a snake rattle, stand still long enough to determine where it is and then leave in the opposite direction. Black bears, not grizzlies, are found in these mountains as well, but they are generally shy. Making some noise as you walk will warn them of your approach so that they can scramble out of the way.

Sun Protection

Not only is skin cancer a serious, potentially fatal problem, but a bad sunburn can ruin a vacation. Sun protection is especially important at higher altitudes, where the amount of ultraviolet radiation (the cancer-causing rays) striking your skin is much greater than at sea level. Natural skin pigmentation alone isn't sufficient sun protection in the Sierra. The major defenses are clothing and sunblock. Instead of T-shirts and tank tops, wear lightweight but opaque, long-sleeved shirts. Consider wearing pants instead of shorts. Wear a hat with a brim sufficient to shade your face. Lightweight gloves will protect hands.

For sunblock, choose the highest "sun protection factor" (SPF) number of water-resistant cream or lotion you can find from a reputable manufacturer. I prefer sunblocks that include a physical blocking agent such as zinc oxide or titanium dioxide. Spray-on products are less effective. Apply as directed to face, ears, neck, and any other areas that may be exposed. Allow 20–30 minutes for the sunblock to react with the skin to form a protective barrier. Reapply as necessary. Don't forget to use a lip-protectant containing sunblock, too.

When using sunblock with insect repellent, apply the sunblock first and give it time to "bond" with the skin before applying the repellent. The only effective repellent, DEET, reduces the effectiveness of sunblock, so this is another reason to get the highest SPF sunblock. Don't waste money on products that combine sunblock and insect repellent; they're self-defeating.

Hypothermia

One of the leading causes of death in the mountains is hypothermia; the old-fashioned term is "death by exposure." As a hiker gets exhausted and chilled, he or she begins to get irrational, too. An irrational hiker often fails to understand what's happening and may fail to halt the insidious downward spiral of progressively greater exhaustion, chilling, and irrationality. A hiker at this stage may vehemently deny that anything's wrong. The person finally makes the bad decision to lie down to rest, falls asleep, and lapses into a coma. Death comes when the body's core temperature drops far enough that vital organs can't perform their functions any more. It only takes hours and happens every year to unprepared hikers.

Most hypothermia cases reportedly occur at temperatures as high as the 50s, not at freezing ones. Perhaps that's because we know enough to be well-prepared when the day starts out icy cold. We get into trouble when the day starts out sunny or unsettled and then turns nasty.

The best "cure" for hypothermia is prevention; don't become hypothermic in the first place. Budget energy; eat and drink often; rest when needed; don't become exhausted; know when to turn around and head home; and stay warm and reasonably dry. Fuel the body by eating high-energy foods and drinking water often. Conserve body heat by wearing appropriate clothing in layers, clothing that won't squander body heat by letting moisture and wind steal it away. Even when it doesn't rain, a hiker gets wet from sweat. So it's imperative to wear clothing made of fabric that insulates when wet. Wool and most synthetics insulate when wet. Cotton not only does not insulate when wet but accelerates heat loss by holding moisture against the body. Cotton can be deadly when the weather turns bad. Most important, put on a warm cap since much of a person's body heat is lost through his or her head. To help keep moisture and wind from carrying away body heat, wear an outer layer of wind- and rainproof clothing. (Most rainproof gear is also windproof.) A poncho with a hood will do; a rain suit (pants and a jacket with a hood) gives more complete protection.

Each member of a party should keep an eye on the others for signs of hypothermia: stumbling, slurred speech, and uncontrollable shivering followed later by no shivering. If a fellow hiker seems hypothermic, help him or her to put on additional, appropriate clothing and, if he or she is fully conscious, to eat and drink properly. However, never give anything by mouth to a person who is not fully conscious. (A fully conscious person is "oriented four by four": knows what day it is, who he or she is, where he or she is, and why he or she is there.) Never give a hypothermic individual alcohol—it just aggravates his or her condition. Don't be surprised if a hypothermia victim resists help. Persist, remembering that he or she is irrational. Above all, turn around, get back to the trailhead, and then get to shelter as soon as possible.

How to Use This Book

Each trip begins with a chart of the sites visited along with the distance to each, elevation of each, the difficulty level for each destination, and the trip type. The summary information also includes the best time of year to visit, the appropriate topographic maps, and nearby lodgings (organized by category). Where applicable, permit information is listed in a notes category. The highlights, directions to the trailhead, and trip description help you know whether a trip's for you, figure out how to get there, and hike to the various destinations.

Trip Summary

Each trip begins with a table summarizing the trip's major "places," from the start to each interim destination to the final destination. The summary information includes place, distance, elevation, difficulty level, and type.

Place

"Trailhead" is self-explanatory. Subsequent names are worthwhile interim destinations you can choose from. Hikers can shorten most hikes to suit their energy and available time by going to an interim destination instead of the final destination. The last place listed is usually the final, farthest destination. There are a few hikes where there is a significant distance to a junction or junctions and so hikers must choose among destinations to stay within the mileage limits (10 miles total) of this book. The hike description describes the options in such cases.

Total Distance

This is typically the total miles to and from a given place. On loop, semiloop, and shuttle trips, the total distance may be to the place only because you don't go back from it; in these cases, the trip description clarifies the situation. The stated mileage for a place typically includes the mileage for all previously listed destinations; if it doesn't, then the write-up will clarify what is included in which mileages.

Elevation

The elevation (in feet) is listed for each named place. If a significant high or low point occurs between destinations, then that is covered in the trip description itself since that can be important in budgeting your energy for a trip.

Difficulty Level

Assigning a hike a particular level of difficulty is a judgment call. Contrary to what most people think, elevation gain/loss and the rate of gain/loss are more important in determining a trip's difficulty level than distance alone. When the elevation gain/loss or gain/loss rate is high, I usually assign a trip the next higher level. I may also assign a trip a higher level if the trail is unusually rough or hard to follow. Each segment of a hike is assigned one of the following four levels:

E An easy hike is no longer than 3 miles, has 500 feet or less of total elevation gain/loss between the start and the named destination, and has no long, steep stretches.

M A moderate hike is no longer than 6 miles, has 1500 feet or less of elevation gain/loss between the start and the named destination, and likely includes some long, steep stretches.

S A strenuous hike is longer than 6 miles, has more than 1500 feet of elevation gain/loss between the start and the named destination, and has steep, long stretches.

U An upside-down hike is one that, unlike most hikes, descends on the way out and ascends on the way back. Keep in mind that, for an upside-down trip, you will need to save some energy for that final climb.

Type

Each of the hikes is one of the following four types:

O&B For out-and-back trips, hikers walk to the destination and return the same way. Most hikes in this book are out-and-back trips.

Loop For loop trips, hikers walk out to the destination by one route and return by a different route.

Semiloop Semiloop trips are composed of a significant loop part and significant out-and-back segments.

Shuttle A shuttle trip begins at one place and ends at a different one. In this book, hikers leave the car at the trip's end and take public transportation to the trip's start.

Loop and semiloop trips may have interim destinations that you can treat as out-and-back trips, and that's how the hike write-up will show all those interim destinations.

Notes

Most Sierra dayhikes don't require permits, but if one is required, this will explain how to get it. It will also include any other important information that doesn't fall into one of the standard categories.

Best Time

This best time of year to take a particular trip is partly a judgment call. For example, waterfalls are best in early season when runoff is high, flowers are best in early and mid-season, fall color belongs to late season, and the previous winter's snow may keep higher elevations snowbound until late summer. The trips in this book start from just under 4200 feet and range as high as 10,230 feet; at those elevations, the winters are longer than at sea level and the other seasons are briefer and compressed into a shorter period. Some very-high-elevation hikes are best late in the year because only then are they snow-free.

Topos

This section lists the topographic maps, or topos, that cover the area the hike traverses. This book provides a simplified trail map for each hike, but since many hikers enjoy having additional maps, the summary information for each hike lists the United States Geological Survey (USGS) 7.5′ maps that cover the area. Most national parks have finely detailed maps of their most visited regions, like Sequoia National Park's Giant Forest and Yosemite's famed Yosemite Valley, which are usually available at the nearest store or ranger station for a few dollars. When appropriate, these maps are listed as well.

Where to Stay

Each region's eligible lodgings are tabulated at the start of the appropriate chapter. Each trip write-up in that region includes a section titled "Where to Stay," which is a listing of lodgings and communities close enough to the trip's trailhead so that hikers would have to drive no more than 30 miles (or one hour) to reach it. As defined in detail in the "Criteria for Lodgings Inclusion" on p. 4, "Mountain" means true mountain lodgings; "Other" means lodgings of interest; and "Towns and Agencies" means nearby chambers of commerce, visitors bureaus, and private travel agencies.

Highlights

The highlights section explains the features of a particular hike that make it worthwhile. These aren't mere Sierra dayhikes, they are the best Sierra dayhikes, and each one has something special to offer. Remember, however, that some highlights, such as waterfalls and wildflowers, are strictly seasonal.

How to Get to the Trailhead

This section conveys driving directions in terms of some reasonable, local reference point. For example, on the Sierra's east-west highways, the reference point is that highway's Sierra crest pass.

On the Trail

This section describes the trail as it would unfold before you, its destinations, pleasures, high points, things to look out for, and so on. In case you wonder, I've walked every mile of every trail that appears as a trip in this book. Be aware of two common hiking terms: duck and use trail. A duck, or cairn, is a small pile of rocks placed to guide hikers. They're often perched on boulders for greater visibility. Ducks mark a route where the trail is faint, confusing, or nonexistent. Follow them only where you need them, such as when crossing granite slabs where it's impossible to have a real trail-tread. Some duck-builders get carried away and put up unnecessary ducks. Or they'll put up ducks on a wrong route and, after discovering the error, not go back to knock the misleading ducks down. Exercise good judgment when following ducks. A use trail is an unofficial, unmaintained track that's created and maintained only by being used. Use trails go, for example, around lakes and from main trails down to streamsides and lakeshores.

Maps

Most trips have their own maps. Some trips share a map with one or more other trips in the same area. If those cases, icons direct you to the correct map page.

Map Legend

Featured Trails	...Trip 22...	Trip Locations	**33**	
Other Trails	- - - - - - - - -	Trailhead	**T**	
Freeways	≡≡≡≡≡	Lodgings	Resort ■ Resort →	
Highways	══════	Picnic	⊼	
Local Roads	══════	Camping	▲	
Dirt Roads	= = = = = =	Peak	x	
		Bridge	⟩⟨	
Interstate Highway	(80)	Creek or River		
U.S. Highway	(395)	Body of Water		
State Highway	(120)			
Forest Road	4N103	North Arrow		

Lone Pine to Convict Lake

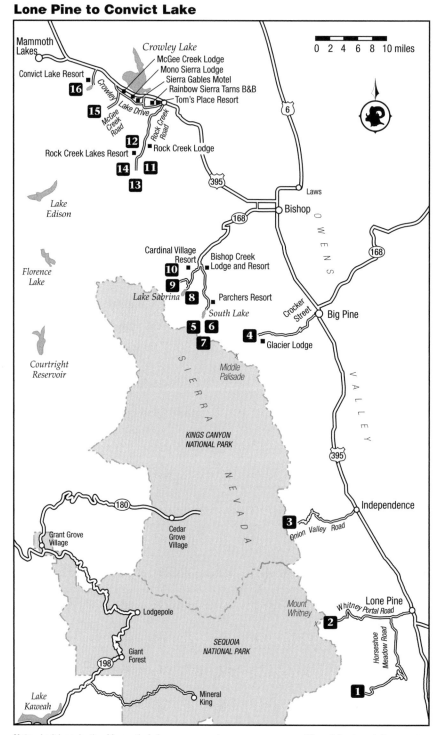

Mammoth Lakes

Crowley Lake
McGee Creek Lodge
Mono Sierra Lodge
Sierra Gables Motel
Rainbow Sierra Tarns B&B
Tom's Place Resort

Convict Lake Resort **16**

15

McGee Creek Road

Crowley Lake Drive

Rock Creek Road

0 2 4 6 8 10 miles

12

Rock Creek Lakes Resort ■ ■ Rock Creek Lodge

14 **11**

13

395

Laws

Lake Edison

Bishop

168

Florence Lake

Cardinal Village Resort
Bishop Creek Lodge and Resort

10

9

Lake Sabrina **8** ■ Parchers Resort

South Lake

Courtright Reservoir

5 **6**

7

4 ■ Glacier Lodge

Crocker Street

Big Pine

SIERRA

Middle Palisade

O W E N S

168

395

V A L L E Y

KINGS CANYON NATIONAL PARK

N E V A D A

180

Independence

3

Onion Valley Road

Grant Grove Village

Cedar Grove Village

Lodgepole

Mount Whitney

Whitney Portal Road

Lone Pine

2

Giant Forest

198

SEQUOIA NATIONAL PARK

Horseshoe Meadow Road

Lake Kaweah

Mineral King

1

Note: Lodgings in the Mammoth Lakes area are shown on map on p. 56 and in June Lake area are shown on p. 86.

CHAPTER 1

Lone Pine to Convict Lake

The Eastern Sierra is simply the best—the most wild and ruggedly scenic—part of the range. The southern part of the Eastern Sierra, from Lone Pine to Bishop, slopes up abruptly to its crest from Owens Valley by as much as 10,000 feet in just a few miles. From the communities along U.S. Highway 395 in Owens Valley, side roads rise swiftly past mountain lodgings to some of the range's highest trailheads. What caused this, to oversimplify millions of years of geological evolution, is that as the Sierra Nevada rose, Owens Valley sank. In the northern part of the Eastern Sierra, from Toms Place to Bridgeport, the range slopes up less abruptly but just as scenically from plateaus at 6000 to 7000 feet. Here again, side roads also rise quickly past mountain lodgings to splendid trailheads.

As indicated in the introduction, the prehistoric Native American inhabitants of the range seasonally used but did not live permanently *in* almost all of the areas explored in this book. In the mid-19th century, people of European descent came to the Eastern Sierra for mineral riches but rarely found them. Some stayed to farm and ranch, but after Los Angeles diverted most of the area's water, the farms and ranches literally dried up. Now the area is devoted largely to recreation. Once people discover the Eastern Sierra, they return again and again.

Almost abreast of Lone Pine, the Sierra Crest rises to its highest point—Mt. Whitney at 14,491 feet. All of the Sierra's jagged 14ers pierce the sky in the region around Lone Pine and north to Convict Lake, along with plenty of 13ers. "Majestic" best describes this part of the crest, and that majesty isn't reserved for climbers. Day-hikers will find a wealth of rugged scenery along the many high trails here, because it is here that the trailheads are the highest—some over 10,000 feet.

At one time, it was thought that the highest peak in the Sierra was Yosemite's 13,053-foot Mt. Dana. It was soon realized that higher peaks lay farther south, and the race was on to identify and climb the highest. Clarence King, an intrepid mountaineer and a member of the California Geological Survey (1860–74), and his fearless climbing partner, Richard Cotter, summated what they thought was the highest peak in 1864, only to see higher peaks to the south. They named the 14,018-foot mountain they had climbed Mt. Tyndall, and they named the highest peak they could see after the survey's leader, Josiah Dwight Whitney. In 1871, King tried to climb Mt. Whitney but picked the wrong peak; he ascended instead what is now Mt. Langley (14,042 feet), the Sierra's southernmost 14er, just a few miles south of Mt. Whitney. Three fishermen from Lone Pine made the first ascent of Mt. Whitney on August 18, 1873, climbing the mountain's easier west side from their camp on the Kern River. They christened it "Fisherman's Peak," but "Mt. Whitney" remained the official name. A chagrined Clarence King, who had returned home to New York, came out West to climb the highest peak soon thereafter—but too late to be first. King's 1872 book *Mountaineering in the Sierra Nevada* is a classic of California literature, although King's accounts are considered to be more vivid in the retelling than they were in actuality.

Recommended Maps

In addition to those listed in the trip write-ups, your library of maps should include the following. Get the latest edition/revision you can find. They're widely available, certainly at any of the local ranger stations.

■ *Inyo National Forest* and *Pacific Southwest Region: A Guide to the John Muir Wilderness and the Sequoia-Kings Canyon Wilderness.* U.S. Forest Service and U.S. Department of Agriculture.

■ *Guide to Eastern Sierra.* Automobile Club of Southern California.

■ *Golden Trout Wilderness, Mt. Whitney High Country, Kearsarge Pass, The Palisades, Bishop Pass,* and *Mono Divide High Country.* Tom Harrison Maps.

Individual Lodgings

Name	Nearest Community	Type	Facilities	Price Range	Contact Information	Website and Email Address
Bishop Creek Lodge and Resort	Bishop	Mountain	Cabins	$$–$$$	Phone: 760-873-4484	http://bishopcreekresort.com bspcrk@schat.com
Cardinal Village Resort	Bishop	Mountain	Cabins	$$–$$$	Phone: 760-873-4789	www.cardinalvillageresort.com info@cardinalvillageresort.com
Convict Lake Resort	Mammoth Lakes	Mountain	Cabins	$$–$$$	HCR 79, Box 204 Mammoth Lakes, CA 93546 Phone: 800-992-2260 or 760-934 - 3800	www.convictlake.com info@convictlake.com
Crystal Crag Lodge	Mammoth Lakes	Mountain	Cabins	$–$$$	Phone: 760-934-2436	www.crystalcrag.com info@crystalcrag.com
Double Eagle Resort and Spa	June Lake	Other	Cabins, rooms	$$–$$$	P.O. Box 736 June Lake, CA 93529 Phone: 760-648-7004	www.doubleeagle.com
Glacier Lodge	Big Pine	Mountain	Cabins	$$–$$$	P.O. Box 3760 Big Pine, CA 93513 Phone: 760-938-2837 or 760-938-2312	www.sonic.net/~kwofford/glacier-lodge/ information@jewelofthesierra.com
Mammoth Mountain Chalets	Mammoth Lakes	Other	Cabins	$$–$$$	P.O. Box 13 Mammoth Lakes, CA 93546 Phone (CA): 800-327-3681 Phone: 760-934-8518 Fax: 760-934-5117	www.mammothmtnchalets.com reservations@mammothmtnchalets.com
Mammoth Mountain Inn	Mammoth Lakes	Other	Rooms, condos	$$–$$$	P.O. Box 353 Mammoth Lakes, CA 93546 Phone: 800-MAMMOTH or 760-934-2581	www.mammothmountain.com
McGee Creek Lodge	Crowley Lake	Other	Rooms	$–$$	Phone: 760-935-4228	http://mcgeecreek.com
Mono Sierra Lodge	Crowley Lake	Other	Rooms	$$	Phone: 800-SADLE UP (723-5387)	www.monosierralodge.com
Parchers Resort	Bishop	Mountain	Cabins, trailer	$–$$$	Phone: 760-873-4177	http://parchersresort.net parchersresort@cebridge.net
Rainbow Tarns Bed and Breakfast	Crowley Lake	Other	Rooms	$$	HC 79 Box 55C Crowley Lake, CA 93546-9702 Phone: 888-0588-6269 760-935-4556	www.rainbowtarns.com innkeeper@rainbowtarns.com
Rock Creek Lakes Resort	Crowley Lake	Mountain	Cabins	$$–$$$	P.O. Box 727 Bishop, CA 93515 Phone: 760-935-4311	www.rockcreeklake.com/resort

Name	Nearest Community	Type	Facilities	Price Range	Contact Information	Website and Email Address
Rock Creek Lodge	Crowley Lake	Mountain	Cabins	$–$$	Route 1, Box 12 Mammoth Lakes, CA 93546 Phone: 877-935-4170 or 760-935-4170 Fax: 760-935-4172	www.rockcreeklodge.com info@rockcreeklodge.com
Sierra Gables Motel	Crowley Lake	Other	Rooms	$ (Rentals are by the month.)	Route 1, Box 94 Crowley Lake, CA 93546 Phone: 760-935-4319	www.sierragables.com
Silver Lake Resort	June Lake	Other	Cabins	$$–$$$	P.O. Box 116 June Lake, CA 93529 Phone: 760-648-7525	www.silverlakeresort.net
Tamarack Lodge and Resort	Mammoth Lakes	Mountain	Rooms, cabins	$–$$$	P.O. Box 69 Mammoth Lakes, CA 93546 Phone: 760-934-2442 or 800-MAMMOTH	www.tamaracklodge.com guestservices@tamaracklodge.com
Tom's Place Resort	Crowley Lake	Other	Rooms, cabins	$–$$	HCR 79, Box 22-A Crowley Lake, CA 93546 Phone: 760-935-4239 Fax: 760-935-9160	www.tomsplaceresort.com tomsplaceresort@earthlink.net
Whispering Pines Resort	June Lake	Other	Rooms, cabins	$–$$$	18 Nevada St. June Lake, CA 93529 Phone (CA): 800-648-7762 Phone: 760-872-6828 or 760-872-6828 Fax: 760-748-7589	www.discoverwhisperingpines.com
Wildyrie Lodge	Mammoth Lakes	Mountain	Rooms, cabins	$–$$$	P.O. Box 109 Mammoth Lakes, CA 93546 Phone: 760-934-2444	www.mammothweb.com/lodging/index.cfm
Woods Lodge	Mammoth Lakes	Mountain	Cabins	$$–$$$	P.O. Box 108 Mammoth Lakes, CA 93546 Phone: 760-934-2261	www.mammothweb.com/lodging/index.cfm

Note: Most Crowley Lake postal addresses are actually in Mammoth Lakes for U.S. Post Office purposes.

Towns and Agencies

Name	Nearest Community	Type	Contact Information	Website and Email Address
Big Pine Chamber of Commerce and Visitors Bureau	Big Pine	Community	P.O. Box 23 Big Pine, CA 93513 Phone: 866-938-2114	www.bigpine.com bigpinechamber@netscape.net
Bishop Area Chamber of Commerce and Visitors Bureau	Bishop	Community	690 N. Main St. Bishop, CA 93514 Phone: 760-873-8405 or 888-395-3952	www.bishopvisitor.com info@bishopvisitor.com
Independence Chamber of Commerce	Independence	Community	P.O. Box 397 Independence, CA 93526 Phone: 760-878-0084	www.independence-ca.com info@independence-ca.com
June Lake Chamber of Commerce	June Lake	Community	P.O. Box 2 June Lake, CA 93529 Phone: 760-648-7584	www.junelakechamber.org
Lone Pine Chamber of Commerce	Lone Pine	Community	P.O Box 749 Lone Pine, CA 93545 Phone: 877-253-8981 or 760-876-4444 Fax: 760-876-9205	www.lonepinechamber.org info@lonepinechamber.org
Mammoth Lakes Visitors Bureau	Mammoth Lakes	Community	P.O. Box 48 Mammoth Lakes, CA 93546 Phone: 888-GO MAMMOTH or 760-934-2712 Fax: 760-934-7066	www.visitmammoth.com info@visitmammoth.com

1 **Chicken Spring Lake**

Place	Total Distance	Elevation	Difficulty Level	Type
Trailhead		9920		
Streamside stop	3	9960	E	O&B
Cottonwood Pass	8	11,200	S	O&B
Chicken Spring Lake	9	11,270	S	O&B

Best Time   Early July–late August
Topo   *Cirque Peak 7.5'*
Where to Stay
   Note: A variety of lodgings are available in Lone Pine.
   Mountain: None
   Other: None
   Towns and Agencies: Lone Pine Chamber of Commerce

HIGHLIGHTS   The drive to the trailhead is very scenic and airy. You're in the high country from the minute you step out of the car. The well-graded trail passes through a wonderfully varied alpine landscape up to superb views at Cottonwood Pass. Chicken Spring Lake, tucked right under Cirque Peak, is starkly beautiful.

HOW TO GET TO THE TRAILHEAD   From the traffic light in Lone Pine, at the intersection of Highway 395 and Whitney Portal Road, turn west on Whitney Portal Road and follow it 3.5 miles to Horseshoe Meadow Road. Turn left (south) onto Horseshoe Meadow Rd. as it snakes up the mountainside to a fork at about 20 miles. Go ahead to the Horseshoe Meadow and Kern Plateau trailheads at the road's end at a parking lot, 0.5 mile more, which has water and restrooms.

ON THE TRAIL   Pick up the sandy trail by a large information sign to the right of the restrooms and head west through an open forest of lodgepole and foxtail pines, soon entering Golden Trout Wilderness. The gradually rising trail stays in the forest edge as you skirt broad, dusty Horseshoe Meadow and bypass a use trail left to Trail and Mulkey passes. Stay on the main trail and near the west end of Horseshoe Meadow cross a couple of forks of Cottonwood Creek one after the other (they look like one crossing on the book's map). Just beyond there's a lovely, shady, streamside stop at 1.5 miles and 9960 feet, with lots of nice rocks to sit on. Sharp-eyed hikers may spot an old log cabin to the south— look but don't disturb.

   Continuing, cross the creek once more, pass a small, flowery meadow, and then begin a moderate, switchbacking climb toward Cottonwood Pass. Views soon open up over Horseshoe Meadow. Cross the creek again partway up, where there's a fine display of flowers in season. Just below the pass, a signed but unmapped stock bypass route branches right; go left, staying on the main trail.

Chicken Spring Lake

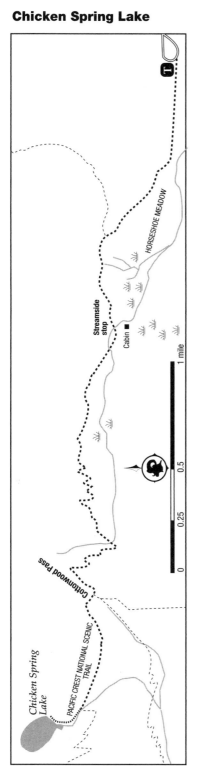

Shortly reach Cottonwood Pass at a little less than 4 miles and 11,200 feet. The view westward, over Kern Plateau and Kern Canyon, toward one of the Sierra's most beautiful subranges, the Great Western Divide, is sublime.

A few steps west of Cottonwood Pass, meet the Pacific Crest Trail (PCT) at a three-way junction. Turn right on the Pacific Crest Trail and follow it for almost 0.6 mile to the rocky outlet stream of Chicken Spring Lake. Turn right and follow the outlet, which is often dry by late season, upstream a short way to reach Chicken Spring Lake at 4.5 miles and 11,270 feet. This beautiful lake is a popular spot, so you'll probably have company.

Return the way you came.

2 Lone Pine Lake

Place	Total Distance	Elevation	Difficulty Level	Type
Trailhead		8365		
Lone Pine Lake	5.5	9940	M	O&B

Note   Permit required to go farther than Lone Pine Lake
Best Time Early July–late August
Topos   WP *Mt. Whitney* 15'; *Mt. Langley, Mount Whitney* 7.5'
Where to Stay
  Note: A variety of lodgings are available in Lone Pine.
  Mountain: None
  Other: None
  Towns and Agencies: Independence Chamber of Commerce, Lone Pine
  Chamber of Commerce

HIGHLIGHTS Experience the easiest and prettiest part of the famous, crowded, and brutal trail to the summit of Mt. Whitney on this delightful, moderate hike to the area's loveliest lake.

HOW TO GET TO THE TRAILHEAD At the traffic light in Lone Pine where Highway 395 intersects Whitney Portal Road, turn west onto Whitney Portal Road and follow it into the steep canyon below Mt. Whitney for 13 miles to its end at Whitney Portal. The trailhead is on the north side of the road (not the parking lot) and is initially lined by information signs. Water, restrooms, a store, a fishing pond, and café are available at the trailhead. Be aware that the trailhead is very crowded, which the facilities can sometimes reflect.

ON THE TRAIL From the information signs, climb northeast gradually to moderately under white firs and Jeffrey pines, on coarse granite sand. A few switchbacks bring you out onto the open, sagebrush-dotted northwest side of the canyon, and this traverse offers good views east over the Owens Valley and west toward Mt. Whitney. In season, there's a good show of fall color in this canyon. On the next switchbacks, note the dashing cascade on Lone Pine Creek.

Lone Pine Lake

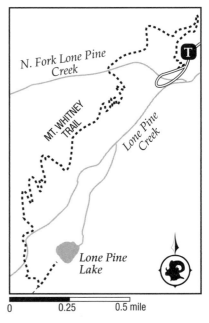

0   0.25   0.5 mile

See It at the Movies!

Whitney Portal may be the most famous trailhead in the Sierra. In the 1941 gangster flick *High Sierra*, the law chases crook Roy "Mad Dog" Earle (played by Humphrey Bogart) and moll Ida-Marie Garson (played by Ida Lupino) to Lone Pine, finally nailing Mad Dog at Whitney Portal. Mt. Whitney itself has appeared in dozens of films, often substituting for the Himalayas.

Cross a couple of streams, soon enter open-to-sparse forest cover, and reach the boundary of John Muir Wilderness. Lodgepole pines now dominate the forest. It's not long before you cross the creek and shortly reach the junction with the spur trail to Lone Pine Lake. Turn left (northeast), leaving the crowds behind, and descend 0.25 mile to the edge of lovely Lone Pine Lake at 2.75 miles and 9940 feet. The views are surprising from the far side of the lake.

Retrace your steps.

3 Kearsarge Trail Lakes

Place	Total Distance	Elevation	Difficulty Level	Type
Trailhead		9200		
Little Pothole Lake	3.3	10,050	M	O&B
Gilbert Lake	5	10,400	M	O&B
Flower Lake	5.3	10,530	M	O&B
Matlock Lake	6.6	10,560	S U	O&B

Best Time   Early July–mid-October
Topo   *Kearsarge Peak 7.5'*
Where to Stay
   Note: A variety of lodgings are available in Lone Pine.
   Mountain: None
   Other: None
   Towns and Agencies: Independence Chamber of Commerce, Lone Pine Chamber of Commerce

HIGHLIGHTS   Four lovely lakes lie along a well-graded trail that also offers fine views over Owens Valley. Each lake has its own charm—can you decide which is your favorite?—and there's a wonderful display of flowers in season.

HOW TO GET TO THE TRAILHEAD   From Highway 395 in Independence, turn west on Market Street, south of the courthouse. Follow this road as it makes a steep, switchbacking climb for 13.3 miles to a circular parking area that serves three trailheads. Day-use parking is by the restrooms, where water is also available.

Kearsarge Trail Lakes

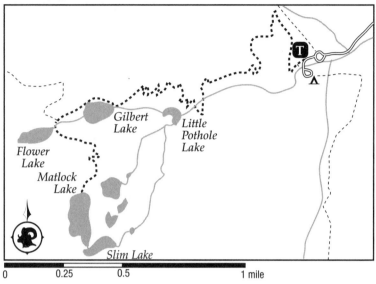

ON THE TRAIL Of the three trailheads here, take the middle one, for Kearsarge Pass, reached by heading southwest on a well-marked trail just past the restrooms. Begin a gradual to moderate ascent on rocky-dusty switchbacks in the scant shade of red fir, foxtail pine, and western white pine; there's a dazzling array of flowers. Near 0.3 mile, be sure to avoid a use trail that veers off to the right. In 0.75 mile reach the John Muir Wilderness boundary and pause to enjoy over-the-shoulder views back to the Owens Valley. The switchbacks grow shorter near a tumbling creek with some cool, shady, flowery nooks. Marshy and dry sections alternate until the trail is above Little Pothole Lake at 1.6 miles and 10,050 feet. The willow-ringed lake is nice, but the real show is the beautiful cascades on the south and west that are the lake's inlets. Enjoy good views of University Peak to the south, Independence Peak to the east-southeast, and Kearsarge Peak to the north-northeast.

Resume the ascent, brushing up to a slopeside meadow before emerging onto a talus slope where the trail has been cleared through the talus. Top a bench, level out, and reach flower-ringed Gilbert Lake at 2.5 miles and 10,400 feet—what a beauty! Leaving Gilbert, the trail switchbacks through some huge boulders to reach a marked junction with the spur trail to Matlock Lake that's right next to the east end of Flower Lake at 2.6 miles and 10,530 feet. Take a minute to follow either of a couple of use trails down to Flower Lake's serene, cliff-backed shoreline.

Back at the spur-trail junction, turn south to cross Flower Lake's outlet and begin switchbacking up the ridge that separates Matlock and its companion lakes from Flower and Gilbert lakes. Just beyond the top of the ridge, at 10,660 feet, there's a view of Matlock Lake and the unnamed, roundish lake to its east, as well as of Dragon and Kearsarge peaks to the northwest and north. Descend moderately to splendid Matlock Lake at 3.3 miles and 10,560 feet, sitting in a beautiful cirque.

Return the way you came, enjoying stunning views eastward, clear over the tops of the Inyo Mountains and on into Nevada.

4 Big Pine Lakes

Place	Total Distance	Elevation	Difficulty Level	Type
Trailhead		7800		
First Falls	0.5+	7950	E	O&B
Second Falls viewpoint	3	8950	E	O&B
First Lake	9	10,000	S	O&B
Second Lake	9.5	10,100	S	O&B

Best Time   Late May–mid-October
Topos   *Split Mountain, Coyote Flat 7.5'*
Where to Stay
  Mountain: Glacier Lodge
  Other: None
  Towns and Agencies: Big Pine Chamber of Commerce and Visitors Bureau, Bishop Area Chamber of Commerce and Visitors Bureau

HIGHLIGHTS   Showy cascades and flower-blessed streamside meadows along North Fork Big Pine Creek make rewarding goals. Beyond them lie splendid alpine lakes that mirror rugged peaks like Temple Crag, whose convoluted face offers at least a score of world-class climbing routes.

HOW TO GET TO THE TRAILHEAD   From the intersection of Highway 395 and Crocker Street, turn west on Crocker Street and follow it for 11 winding miles to the trailhead, which is at the roadend past the spur road to Glacier Lodge. Trailhead parking is for day users only; overnight users must use the lot 0.7 mile back down and just off the road. If the trailhead parking is full, there's limited day-use parking along the spur road to Glacier Lodge. The trailhead has restrooms.

ON THE TRAIL   From the roadend, head west-southwest past a locked gate, on a continuation of the road and next to rushing Big Pine Creek. The trail is marked SOUTH FORK BIG PINE TRAIL TO NORTH FORK BIG PINE TRAIL. Pass a number of summer cabins, but don't take the numerous paths to any of them. At a second wide spot in the road, turn right (uphill) and shortly veer left toward the creek on a signed, rocky footpath. A switchback leg leads to a bridged crossing of the creek over the handsome cascades known as First Falls at a little over 0.25 mile and 7950 feet.

Just beyond the bridge, there's a junction. The left (southwest) trail along Big Pine Creek South Fork has fine wildflower displays but no destinations meeting this book's criteria, so turn right, up the North Fork, and begin a series of very short, moderate to steep, open switchbacks next to the creek. Soon there's a view over the bouldery wash of South Fork Big Pine Creek. The grade eases as the shade increases, and use trails dart off to the creekside. Staying on the main

Big Pine Lakes

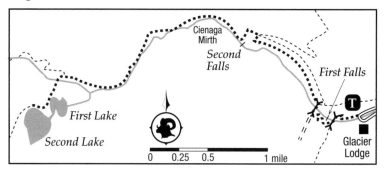

trail, meet an old road at a T-junction near 0.6 mile. Go right (north) on the old road—the part you walk is shown as a trail on the book's map—almost immediately crossing the creek on another bridge and reaching another junction: left (north-northwest) on the old road right (east-southeast) and up to the sometimes-unsigned upper trail, and hard right (southeast) and level to the often-unsigned First Falls Walk-in Campground. For this hike, go either left on the old road or right on the upper trail, which soon switchbacks and heads in the same general direction as the old road but many feet above it. The confusion of roads and trails here reflects a long-gone era when there was a car campground here, Second Falls Campground on the topo. (The ex-roads and that campground are casualties of floods in the 1980s.)

On the road, the route remains level as it passes use trails that lead left to the stream; below Second Falls, moderate switchbacks climb to meet the upper trail. Or, on the upper trail, climb steeply but briefly, make a switchback turn, and then climb gradually on an open, scenic slope. Either way, the long cascades of Second Falls soon come into view ahead as the trail heads northwest, skirting Mt. Alice to the southwest. If you're on the road, the road narrows back to a trail as it passes under some cottonwoods and begins climbing; avoid a use trail left toward the falls near a switchback turn—it goes nowhere.

Both routes have a good view of Second Falls near 1.5 miles and 8590 feet at a junction where the routes rejoin. After taking in the view, go left (northwest) on the hot, open trail, switchbacking moderately up to the brink of Second Falls. The trail straightens out just above the falls and begins a gradual climb on the north side of the creek. A flower-filled meadow lines the creek, while the trail stays somewhat higher on open, sandy soil. Around 2.3 miles, the trail alternates through patches of cool forest and squishy, flowery meadow. At 2.6 miles pass a spur trail (not on the map) left to signed BIG PINE CREEK WILDERNESS RANGER CAMP. This handsome, streamside stone cabin at Cienaga Mirth was once a vacation home for actor Lon Chaney. Now it's a backcountry summer ranger station.

After a brief, sunstruck stretch, ascend to a lodgepole-studded granite bench. Meadow and forest alternate atop the bench here, the flower display is delightful, and the creek is never far away. Cross the stream near the 4-mile mark and again shortly beyond 4 miles.

Then, with the inspiring sight of Temple Crag to the southwest, begin a series of hot switchbacks to a junction at 4.3 miles. Turn left (west), cross a tiny stream, duck into forest cover, and soon pass a use trail that goes left down to campsites on First Lake's shore. Keep going to the next switchback turn, to a viewpoint above beautiful First Lake at 10,000 feet and 4.5 miles. The rugged peaks surrounding First and Second lakes make perfect settings for these two alpine gems.

To continue to Second Lake, stay on the main trail and ascend gradually, at 4.6 miles passing another use trail left to campsites above First Lake. It's just a few more steps to a big erratic near which there are picnic sites overlooking splendid Second Lake at 10,100 feet and 4.75 miles.

Return the way you came.

5 Treasure Lakes

Place	Total Distance	Elevation	Difficulty Level	Type
Trailhead		9800		
Treasure Lakes	6	10,688	S	O&B

Note   A stream crossing a little below the lakes can be very dangerous in early season.

Best Time   Early July–mid-October

Topos   *Mt. Thompson 7.5'*

Where to Stay

Mountain: Bishop Creek Lodge and Resort, Cardinal Village Resort, Parchers Resort

Other: None

Towns and Agencies: Bishop Area Chamber of Commerce and Visitors Bureau

Southernmost Treasure Lake

HIGHLIGHTS Cross one flower-lined stream after another before climbing to the Treasure Lakes, the lower two of which are breathtakingly lovely. There are stunning views along the way.

HOW TO GET TO THE TRAILHEAD From the traffic-light-controlled intersection of U.S. Highway 395 and West Line Street in Bishop, turn west onto West Line Street (State Route 168) and follow it up into the mountains to its junction with the marked road to South Lake. Turn left onto the South Lake road and follow it for 7 more miles, past Bishop Creek Lodge and Resort and Parchers Resort, to its end at a day-use parking lot just above South Lake at 22.3 miles, which has restrooms.

ON THE TRAIL Head south on the Bishop Pass Trail, into John Muir Wilderness and past an information sign, almost immediately crossing two tiny footbridges over a marshy, wonderfully flowery spot. In a few steps reach a junction where a stock trail from the pack station comes in sharply from the left; note this in order to avoid it on the way back. The trail dips briefly, and use trails dart off toward the shoreline (right).

Soon the trail climbs gradually to moderately, and the scenery over the lake is simply spectacular. At a marked junction with the Treasure Lakes Trail at a little over 0.75 mile, go right (south) to Treasure Lakes.

Head toward four-pronged Hurd Peak, and descend gradually to a footbridge over the first of South Lake's many inlets, many of which don't appear on the map and are seasonal. Curve down and around the head of the valley in which South Lake lies and cross several inlets. Bob over a low ridge and make a dry southwest traverse, at times heading for a prominent crag between Mts. Gilbert and Johnson. A patch of thinning forest along this traverse allows for good views over South Lake's south bay.

The roar of a runoff stream heralds the next inlet. Descend steeply to moderately to cross it on a footbridge. Beyond it, the

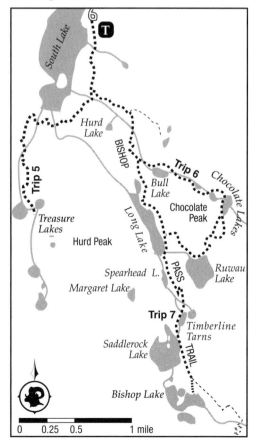

Treasure, Chocolate, and Bishop Lakes

next inlet is unbridged, and multiple tracks tell of hikers' searches for places to cross safely. Depending on the season, there may be one or more other streams before the last major one, where the stock crossing is obvious but a good foot crossing isn't. Avoid a use trail that strikes north near the stock crossing.

Pick up the Treasure Lakes Trail on the west side of the stream near the stock crossing and cross an intermittent stream before beginning to climb moderately to steeply on rocky and dusty switchbacks, up the valley wall. It's not long before the forest thins and the grade eases near an outstanding viewpoint of South Lake to the north, the rugged Inconsolable Range to the east, and Hurd Peak to the southeast.

Soon the trail begins a southward ascent over open granite slabs, toward Peak 12047. Look for ducks as well as for the trail tread in the soil between the slabs. Curve eastward briefly to cross the Treasure Lakes' raging outlet—dangerous in early season and dicey just about any time. Climbing again, pass some seasonal ponds and then begin a steep, switchbacking climb on a trail blasted out of the polished granite slabs of knoll 10718.

The climb soon ends as the trail reaches the shore of the first Treasure Lake at just under 3 miles and 10,668 feet. With Peak 12047 towering over it and red heather blooming along its edges, the lake is glorious—well worth the hike. You may want to climb trailless knoll 10718, just north of the lake, for a spectacular view of the entire area. The trail continues around the lowest lake's northeast shore and reaches another alpine gem, the second Treasure Lake at 3 miles and 10,688 feet (after that, there's only a use trail).

Return the way you came.

6 Chocolate Lakes Loop

Place	Total Distance	Elevation	Difficulty Level	Type
Trailhead		9800		
Bull Lake only	4.5	10,780	M	O&B
Long Lake only	4.5	10,753	M	O&B
Ruwau Lake only	6.5	11,044	S	O&B
Entire semiloop	7.5	11,340	S	Semi

Best Time Early July–mid-October
Topo *Mt. Thompson 7.5'*
Where to Stay
  Mountain: Bishop Creek Lodge and Resort, Cardinal Village Resort, Parchers Resort
  Other: None
  Towns and Agencies: Bishop Area Chamber of Commerce and Visitors Bureau

See map on page 30

HIGHLIGHTS This full trip is one of the most rugged, demanding, scenic, and rewarding, but there are lots of wonderful shorter and scenic options.

HOW TO GET TO THE TRAILHEAD From the traffic-light-controlled intersection of U.S. Highway 395 and West Line Street in the town of Bishop, turn west onto West Line Street (State Route 168) and follow it up into the mountains to its junction with the marked road to South Lake. Turn left onto the South Lake road and follow it for 7 more miles, past Bishop Creek Lodge and Resort and Parchers Resort, to its end at a day-use parking lot, which has restrooms, just above South Lake at 22.3 miles.

ON THE TRAIL Head south on the Bishop Pass Trail, into John Muir Wilderness and past an information sign, almost immediately crossing two tiny footbridges over a marshy, wonderfully flowery spot. In a few steps reach a junction where a stock trail from the pack station comes in sharply from the left; note this in order to avoid it on the way back. The trail dips briefly, and use trails dart off on the right side toward the shoreline (right). Soon the trail climbs gradually to moderately, and the scenery over the lake is simply spectacular. At a marked junction with the Treasure Lakes Trail at a little over 0.75 mile, go left (southeast) at the Treasure Lakes Trail junction, and then right (south) at the obscure Marie Louise Lakes Trail junction, which may or may not be marked. (These tiny puddles aren't worth a visit.)

Cross a meadow on a footbridge and then wind up short switchbacks to a fine view of Hurd Lake. Continue zigzagging up with cocoa-topped Chocolate Peak visible ahead, and at almost 2 miles reach the junction with the trail to Bull Lake: The left (southeast) trail heads to Bull and Chocolate lakes, and the right (south) fork goes to Long Lake and Bishop Pass. The loop part of this trip starts and ends here. Bull Lake at 2.25 miles and 10,780 feet—just 0.25 mile away on the left fork—is a great destination for those wanting a shorter trip.

Continuing the trip, head for Long Lake, a little over 0.25 mile more on the right fork, staying right on the Bishop Pass Trail. Islet-dotted Long Lake at 2.25 miles and 10,753 feet is breathtaking—a deep-blue jewel in a setting of awesome peaks. The trail rolls along beside the lake for another half mile before reaching a junction at 2.75 miles with the trail to Ruwau Lake: The left (east-northeast) branch heads to Ruwau, Chocolate, and—yes—Bull lakes, and the right (south) fork continues to Bishop Lake (Trip 7) and Bishop Pass.

Go left on the narrow track to Ruwau Lake, climbing very steeply for about 0.3 mile, to a bench overlooking Margaret Lake. Continue climbing moderately to rocky, sparkling Ruwau Lake at 3.25 miles and 11,044 feet. Trace Ruwau's north shore to an unmarked, unmapped junction where an angler's trail forks right along the shore and the main trail begins a sometimes-steep, sometimes-rocky, sometimes-hard-to-follow ascent on the left fork.

The trail breaks its climb by dipping across a rocky chute that trends south to Ruwau and then climbs again to the saddle between Ruwau and the Chocolate lakes at 4 miles. The high point of this trip, this saddle is an 11,340-foot perch where it seems as if 13,525-foot Cloudripper, the highest peak of the Inconsolable Range—a subrange of the Sierra—is so close you could reach out and touch it.

Below to the northeast lies the highest and largest Chocolate Lake, and the steep chute that the route descends is often filled with snow until late season. (If that's the case, retrace your steps from here.) If the chute is snow-free, the route is still rough, more like an angler's route than a maintained trail. The topo shows two routes, one to the west, clinging to the side of Chocolate Peak, and another to the east that's largely under talus.

The west route is the better choice, so carefully work down it. The highest Chocolate Lake is surrounded by talus, and the trail makes a rocky, loose, up-and-down angler's route along its western edge. In descending along the Chocolate Lakes, you'll see many confusing use trails, but the standard route follows the highest lake's west shore, the middle lake's east shore, and the lowest lake's west shore.

With that in mind, squish through a marsh and cross the stream that connects the highest and middle lakes. Scramble along the middle lake's pretty east shore and then descend to cross the stream between the middle and lowest lakes below the stream's cascade from the middle lake. Climb up and over an outcrop, cross a patch of scree, and descend the meadow that stretches along the lowest lake's west side. Near the north end of the lowest lake, meet a use trail leading to the lake's east side. Continue north to begin a long, steep, rocky, often damp, northwest-trending descent to Bull Lake, 200 feet below, along the stream that connects the lakes.

Just before Bull Lake, cross the stream and curve northwest around Bull Lake's lovely north shore. The sight of Chocolate Peak—which should be named "Chocolate Sundae Peak"—reflected in Bull Lake is unforgettable. Use trails lead to campsites here and there, so keep a sharp eye out for the main trail. Make a short, steep, loose descent, and then rise slightly to meet the Bishop Pass Trail, 5.5 miles from the start at South Lake and 1.5 miles from the saddle.

Turn right (north) onto the Bishop Pass Trail and retrace your steps to the parking lot at South Lake.

7 Bishop Lake

Place	Total Distance	Elevation	Difficulty Level	Type
Trailhead		9800		
Long Lake	4.5	10,753	M	O&B
Timberline Tarns	7.3	11,080	S	O&B
Saddlerock Lake	8	11,128	S	O&B
Bishop Lake	8.6	11,240	S	O&B

Best Time   Early July–mid-October

Topos   *Mt. Thompson, North Palisade 7.5'*

Where to Stay

Mountain: Bishop Creek Lodge and Resort, Cardinal Village Resort, Parchers Resort

Other: None

Towns and Agencies: Bishop Area Chamber of Commerce and Visitors Bureau

See map on page 30

HIGHLIGHTS Like Trip 6, this is one of the most scenic trips in this book, but unlike Trip 6, it's leisurely, with only gradual to moderate climbs. Wander up a magnificent chain of lakes—one of the most beautiful Sierra chains accessible by dayhiking—in a setting of spectacular peaks. Twelve-thousand-foot peaks are so common in this region that most of them aren't even named!

HOW TO GET TO THE TRAILHEAD From the traffic-light-controlled intersection of U.S. Highway 395 and West Line Street in Bishop, turn west onto West Line Street (State Route 168) and follow it up into the mountains to its junction with the marked road to South Lake. Turn left onto the South Lake road and follow it for 7 more miles, past Bishop Creek Lodge Resort and Parchers Resort, to its end at a day-use parking lot, which has restrooms, just above South Lake at 22.3 miles.

ON THE TRAIL Head south on the Bishop Pass Trail, into John Muir Wilderness and past an information sign, almost immediately crossing two tiny footbridges over a marshy, wonderfully flowery spot. In a few steps reach a junction where a stock trail from the pack station comes in sharply from the left; note this in order to avoid it on the way back. The trail dips briefly, and use trails dart off on the right side toward the shoreline. Soon the trail climbs gradually to moderately, and the scenery over the lake is simply spectacular. At a marked junction with the Treasure Lakes Trail at a little over 0.75 mile, go left (southeast) at the Treasure Lakes Trail junction and then right (south) at the obscure Marie Louise Lakes Trail junction, which may or may not be marked. Cross a meadow on a footbridge and then wind up short switchbacks to a fine view of Hurd Lake. Continue zigzagging up with cocoa-topped Chocolate Peak visible ahead, and at almost 2 miles reach the junction with the trail to Bull Lake.

To head toward Bishop Lake, take the right (south) fork, staying on the Bishop Pass Trail. Islet-dotted Long Lake at 2.25 miles and 10,753 feet is breathtaking—a deep-blue jewel in a setting of awesome peaks. The trail rolls along beside the lake for another 0.5 mile before reaching a junction at 2.75 miles with the trail to Ruwau Lake. Continue ahead (south) on the Bishop Trail toward Bishop Lake, traversing above Long Lake and, nearing 3 miles from the start, descend to cross one of its inlets, which happens to be the outlet of Ruwau Lake. There's a sublime over-the-shoulder view of Long Lake and Chocolate Peak from here. Now begin a steady, gradual to moderate climb, passing well above Spearhead Lake, which is quickly becoming a meadow. Switchbacks above Spearhead also offer excellent views of Long Lake.

At the top of the climb, descend a little, cross an outlet stream, pass the westernmost of the pretty Timberline Tarns at 3.6 miles and 11,080 feet, and then climb along the lovely cascades that connect Saddlerock Lake above with the Timberline Tarns. Cross the stream to reach austerely beautiful Saddlerock Lake near 4 miles and at 11,128 feet, whose rocky setting is softened a little by alpine flowers and by the sparse pines on its northwest shore.

While climbing past Saddlerock Lake, look over to the bench that forms its northwest shore for a glimpse of small Ledge Lake. Soon the route passes a seasonal tarn, noted on the topo as a marsh, and then passes a meadow with snow-survey markers. At an unmarked junction near the snow-survey markers, a well-trod use trail veers right (south) to a rise above multi-lobed Bishop Lake, the highest and starkest large lake in the drainage of South Fork Bishop Creek.

Follow that use trail right and a short distance up to the top of the rise, where you find a good perch above Bishop Lake at 4.3 miles and 11,240 feet, and also some storm-stunted whitebark pines that offer a little shelter from the fierce winds that sweep across the lake. Stop here and savor the awe-inspiring view. Ahead to the south is the headwall of this glacier-carved cirque you've been ascending. To the west is 13,085-foot Mt. Goode; to the north are Peaks 12,916, 12,689, and 12,286; to the south is Bishop Pass; to the southeast is 13,893-foot Mt. Agassiz; and to the east 13,265-foot Aperture Peak at the southeast end of the Inconsolable Range.

Here, even after the hottest days, nighttime temperatures often drop to freezing, and people camped at Bishop Lake may wake to find ice in their water bottles. All seems stark and lifeless at first, but watch for scurrying rodents, dwarf willows, and some of the loveliest Sierra wildflowers, like Davidson's penstemon and Coville's columbine.

Retrace your steps.

8 Lake Sabrina and Blue, Donkey, Emerald, and Dingleberry Lakes

Place	Total Distance	Elevation	Difficulty Level	Type
Trailhead		9060		
Blue Lake	6	10,380	S	O&B
Donkey Lake	8.5	10,580	S	O&B
Emerald Lakes	8+	10,460	S	O&B
Dingleberry Lake	9.6	10,489	S	O&B

Best Time   Early July–mid-October
Topos   *Mt. Darwin, Mt. Thompson 7.5'*
Where to Stay
   Mountain: Bishop Creek Lodge and Resort, Cardinal Village Resort, Parchers Resort
   Other: None
   Towns and Agencies: Bishop Area Chamber of Commerce and Visitors Bureau

HIGHLIGHTS   Lovely Lake Sabrina makes an inviting start to this wonderful but demanding hike. The long climb from Sabrina to spectacular Blue Lake, "gateway" to the lovely lakes beyond, is worth it.

HOW TO GET TO THE TRAILHEAD   From the intersection of U.S. Highway 395 and West Line Street in the town of Bishop, turn west onto West Line Street (State Route 168) and follow it up into the mountains past the turnoff to South

Lake. Stay on Highway 168 (ahead, right) and continue past the turnoff to North Lake to day-use parking just beyond that turnoff at Lake Sabrina at a total of 22.1 miles.

ON THE TRAIL Find the trailhead on the left side of the road as you face Lake Sabrina's dam, below that dam and well-signed. Head south and soon switchback up to level out overlooking the pine- and aspen-ringed lake, up whose southwest headwall you'll hike to get to this trip's destinations. But for now, enjoy an easy stroll, climbing very gradually, along Sabrina's rocky, flowery shore.

Nearing 1 mile, begin climbing more steeply and presently reach the junction with the trail to George Lake. Go right (south) here, ducking into aspens and crossing George Lake's seasonally roaring outlet. Zigzag up a lodgepole-pine-clad slope, and at the next stream crossing (seasonal), revel in a great view north over Sabrina toward the White Mountains. The switchbacks rise generally northwest across a ridge overlooking Lake Sabrina and offering sweeping views.

At last curve south-southeast into a forested draw and follow the trail up short switchbacks to top out by some picturesque tarns above Blue Lake at 3 miles and 10,380 feet, spectacularly set beneath Thompson Ridge and the Sierra crest—a sight guaranteed to take your breath away. Following the trail, which is marked by lines of rocks, cross granite slabs lining Blue Lake's west shore. Near 3.25 miles, descend a little to a junction with the trails to Donkey Lake (left, south) and Emerald and Dingleberry lakes (right, northwest). From Blue Lake hikers can go to either Donkey Lake (8.5-mile round-trip) or to Emerald and Dingleberry lakes (9.6-mile round-trip). Going to all is certainly possible for sturdy hikers who get an early start.

Lake Sabrina and Blue, Donkey, Emerald, and Dingleberry Lakes

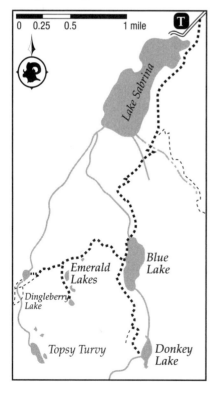

To go to Donkey Lake, turn left, strolling along the duff trail through still meadows, past fine old lodgepoles, and over rocky outcrops. A little beyond 3.75 miles, meet the Baboon Lakes' outlet stream and reach a faint junction that may be unmarked: left (east-southeast) on a rocky trail down toward the stream and to Donkey Lake or right (south-southwest) on a rocky track toward the Baboon Lakes. (The trail to the Baboon Lakes, which still appears on some maps, shortly vanishes, and the route requires boulder-scrambling skills.)

Go left again to continue to Donkey Lake, crossing the stream and picking up the increasingly faint trail on the other side. Bear right (south-southeast) on the other side of the stream, past a campsite, and wind up a little knoll. With the help of ducks, head south-southeast, past a little tarn on the right, and come out on the rocks above pretty Donkey Lake's west shore at 4.25 miles and 10,580 feet. Retrace your steps from here.

To go to Emerald and Dingleberry lakes, go right at the junction on Blue Lake's west shore, bobbing up and down through lodgepoles and then zigzagging across a slope where the trail has been blasted out of the granite. Curving toward the Sierra crest, meet a spur trail at 3.75 miles—the unsigned Emerald-Dingleberry junction. The left (south) trail goes to the rest of the Emerald Lakes, and the right (southwest) heads to Dingleberry Lake.

To reach the rest of the Emerald Lakes, go left on the spur trail, across a meadow that may be very muddy, and follow a well-beaten path generally southward with the help of ducks, past the meadow-ringed ponds and lakelets that make up lower Emerald Lakes, to an overlook of upper Emerald Lake. Veer right to descend to the grassy shore of upper Emerald Lake at a little over 4 miles and 10,460 feet. The lake is cupped in a little cirque under Peak 11,800.

To reach Dingleberry Lake, turn left (southwest) at the Emerald-Dingleberry junction. As the path climbs gradually, pass a tarn that resembles a giant's bathtub. Hike over granite slabs to emerge high above the south end of delightful Dingleberry Lake. When abreast of the inlet, pick a use trail and descend to the shore, where there are good rocks to lounge on. Dingleberry Lake is at 4.75 miles and 10,489 feet—including the 0.6 mile to and from upper Emerald Lake. The lake was named, according to *Place Names of the Sierra Nevada* by Peter Browning, for "dingleberries" on the fannies of the sheep that once grazed in this area.

Return the way you came.

9 Grass and Lamarck Lakes

Place	Total Distance	Elevation	Difficulty Level	Type
Trailhead		9260/9362		
Grass Lake	3.5	9860	M U	O&B
Lower Lamarck Lake	6.25	10,662	S	O&B
Upper Lamarck Lake	7.5	10,918	S	O&B

Note   The elevation is 9260 at the parking lot but is 9362 at the trailhead.

Best Time   Early July–mid-October

Topos   *Mt. Thompson, Mt. Darwin 7.5'*

Where to Stay

Mountain: Bishop Creek Lodge and Resort, Cardinal Village Resort, Parchers Resort

Other: None

Towns and Agencies: Bishop Area Chamber of Commerce and Visitors Bureau

Grass, Lamarck, Loch Leven, and Piute Lakes

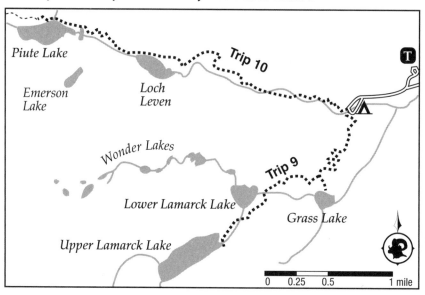

HIGHLIGHTS Few high Sierra trips offer both the sheltered feel of little Grass Lake and the open, wild feel of the Lamarck Lakes. Surprisingly few people head for this lovely area; most hikers are bound for the next drainage north, toward Piute Pass (Trip 10). Fine scenery on the way adds to your enjoyment of this trip, and aspens along the trail provide good fall color in season.

HOW TO GET TO THE TRAILHEAD From the traffic-light-controlled intersection of U.S. Highway 395 and West Line Street (State Route 168) in Bishop, turn west and follow State Route 168 up into the mountains past the turnoff to South Lake to the turnoff to North Lake, just before Lake Sabrina. Turn right onto the North Lake road and follow this narrow, sometimes unpaved road on an airy traverse of the ridge separating North Lake and Lake Sabrina. Turn into the pretty valley that holds little North Lake, pass it on your right, and turn right on the marked spur to the pack station and parking. Pass the pack station's entrance and continue to one of two hiker parking lots at a total of 19.7 miles. The official trailhead is 0.5 mile farther up the road, at the upper end of North Lake Campground. Since you can't park there, for all practical purposes, the trip starts at the parking lots. Restrooms are available at the parking lots, and both restrooms and water are available in the campground.

ON THE TRAIL From the parking lot, walk on the spur road past the pack station, and turn right onto the North Lake Road. Follow the road to the campground and take either branch of the campground road—the right branch is slightly shorter—to a parking spot for some walk-in sites at 0.5 mile at the upper end of the campground. Continue a few more feet to the marked trailhead.

Go left (south) through a delightful mix of forest and flowers. Cross three little footbridges (not shown on the book's map), pass a use trail on the left, and shortly begin a long series of moderate switchbacks. The orange-tinted, rugged Piute Crags backdrop the shimmering green aspens along the trail. Slant up a boulder-strewn slope and then briefly level out on a delightful, lodgepole-shaded bench. Resume the switchbacks, and at 1.5 miles reach the junction of Grass and Lamarck lakes trails.

Go left (south) to Grass Lake, at first proceeding levelly across a lodgepole- and boulder-studded moraine at about 9960 feet. Then begin a rocky, 100-foot descent toward a broad meadow and Grass Lake at 1.75 miles and 9860 feet, cupped by forested slopes.

Back at the Grass and Lamarck lakes junction—2 miles into the trip now—turn right (northwest) to the Lamarck Lakes. Soon resume the switchbacking ascent and get a view over the saddle south of Grass to the beautiful glaciers and peaks of distant Thompson Ridge, on the far side of Lake Sabrina. Leave the forest behind and switchback across open sagebrush slopes, enjoying wonderful views of the North Fork Bishop Creek drainage east to the White Mountains. Pass a pond on the right and then reach beautiful Lower Lamarck Lake at 3 miles and 10,662 feet, to your right. Under the stern gaze of Peaks 12153 and 12691, it is cradled in granite, outlined by stunted lodgepoles and whitebarks, and has some nice picnic rocks around its edge.

Leaving Lower Lamarck Lake, dip across its outlet below a lovely pool, round an outcrop, and begin walking up a narrow valley. The sandy trail crosses the valley and traverses rocky slopes, where a wonderful view of Lower Lamarck Lake and its dashing inlet stream opens up on the right. Bypass a use trail to the lake's shore and instead begin switchbacking steeply up the east side of the inlet-outlet stream's gully, curving southwest with the gully. Cross the stream about halfway up and continue the loose ascent on the gully's west side to a beautiful, stream-threaded meadow below Upper Lamarck Lake.

Turn west-southwest on the main trail, cross the outlet stream once more below the lake, and emerge at Upper Lamarck Lake at 3.75 miles and 10,918 feet. The lake is big by high Sierra standards, a long sheet of brilliant blue water that ends abruptly at a steep moraine. On the crest, slightly to the left of the far end, is Mt. Lamarck; Lamarck Col is a little left of it; and Peak 12153 towers to the right.

Return the way you came.

10 Loch Leven and Piute Lake

Place	Total Distance	Elevation	Difficulty Level	Type
Trailhead		9260/9362		
Loch Leven	6.6	10,743	S	O&B
Piute Lake	8.6–9+	10,958	S	O&B

Note	The elevation is 9260 at the parking lot but is 9362 at the trailhead.
Best Time	Early July–mid-October
Topos	*Mt. Thompson, Mt. Darwin 7.5'*

See map on page 38

Where to Stay

Mountain: Bishop Creek Lodge and Resort, Cardinal Village Resort, Parchers Resort
Other: None
Towns and Agencies: Bishop Area Chamber of Commerce and Visitors Bureau

HIGHLIGHTS The walk up North Fork Bishop Creek toward Piute Pass ranks as one of the most scenic in the Sierra. The first leg is famous for its summer flower gardens and fall color; the third leg leads along a string of glorious ponds and lakes. Marking the abrupt altitude change on the second leg, the creek splashes out of a pool below Loch Leven and more than 300 feet down a narrow slot in the rocks—a cool sight for a hot climb.

HOW TO GET TO THE TRAILHEAD From the traffic-light-controlled intersection of U.S. Highway 395 and West Line Street (State Route 168) in Bishop, turn west and follow State Route 168 up into the mountains past the turnoff to South Lake to the turnoff to North Lake, just before Lake Sabrina. Turn right onto the North Lake road and follow this narrow, sometimes unpaved road on an airy traverse of the ridge separating North Lake and Lake Sabrina. Turn into the pretty valley that holds little North Lake, pass it on your right, and turn right on the marked spur to the pack station and parking. Pass the pack station's entrance and continue to one of two hiker parking lots at a total of 19.7 miles. The official trailhead is 0.5 mile farther up the road, at the upper end of North Lake Campground. Since you can't park there, for all practical purposes, your trip starts at the parking lots. Restrooms are available at the parking lots, and both restrooms and water are available in the campground.

ON THE TRAIL From the parking lot, walk on the spur road, pass the pack station, turn right on the main road, and follow it into the upper campground to the junction of the trails to Grass and Lamarck lakes and Loch Leven and Piute Lake.

Go right (west) toward Piute Pass on a rocky, very dusty trail favored by equestrians. Moderate forest cover is interspersed with openings that offer lush, brilliantly colored wildflowers in season. The trail gradually swings nearer the creek, where the flower display gets even better, and you have occasional glimpses of orange-y Piute Crags and of Mt. Emerson. Around 1.25 miles, cross the creek twice, which may be difficult early in the season. Beyond here, open spots begin to offer wonderful over-the-shoulder views down-canyon. Nearing 2 miles, the forest cover dwindles to scattered whitebark pines on the scree and talus slopes below Piute Crags and Mt. Emerson; this leg can get very hot on a warm day. The trail ascends in lazy, dusty switchbacks, and the roar of water signals the cascade below Loch Leven.

At 2.75 miles begin winding moderately to steeply up stone "stairs" through granite outcrops on a reconstructed segment of the trail. Back on the older trail, turn west past a pond below Loch Leven, climb a little more, and emerge above

Loch Leven at 3.3 miles and 10,743 feet—the prettiest lake in this chain. The trail descends to Loch Leven's shore, where there's an exhilarating view west over it toward Piute Pass. The trail then follows the rocky shore, where there are plenty of picnic spots under the whitebark pines. As if to defy the high altitude and the long, bitter winters, abundant wildflowers carpet the shoreline and shelter among the boulders in season.

Continuing, wander through beautiful meadows and up past several more picturesque ponds and lakelets, each different, yet all brightened by the same sturdy alpine wildflowers.

Reach windswept Piute Lake at 4.3 miles and 10,958 feet, the largest in this chain. Be careful not to disturb the snow-survey cabin on the south side of its outlet. Follow the trail along the north side of this beautiful lake as far as a multibranched inlet stream at 4.5 miles. Beyond here, the trail climbs again; take in the incredible panorama up toward the crest and down toward Owens Valley. Although it doesn't look far away, Piute Pass lies almost 1.5 miles farther on at 11,423 feet, so this is a great place to stop.

Retrace your steps to the trailhead.

11 Francis and Dorothy Lakes

Place	Total Distance	Elevation	Difficulty Level	Type
Trailhead		9695		
Francis Lake only	5.5	10,860	M	O&B
Dorothy Lake only	6	10,500	M	O&B
Both lakes	8.5	10,860	S	O&B

Best Time Early July–mid-October
Topo *Mt. Morgan 7.5'*
Where to Stay
  Mountain: Convict Lake Resort, Rock Creek Lakes Resort, Rock Creek Lodge
  Other: McGee Creek Lodge, Mono Sierra Lodge, Rainbow Tarns Bed and Breakfast, Sierra Gables Motel, Tom's Place Resort
  Towns and Agencies: Mammoth Lakes Visitors Bureau

HIGHLIGHTS Don't be fooled by the first part of this trip, which is up and across the top of a large, dry, sandy moraine. That makes beautiful, meadow-blessed Francis and Dorothy lakes all the more fun to discover. Francis's setting is more rugged, while Dorothy's is more flowery and tranquil; both are delightful.

HOW TO GET TO THE TRAILHEAD From U.S. Highway 395, turn west on Rock Creek Road at Tom's Place and cross Crowley Lake Drive. Follow the road through a dry pinyon pine forest and past several turnoffs into campgrounds,

Francis and Dorothy Lakes

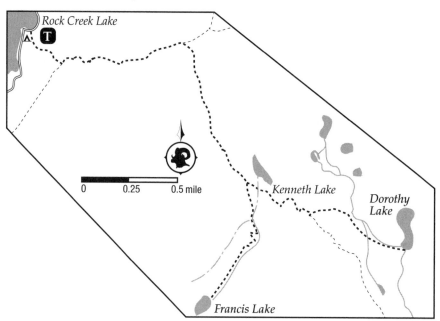

past the turnoff to Rock Creek Lodge, as far as the turnoff left to Rock Creek Lake and the lake's campground. Turn left as if for the campground and follow the spur road past picnic areas and into the campground parking lot. The trailhead is in the campground; look for parking spaces marked for day use rather than camping, on the east side of the spur road, opposite a cinderblock restroom, about 9.2 miles from 395. Park carefully as some spaces are reserved for those camping here. The trailhead has restrooms and water. Nearby Rock Creek Lakes Resort has a store and café.

ON THE TRAIL At the TAMARACK TRAILHEAD sign, curve right at the sign and begin a steady, moderate to steep climb under sparse lodgepole cover on a rocky and sandy trail, east-northeast up a gully on the moraine east of Rock Creek Lake. This initial climb can be hot on a sunny day. In 0.25 mile reach a T-junction with an old road (shown as a trail on the book's map); turn left (north) here and follow the old road up, heading generally east and enjoying views toward Mono Pass (south) and over Rock Creek Lake. From here to the turnoff to Kenneth Lake, the hiking route overlaps the Sand Canyon Mountain Bike Trail.

A little beyond 0.5 mile, the grade eases in the welcome shade of a clump of lodgepoles, with fine over-the-shoulder views of Mt. Huntington, Mt. Stanford, and Rock Creek Lake. Still on the old road, ramble through dry forest, climbing gradually, to a junction at nearly 1 mile. Go right (east) onto a foot trail and toward Kenneth Lake, shortly entering John Muir Wilderness, crossing a low ridge, and skirting a meadow. Hike up a shallow draw to a sandy, lupine-dotted saddle, from which there are magnificent views of Mt. Morgan, Broken Finger Peak, and Wheeler Ridge. Descending, you cross another meadow, wander over another low ridge, and reach the Francis-Kenneth junction at 1.6 miles: right (south) to Francis Lake and left (ahead, east) to Kenneth, Dorothy, and Tamarack lakes.

To go to Francis Lake, take the right fork and begin climbing steeply. The grade soon eases to a gradual to moderate traverse of this slope. After crossing a seasonal trickle, reach the willow-choked outlet of Francis Lake and ascend moderately to steeply, with the help of a few switchbacks. Whitebarks replace the lodgepoles as you climb; midway, swing west of the outlet. The trail levels off as it swings back toward the outlet, and there are wonderful flower gardens along the stream here. Continue along the outlet to the north shore of sparkling Francis Lake at 2.75 miles and 10,860 feet. The gentle meadow immediately around this pretty lake contrasts wonderfully with the surrounding rugged slopes that are outliers of Mt. Morgan and Broken Finger Peak. Retrace your steps.

To go to Dorothy Lake, take the left fork at the Francis-Kenneth junction over one more ridgelet and descend to pretty Kenneth Lake, which by late season in a dry year may dry up. But there's a fine wildflower display here, deep in the meadow that Kenneth's shrinkage has left behind. After crossing a seasonal inlet, ascend another ridge moderately to steeply, enjoying good views from open spots. At 2.25 miles from the start, not including the side trip to Francis Lake, reach another junction. Go left (east) to Dorothy, soon spotting a broad, flower-strewn meadow along a bright stream below to your left. Descending from the ridge to the meadow, walk through the meadow, hopping over streamlets, toward Broken Finger Peak. Arrive at the south end of lovely Dorothy Lake at 3 miles and 10,500 feet, where the inlet and outlet streams are only a few steps apart. In late season, the display of gentians in Dorothy Lake's meadow is dazzling. Retrace your steps.

12 Hilton Lakes

Place	Total Distance	Elevation	Difficulty Level	Type
Trailhead		9860		
Hilton Lake 3	8.6	10,300	S U	O&B
Hilton Lake 4	10	10,353	S U	O&B

Best Time   Early July–mid-October

Topos   *Mt. Morgan, Mt. Abbot, Convict Lake 7.5'*

Where to Stay

Mountain: Convict Lake Resort, Rock Creek Lakes Resort, Rock Creek Lodge

Other: McGee Creek Lodge, Mono Sierra Lodge, Rainbow Tarns Bed and Breakfast, Sierra Gables Motel, Tom's Place Resort

Towns and Agencies: Mammoth Lakes Visitors Bureau

HIGHLIGHTS After a very long traverse and a climb over the ridge between Rock and Hilton creeks, this trail leads to a junction. To the south and higher are

Hilton Lakes 3 and 4, which will appeal to lovers of open, alpine lakes. To the north and lower are Hilton Lake 2 and Davis Lake; both are heavily used by packers and, therefore, omitted from this trip.

HOW TO GET TO THE TRAILHEAD

From U.S. Highway 395 turn west on Rock Creek Road at Toms Place, cross Crowley Lake Drive, and follow the road past Rock Creek Lake to a parking area on the right side of the road, 9.3 miles from the highway. The Hilton Lakes Trailhead, which has no facilities, is about 400 feet back down the road from here. Restrooms and water are available in Rock Creek Lake Campground. Nearby Rock Creek Lakes Resort has a store and café.

ON THE TRAIL Walk back down the road those 400 feet to the trailhead.

Mt. Huntington over Hilton Lake 3

From there, immediately begin a gradual to moderate climb north-northeast, first through a lodgepole-aspen forest and then on exposed slopes that boast an amazing array of flowers in season. A switchback turn affords excellent views over Rock Creek Lake and the peaks south, around Little Lakes Valley. Nearing 0.5 mile, cross a seasonal channel, and at 0.6 mile cross a stream and reach the John Muir Wilderness boundary. Ford a few more creeks and dry channels and note that a junction shown on the topo, with a steep trail down to Pine Grove Campground, no longer exists.

A little past 1.6 miles, the trail curves northwest, dips across a forested gully, and then swings up the next ridge, through shrubby aspens. A little past 2 miles, reach a junction whose left fork has been intentionally blocked off; go right (northwest) and enjoy glimpses of Peaks 11950 and 11962 upslope on the left. Curve through an open, sandy forest of lodgepoles and skirt a large meadow that's fringed with aspen and invaded by lodgepoles. Then curve generally west around the bases of Peaks 11950 and 11962. Around 2.6 miles, the grade increases. Slog uphill on the wide, sandy trail to top out on a saddle at 10,380 feet—higher than any of the lakes—north of Peak 11962, where you glimpse the Sierra crest through breaks in the forest. Heading west toward Peak 12508, cross an area covered by the sun-bleached trunks of trees felled by an avalanche in the early 1980s. The reestablished trail dodges through this giant-sized game of pick-up sticks and descends on gradual to moderate switchbacks to a pocket meadow and then a trail junction at 4 miles: The left (southwest) trail heads to Hilton Lakes 3 and 4; and the right (north) branch continues to Hilton Lake 2 and Davis Lake.

Go left at the junction to cross a seasonal stream, pass a small meadow, and begin a series of unrelenting switchbacks up, leveling out at fabulous views

Hilton Lakes

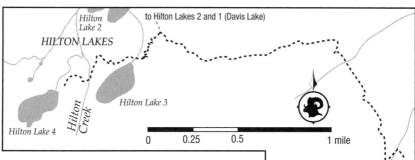

northward over Hilton Lake 2 and Davis Lake and across Long Valley to Glass Ridge. Cross the stream connecting Lakes 2 and 3; Hilton Lake 3 is visible upstream. The main trail is rather faint around here. Leave it and briefly follow a use trail upstream to the lake's edge, where you find a breathtaking alpine scene: flower-ringed Hilton Lake 3 at 4.3 miles and 10,300 feet, with a dramatic backdrop of Mts. Huntington and Stanford.

Now return to the main trail, which crosses the stream and curves southwest along the lake's northwest shore; contrary to what the topo says, there's no trail branching left to the next higher set of lakes. The trail then veers west across a low ridge from which there's a fine view of the dashing cascades of Hilton Lake 5's outlet. Descend to cross the outlet in a meadow, bob over another ridgelet, and reach Hilton Lake 4 at almost 5 miles and 10,353 feet—another glorious alpine sight. The stunning peak on the lake's far side is Mt. Huntington. Retrace your steps.

13 Little Lakes Valley

Place	Total Distance	Elevation	Difficulty Level	Type
Trailhead		10,230		
Viewpoint by Mono-Morgan Junction	1	10,460	E	O&B
Marsh Lake	2	10,420	E	O&B
Heart Lake	2.5	10,420	E	O&B
Long Lake (south end)	4	10,540	M	O&B
Gem Lake	6.5	10,940	S	O&B

Best Time Early July–mid-October
Topos WP *Mt. Abbot* 15'; *Mt. Morgan, Mt. Abbot* 7.5'
Where to Stay
   Mountain: Convict Lake Resort, Rock Creek Lakes Resort, Rock Creek Lodge
   Other: McGee Creek Lodge, Mono Sierra Lodge, Rainbow Tarns Bed and Breakfast, Sierra Gables Motel, Tom's Place Resort
   Towns and Agencies: Mammoth Lakes Visitors Bureau

HIGHLIGHTS If you are interested in a trail that starts at the Sierra's highest trailhead and, climbing gradually for the most part, passes spectacular flower gardens and one pretty lake after another, all in a valley ringed by some of the range's loveliest peaks, this trip is for you. Get an early start though. The midsummer crowds are huge.

HOW TO GET TO THE TRAILHEAD From U.S. Highway 395, turn west on Rock Creek Road at Toms Place, cross Crowley Lake Drive, and follow the road past the Hilton Lakes Trailhead. The road gets quite narrow beyond Rock Creek Lake. Follow it to its end at Mosquito Flat, 10.7 miles from the highway. There's plenty of parking, as well as restrooms, for this trailhead.

ON THE TRAIL Roughly paralleling Rock Creek on the creek's west side, the broad, sandy trail is nearly level at first, soon enters John Muir Wilderness, and begins climbing moderately through a dazzling flower garden that's perhaps the best in the Eastern Sierra in season. A little short of 0.5 mile, reach a Y-junction: The left (south) trail heads to Little Lakes Valley and Morgan Pass, and the right (southwest) heads to Mono Pass—the southern of two passes with that name in the Eastern Sierra. Go left. A few steps away, find a spectacular viewpoint at 0.5 mile and 10,460 feet of Mack Lake below to the left (east) and beyond it of Mt. Morgan; of

Marsh Lake

Little Lakes Valley and Ruby Lake

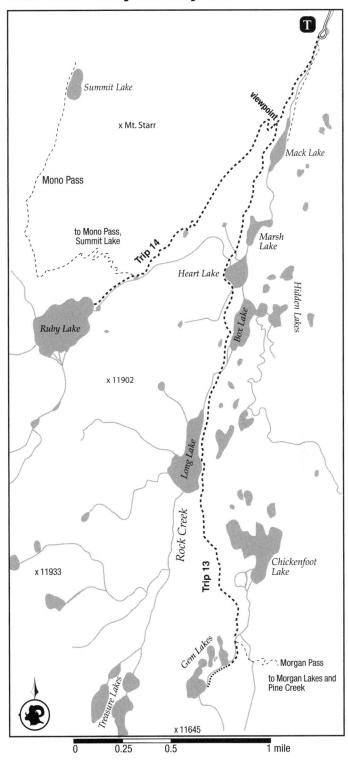

T

Summit Lake

x Mt. Starr

viewpoint

Mack Lake

Mono Pass

to Mono Pass,
Summit Lake

Trip 14

Marsh
Lake

Heart Lake

Hidden Lakes

Ruby Lake

Box Lake

x 11902

Long Lake

x 11933

Rock Creek

Trip 13

Chickenfoot
Lake

Gem Lakes

Morgan Pass

to Morgan Lakes and
Pine Creek

Treasure Lakes

x 11645

| 0 | 0.25 | 0.5 | | 1 mile |

hulking, bare Mt. Starr to the west; and of the glorious semicircle of peaks at the head of Little Lakes Valley to the south, including Bear Creek Spire and Mts. Mills, Abbot, and Dade.

Continue to Little Lakes Valley, descending across a noisy, flower-lined inlet and leveling out near the grassy south end of Mack Lake at nearly 0.6 mile. The trail rises and falls gradually as it passes broad-meadowed Marsh Lake at 1 mile at 10,420 feet and then sparkling Heart Lake near 1.25 miles and 10,420 feet. Heart Lake has multiple inlets; boulder-hop one and cross another on a footbridge that isn't shown on the book's map. At the south end of Heart Lake, a use trail veers left toward the east shore, but stick to the main trail, which rises a little along another of Heart's inlets, up a tiny, narrow, meadowed valley, topping out above handsome Box Lake. From this viewpoint, look for two more little lakes east of Box. They belong to a cluster of lakelets, the Hidden Lakes, that are almost completely surrounded by very wet meadows. Descend to the south end of Box Lake at 1.5 miles.

After a gentle to moderate ascent along the stream connecting Box and Long lakes, cross it, which may be difficult in early season, at 1.75 miles and soon reach splendid Long Lake, perhaps the most beautiful lake in this chain. Across the lake rise peaks whose rocks form bands of black and white. Traverse Long Lake's east shore to its grassy south end at a little more than 2 miles and 10,540 feet.

Now make a gradual ascent to a junction at a little beyond 2.6 miles with a spur trail (that is not shown on the map) that goes left (northeast) to Chickenfoot Lake, a total out-and-back excursion of about 0.25 mile (recommended!). The wide main trail goes right (south) here, dipping across a culvert. This trail was once a road to the tungsten mines in the next drainage south, Pine Creek, via Morgan Pass, and along this next stretch are a few rusting remnants of mining vehicles. (Nowadays, there's a far better road to the mines, which are currently inactive, right up Pine Creek.)

The trail curves left (east) toward Morgan Pass and crosses a rock-filled stream. Ahead, the old road climbs steeply to Morgan Pass, which has a nice view of the Gem Lakes. Just across a rocky streambed at nearly 3 miles, reach an unsigned and rather obscure junction. Turn right (south) to the three lovely Gem Lakes, reaching the shore of the easternmost Gem Lake at 3 miles—truly worthy of its name. Angler's trails form an up-and-down route to the next two lakes. Reach the third and highest Gem Lake at almost 3.25 miles and 10,940 feet, nestled below Peak 11645.

Retrace your steps to the trailhead.

14 Ruby Lake

Place	Total Distance	Elevation	Difficulty Level	Type
Trailhead		10,230		
Viewpoint by Mono-Morgan Junction	1	10,460	E	O&B
Ruby Lake	4.5	11,121	S	O&B

Best Time   Early July–mid-October
Topos   WP *Mt. Abbot* 15'; *Mt. Morgan, Mt. Abbot* 7.5'
Where to Stay

See map on page 47

    Mountain: Convict Lake Resort, Rock Creek Lakes Resort, Rock Creek Lodge

    Other: McGee Creek Lodge, Mono Sierra Lodge, Rainbow Tarns Bed and Breakfast, Sierra Gables Motel, Tom's Place Resort

    Towns and Agencies: Mammoth Lakes Visitors Bureau

HIGHLIGHTS   After enjoying the flowers and the excellent views on the first leg of this trip, climb steeply to a spur to high, dramatic Ruby Lake.

HOW TO GET TO THE TRAILHEAD   From U.S. Highway 395, turn west on Rock Creek Road at Tom's Place, cross Crowley Lake Drive, and follow the road past the Hilton Lakes Trailhead. The road gets quite narrow beyond Rock Creek Lake. Follow it to its end at Mosquito Flat, 10.7 miles from the highway. There's plenty of parking, as well as restrooms, for this trailhead.

ON THE TRAIL   Roughly paralleling Rock Creek on its west side, the broad, sandy trail is nearly level at first, soon enters John Muir Wilderness, and begins climbing moderately through a dazzling flower garden that's perhaps the best in the Eastern Sierra in season. A little short of 0.5 mile reach a Y-junction: The left (south) trail heads to Little Lakes Valley and Morgan Pass, and the right (southwest) heads to Ruby Lake and Mono Pass—the southern of two passes with the same name in the Eastern Sierra. Go right. A few steps away, find a spectacular viewpoint at 0.5 mile and 10,460 feet—of Mack Lake, below to the left (east) and beyond it of Mt. Morgan; of hulking, bare Mt. Starr to the west; and of the glorious semicircle of peaks at the head of Little Lakes Valley to the south, including Bear Creek Spire and Mts. Mills, Abbot, and Dade.

    Climb moderately to steeply and soon meet a junction with a spur trail, which is not shown on the book's map, from the pack station. Turn left (southwest) here and continue climbing, passing a beautiful little tarn near 1.5 miles and enjoying the view of the white granite walls and peaks to the south.

    At almost 2 miles reach a junction with the spur to Ruby Lake, by a lovely pond on Ruby's outlet. Go left (southwest) on the spur trail, passing an obvious campsite, crossing a meadow, and climbing a little along the outlet. Reach Ruby Lake at 2.25 miles and 11,121 feet. A real treat, it's ringed by whitebarks and almost completely surrounded by beautiful, light-colored granite cliffs. More ambitious hikers may want to continue another 2.25 steep miles ahead on the main trail to Mono Pass at 12,060 feet and its tarn, Summit Lake.

Whatever your turnaround point, retrace your steps.

15 McGee Canyon to Grass Lake

Place	Total Distance	Elevation	Difficulty Level	Type
Trailhead		8136		
Meadow along McGee Creek	6	9055	M	O&B
Grass Lake	10+	9826	S	O&B

Best Time   Early July–mid-October

Topo   *Convict Lake 7.5'*

Where to Stay

Mountain: Convict Lake Resort, Rock Creek Lakes Resort, Rock Creek Lodge

Other: McGee Creek Lodge, Mono Sierra Lodge, Rainbow Tarns Bed and Breakfast, Sierra Gables Motel, Tom's Place Resort

Towns and Agencies: Mammoth Lakes Visitors Bureau

HIGHLIGHTS   In season, one of the Eastern Sierra's finest flower gardens blooms along and above McGee Creek on the first leg of this hike. Just past it is one of the area's best fall color displays. Beyond, an idyllic meadow beckons; farther on and high above the canyon, you find meadowed Grass Lake—a common name in the Sierra. Colorful layers of metamorphosed rock make the McGee Canyon's walls a delight to the eye, and the aspen-lined creek is an explosion of fall color in season.

HOW TO GET TO THE TRAILHEAD   From U.S. Highway 395, turn southwest onto signed McGee Canyon Road. You have overshot this turnoff if you get to the Mammoth Lakes junction with State Route 203 while northbound or Toms Place while southbound. Shortly cross Crowley Lake Drive and continue southwest deeper into the canyon. Pass a campground turnoff and the pack station, and continue to the parking loop, which has restrooms, at the roadend, 3.2 miles, east of the old trailhead shown on the topo.

ON THE TRAIL   An old road that once served a now-vanished campground runs nearer the stream and its sheltering aspens, but your official trail leaves from the upper end of the parking loop, on the right as you face into the canyon. Begin a gradual southwest ascent up a treeless, sandy moraine covered with low, colorful, fragrant high-desert shrubs.

The lack of trees allows spectacular views of McGee Canyon's walls—layers, sometimes swirled, of brick reds, a range of browns, grays from light to charcoal, and, in the right light, tints of lavender and green.

Second crossing of McGee Creek in McGee Canyon

The route, which looks desert-like from a distance, often intersects seeps, springs, and tributary streams that nourish wonderful flower gardens. The rising trail brings Mt. Baldwin and its handsome outliers into view. Traverse a thicket of stunted aspens, cross multiple streams, and look upslope and right for pretty cascades, including a long, prominent one named Horsetail Falls. Curving south, traverse a ledge offering nice views up- and down-canyon. The next trail section is exposed and rocky, and use trails dart off to the stream. However, soon the route crosses McGee Creek on a bridge of flattened logs and continues upstream.

Gray cliffs define the canyon's west wall as you reach a beautiful meadow near 3 miles and 9055 feet, where the stream slows down to form sandy-bottomed pools as it meanders amid willows and grasses. Use trails lead down to the meadow—a temptation for anglers.

Back on the main trail, traverse a boulder field as the canyon narrows, and the path crosses the stream again on a flattened-log bridge to an outcrop. Curve north around the outcrop and then ascend gradually through moderate forest cover, to a fork at 3.6 miles: The left (east and then south) branch is for foot traffic, and the right (south) is for stock. Go left here, soon crossing a tributary creek, and then regaining the main creek, to a junction near 4.5 miles. Go left (south), cross the creek, and begin a steep climb on lodgepole-shaded switchbacks, enjoying great views down-canyon as well as toward the peaks to the west. The grade eases near a junction near 5 miles. Go left (northeast) and reach pretty Grass Lake a little past 5 miles and 9826 feet, fed at its south end by

McGee Canyon to Grass Lake

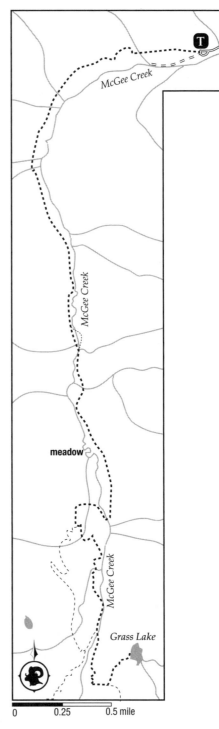

Roof Pendants

Some of the most beautiful canyon walls in the Sierra, these are made largely of metamorphosed ancient seafloor that once overlay the gray granite for which the Sierra is better known. The forces that thrust the granite up also pushed the seafloor layers up and aside, crushed them, tilted them, twisted them, and left them to be stripped away by erosion, exposing the granite. Because the metamorphic layers once formed a "roof" over the buried granite but now consist of scattered remains left "pendant" in the great bodies of granite, the remnants are referred to as roof pendants. Roof pendants can be huge, making up entire mountains, like Red and Gold Mountain, the site of the Mammoth Consolidated Gold Mine near Mammoth Lakes (see Trip 19), and entire subranges, like the Tioga Crest between Lee Vining and Yosemite (see Chapter 7). Dissolved minerals are especially likely to precipitate out of solution and be deposited at the junctions of roof pendants and granite, called contact zones. Miners associated deposits with contact zones, so many Sierra mines were located on or near such areas.

the long, cascading outlet of Steelhead Lake and seemingly set right underneath Mt. Stanford (to the east-southeast). Its meadowy shore offers some nice picnic spots. Retrace your steps.

16 Convict Lake

Place	Total Distance	Elevation	Difficulty Level	Type
Trailhead		7620		
Entire trip	3	7660	E	Semi

Best Time   Late May–mid-October

Topos   *Convict Lake 7.5'*

Where to Stay

Mountain: Convict Lake Resort, Crystal Crag Lodge, Double Eagle Resort and Spa, Rock Creek Lakes Resort, Rock Creek Lodge, Silver Lake Resort, Tamarack Lodge and Resort, Whispering Pines Resort, Wildyrie Lodge, Woods Lodge

Other: Mammoth Mountain Chalets, Mammoth Mountain Inn, McGee Creek Lodge, Mono Sierra Lodge, Rainbow Tarns Bed and Breakfast, Sierra Gables Motel, Tom's Place Resort

Towns and Agencies: June Lake Chamber of Commerce, Mammoth Lakes Visitors Bureau

HIGHLIGHTS   Like adjacent McGee Canyon, the canyon cradling Convict Lake is a marvelous layer-cake of metamorphic rock. Aspens and cottonwoods along Convict Creek and Convict Lake glow with color in the fall. (To shorten the hike by nearly 2 miles, start from one of the parking lots on Convict Lake's east or southeast shore, which makes the trip a loop.)

HOW TO GET TO THE TRAILHEAD On U.S. Highway 395, 2 miles south of the Mammoth Lakes junction (State Route 203) and north of Toms Place, turn south-southwest onto signed Convict Lake Road. You have overshot this turnoff if you get to the Mammoth Lakes junction with State Route 203 while northbound or Toms Place while southbound. Follow this road uphill across a moraine, almost to Convict Lake Resort. The trailhead and its big parking lot with restrooms are not at the roadend; rather, they're on a short, signed spur to your right as you approach the resort at 2 miles. A store, gourmet restaurant (serving lunch in summer only and dinner), and boat rentals are available at adjacent Convict Lake Resort.

ON THE TRAIL You can't see Convict Lake from this trailhead, so, from the trailhead sign, head southwest up a sandy, sagebrush-dotted moraine, topping out at 0.25 mile at a wonderful overlook of the lake. Mt. Morrison is obvious, ahead; on the right is Laurel Mountain; on the left are the reddish slopes of Mt. McGee. Descending moderately to steeply on this sandy trail—the route is confusing because of use trails back toward the resort—level out well above the shore a little past 0.3 mile. Continue southwest on a shadeless, sandy and dusty trail that bobs up and down some 20 to 40 feet above the water. Steep anglers' trails lead down to the water.

Look for a pair of particularly tall Jeffrey pines at the lake's head: "Two Jeffreys," an easy-to-spot landmark for the pleasant stretch of lakeshore around the multistranded inlet. At 1 mile, you reach a junction. Go left (south) on a well-tramped trail around the lake. Pause to study the wonderfully twisted, colorful rock layers to the west. Reach another junction almost immediately: Hikers and anglers go left while stock users go right. You're soon at "Two Jeffreys" at 1 mile and 7620 feet.

Near 1.25 miles, reach the long boardwalk that spans most of the stony distributaries of Convict Creek, some of which may be dry by late season. The boardwalk threads its way between tall willows and cottonwoods before ending

Convict Lake

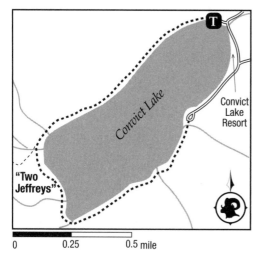

near 1.3 miles. Almost immediately cross the last distributary on a log bridge.

The trail resumes in aspens as it begins to curve around the lake's southwest end and comes to a "stairway" that leads to a traverse of the steep southern shoreline. At first the track is rocky through moisture-loving plants and trees. Numerous steep anglers' trails dash down to the water as the trail turns sandy and dusty on a sunstruck chaparral slope before reaching the day-use/picnic area and the parking loop on the lake's south shore at 2 miles.

The Story Behind the Name

The striking peak whose vertical face overlooks Convict Lake on the lake's south side is Mt. Morrison. At this lake in 1871 a posse shot it out with and then captured 6 of 29 convicts who'd escaped from a Carson City prison—hence the name "Convict Lake." Posse member Robert Morrison died in the shootout—hence the name "Mt. Morrison" in his memory.

An easy way to continue is to climb up to the parking loop and walk along the road past the restrooms and water facilities and a rough launching ramp. Just past the loop, pick up a roadside walkway with a wooden fence on its lake side. Where the fence ends, turn left down a dirt track that makes one switchback on its short, steep way to the water. Past the switchback and about halfway down, pick up a trail on the right in order to continue this shoreline traverse, now through snowberry, sage, tobacco brush, and wild rose.

Soon the path intersects a paved trail coming down from the road. Turn left to continue the traverse past the occasional bench and under the welcome shade of cottonwoods. Thickets of wild rose here offer colorful seasonal treats: intensely fragrant, pink, single flowers in early season; lipstick-red seed pods called "hips" in mid- to late season; and small red leaves in the fall.

As the walkway begins to curve around the east end of the lake, find an area with informational displays about the area's geology and history as well as great views across the lake. The trail shortly angles up to meet the road at another set of informational displays. After studying them, cross the bridged outlet and stick to the road's west shoulder as you pass a memorial to Clay Cutter, who died here in February 1990 while trying to save others in a tragedy that took seven lives.

Pick up a sidewalk while passing the official dock, boat rental shack, and launching ramp. Just beyond the ramp, find the sandy and dusty trail around the lake's northeast side. Ignore a steep use trail on the right and continue around the lake to close the loop part of this hike at the junction with the trail back to the parking lot at almost 2.6 miles.

Retrace your steps from here.

Convict Lake and "Two Jeffreys"

Mammoth Lakes

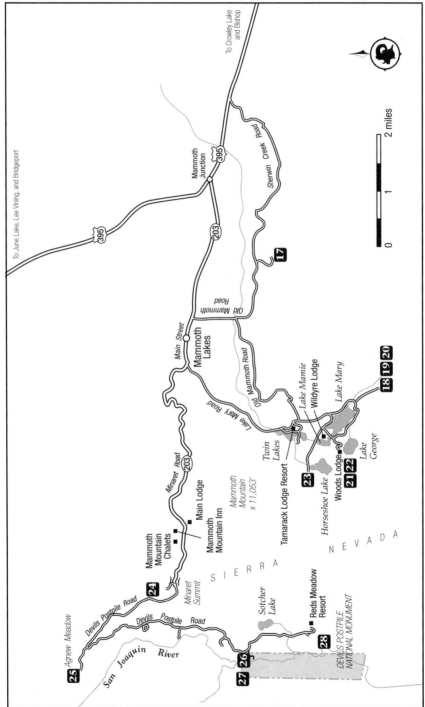

Note: All lodgings outside the Mammoth Lakes area yet convenient to hikes in this chapter are shown on map on p. 16.

CHAPTER 2

Mammoth Lakes

From Mammoth Lakes, the Eastern Sierra's largest town, roads lead to many fine trailheads, most of them out of the Lakes Basin four miles southwest of town or out of the Devils Postpile area west of town. Leave plenty of time to enjoy these wonderful hiking opportunities. Mammoth Mountain Ski Area is the town's largest employer by far, and the ski area has long been popular with Southern Californians. In the summer, it becomes a mountain biking park with a variety of terrain. Thrill-seekers favor "Kamikaze," a steep trail that allows a wild ride down 2000 feet of dusty pumice.

The area is full of volcanic features. Mammoth Mountain itself is the west wall of a dormant volcano that arose about 110,000 years ago on the west edge of the Long Valley Caldera; that volcano continued erupting and building its cone until about 50,000 years ago. Some time later, much of the volcano's cone collapsed, leaving only 11,053-foot Mammoth Mountain standing. There are active fumaroles on the mountain, and tremors under the area declare that future volcanic activity is still possible. Three ski patrollers died and one more was hospitalized in February 2006 after they tumbled into one of the fumaroles, where toxic gases displace oxygen.

The Long Valley Caldera is the result of a gigantic eruption about 760,000 years ago, which blew ash as far east as Nebraska. Glass Ridge, visible to the east from many viewpoints, is a remnant of that older and far larger volcano's east wall. Another notable remnant of that explosion is the pinkish rock that is so visible along U.S. Highway 395 between Bishop and Mammoth. This rock is the Bishop tuff, which is the consolidated volcanic ash of the great eruption.

Mammoth Mountain itself is short by Sierra standards and is also an unattractive lump. But its location in the range ensures that it attracts the most storms from the Pacific and therefore that it normally gets the most snow of any area in the Eastern Sierra. Gondola rides to its top are available year-round, weather permitting, and the 360-degree view is one of the best in the Sierra.

The area gets its name from a short-lived, illusory gold frenzy back in the 1870s. Gold-mining activity continued well into the 20th century, and it still revives periodically, only to arouse strong opposition from environmental groups. Back in the 1870s, someone modestly dubbed the gold strike "mammoth," but it was never a rich one. Ruins of the gold mines and the short-lived town that popped up to serve them attract many visitors.

Unless otherwise specified, all driving directions are from the intersection of State Route 203 (Main Street), Minaret Road, and Lake Mary Road in the town of Mammoth Lakes. This is the second traffic light on SR 203 as you drive west through town.

Recommended Maps

In addition to those listed in the trip write-ups, your library of maps should include the following. Get the latest edition/revision you can find. They're widely available, certainly at any of the local ranger stations.

- *Inyo National Forest* and *A Guide to the John Muir Wilderness and the Sequoia-Kings Canyon Wilderness.* U.S. Forest Service and U.S. Department of Agriculture.
- *Guide to Eastern Sierra.* Automobile Club of Southern California.
- *Mammoth High Country and Devils Postpile.* Tom Harrison Maps.

Individual Lodgings

Name	Nearest Community	Type	Facilities	Price Range	Contact Information	Website and Email Address
Convict Lake Resort	Mammoth Lakes	Mountain	Cabins	$$–$$$	HCR 79, Box 204 Mammoth Lakes, CA 93546 Phone: 800-992-2260 or 760-934-3800	www.convictlake.com info@convictlake.com
Crystal Crag Lodge	Mammoth Lakes	Mountain	Cabins	$–$$$	P.O. Box 88 Mammoth Lakes, CA 93546 Phone: 760-934-2436	www.crystalcrag.com info@crystalcrag.com
Double Eagle Resort and Spa	June Lake	Other	Cabins, rooms	$$–$$$	P.O. Box 736 June Lake, CA 93529 Phone: 760-648-7004	www.doubleeagle.com
Mammoth Mountain Chalets	Mammoth Lakes	Other	Cabins	$$–$$$	P.O. Box 13 Mammoth Lakes, CA 93546 Phone (CA): 800-327-3681 Phone: 760-934-8518 Fax: 760-934-5117	www.mammothmtnchalets.com reservations@mammothmtnchalets.com
Mammoth Mountain Inn	Mammoth Lakes	Other	Rooms, condos	$$–$$$	P.O. Box 353 Mammoth Lakes, CA 93546 Phone: 800-MAMMOTH or 760-934-2581	www.mammothmountain.com
McGee Creek Lodge	Crowley Lake	Other	Rooms	$–$$	Phone: 760-935-4228	http://mcgeecreek.com
Mono Sierra Lodge	Crowley Lake	Other	Rooms	$$	Phone: 800-SADLE UP (723-5387)	www.monosierralodge.com
Rainbow Tarns Bed and Breakfast	Crowley Lake	Other	Rooms	$$	HC 79 Box 55C Crowley Lake, CA 93546 Phone: 888-588-6269 or 760-935-4556	www.rainbowtarns.com innkeeper@rainbowtarns.com
Red's Meadow Resort	Mammoth Lakes	Mountain	Rooms, cabins	$–$$	P.O. Box 395 Mammoth Lakes, CA 93546 Phone: 800-292-7758 or 760-934-2345	www. rmps395@aol.com redsmeadow.com
Rock Creek Lakes Resort	Crowley Lake	Mountain	Cabins	$$–$$$	P.O. Box 727 Bishop, CA 93515 Phone: 760-935-4311	www.rockcreeklake.com/resort creekinfo@rockcreeklake.com
Rock Creek Lodge	Crowley Lake	Mountain	Cabins	$–$$	Route 1, Box 12 Mammoth Lakes, CA 93546 Phone: 877-935-4170 or 760-935-4170 Fax: 760-935-4172	www.rockcreeklodge.com info@rockcreeklodge.com
Silver Lake Resort	June Lake	Other	Cabins	$$–$$$	P.O. Box 116 June Lake, CA 93529 Phone: 760-648-7525	www.silverlakeresort.net

Name	Nearest Community	Type	Facilities	Price Range	Contact Information	Website and Email Address
Tamarack Lodge and Resort	Mammoth Lakes	Mountain	Rooms, cabins	$–$$$	P.O. Box 69 Mammoth Lakes, CA 93546 Phone: 760-934-2442 or 800. MAMMOTH	www.tamaracklodge.com guestservices@tamaracklodge.com
Tioga Lodge	Lee Vining	Other	Rooms, cabins	$–$$	P.O. Box 580 Lee Vining, CA 93541 Phone: 760-647-6423 Fax: 760-647-6074	www.tiogalodge.com lodging@tiogalodge.com
Tom's Place Resort	Crowley Lake	Other	Rooms, cabins	$–$$	HCR 79, Box 22-A Crowley Lake, CA 93546 Phone: 760-935-4239 Fax: 760-935-9160	www.tomsplaceresort.com tomsplaceresort@earthlink.net
Whispering Pines Resort	June Lake	Other	Rooms, cabins	$–$$$	18 Nevada St. June Lake, CA 93529 Phone (CA): 800-648-7762 Phone: 760-872-6828 or 760-872-6828 Fax: 760-748-7589	www.discoverwhisperingpines.com
Wildyrie Lodge	Mammoth Lakes	Mountain	Rooms, cabins	$–$$$	P.O. Box 109 Mammoth Lakes, CA 93546	www.mammothweb.com/lodging/index.cfm
Woods Lodge	Mammoth Lakes	Mountain	Cabins	$$–$$$	P.O. Box 108 Mammoth Lakes, CA 93546 Phone: 760-934-2261	www.mammothweb.com/lodging/index.cfm

Note: Most Crowley Lake postal addresses are actually in Mammoth Lakes for U.S. Post Office purposes.

Towns and Agencies

Name	Nearest Community	Type	Contact Information	Website and Email Address
June Lake Chamber of Commerce	June Lake	Community	P.O. Box 2 June Lake, CA 93529 Phone: 760-648-7584	www.junelakechamber.org
Lee Vining Chamber of Commerce	Lee Vining	Community	Phone: 760-647-6629	www.leevining.com info@leevining.com
Mammoth Lakes Visitors Bureau	Mammoth Lakes	Community	P.O. Box 48 Mammoth Lakes, CA 93546 Phone: 888-GO MAMMOTH or 760-934-2712 Fax: 760-934-7066	www.visitmammoth.com info@visitmammoth.com

17 Sherwin and Valentine Lakes

Place	Total Distance	Elevation	Difficulty Level	Type
Trailhead		7840		
Largest Sherwin Lake	4+	8680	M	O&B
Valentine Lake	9.5	9700	S	O&B

Best Time   Late May–mid-October
Topo   *Bloody Mountain 7.5'*
Where to Stay

Mountain: Convict Lake Resort, Crystal Crag Lodge, Rock Creek Lakes Resort, Rock Creek Lodge, Tamarack Lodge and Resort, Wildyrie Lodge, Woods Lodge

Other: Double Eagle Resort and Spa, Mammoth Mountain Chalets, Mammoth Mountain Inn, McGee Creek Lodge, Mono Sierra Lodge, Rainbow Tarns Bed and Breakfast, Silver Lake Resort, Tioga Lodge, Tom's Place Resort, Whispering Pines Resort

Towns and Agencies: June Lake Chamber of Commerce, Lee Vining Chamber of Commerce, Mammoth Lakes Visitors Bureau

HIGHLIGHTS Besides being one of the earlier trails to open in the Mammoth Lakes area, this trail offers wonderful views over the town and Long Valley as you ascend the Sherwin Creek moraine to the pretty Sherwin Lakes, sky-blue surprises in their chaparral setting. Beyond, larger Valentine Lake offers more typical Sierra beauty in a setting of rugged peaks.

HOW TO GET TO THE TRAILHEAD From Highway 395 a short distance south of the junction with State Route 203 and north of the Convict Lake junction, turn off on signed Sherwin Creek Road, which is mostly dirt. Follow the road past Sherwin Creek Campground. Turn left at a road signed for the Sherwin Creek Trailhead and the motocross course at 4.1 miles. Continue 0.3 mile to a spur road signed for Sherwin Lakes and Voorhis Viking Camp. Turn left again, 0.1 mile to a parking area with a restroom at the trailhead at 4.5 miles total.

ON THE TRAIL The trail heads generally south past the restroom, under sparse Jeffrey pines. Dip across aspen-lined Sherwin Creek on a footbridge and enter moderate forest cover, passing a sign noting that, while this is not yet official wilderness, it is backcountry and should be treated as wilderness.

The trail curves east, passing a spur left (north-northeast) to some buildings—part of private Voorhis Viking Camp. Continue ahead (right), soon working gradually up a moraine and curving around the head of a gully. Beyond here, begin a series of long, lazy, sandy switchbacks up the moraine. Views open up over the dry meadows south of town to the volcanic knolls north of it and the distant White Mountains to the northeast.

At 1.75 miles top out, traverse the moraine through chaparral and sparse forest, and spot one or two of the smaller Sherwin Lakes well below the trail to the right (west). Curving around a knob, you're a few steps away from the northernmost bay on a shallow but lovely lake, one of the two largest Sherwin Lakes at a little more than 2 miles and 8680 feet. In early season, these two lakes may overflow their short connecting stream and become one.

To continue, follow the trail through boulders to a signed junction at 2.25 miles: The left (southeast) trail heads to Valentine Lake, and the right (west) is on a short spur trail to upper Sherwin Lakes. Go left. Walk generally east through sparse forest, dip across a sandy flat dotted with blue lupine and immense Western junipers, cross an aspen-lined channel, traverse another flat, and at 2.75 miles curve south past a sign on a big juniper that says VALENTINE LAKE. It's a short way to a blocked-off junction with a very faint trail that leads to a different trailhead off Sherwin Creek Road.

Nearing 3 miles, enter John Muir Wilderness and begin climbing a little valley that varies among open and sandy, densely forested, filled with fluttering green aspen leaves, and marshy and provided with logs laid to form a "corduroy" tread in the mud. Emerge to views of the steep east faces of unnamed crags on the Sierra Crest and to the invigorating sound of a cascading creek. At 3.5 miles cross this tributary creek and soon catch over-the-shoulder glimpses of Lost Lake below. Presently cross yet another seasonal trickle.

Around 4 miles pass a shallow lakelet bordered by Labrador tea and fragrant red heather. At 9460 feet begin to switchback, playing tag with the creek, staying on its east side instead of crossing to its west side as shown on the topo. Near the top of the climb, reach the north end of beautiful, peakbound Valentine Lake at 4.75 miles and 9700 feet, on the east side of its outlet.

Return the way you came.

Sherwin and Valentine Lakes

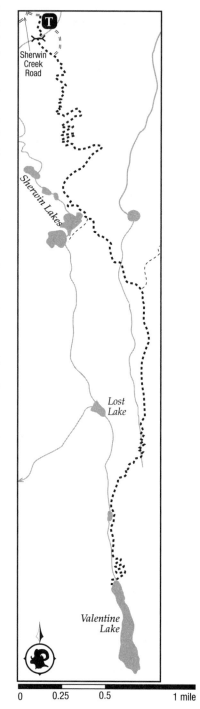

Sherwin Creek Road

Sherwin Lakes

Lost Lake

Valentine Lake

0   0.25   0.5   1 mile

18 Heart Lake

Place	Total Distance	Elevation	Difficulty Level	Type
Trailhead		9120		
Heart Lake	2	9610	E	O&B

Best Time Late May–mid-October
Topo *Bloody Mountain 7.5'*
Where to Stay
  Mountain: Convict Lake Resort, Crystal Crag Lodge, Rock Creek Lakes Resort, Rock Creek Lodge, Tamarack Lodge and Resort, Wildyrie Lodge, Woods Lodge

  Other: Double Eagle Resort and Spa, Mammoth Mountain Chalets, Mammoth Mountain Inn, McGee Creek Lodge, Mono Sierra Lodge, Rainbow Tarns Bed and Breakfast, Silver Lake Resort, Tom's Place Resort, Whispering Pines Resort

  Towns and Agencies: June Lake Chamber of Commerce, Mammoth Lakes Visitors Bureau

HIGHLIGHTS The route to charming Heart Lake crosses slopes that support an amazing array of flowers in season, and the view from the knoll west of Heart Lake is breathtaking. While the lake's popularity with equestrians can be a drawback for walkers, the trip is worth the trouble. A bonus is that the ruins of the Mammoth Consolidated Gold Mine are located at the trailhead; it's a popular detour, though not part of this trip as described here.

HOW TO GET TO THE TRAILHEAD Go straight (southwest) on Lake Mary Road, climbing away from Mammoth Lakes toward the Lakes Basin. Go left at both junctions you pass. Climbing, pass the Mammoth Lakes Pack Station and soon reach a Y-junction. Go left to skirt beautiful Lake Mary on the right and Pine City Campground on the left. Shortly turn left into Coldwater Campground and follow the road through the campground to a large parking area about 5 miles from your turnoff onto Lake Mary Road. This parking area, which has restrooms and water, serves three trailheads that are 0.1 mile apart: Heart Lake, Duck Pass (Trip 19), and Emerald Lake (Trip 20). The Heart Lake Trailhead is on the east side of the parking area.

ON THE TRAIL From the stone monument marking the entrance to Mammoth Consolidated Gold Mine at the parking lot, follow the trail east-northeast under a wooden archway and across Mammoth Creek. The area is webbed with use trails, many made by visitors to the mine as they scramble around in search of more ruins. Keep your eyes peeled in order to stay on the main trail.

In the first few steps pass an information sign, where inexpensive brochures for a self-guided tour of the mine are sometimes available, and cross two equestrian trails. At a Y-junction, take the right fork east past an old pumphouse. In a few more steps reach another Y-junction and go right (east-northeast) again, past a spur trail that comes in from the left, from the mine.

Continue ahead, climbing, to meet yet another trail from the mine. At this junction, turn right (east) onto that trail, emerging onto a slope sparsely shaded by lodgepoles. This leg is steep and rocky but compensates by offering views of Red and Gold Mountain to the north and of Mammoth Crest to the south. The creek's roar below reminds you that water is nearby, in spite of the dryness of this rocky slope, which sports a wonderful variety of flowers in season.

At a switchback turn between 0.25 and 0.3 mile, a use trail darts southeast toward the creek as the main trail jogs north, and then east, continuing a steady, moderate to steep climb. The trail itself is unpleasantly deep in horse droppings and dust, but the ever-expanding views make up for that. A northwestward leg offers great views that include Crystal Crag to the south.

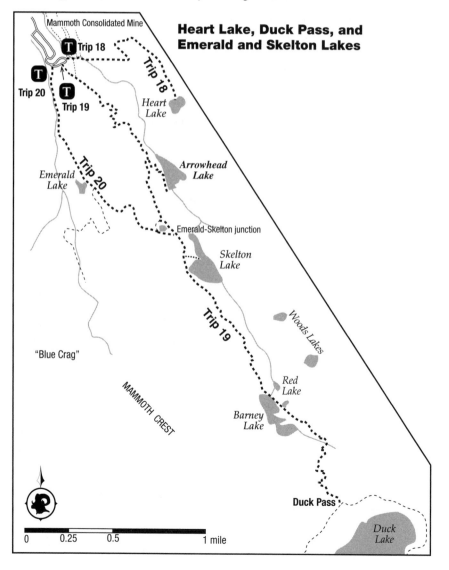

Around 0.5 mile, multiple use trails make the area confusing, so if in doubt, follow the horse droppings. The grade eases as the path begins an eastward leg, and more than once, the trail splits into multiple tracks, most of which presently rejoin. Near 0.6 mile meet a use trail joining the main trail from the left; continue ahead.

At a fork near 1 mile, the trail splits into two routes, upper and lower, to the lake; only one appears on this book's map. Take either, as they rejoin, but if you take the upper fork, ignore a use trail going uphill to the left, just before the forks rejoin. Find Heart Lake at 1 mile and 9610 feet. A use trail makes a short, steep-ish climb up the knoll west of Heart Lake, and from the knoll's summit there are outstanding views down-canyon across the Lakes Basin to Crystal Crag, to the great, bare hulk of Mammoth Mountain, to Mammoth Crest, and beyond to the distant Ritter Range.

Retrace your steps from here.

19 Duck Pass

Place	Total Distance	Elevation	Difficulty Level	Type
Trailhead		9120		
Arrowhead Lake	2.6	9678	E U	O&B
Skelton Lake	4.6	9915	M	O&B
Barney Lake	6.3	10,203	S	O&B
Duck Pass	9.3+	10,797	S	O&B

Best Time Early July–mid-October
Topo *Bloody Mountain 7.5'*

See map on page 64

Where to Stay

Mountain: Convict Lake Resort, Crystal Crag Lodge, Rock Creek Lakes Resort, Rock Creek Lodge, Tamarack Lodge and Resort, Wildyrie Lodge, Woods Lodge

Other: Double Eagle Resort and Spa, Mammoth Mountain Chalets, Mammoth Mountain Inn, McGee Creek Lodge, Mono Sierra Lodge, Rainbow Tarns Bed and Breakfast, Silver Lake Resort, Tom's Place Resort, Whispering Pines Resort

Towns and Agencies: June Lake Chamber of Commerce, Mammoth Lakes Visitors Bureau

HIGHLIGHTS Winding up Mammoth Creek past several lovely lakes to knockout views at Duck Pass, you'll see why the beautiful Duck Pass Trail is one of the most popular hikes in the Mammoth Lakes area.

HOW TO GET TO THE TRAILHEAD Go straight (southwest) on Lake Mary Road, climbing away from Mammoth Lakes toward the Lakes Basin. Go left at both junctions you pass. Climbing, pass the Mammoth Lakes Pack Station and soon reach a Y-junction. Go left to skirt beautiful Lake Mary on the right and Pine City Campground on the left. At Lake Mary's head, turn left into Coldwater Campground and follow the road up through the campground to a large parking area about 5 miles from your turnoff onto Lake Mary Road. This parking area, which has restrooms and water, serves three trailheads that are 0.1 mile apart: Heart Lake (Trip 18), Duck Pass, and Emerald Lake (Trip 20). The Duck Pass Trailhead is the middle of the three.

ON THE TRAIL Head generally southeast past an information sign, soon crossing an unmapped streamlet to enter John Muir Wilderness at a junction, where you turn right (southeast) to continue to Duck Pass. Under moderate lodgepole-red fir cover, the Duck Pass Trail climbs gradually to moderately before beginning a series of lazy switchbacks that offer over-the-shoulder views of Mammoth Mountain and Lake Mary where the trees permit.

At 1 mile reach an inconspicuously marked junction at 9776 feet. Go left (southeast) to Arrowhead Lake, nearly 100 feet and 0.3 mile below, its sparkling waters barely visible from this junction. Arrowhead Lake at 1.3 miles and 9678 feet lies in a steep canyon. The spur trail goes near its cascading inlet, which supports a lovely flower garden in season. Return to the Duck Pass Trail, now with 1.6 miles of this journey on your boots, and turn left to continue to Duck Pass.

Climb through lightly wooded granite outcrops and then between a picturesque tarn on the right (may be dry late in a dry year) and on the left, one of the outlets linking Arrowhead and Skelton lakes. This outlet is not on the topo. An unmarked but well-traveled trail branching right (west) past the tarn at the Emerald-Skelton junction connects this Mammoth Creek drainage with that of Coldwater Creek (see Trip 20). A little farther on, use trails branching left lead to camping and picnic sites along Skelton Lake, as yet unseen from the Duck Pass Trail. Scamper off on one that's one-sixth mile from the Emerald-Skelton junction, out to a peninsula, to find a sublime spot at beautiful Skelton Lake at about 2.3 miles and 9915 feet. From here there are wonderful views across the lake to "Red and Gold Mountain," the huge roof pendant between Mammoth and Sherwin creeks; of the jagged ridge that connects Red and Gold Mountain to the Sierra Crest; and of the crest itself.

Until late season, especially after a heavy winter, the Duck Pass Trail may be under snow beyond Skelton Lake. If conditions permit, continue on a brief traverse above Skelton's west shore—idyllic views—and then climb moderately through more outcrops. Passing through a rocky slot, cross streamlets at the base of an alpine meadow with a splintered, isolated peak ahead to the southeast and pass richly varied flower gardens.

Top a rise overlooking desolate Barney Lake; lodgepoles on its northwest shore shelter camping and picnicking spots. Descend to cross its outlet and begin a longish traverse of Barney Lake's east shore at 3 miles and 10,203 feet, with tiny Red Lake to the northeast. A scree slope plunges to Barney's west shore, and there may be seasonal ponds east of the trail. Peak 3592T rises to the east-northeast, beyond a granite knoll.

The final, sometimes steep, winding ascent to Duck Pass brings spectacular views northwest as the trail passes pocket gardens of alpine flowers. At unmarked Duck Pass at 4.6 miles and 10,797 feet, traverse briefly southeast through boulders a few more steps to discover a spectacular overlook of huge Duck Lake and its companion to the east, Pika Lake. Far beyond are the peaks of the Silver Divide. A few energetic hikers may want to follow an obvious spur trail down to Duck's and Pika's open shores (the main trail stays well above Duck's shore almost to the lake's outlet).

Retrace your steps from here.

20 Emerald and Skelton Lakes

Place	Total Distance	Elevation	Difficulty Level	Type
Trailhead		9120		
Emerald Lake	1.5	9482	E	O&B
Entire loop	3.25	9915	M	Loop

Best Time   Early July–mid-October
Topo   *Bloody Mountain 7.5'*
Where to Stay

Mountain: Convict Lake Resort, Crystal Crag Lodge, Rock Creek Lakes Resort, Rock Creek Lodge, Tamarack Lodge and Resort, Wildyrie Lodge, Woods Lodge

Other: Double Eagle Resort and Spa, Mammoth Mountain Chalets, Mammoth Mountain Inn, McGee Creek Lodge, Mono Sierra Lodge, Rainbow Tarns Bed and Breakfast, Silver Lake Resort, Tom's Place Resort, Whispering Pines Resort

Towns and Agencies: June Lake Chamber of Commerce, Mammoth Lakes Visitors Bureau

HIGHLIGHTS A flower- and meadow-blessed walk along Coldwater Creek leads to charming Emerald Lake, from which there's an exciting climb to beautiful Skelton Lake and a downhill stroll with an optional detour to Arrowhead Lake.

HOW TO GET TO THE TRAILHEAD Go straight (southwest) on Lake Mary Road, climbing away from Mammoth Lakes toward the Lakes Basin. Go left at both junctions you pass. Climbing, pass the Mammoth Lakes Pack Station and soon reach a Y-junction. Go left to skirt beautiful Lake Mary on the right and Pine City Campground on the left. At Lake Mary's head, turn left into Coldwater Campground and follow the road through the campground to a large parking area about 5 miles from your turnoff onto Lake Mary Road. This parking area, which has restrooms and water, serves three trailheads that are 0.1 mile apart: Heart Lake (Trip 18), Duck Pass (Trip 19), and Emerald Lake. The Emerald Lake Trailhead is nearest the west end of the parking lot.

ON THE TRAIL You can do this loop in reverse, but the route connecting Emerald and Skelton lakes is much easier to find and follow from the Emerald Lake Trail.

The trailhead is marked but the trail's start is indistinct because of multiple tracks beaten out by its many users. Just keep the restroom building on the left, funneling up and into the narrow canyon of Coldwater Creek. Meet a spur road (not on the map) that goes left to a water tank. A sign identifies the equestrian route as the main trail rather than the creekside trail I recommend. The latter is easier for first-time visitors. Those hikers going only to Emerald Lake can use both routes to turn their hike into a semiloop.

The trail nearly levels out along the shady creek except where it must climb over obstacles like tree roots exposed by runoff and foot traffic—this streambank erodes easily. Bright yellow blossoms of monkeyflower and mountain helenium color the banks here and there. Ascend very gradually to the point where a tributary, Emerald Lake's outlet, which is not on the topo, elbows in from the east.

Don't cross the tributary; instead, follow the trail along its northern bank, entering John Muir Wilderness at an unsigned point. Here, the tributary forms a long, sandy-bottomed pool of that wonderful green tint peculiar to mid-mountain streams. In early season, the water may be high enough to cover the trail; in that case, just trace the stream's edge.

Soon leave the stream and begin a moderate ascent up a sandy slope, meeting the official route coming from the left. Turn right and continue ascending past granite boulders to level out at Emerald Lake at 0.75 mile and 9482 feet. The handsome, nameless crag towering over the lake is locally called Blue Crag.

Continuing along Emerald Lake's north shore, shortly reach a junction. Go left (southeast) toward Skelton Lake and begin a moderate to steep climb above a seasonal tributary of Emerald Lake, through moderate to open forest. Presently veer east, away from the tributary, to climb steeply up a ridge that's been on the left. Near the top of the climb, pass a seasonal pond on the left and head for a large gray outcrop. Curve around the outcrop to climb along its east face through a very rocky, narrow gully. The trail grows very steep, rough, and faint as it nears the head of the gully. Although the trail seems to split three ways at the head of the gully, the middle fork is its real continuation. An outcrop on the right after exiting from the gully offers excellent views: Red and Gold Mountain, Lake Mary, Mammoth Mountain, Crystal Crag and the Mammoth Crest, and beyond, Banner Peak and Mt. Ritter. (If you are coming from Skelton Lake, taking this trip in reverse, be aware that in this area, even though the obvious route goes out to the outcrop, the route connecting with Emerald Lake drops into the rough, narrow gully on your right.)

There are many confusing use trails in this area. Follow the track that puts the very top of the outcrop and Blue Crag on the right and a wooded swale with seasonal tarns on the left. Soon dip into the swale and presently approach a particularly large tarn or two—one huge tarn if the water is high, sometimes just a dry tarn-bed late in the season. Tracks curve around the tarn's left and right sides, and the right side is the better track. Taking it, squish along the tarn as the track seems to fade out, ascend a low rise, and at its top pick up a faint trail that descends between parallel lines of rocks to meet the Duck Pass Trail at 1.5 miles at the unsigned Emerald-Skelton junction. (If you are taking this trip in reverse, leave the Duck Pass Trail *after* passing the tarn, at the place where parallel lines of rocks on the right indicate a faint, unsigned trail branching up and west.)

Turn right onto the Duck Pass Trail, toward Duck Pass, and shortly find use trails branching left to camping and picnic sites along Skelton Lake, as yet unseen from the Duck Pass Trail. As recommended in Trip 19, take one of them to find a sublime spot along beautiful Skelton Lake at 1.75 miles and 9915 feet.

To return to the parking lot, retrace your steps from Skelton Lake to the Duck Pass Trail and turn right (northwest). From the Emerald-Skelton junction, it's 0.5 mile to the junction with the spur trail to Arrowhead Lake and a 0.6-mile detour (turn right) and a nearly 100-foot descent/ascent to visit attractive Arrowhead Lake (see Trip 19).

Back on the Duck Pass Trail, turn right to continue to the Duck Pass Trailhead at 3.25 miles, from which you'll close this loop by returning to your car.

21 Barrett and T J Lakes

Place	Total Distance	Elevation	Difficulty Level	Type
Trailhead		9055		
Barrett Lake	1	9284	E	O&B
T J Lake	1.5	9284	E U	O&B

Best Time   Late July–mid-October
Topos   WP *Devils Postpile* 15'; *Crystal Crag* 7.5'
Where to Stay

Mountain: Convict Lake Resort, Crystal Crag Lodge, Rock Creek Lakes Resort, Rock Creek Lodge, Tamarack Lodge and Resort, Wildyrie Lodge, Woods Lodge

Other: Double Eagle Resort and Spa, Mammoth Mountain Chalets, Mammoth Mountain Inn, McGee Creek Lodge, Mono Sierra Lodge, Rainbow Tarns Bed and Breakfast, Silver Lake Resort, Tom's Place Resort, Whispering Pines Resort

Towns and Agencies: June Lake Chamber of Commerce, Mammoth Lakes Visitors Bureau

HIGHLIGHTS   Two pretty lakes lie along this short and occasionally steep hike, which has delightful scenery.

HOW TO GET TO THE TRAILHEAD   Go straight (southwest) on Lake Mary Road, climbing away from Mammoth Lakes toward the Lakes Basin. Go left at both junctions you pass. Climbing, pass the Mammoth Lakes Pack Station and soon reach a Y-junction. Bear right and soon pass an overlook of Lake Mary and then the Pokenobe Store. At a junction, go left on a spur road, signed for Lake George. Pass the Lake Mary Campground, cross a small bridge over the stream linking Lakes Mary and Mamie, and reach a T-junction. Turn right here, onto the spur road to Lake George, and follow it uphill to the lake, where there's a parking lot, with restrooms and water and an adjacent campground next to the Barrett and TJ Lakes trailhead, at 4.7 miles. This trailhead is on the *south* side

Barrett and T J Lakes and Crystal Lake and Crest

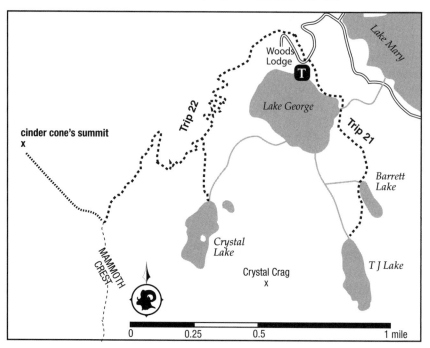

of the lot—your left as you enter the lot. (The Crystal Lake-Mammoth Crest trailhead for Trip 22 is on the north side of the lot.) Avoid the signed service road that leads into Woods Lodge unless you're staying there.

ON THE TRAIL The broad, sandy trail passes in front of the restrooms, heading south on a level grade through moderate to open lodgepole forest. Lake George lies a little below; majestic Crystal Crag and the Mammoth Crest soar above the other shore. Picnic tables dot the shoreline here. Presently cross the lake's outlet on a footbridge and curve southwest past a charming summer cabin; avoid a use trail left here—it leads only to the cabin.

A little past the cabin, follow the main trail left (south-southeast) at a fork and ascend moderately to steeply on an open slope, paralleling one of Lake George's inlets, which is not shown on the topo and this book's map. At one point, rocks may require a little bouldering skill. Near the top of the ascent, walk on shallow "terraces" made by the roots of a stout lodgepole. As the grade eases, cross the little stream and then briefly resume climbing. Puff up over another root-terrace to a junction a little short of 0.5 mile. Go right (south) to reach peaceful, wooded, little Barrett Lake at 0.5 mile and 9284 feet, from whose northwest shore there's a view of Red and Gold Mountain and the Mammoth Crest.

Cruise along Barrett's shoreline until, about halfway along it, the trail veers right over a low ridge and to a junction at about 0.6 mile. Go right (southwest), almost immediately reaching an apparent junction where a prominent use trail branches right. Go left to keep on the main trail, which tops out at 0.6 mile on the 9350-foot ridge overlooking dramatic T J Lake. From here, the trail descends steeply toward the lakeshore, veering right toward the outlet partway down. There are good spots just off the trail, before the outlet, to rest and enjoy T J Lake at 0.75 mile and also at 9284 feet. Lichen-streaked granite cliffs bound the northwest shore, and Crystal Crag and the Mammoth Crest seem to leap into the sky above.

Retrace your steps from T J Lake.

22 Crystal Lake and Crest

Place	Total Distance	Elevation	Difficulty Level	Type
Trailhead		9055		
Crystal Lake	2.75	9613	E	O&B
Cinder cone's summit	6	10,480	S	O&B

Best Time   Early July–mid-October

Topos   WP *Devils Postpile* 15'; *Crystal Crag* 7.5'

See map on page 70

Where to Stay

Mountain: Convict Lake Resort, Crystal Crag Lodge, Rock Creek Lakes Resort, Rock Creek Lodge, Tamarack Lodge and Resort, Wildyrie Lodge, Woods Lodge

Other: Double Eagle Resort and Spa, Mammoth Mountain Chalets, Mammoth Mountain Inn, McGee Creek Lodge, Mono Sierra Lodge, Rainbow Tarns Bed and Breakfast, Silver Lake Resort, Tom's Place Resort, Whispering Pines Resort

Towns and Agencies: June Lake Chamber of Commerce, Mammoth Lakes Visitors Bureau

Crystal Crag over Tarn

HIGHLIGHTS   This is an extremely scenic hike: one wonderful view after another, a gem of a little alpine lake, and at the top a volcanic landscape of colorful cinders and a cinder cone reminiscent of Haleakala on Maui.

HOW TO GET TO THE TRAILHEAD

Go straight (southwest) on Lake

Mary Road, climbing away from Mammoth Lakes toward the Lakes Basin. Go left at both junctions you pass. Climbing, pass the Mammoth Lakes Pack Station and soon reach a Y-junction. Turn right and soon pass an overlook of Lake Mary and then the Pokenobe Store. At a junction go left on a spur road signed for Lake George. Pass the Lake Mary Campground, cross a small bridge over the stream linking Lakes Mary and Mamie, and reach a T-junction. Turn right here, onto the spur road to Lake George, and follow it uphill to the lake, where there's a parking lot, with restrooms and water and an adjacent campground next to the Barrett and T J Lakes trailhead, at 4.7 miles. *This* trip's trailhead is on the *north* side of the lot—your right as you enter the lot. (The Barrett and T J Lakes trailhead for Trip 21 is on the south side of the lot.) Avoid the signed service road that leads into Woods Lodge unless you're staying there.

ON THE TRAIL The first part of this trail passes around and above, not through as incorrectly shown on the topo, the cabins of Woods Lodge. Head north-northwest, up long, gradual to moderate switchbacks and through a moderate forest of species typical of this area: lodgepole, western white pine, hemlock, and red fir. The sandy and dusty trail passes behind Woods Lodge and through a scattering of dry-slope flowers. Beyond the lodge, the trail bursts out of the forest to a beautiful overlook of Lakes George and Mary and beyond them of Red and Gold Mountain. Views like this just improve on the ascent. In season, Crystal Lake's outlet splashes down the slope ahead in delightful cascades.

At last turn away from the slope and back into the forest, where just shy of 1.25 miles there's a junction: left (south) to Crystal Lake or right (southwest) to the Mammoth Crest. The out-and-back detour of 0.5-mile-plus to Crystal Lake with a 131-foot elevation loss/gain is well worth the trouble! Turning left, you cross a saddle (9744 feet) and then make a moderate to steep descent to the lake's outlet stream. Turn right along a beaten track paralleling the outlet to reach Crystal Lake at a little under 1.5 miles and 9613 feet. This jewel of a lake is tucked right under Crystal Crag and the Mammoth Crest in a wonderfully picturesque, tranquil alpine setting. Near its mouth and along its outlet stream there's an eye-catching array of wildflowers.

Back at the junction with the main trail, with 1.6 miles now on your boots, turn left to continue up to the Mammoth Crest. The trail corkscrews moderately to steeply away from the junction. As the grade eases, reach an airy perch with fabulous views: peaks in southern Yosemite; San Joaquin Ridge; Mammoth Mountain; McCloud Lake, Horseshoe Lake, Twin Lakes, and Lakes Mamie, Mary, and George in this lakes basin; Panorama Dome; the town of Mammoth Lakes; beyond, Bald Mountain, Glass Ridge, the White Mountains; across the lakes basin, Red and Gold Mountain and the Sherwin Range; Blue Crag; and Crystal Crag. Views continue to develop on the climb while the forest dwindles to a few stunted whitebark pines. The slope soon turns to volcanic material—pumice and cinders—and the trail is loose and dusty.

A little past 2.5 miles, a sign announces John Muir Wilderness at a huge, dark red boulder—possibly a lava bomb. The true boundary is actually a little farther on, at the crest. Cross over a ridge and descend a little among brick-red lava rocks. To the west there's a red cinder cone with a long, gentle, south slope and, facing you, an abrupt east slope up which an obvious use trail winds. At an unmarked Y-junction just beyond the ridge, the main trail goes left (southwest) to Deer Lakes and an obvious use trail goes right (west) to the cinder cone.

Go right here, curving around the top of the Mammoth Crest's cliffs, enjoying thrilling views and an amazing display—colorful volcanic rocks contrasting with the severe, light-gray granites more typical of the Sierra. Ascend the cone on a series of steep, tiny, tight switchbacks. The view from the cinder cone's summit at nearly 3 miles and 10,480 feet is spectacular, including the Minarets, Mt. Ritter, Banner Peak, and many of the features you saw earlier from the "airy perch." The volcanic rubble here offers a fine array of colors: reds, ochres, blacks, grays, soft oranges, dusty lavenders, and golden browns. This is as close to being in Maui's famous Haleakala Crater as you can get in the Eastern Sierra.

Return the way you came.

23 McCloud Lake and Red Cones

Place	Total Distance	Elevation	Difficulty Level	Type
Trailhead		8990		
McCloud Lake	1	9285	E	O&B
Entire semiloop	7.6	9350	S U	Semi

Best Time   Early July–mid-October

Topos   WP *Devils Postpile* 15'; *Crystal Crag* 7.5'

Where to Stay

Mountain: Convict Lake Resort, Crystal Crag Lodge, Rock Creek Lakes Resort, Rock Creek Lodge, Tamarack Lodge and Resort, Wildyrie Lodge, Woods Lodge

Other: Double Eagle Resort and Spa, Mammoth Mountain Chalets, Mammoth Mountain Inn, McGee Creek Lodge, Mono Sierra Lodge, Rainbow Tarns Bed and Breakfast, Silver Lake Resort, Tom's Place Resort, Whispering Pines Resort

Towns and Agencies: June Lake Chamber of Commerce, Mammoth Lakes Visitors Bureau

HIGHLIGHTS   Pretty McCloud Lake is easy to get to and a favorite family destination. The adventure continues over highly varied terrain with a visit to a pair of beautiful meadows and a pair of brick-red cinder cones. Climb one of them for knockout views.

HOW TO GET TO THE TRAILHEAD   Go straight (southwest) on Lake Mary Road, climbing away from the town toward the Lakes Basin. Pass a couple of junctions on the right; go left at both. Climbing, pass the Mammoth Lakes Pack Station and soon reach a Y-junction. Bear right and soon pass an overlook of Lake Mary and then the Pokenobe Store. Bypass the junction with a spur road on the left signed for LAKE GEORGE. Continue ahead to the large parking area with restrooms and water at the roadend next to pale blue Horseshoe Lake.

McCloud Lake and Red Cones

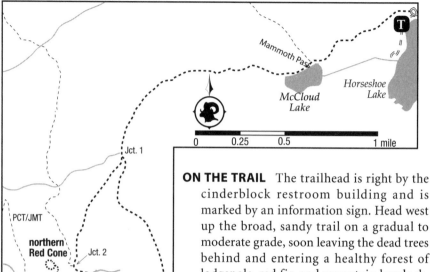

ON THE TRAIL The trailhead is right by the cinderblock restroom building and is marked by an information sign. Head west up the broad, sandy trail on a gradual to moderate grade, soon leaving the dead trees behind and entering a healthy forest of lodgepole, red fir, and mountain hemlock. The multiple tracks may be confusing, but keep going generally west, then southwest, and find McCloud Lake at 0.5 mile and 9285 feet. It's a breathtakingly lovely sight on a still, bright morning, when the magnificent, light gray cliffs of the Mammoth Crest are reflected in the lake's sky-blue waters.

Leaving this pretty spot, almost immediately reach a Y-junction overlooking the lake. Go left (southwest), skirting McCloud Lake and then climbing a little to the very broad, heavily forested saddle that's Mammoth Pass—sorry, the high point of this hike, at 9350 feet, has no views. Presently begin a gradual to moderate descent, and at 1.6 miles, reach a junction near a noisy spring, where the loop part of this trip begins. The right (south) branch heads to the Red Cones, and the left (south-southeast) branch goes to Upper Crater Meadow. Go right at what we'll call "Junction 1," shortly crossing a stream and descending moderately to steeply to glimpses of the brick-red cinders of the Red Cones.

At 2.25 miles, you reach what we'll call "Junction 2." Go left (east) to continue this hike on a sandy slope, presently skirting below the Red Cones. Several obvious use trails scamper up the northern Red Cone's steep slopes. I recommend the use trail nearest the next junction ("Junction 3") at about 3 miles. From the summit of the northern Red Cone at about 3.5 miles and 9000 feet there's a not-to-be-missed, 360-degree view over the drainage of Middle Fork San Joaquin River, including the back of Mammoth Mountain and Mammoth Crest; San Joaquin Ridge; the Middle Fork's canyon, including Devils Postpile National Monument; the Ritter Range (the Minarets, Mt. Ritter, and Banner Peak); and south to the

Why All the Dead Trees?

Carbon dioxide gas seeping up through the soil in measurable amounts around this trailhead is apparently responsible for the dead trees around here; it's suffocating the trees' roots. This seepage comes in small amounts that are harmless if you're in the open air; its source is magma moving deep underground. However, hanging around here or lingering in an enclosed space like the restroom may be unsafe: when concentrated, as inside a building, the odorless, invisible gas could suffocate you.

peaks around Fish Valley. After you've taken in the view, return to Junction 3 (about 1 mile out and back).

Back at Junction 3, with 4 miles on your boots, go left (southeast) to Upper Crater Meadow. Go left to make a moderate to steep ascent of a sandy gully that's home to a fork of Crater Creek, crossing the saddle between the northern and southern Red Cones. The grade eases near "Junction 4" in flowery, squishy Upper Crater Meadow at 4.75 miles and 8890 feet. The right (south) fork is the Pacific Crest Trail/John Muir Trail to Mt. Whitney.

Take the middle (north) fork for Horseshoe Lake, beginning a pleasant but unremarkable leg of this trip by climbing over a broad, gentle, forested ridge whose summit at 9150 feet is the high point of this leg. Cross another fork of Crater Creek at 5.25 miles before climbing yet another gentle, forested ridge and then descending to close the loop part of this trip at 6 miles at Junction 1.

From here, turn right (north) and retrace your steps to Horseshoe Lake, 1.6 miles more, for a total of 7.6 miles.

24 San Joaquin Ridge

Place	Total Distance	Elevation	Difficulty Level	Type
Trailhead		9175		
Deadman Peak	4.5	10,255	M	O&B

Best Time   Early July–mid-October

Topos   WP *Devils Postpile* 15'; *Mammoth Mountain* 7.5'

Where to Stay

Mountain: Convict Lake Resort, Crystal Crag Lodge, Rock Creek Lakes Resort, Rock Creek Lodge, Tamarack Lodge and Resort, Wildyrie Lodge, Woods Lodge

Other: Double Eagle Resort and Spa, Mammoth Mountain Chalets, Mammoth Mountain Inn, McGee Creek Lodge, Mono Sierra Lodge, Rainbow Tarns Bed and Breakfast, Silver Lake Resort, Tom's Place Resort, Whispering Pines Resort

Towns and Agencies: June Lake Chamber of Commerce, Mammoth Lakes Visitors Bureau

HIGHLIGHTS   A 4WD road, very rough and sometimes very steep, climbs pumice-covered San Joaquin Ridge and offers astonishing views and seasonal flower displays. Minaret Vista, almost next to the trailhead, offers views nearly as expansive together with aids to help identify many of the spectacular peaks around here.

HOW TO GET TO THE TRAILHEAD From the Main-Minaret-Mary junction, turn right onto Minaret Road (now State Route 203). Follow it uphill to Mammoth Mountain Ski Area/Bike Park. If there is a road-control point here, explain that you are going only to Minaret Vista. Continue between the ski area buildings and wind up toward Minaret Summit. At Minaret Summit, there's an entrance station and a road closure, along with a paved spur road that goes right. Take that spur road to its end at a paved parking loop, 6 miles from the Main-Minaret-Mary junction, passing a blocked-off 4WD road that branches right and is the trail. If the parking loop, which has restrooms, at the road-end is full, you'll find a couple of informal, unpaved parking areas back here.

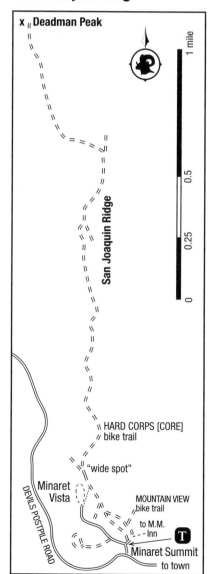

San Joaquin Ridge

AT THE TRAILHEAD Just beyond the parking loop's far end is a vista point, Minaret Vista. The views over the canyon of the Middle Fork San Joaquin River from Minaret Vista are breathtaking, and you'll find viewing tubes with bases scribed to help you spot named peaks as well as a mounted metal silhouette of the peaks, labeled so you can identify them. There's also a rough little "nature trail" around the vista. This is one of the finest road-accessible viewpoints in the entire Sierra.

ON THE TRAIL Be sure to take in the view at Minaret Vista. Then, backtrack downhill to the 4WD road. Optionally, make your way downhill from Minaret Vista to the 4WD road on a use trail east of the toilets. Turn left (north) onto the road, which cuts across coarse, light-colored pumice—volcanic rock so light it floats on water—spewed from one of the lava domes east of San Joaquin Ridge. At a fork with a closed-off road, go left, passing a foot trail to Mammoth Mountain Inn. The road is open to 4WD vehicles and mountain bikes (marked MOUNTAIN VIEW and HARD CORPS trails—the latter is spelled

"Hard Core" later on). Multiple tracks diverge and converge where vehicles have passed each other and tried to avoid the rougher spots, but the well-traveled main road is obvious. Mountain View bike route soon branches right; continue left (ahead) on HARD CORPS. At about 0.3 mile, a road comes from the left and you continue ahead—right—on the main road, steeply ascending a broad knoll whose pumice-flat top offers stupendous views westward. From here on, the flower display on these open pumice flats gets better and better. A little beyond 1.25 mile, where a road comes in from the south on the right, the road curves left and ascends very steeply for a while. Top out on a nearly level grade around 1.5 miles and pass a snow-depth marker on the right. Near 1.75 miles, reach a Y-junction and take the left fork—signed HARD CORE—toward a knob to the northwest. Make another steep climb, earning superb views to the east and west.

Approaching 2 miles, see the final goal, a summit with a tuft of trees like a wisp of hair on a baby's head. This is Peak 10,255, locally called "Deadman Peak," as it's above officially named Deadman Pass, which takes its name from Deadman Creek, which is in turn named for "the headless body of a man" found near the creek in 1868, according to *Place Names of the Sierra Nevada* by Peter Browning. The canyon of the Middle Fork San Joaquin River yawns below to the west; distant red-brown patches of dead trees are largely from the lightning-caused 1992 Rainbow Fire. The Ritter Range fills the western skyline, and there's a sweeping view over the rugged lava terrain between San Joaquin Ridge and Long Valley to the east. These views get better and better on the way to Deadman Peak at nearly 2.25 miles and 10,255 feet, where the trees turn out to be shrub-sized and the 360-degree panoramas awe-inspiring.

Retrace your steps to your car.

25 Olaine and Shadow Lakes

Place	Total Distance	Elevation	Difficulty Level	Type
Trailhead		8335		
Olaine Lake	3	8038	M U	O&B
Shadow Lake	6–7	8737	S U	O&B

Best Time   Early July–mid-October

Topos   WP *Devils Postpile* 15'; *Mammoth Mtn., Mt. Ritter* 7.5'

Where to Stay

Mountain: Convict Lake Resort, Crystal Crag Lodge, Red's Meadow Resort, Rock Creek Lakes Resort, Rock Creek Lodge, Tamarack Lodge and Resort, Wildyrie Lodge, Woods Lodge

Other: Double Eagle Resort and Spa, Mammoth Mountain Chalets, Mammoth Mountain Inn, McGee Creek Lodge, Mono Sierra Lodge, Rainbow Tarns Bed and Breakfast, Silver Lake Resort, Tom's Place Resort, Whispering Pines Resort

Towns and Agencies: June Lake Chamber of Commerce, Mammoth Lakes Visitors Bureau

HIGHLIGHTS Grassy Olaine Lake is a little gem set off by the handsome cliffs that here bound the Middle Fork San Joaquin River. Shadow Lake is a famous beauty spot at the foot of the magnificent Ritter Range.

HOW TO GET TO THE TRAILHEAD From the Main-Minaret-Mary junction, turn right onto Minaret Road (now State Route 203). Follow it uphill to Mammoth Mountain Ski Area/Bike Park. Unless it's very early, expect to take the shuttle-bus (for a fee)—visit www.nps.gov/depo for details. One way or another, get down the Devils Postpile Road 8.2 miles to the hairpin turn from which the spur road to Agnew Meadows Pack Station takes off. Follow this spur road past the Agnew Meadows Pack Station to either of two parking lots, which have restrooms, at about 8.5 miles from the Main-Minaret-Mary junction. The trailhead is on the south side of the first of the two lots.

ON THE TRAIL Look for a Pacific Crest Trail marker on a double-trunked lodgepole on the south side of the first parking lot. The well-beaten trail leaves from here, southbound, where a creek gurgles into the meadow on the left. Cross a

Olaine and Shadow Lakes

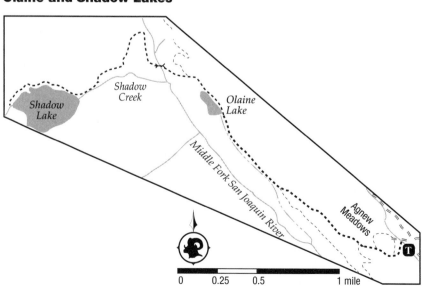

Olaine Lake

couple of arms of the little creek, bob over a low ridge, and skirt part of exten-
sive Agnew Meadows on the right. Colorful San Joaquin Ridge rises steeply to
the north. Cross the creek again as you leave the meadow behind and follow the
lodgepole-shaded, nearly level trail as it threads its way between rocky knobs.
Pass an unsigned track coming in on the right and continue ahead to a junction
at nearly 0.6 mile.

Go right (northwest) on the River Trail, gradually descending an open,
scrubby trail along rocky bluffs. A little after 1 mile, the trail reaches flats flank-
ing the river and then reenters forest cover. Now the going is level again, and the
trail soon reaches the southeast end of charming Olaine Lake at 1.5 miles and
8038 feet, reed-fringed and water-lily-dotted, set among lodgepoles and aspens,
cupped by rocky bluffs.

Continuing beyond Olaine Lake, reach a Y-junction just beyond 1.75 miles.
Turn left (west), leaving the River Trail, and cross a sandy flat. Avoid use trails
branching to the river, and then curve through aspens to a handsome footbridge
across the Middle Fork San Joaquin. Once across the river, begin a series of rocky
but gentle switchbacks up the open slopes below Shadow Lake. Views open up;
there's a particularly stunning view to the southeast of Mammoth Mountain
framed by the river canyon's walls.

The trail turns southwest into Shadow Creek's canyon, where fine cascades
plunge down its rocky throat. Near the top of the climb, the trail eases alongside
Shadow Creek in thickets of alder and willow. Beyond one final ledge of rock, exquisite Shadow Lake at 3 miles and 8737 feet comes into view. Peaks of the Ritter
Range tower over the west end of the lake, and Volcanic Ridge rises on the lake's
south side. The lake's west end, at its inlet, is at 3.5 miles at a junction with the
famed John Muir Trail.

Retrace your steps.

26 **Minaret Falls**

Place	Total Distance	Elevation	Difficulty Level	Type
Trailhead		7559		
Devils Postpile semiloop	1	7775	M	Semi
Minaret Falls	3.5	7610	M	O&B

Best Time   Early July–mid-October

Topos   WP *Devils Postpile* 15'; *Mammoth Mountain, Crystal Crag* 7.5'

Where to Stay

Mountain: Convict Lake Resort, Crystal Crag Lodge, Red's Meadow Resort, Rock Creek Lakes Resort, Rock Creek Lodge, Tamarack Lodge and Resort, Wildyrie Lodge, Woods Lodge

Other: Double Eagle Resort and Spa, Mammoth Mountain Chalets, Mammoth Mountain Inn, McGee Creek Lodge, Mono Sierra Lodge, Rainbow Tarns Bed and Breakfast, Silver Lake Resort, Tom's Place Resort, Whispering Pines Resort

Towns and Agencies: June Lake Chamber of Commerce, Mammoth Lakes Visitors Bureau

HIGHLIGHTS   Devils Postpile National Monument hosts the eponymous columnar-basalt formation in a beautiful setting that would be worth a visit even without the Devils Postpile. Close to the monument, Minaret Falls, while not a classical waterfall, is a thrilling spectacle of wild cascades at peak runoff. In spring, Minaret Falls is easy to spot from viewpoints on the upper Devils Postpile road, and you may even hear its roar that far away!

HOW TO GET TO THE TRAILHEAD   From the Main-Minaret-Mary junction, turn right onto Minaret Road (now State Route 203). Follow it uphill to Mammoth Mountain Ski Area/Bike Park. Unless it's very early, expect to take the shuttlebus (for a fee)—visit www.nps.gov/depo for details. One way or the other, it's 12.3 miles from the Main-Minaret-Mary junction to the turnoff to Devils Postpile National Monument. Turn right here and follow this access road 0.3 mile more to a large parking area that's often very crowded by midday in the summer. The parking area has restrooms and water, as well as a National Park Service ranger station.

ON THE TRAIL   To find the trailhead, walk over to the ranger station to pick up a Devils Postpile brochure; the trail is just beyond the front of the ranger station, a broad gravel path heading south-southeast across a meadow. Beyond the meadow, the trail climbs moderately to level out overlooking the river as it meanders lazily through a broad meadow. In less than 0.25 mile reach a junction with a spur trail to the Pacific Crest and John Muir trails: The left (ahead) branch heads to Devils Postpile, and the right crosses the river to Minaret Falls and Johnston Lake. For now, go left to the first glimpse of the Postpile at 0.25 mile and a junction with a side trail that loops over the top of the Postpile. Though it's spectacular, the side trail is quite steep; if you're disinclined to tackle it, just continue ahead a few steps to enjoy a wonderful view of the tall, angular columns of the Devils Postpile at 0.25-plus mile and 7595 feet. Many still stand, but even more lie, broken and shattered, spilled at the Postpile's base.

To loop over the formation, turn left at the junction with the side trail and climb very steeply to reach the Postpile's top at 7775 feet in a little over 0.3 mile from the start. Sunlight glints off the polished "tiles" of the Postpile's top, and there's an amazingly steep drop to the river from here. Continue by leaving this overlook of the "tiles" and descending steeply on the side trail as it zigzags past columns tilted onto their sides and through the remains of a forest burnt by the lightning-caused 1992 Rainbow Fire. At a junction at 0.75 mile, reach a junction: left (southeast) to Rainbow Falls, right (west) to close the loop. Turn right (west) to

Minaret Falls, Johnston Lake, and Rainbow and Lower Falls

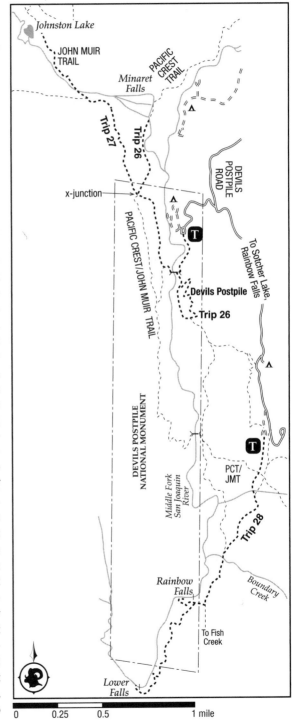

About the Devils Postpile

An interpretive sign at the formation's base explains this phenomenon. According to Mary Hill's *Geology of the Sierra Nevada*, the Postpile is a remnant of a 600,000-year-old lava flow. Here, liquid rock pooled deep, and conditions during the mass's cooling were quite uniform. A cooling mass shrinks, and a uniformly cooling mass like the Postpile flow tends to crack apart "more or less all at once" from top to bottom into unusually regular polyhedrals, yielding three- to eight-sided columns. As every honeybee knows, six-sided structures are the most efficient, and six-sided columns predominate here (various sources categorize anywhere from 44.5% to 55% of the Postpile's columns as such). At what is now the top of the formation, glaciers have planed off and exposed cross-sections of the columns, leaving a now-small, shiny "pavement" of polygons that looks remarkably like a tiled floor.

---

soon pass the interpretive sign at the Postpile's base and close the loop around Devils Postpile at a little over 1 mile. Mileages given from now on assume you've taken the 1-plus-mile semiloop around Devils Postpile. Retrace your steps to the junction with the spur to the Pacific Crest and John Muir trails. From here, either continue this trip (below) or retrace your steps to the parking lot.

Head for Minaret Falls by turning left (west) onto the spur to the Pacific Crest and John Muir trails, and shortly cross a handsome footbridge over the roiling Middle Fork San Joaquin. The spur trail curves right on the west side of the bridge. Go right at the next junction, at 1.25 miles, toward the Pacific Crest and John Muir trails.

A little shy of 1.75 miles, reach a well-signed multiway junction. Take the lower right-hand branch, the Pacific Crest Trail, northeast toward Minaret Falls. Soon leave the monument and descend to cross an unnamed creek, which can be difficult when the water is high, near its junction with Minaret Creek. In early season, it's not long before hikers hear the roar of Minaret Falls ahead (the falls are seasonal). Soon the trail reaches the south side of a very wide, boulder-choked creekbed—broad and shallow Minaret Creek as it comes to rest below the beautiful series of cascades called Minaret Falls at 2.25 miles and 7610 feet. Individually, no cascade is particularly spectacular, but all together, they're impressive! Gaze up to enjoy the sight of the water leaping free of the rock shelves at the top of the falls.

Retrace your steps.

27 Johnston Lake

Place	Total Distance	Elevation	Difficulty Level	Type
Trailhead		7559		
Devils Postpile semiloop	1	7775	M	Semi
Johnston Lake	5	8100	M	O&B

Best Time   Late May–early July

Topos   WP *Devils Postpile* 15'; *Mammoth Mtn., Crystal Crag* 7.5'

Where to Stay

Mountain: Convict Lake Resort, Crystal Crag Lodge, Red's Meadow Resort, Rock Creek Lakes Resort, Rock Creek Lodge, Tamarack Lodge and Resort, Wildyrie Lodge, Woods Lodge

Other: Double Eagle Resort and Spa, Mammoth Mountain Chalets, Mammoth Mountain Inn, McGee Creek Lodge, Mono Sierra Lodge, Rainbow Tarns Bed and Breakfast, Silver Lake Resort, Tom's Place Resort, Whispering Pines Resort

Towns and Agencies: June Lake Chamber of Commerce, Mammoth Lakes Visitors Bureau

HIGHLIGHTS   Take in the Devils Postpile before heading off toward pretty Johnston Lake, which is surrounded by a deep meadow full of low bilberry shrubs whose leaves turn fiery red in the fall.

HOW TO GET TO THE TRAILHEAD   From the Main-Minaret-Mary junction, turn right onto Minaret Road (now State Route 203). Follow it uphill to Mammoth Mountain Ski Area/Bike Park. Unless it's very early, expect to take the shuttlebus (for a fee)—visit www.nps.gov/depo for details. Either way, it's 12.3 miles from the Main-Minaret-Mary junction to the turnoff to Devils Postpile National Monument. Turn right here and follow this access road 0.3 mile more to a large parking area that's often very crowded by midday in the summer. The parking area has restrooms and water, as well as a National Park Service ranger station.

ON THE TRAIL   Before you begin hiking, walk over to the ranger station to pick up a Devils Postpile brochure. The trailhead is just beyond the front of the ranger station, a broad gravel path heading south-southeast across a meadow. Beyond the meadow, the trail climbs moderately to level out overlooking the river as it meanders lazily through a broad meadow. In less than 0.25 mile reach a junction with a spur trail to the Pacific Crest and John Muir trails: The left (ahead) branch heads to Devils Postpile, and the right crosses the river to Minaret Falls and Johnston Lake. For now, go left to the first glimpse of the Postpile at 0.25 mile and a junction with a side trail that loops over the top of the Postpile. Though it's spectacular, the side trail is quite steep; if you're disinclined to tackle it, just continue ahead a few steps to enjoy a wonderful view of the tall, angular columns of the Devils Postpile at 0.25-plus mile and 7595 feet. Many still stand, but even more lie, broken and shattered, spilled at the Postpile's base.

Head for Johnston Lake by turning left (west) onto the spur to the Pacific Crest and John Muir trails, and shortly cross a handsome footbridge over the roiling Middle Fork San Joaquin. The spur trail curves right on the west side of the bridge. Go right at the next junction, at 1.25 miles, toward the Pacific Crest and John Muir trails.

A little shy of 1.75 miles, reach a well-signed multiway junction. Take the upper right-hand branch northwest toward Johnston and Shadow lakes. The dusty trail is deep in pumice sand as it rises through a moderate to dense cover of fir and lodgepole. Shortly walk out of Devils Postpile National Monument and, near

2.3 miles, follow the trail as it swings near the edge of a bluff with views southeast to the Mammoth Crest area, scarred by the lightning-caused 1992 Rainbow Fire; east to Mammoth Mountain; and north along San Joaquin Ridge.

At 2.5 miles meet Minaret Creek, running deep in a rocky channel below the trail, and veer west near its south bank. Use trails branch off to the creek, but the main trail curves slightly away from it. At a junction in a few more steps, go right (northwest) on the John Muir Trail to continue to Johnston Lake. Curve right toward the creek, cross a meadow, and ford the creek at a spot that suits you around 2.6 miles—ignore a use trail leading upstream on the south side of the creek.

Now on the north bank, the nearly level trail heads away from the creek before curving generally northwest to offer occasional views of the Minarets through breaks in the forest cover. Soon you glimpse big Johnston Meadow and little Johnston Lake at just over 3 miles and 8100 feet. Use trails dart left off to the lakeshore. In the fall, the vibrant red of the dwarf bilberry leaves here is dazzling.

Retrace your steps.

28 Rainbow and Lower Falls

Place	Total Distance	Elevation	Difficulty Level	Type
Trailhead		7610		
Rainbow Falls (first viewpoint)	2	7400	E	O&B
Lower Falls	3	7220	M U	O&B

Best Time   Early July–mid-October

Topos   WP *Devils Postpile* 15′; *Crystal Crag* 7.5′

Where to Stay

Mountain: Convict Lake Resort, Crystal Crag Lodge, Red's Meadow Resort, Rock Creek Lakes Resort, Rock Creek Lodge, Tamarack Lodge and Resort, Wildyrie Lodge, Woods Lodge

Other: Double Eagle Resort and Spa, Mammoth Mountain Chalets, Mammoth Mountain Inn, McGee Creek Lodge, Mono Sierra Lodge, Rainbow Tarns Bed and Breakfast, Silver Lake Resort, Tom's Place Resort, Whispering Pines Resort

Towns and Agencies: June Lake Chamber of Commerce, Mammoth Lakes Visitors Bureau

HIGHLIGHTS It's an easy hike to see Rainbow Falls, justly regarded as the most classically beautiful waterfall in the Sierra outside Yosemite. If that hike is not long enough for you, extend your stroll south to pretty little Lower Falls.

HOW TO GET TO THE TRAILHEAD From the Main-Minaret-Mary junction, turn right onto Minaret Road (now State Route 203). Follow it uphill to Mammoth Mountain Ski Area/Bike Park. Unless it's very early, expect to take the shuttlebus (for a fee)—visit www.nps.gov/depo for details. The bus will drop you

See map on page 81

off 0.1 mile from the trailhead. If you are driving, descend the Devils Postpile Road past the turnoff to Devils Postpile. Continue almost to the road's end, to a Y-junction at 13.6 miles. Take the right fork onto a dirt road and into a large dirt parking lot, about 13.7 miles from the Main-Minaret-Mary junction. The trailhead is on the south side of the parking lot, which has restrooms.

ON THE TRAIL Head south on a very broad, dusty and sandy trail under moderate forest cover. The forest soon becomes patchy and includes a number of burnt trees, victims of the lightning-caused August 1992 Rainbow Fire. For now, the thinned forest cover permits these sandy flats to support a wonderful, seasonal display of lupine. Numerous use trails dart off here and there in this heavily used area, but the main trail is easily distinguished by its considerable width. Step across an intersecting trail—the John Muir/Pacific Crest Trail—and soon pass a trail that comes in from the left. Approaching the boundary of Devils Postpile National Monument, bypass a trail that comes in from the right and then cross Boundary Creek. Soon there's a fork: ahead (south) to Fish Creek, right (west) to Rainbow Falls. Go right.

At the Devils Postpile boundary, the trail forks, with the horse trail leading left. Middle Fork San Joaquin River rolls along on the right, and Rainbow Falls thunders just downstream. Turn right here to a dramatic overlook a little above the top of Rainbow Falls marked FIRST VIEWPOINT at 1 mile and 7400 feet. Descend a little to Second Viewpoint, with another splendid eyeful of the 101-foot sheer waterfall. Look for a trail to Lower Falls branching left.

Continuing along the brink of the falls for now, the trail angles sharply right to the top of an extremely steep "staircase." Don't take this descent if you wish to keep your hike an "easy" one. At the bottom of the descent at about 7250 feet, the rocks are perpetually wet with the dense mist from Rainbow Falls, just upstream, which makes the rocks dangerous to scramble on.

To continue to Lower Falls, return to the junction near Second Viewpoint and pick up the trail to Lower Falls. The dusty trail rolls generally southward on increasingly sunstruck terrain. Near its end, the trail drops steeply to the river (on the right), passing a junction with a prominent but unmapped use trail. The trail hooks right to big rocks at the top of little Lower Falls at 1.5 miles and 7224 feet, only about 15 feet high but falling into a large, lovely pool. Here I once saw a frustrated, waders-clad angler waist-deep in the pool, slapping the water with his fishing rod while yelling, "Here, fishie, fishie, fishie!"

Retrace your steps.

June Lake to Bridgeport

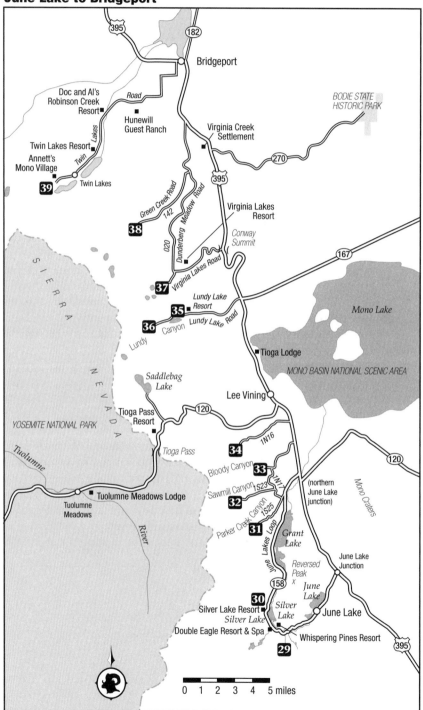

Note: Lodgings in the Mammoth Lakes area are shown on map on p. 56 and in Crowley Lakes areas are shown on map on p. 16.

CHAPTER 3

June Lake to Bridgeport

There's so much to enjoy on the Sierra hikes between June Lake and Bridgeport: wonderful views and beautiful trails to secluded, spectacular destinations. This doesn't even include Yosemite National Park's trails, which are covered in Chapters 5 and 6. Along the way, there are recreational opportunities that are beyond the scope of this book but which you'll want to make time to enjoy: The town of Lee Vining sits on the east edge of Mono Lake and the surrounding Mono Basin National Forest Scenic Area, a California state park. See www.monolake.org. In town, the Mono Lake Committee's office offers books and maps of the area. The attractive U.S. Forest Service visitors center just north of town offers interpretive displays and videos, books, and maps that will guide you to the area's best features. National forest and national park information are available here, too; Yosemite National Park is just west of Lee Vining. In the Mono Basin, the South Tufa Area with its otherworldly tufa formations is a popular hike, as is Panum Crater, a lava dome just southwest of Mono Lake.

South of Bridgeport is the turnoff to Bodie State Historic Park, where the ruins of Bodie Ghost Town are preserved in a state of "arrested decay." About a tenth of the town still stands. Bodie was the site of one of the richest gold strikes in the Eastern Sierra. In its heyday, Bodie was notorious for its violence and lawlessness. One story claims that a young girl from the East Coast, upon being told that her family was moving to Bodie, wrote in her diary, "Goodbye, God, I'm going to Bodie!" Insulted Bodie-ites retorted that what she had really written was, "Good, by God, I'm going to Bodie!" Whichever story is true, the town that began in 1877 and once boasted 10,000 residents is today unoccupied and, according to California State Parks, visited only by ". . . tourists, howling winds, and an occasional ghost."

All driving directions in this chapter are from points on U.S. Highway 395.

Recommended Maps

In addition to those listed in the trip write-ups, your library of maps should include the following. Get the latest edition/revision you can find. They're widely available; you can almost certainly find them at any of the local ranger stations.

■ *Hoover Wilderness, Inyo National Forest,* and *Pacific Southwest Region: A Guide to the John Muir Wilderness and the Sequoia-Kings Canyon Wilderness.* U.S. Forest Service and U.S. Department of Agriculture.

■ *Guide to Eastern Sierra.* Automobile Club of Southern California.

■ *Hoover Wilderness Region.* Tom Harrison Maps.

Individual Lodgings

Name	Nearest Community	Type	Facilities	Price Range	Contact Information	Website and Email Address
Annett's Mono Village	Bridgeport	Mountain	Rooms, cabins, trailers	$–$$	P.O. Box 455 Bridgeport, CA 93517 Phone: 760-932-7071 Fax: 760-932-7468	www.monovillage.com
Convict Lake Resort	Mammoth Lakes	Mountain	Cabins	$$–$$$	HCR 79, Box 204 Mammoth Lakes, CA 93546 Phone: 800-992-2260 or 760-934 - 3800	www.convictlake.com info@convictlake.com
Crystal Crag Lodge	Mammoth Lakes	Mountain	Cabins	$–$$$	P.O. Box 8 Mammoth Lakes, CA 93546 Phone: 760-934-2436	www.crystalcrag.com info@crystalcrag.com
Doc and Al's Robinson Creek Resort	Bridgeport	Mountain	Cabins, trailers	$–$$	P.O. Box 266 Bridgeport, CA 93517 Phone: 760-932-7051	None
Double Eagle Resort and Spa	June Lake	Other	Cabins, rooms	$$–$$$	P.O. Box 736 June Lake, CA 93529 Phone: 760-648-7004	www.doubleeagle.com
Hunewill Guest Ranch	Bridgeport	Mountain	Cabins	$$$	*Summer:* P.O. Box 368 Bridgeport, CA 93517 Phone: 760-932-7710 *Winter:* 200 Hunewill Lane Wellington, NV 89444 Phone: 775-465-2201	www.hunewillranch.com
Lundy Lake Resort	Lee Vining	Mountain	Cabins, trailers	$	P.O. Box 550 Lee Vining, CA 93541 Phone: 626-309-0415	None
Mammoth Mountain Chalets	Mammoth Lakes	Other	Cabins	$$–$$$	P.O. Box 13 Mammoth Lakes, CA 93546 Phone (CA): 800-327-3681 Phone: 760-934-8518 Fax: 760-934-5117	www.mammothmtnchalets.com reservations@mammothmtn chalets.com
Mammoth Mountain Inn	Mammoth Lakes	Other	Rooms, condos	$$–$$$	P.O. Box 353 Mammoth Lakes, CA 93546 Phone: 800-MAMMOTH or 760-934-2581	www.mammothmountain.com
McGee Creek Lodge	Crowley Lake	Other	Rooms	$–$$	Phone: 760-935-4228	http://mcgeecreek.com
Mono Sierra Lodge	Crowley Lake	Other	Rooms	$$	Phone: 800-SADLE UP (723-5387)	www.monosierralodge.com
Sierra Gables Motel	Crowley Lake	Other	Rooms	$ (Rentals are by the month)	Route 1, Box 94 Crowley Lake, CA 93546 Phone: 760-935-4319	www.sierragables.com

Name	Nearest Community	Type	Facilities	Price Range	Contact Information	Website and Email Address
Silver Lake Resort	June Lake	Other	Cabins	$$–$$$	P.O. Box 116 June Lake, CA 93529 Phone: 760-648-7525	www.silverlakeresort.net
Tamarack Lodge and Resort	Mammoth Lakes	Mountain	Rooms, cabins	$–$$$	P.O. Box 69 Mammoth Lakes, CA 93546 Phone: 760-934-2442 or 800-MAMMOTH	www.tamaracklodge.com guestservices@tamaracklodge.com
Tioga Lodge	Lee Vining	Other	Rooms, cabins	$–$$	P.O. Box 580 Lee Vining, CA 93541 Phone: 760-647-6423 Fax: 760-647-6074	www.tiogalodge.com lodging@tiogalodge.com
Tioga Pass Resort	Lee Vining	Mountain	Cabins, rooms	$$–$$$	P.O. Box 7 Lee Vining, CA 93541	www.tiogapassresort.com reservations@tiogapassresort.com
Tuolumne Meadows Lodge	Lee Vining	Mountain	Tent cabins	$	Phone: 559-253-5635	www.yosemitepark.com/accommodations.aspx
Twin Lakes Resort	Bridgeport	Mountain	Cabins	$$	P.O. Box 248 Bridgeport, CA 93517 Phone: 877-932-7751	www.twinlakesresort.com
Virginia Creek Settlement	Bridgeport	Other	Rooms, cabins, tent cabins	$–$$	HCR 62, Box 1050 Bridgeport, CA 93517 Phone: 760-932-7780	http://virginiacreeksettlement.com info@virginiacreeksettlement.com
Virginia Lakes Resort	Lee Vining and Bridgeport	Mountain	Cabins	$–$$$	HC 62, Box 1065 Bridgeport, CA 93517-1065 Phone and Fax: 760-647-6484	www.virginialakesresort.com
Whispering Pines Resort	June Lake	Other	Rooms, cabins	$–$$$	18 Nevada St. June Lake, CA 93529 Phone (CA): 800-648-7762 Phone: 760-872-6828 or 760-872-6828 Fax: 760-748-7589	www.discoverwhisperingpines.com
Wildyrie Lodge	Mammoth Lakes	Mountain	Rooms, cabins	$–$$$	P.O. Box 109 Mammoth Lakes, CA 93546 Phone: 760-934-2444	www.mammothweb.com
Woods Lodge	Mammoth Lakes	Mountain	Cabins	$$–$$$	P.O. Box 108 Mammoth Lakes, CA 93546 Phone: 760-934-2261	www.mammothweb.com

Note: Most Crowley Lake postal addresses are actually in Mammoth Lakes for U.S. Post Office purposes.

Towns and Agencies

Name	Nearest Community	Type	Contact Information	Website and Email Address
Bridgeport Chamber of Commerce	Bridgeport	Community	P.O. Box 541 Bridgeport, CA 93517 Phone: 760-932-7500	www.bridgeportcalifornia.com bridgeportcalifornia@bridgeport california.com
June Lake Chamber of Commerce	June Lake	Community	P.O. Box 2 June Lake, CA 93529 Phone: 760-648-7584	www.junelakechamber.org
Lee Vining Chamber of Commerce	Lee Vining	Community	P.O. Box 130 Lee Vining, CA 93541 Phone: 760-647-6629	www.leevining.com info@leevining.com
Mammoth Lakes Visitors Bureau	Mammoth Lakes	Community	P.O. Box 48 Mammoth Lakes, CA 93546 Phone: 888-GO MAMMOTH or 760-934-2712 Fax: 760-934-7066	www.visitmammoth.com info@visitmammoth.com

29 Fern and Yost Lakes

Place	Total Distance	Elevation	Difficulty Level	Type
Trailhead		7300		
Fern Lake	3	8890	M	O&B
Yost Lake	4.6	9090	M	O&B
Both lakes	5.6	9090	S	O&B

Best Time   Late May–mid-October

Topos   *June Lake, Mammoth Mtn. 7.5′*

Where to Stay

Mountain: Convict Lake Resort, Crystal Crag Lodge, Lundy Lake Resort, Tamarack Lodge and Resort, Wildyrie Lodge, Woods Lodge

Other: Double Eagle Resort and Spa, Mammoth Mountain Chalets, Mammoth Mountain Inn, McGee Creek Lodge, Mono Sierra Lodge, Sierra Gables Motel, Silver Lake Resort, Tioga Lodge, Tioga Pass Resort, Whispering Pines Resort

Towns and Agencies: June Lake Chamber of Commerce, Lee Vining Chamber of Commerce, Mammoth Lakes Visitors Bureau

HIGHLIGHTS   A steep trail with lovely views over the June Lake area also leads to two wonderful lakes. See one, see the other, or (best of all) see both!

HOW TO GET TO THE TRAILHEAD The trailhead is just off State Route 158, the June Lakes Loop, which meets U.S. Highway 395 at two points 5.6 miles apart, between the turnoff to Mammoth Lakes (State Route 203) and the town of Lee Vining. This trailhead is much closer to the more southerly of the two junctions, which is signed as JUNE LAKE JUNCTION. From there, turn southwest, toward the Sierra and follow State Route 158 over Oh! Ridge. Odd name, you will likely think, until you top the ridge and take in the breathtaking spectacle of June Lake backed by rugged, snow-dashed peaks—oh! Drive past June Lake, through charming June Lake village, past Gull Lake, and then past June Mountain Ski Area's base. Between 5.2 and 5.3 miles from the south junction of Highway 395 and State Route 158, spot an obscurely marked trailhead turnoff on the left. Turn here and go about 100 yards on a dirt road to a parking area.

ON THE TRAIL The trailhead is at the south end of the parking lot, past a row of large boulders. Pass an interpretive display and begin a moderate climb, avoiding use trails and enjoying the sight of Carson Peak's rugged face when the forest cover permits. Views over Silver Lake and of Reversed Peak open up on the climb.

The trail makes a switchback turn a little before 0.5 mile and begins to climb more steeply. Views toward fantastically shaped Mono Craters open up between Reversed Peak and June Mountain, and hikers can hear rushing Fern Creek. Just beyond 1 mile and just before the cascades called Fern Creek Falls, reach the fork for the separate trails to Fern and Yost Lakes. Fern Lake is the more spectacular, and most people head for it, leaving quiet Yost Lake a more desirable choice for those seeking to escape the crowds.

To go to Fern Lake, turn right (south) to Fern Lake,

Fern and Yost Lakes

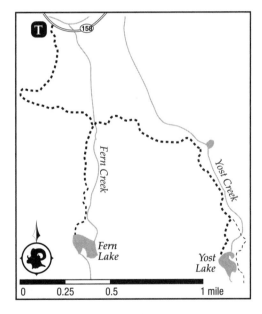

Reversed Peak

Reversed Peak is named for Reversed Creek, which connects Gull Lake (between June and Silver lakes) with Rush Creek and Silver Lake. The creek is named for the direction of its flow: The unusual shape of the glacial valley between Reversed and Carson peaks, in which Gull Lake lies, makes the creek flow briefly toward, rather than away from, the Sierra Crest. Thus, its flow is reversed from normal, which would be away from the crest.

Missing Trails

Since this is the first hike in the June Lake Area, it's useful for you to note that the USFS *Ansel Adams Wilderness* map, as well as some June Lake area handouts based on it, have a couple errors. First, the "trail" to the top of Reversed Peak doesn't exist. You can follow some four-wheel-drive roads for a little way and then scramble up a steep, rough use trail a bit farther, but eventually it's just bushwhacking through tick-laden shrubbery. The use trail leads to the ponds south of Reversed Peak; they're not worth your trouble. Second, most of the trail shown between Yost Lake and Obsidian Dome, via Glass Creek Meadow, has disappeared.

climbing very steeply on a rocky, twisting trail. At 1.5 miles top out 300 feet north of Fern Lake's shore, where there's spectacular scenery. Fern Lake at more than 1.5 miles and 8890 feet sits in a steep-sided cup formed by rugged outliers of Carson Peak and San Joaquin Ridge. San Joaquin Mountain dominates views to the south, and the lake itself is exquisite. Retrace your steps to the fork, enjoying excellent views of June and Gull lakes and of Mono Craters on the way back.

To go to Yost Lake, turn right (east) for Yost Lake if you've come from Fern Lake (now with 2 miles on your boots), or left if you've come from the parking lot. Cross Fern Creek Falls, which may be difficult in early season. Fern Creek Falls isn't much to look at from here but is seasonally showy from vantage points near Silver Lake and on the Rush Creek Trail (Trip 30). Now climb eastward, moderately to steeply, on open slopes offering fine views of the June Lake area. Abruptly veering through a densely forested gully, leave the views behind and climb steadily within hearing of Yost Creek. Curve generally south, paralleling the creek for a time, before climbing gradually to a junction at nearly 3.25 miles. Go right (south) to Yost Lake, topping a low ridge before descending a little to Yost Lake at a little more than 3.3 miles and 9090 feet, a pretty spot guarded by an outlier of San Joaquin Ridge.

Retrace your steps.

30 Agnew and Gem Lakes

Place	Total Distance	Elevation	Difficulty Level	Type
Trailhead		7240		
Agnew Lake	5	8520	S	O&B
Gem Lake overlook	7	9100	S	O&B

Best Time   Early July–mid-October
Topo   *Koip Peak 7.5'*
Where to Stay

Mountain: Convict Lake Resort, Crystal Crag Lodge, Lundy Lake Resort, Tamarack Lodge and Resort, Wildyrie Lodge, Woods Lodge

Other: Double Eagle Resort and Spa, Mammoth Mountain Chalets, Mammoth Mountain Inn, McGee Creek Lodge, Mono Sierra Lodge, Sierra Gables Motel, Silver Lake Resort, Tioga Lodge, Tioga Pass Resort, Whispering Pines Resort

Towns and Agencies: June Lake Chamber of Commerce, Lee Vining Chamber of Commerce, Mammoth Lakes Visitors Bureau

HIGHLIGHTS The view-filled ascent of the Rush Creek Trail is a treat in itself, and the strenuous climb is amply rewarded by the visit to attractive Agnew and splendid Gem lakes. The route passes near or offers good views of several beautiful waterfalls in season. Get an early start, as the trail is mostly shadeless and can be very hot.

HOW TO GET TO THE TRAILHEAD The trailhead is off State Route 158, the June Lakes Loop, which meets U.S. Highway 395 at two points 5.6 miles apart, between the turnoff to Mammoth Lakes (State Route 203) and the town of Lee Vining. Begin at the more southerly of the two junctions, which is signed as JUNE LAKE JUNCTION. From there, turn southwest, toward the Sierra and follow State Route 158 over Oh! Ridge, past June Lake, through June Lake village, past Gull Lake, past June Mountain Ski Area's base, and past the turnoff to the trailhead for Fern and Yost lakes. As the highway curves north past Silver Lake Resort to the west

Agnew and Gem Lakes

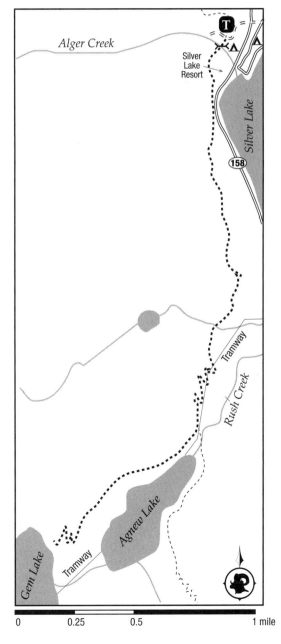

and Silver Lake to the east, look for a marked trailhead turnoff on the west side, beyond the resort and just past a campground and trailer park. Turn into parking here, 7.2 miles from the 395 and 158 junction; there is a restroom and a seasonally staffed ranger kiosk.

ON THE TRAIL Straight ahead from the trailhead sign, note the showy waterfall Alger Creek forms as it thunders down to swell Silver Lake in season. Almost immediately reach a T-junction. Go left (south), crossing one unmapped dirt road and then picking up the next briefly as the trail jogs west to cross Alger Creek on a footbridge. (This stretch of dirt road is shown as part of the trail on the book's map.) The trail jogs south again and fords a placid creek-branch before curving behind the trailer park and cabins of Silver Lake Resort. The view of Carson Peak's convoluted north face over Silver Lake is stunning.

Climb moderately and in 0.75 mile enter Ansel Adams Wilderness abreast of Silver Lake's inlet, a bright stream that meanders through a deep meadow. The upper runs of June Mountain Ski Area are visible ahead. Seasonally, spy the long cascade of Fern Creek Falls tucked into a deep crevice on June Mountain's west flank. In just a few more steps, curve around an outcrop and into Rush Creek's steep canyon, where an unnamed, seasonal waterfall on a tributary of Rush Creek dashes down the cliffs very high up on the right. Cross the tributary; from here to Agnew Lake, snowbanks stuck in the throat of this narrow canyon can be very difficult to cross safely in early season.

At 1.6 miles reach the tracks of the tramway that helps move supplies between the Southern California Edison powerhouse below and the dammed Agnew and Gem lakes ahead, all of which are part of a hydroelectric project. Cross the tracks, switchback up, sometimes on concrete stairs, traverse a section that's blasted out of the rock, cross the tracks again, and switchback up again. Then, rounding an outcrop, you emerge above Agnew Lake and its dam at 2.5 miles and 8520 feet, where use trails lead off to the dam and its buildings as well as to some picnic spots. Gem Lake's dam and the tramway tracks leading to it are visible across little Agnew Lake to the southwest. Carson Peak (10,909 feet) looms above. Spurning the trails to the dam, you stick to the main trail, switchbacking up and climbing moderately to steeply, high above the lake. Near the head of Agnew Lake, switchback steeply up on a rocky track, crossing a huge, rusty pipe. Pause to enjoy the fine over-the-shoulder views down-canyon.

At last, cross a low saddle and find a scrub-dotted knob (to the left) of shattered, rusty rock, above big, beautiful Gem Lake and its dam at nearly 3.5 miles and 9100 feet. This knob has many scenic, if windy, picnic spots overlooking Gem Lake, Donohue Pass, and the grand peaks of the Sierra Crest, beyond which lies the southern backcountry of Yosemite National Park. *Mammoth Lakes Sierra* described this spot as "Hat Ridge, where the wind blows hats off"—very apt. It's an easy scramble up the knob to take in the spectacular scenery, which includes great views back to Agnew Lake.

Retrace your steps.

31 Parker Lake

Place	Total Distance	Elevation	Difficulty Level	Type
Trailhead		7680		
Parker Lake	3+	8318	M	O&B

Best Time   Early July–mid-October
Topo   *Koip Peak 7.5'*
Where to Stay

Mountain: Convict Lake Resort, Crystal Crag Lodge, Lundy Lake Resort, Tamarack Lodge and Resort, Wildyrie Lodge, Woods Lodge

Other: Double Eagle Resort and Spa, Mammoth Mountain Chalets, Mammoth Mountain Inn, McGee Creek Lodge, Mono Sierra Lodge, Sierra Gables Motel, Silver Lake Resort, Tioga Lodge, Tioga Pass Resort, Whispering Pines Resort

Towns and Agencies: June Lake Chamber of Commerce, Lee Vining Chamber of Commerce, Mammoth Lakes Visitors Bureau

HIGHLIGHTS Pretty Parker Lake and the idyllic meadow below it come as wonderful surprises, because the hike begins with a sandy, sunblasted, but flower-strewn moraine.

HOW TO GET TO THE TRAILHEAD It's easier to approach Parker Lake and neighboring Walker Lake (Trips 32 and 33) from the northern junction of U.S. Highway 395 and State Route 158 (the June Lakes Loop). Turn west, toward the Sierra, and follow State Route 158 1.4 miles to a signed

Parker Lake

turnoff onto dirt roads to Parker and Walker lakes. (There are actually three turnoffs here within 0.1 mile; take any of them. By the end of summer, they may look like a single huge, dusty turnoff.) Turn right here and follow the road 0.5 mile more to another junction. Turn left and follow the road generally west toward the Parker Lake Trailhead, 3.7 miles from 395. At a fork with the road to Parker Creek, go left for Parker Lake. At a fork near the end, take the right branch to the trailhead. After a heavy winter, the road may wash out in the area of this fork. In that case, park off the road and walk to the trailhead—it's not far.

ON THE TRAIL From the information sign at the trailhead, climb moderately southwest, up a hot, scrub-dotted slope of the moraine left behind by Parker Creek's glacier. In less than 0.25 mile you enter Ansel Adams Wilderness and continue to climb, sometimes steeply. Well below the trail and on the right, Parker Creek makes a noisy descent through aspens. The trail's grade eases as it crosses flats dominated by sagebrush and bitterbrush, although there are a couple of short, steep hauls over wrinkles in the moraine.

After a mile, the trail curves near the stream at last and becomes nearly level, while the terrain turns from high desert to appealing forest and meadow, with Parker Creek winding lazily between grassy banks. Aspens growing near the streambanks provide wonderful color in the fall.

Soon after passing a junction with a trail descending from Parker Bench and coming in on the left, emerge on the southeast side of the forested outlet at lovely Parker Lake at a little more than 1.5 miles and 8318 feet; Parker and Kuna peaks and Mt. Wood tower over the lake. Across the lake is the upper part of the narrow valley down which the lake's inlet flows, and in season there's a large waterfall high in that valley. I don't recommend bashing your way all around the lake because the use trails eventually vanish, and the way becomes a bushwhack through tick-laden scrub.

Retrace your steps.

32 Walker and Sardine Lakes

Place	Total Distance	Elevation	Difficulty Level	Type
Trailhead		8420		
Walker Lake	0.5	7935	M U	O&B
Lower Sardine Lake	7+	9888	S	O&B

Best Time Late May–mid-October
Topo *Koip Peak 7.5'*
Where to Stay

Mountain: Convict Lake Resort, Crystal Crag Lodge, Lundy Lake Resort, Tamarack Lodge and Resort, Wildyrie Lodge, Woods Lodge

Other: Double Eagle Resort and Spa, Mammoth Mountain Chalets, Mammoth Mountain Inn, McGee Creek Lodge, Mono Sierra Lodge, Sierra Gables Motel, Silver Lake Resort, Tioga Lodge, Tioga Pass Resort, Whispering Pines Resort

Towns and Agencies: June Lake Chamber of Commerce, Lee Vining Chamber of Commerce, Mammoth Lakes Visitors Bureau

HIGHLIGHTS From the lush meadows and aspens of beautiful Walker Lake to the barren rocks and wild peaks around Lower Sardine Lake, this is a journey of wonderful contrasts. The stand of aspens around the head of Walker Lake is exceptionally lovely in the fall.

HOW TO GET TO THE TRAILHEAD You may need a high-clearance vehicle for this drive. From the northern junction of U.S. Highway 395 and State Route 158 (the June Lakes Loop) turn west, toward the Sierra and follow State Route 158 1.4 miles to a signed turnoff onto dirt roads to Parker and Walker lakes. (There are actually three turnoffs here within 0.1 mile; take any of them. By the end of summer, they may look like one, huge, dusty turnoff.) Turn right here and follow the road 0.5 mile more to another junction. Turn right and continue, taking the right fork at all junctions except for the one that goes through a ranch's fence—there, go left—for 0.9 mile more to a marked turnoff for Walker Lake. Follow this road west into the mountains to trailhead parking, with restrooms and four walk-in campsites/picnic sites with tables and fireplaces, at 2.7 more miles, a total of 4.9 miles from Highway 395.

ON THE TRAIL The sandy trail heads up a short, steep slope, soon topping out at about 8500 feet under an immense mountain mahogany and an overlook of long, beautiful Walker Lake. The docks, boats, and cabins at the northeast end of the lake are private property—don't trespass. The trail heads moderately to steeply down the moraine toward the lake, making one long switchback and bypassing a breathtakingly steep, loose use trail that darts off on the right, straight down to the lake's edge. Staying on the main trail (left), shortly reach a junction. For now, go right (northwest) to Walker Lake in order to enjoy the wonderful aspen grove at Walker Lake's west end. In a few more steps, nearly reach the shore of Walker Lake at 0.25 mile and 7935 feet, where use trails branch left and right. From the shoreline, a few steps away, there are wonderful views north-northwest across the lake and west toward Mono Pass (the northern one on the boundary of Yosemite National Park in Trip 72, not the one out of Mosquito Flat mentioned in Trip 14). In the fall, currents raft masses of golden aspen leaves ashore here.

Walker and Sardine Lakes

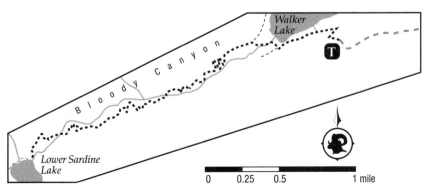

Topo Errors

The topo showing this trailhead and the first section of this trail is quite inaccurate. The trailhead used to be at the end of the road extending up what's marked "Sawmill Canyon." Recently, the road has been extended another 0.5 mile to a new, higher trailhead. There is no four-wheel-drive road extending from the next canyon south (from point 7678T) and northwest over the moraine to Walker Lake.

Retrace your steps to the junction and take the main Mono Pass Trail northwest here, crossing Walker Lake's inlet at a little under 0.6 mile. On the other side, parallel the inlet briefly before curving through a lovely meadow beneath the aspens to a trail junction. To continue to Lower Sardine Lake, turn left (west) at this junction to enter Ansel Adams Wilderness at 0.75 mile, where the trail crosses a slab of dark rock. Ahead to the southwest, Peak 11092T is so rugged and imposing that it's impossible that it's unnamed. On the northwest, rust-colored outliers of Mt. Gibbs pierce the blue sky.

The trail curves southwest, back toward the inlet stream and through dense forest, before beginning a steep, switchbacking climb on the north side of the stream. A couple of open switchback turns offer good over-the-shoulder views of Walker Lake and far beyond it to Mono Lake. The grade eases where the trail crosses a bench within this narrow, northeast-angling canyon, infamous Bloody Canyon. The canyon is named, according to *Place Names of the Sierra Nevada* by Peter Browning, for blood spattered from cuts on the legs of mules and horses, cuts made by the sharp rocks along this once-dreaded trail.

At a little over 1.5 miles, cross the flower-decked creek while on a bench. Look west-northwest near here for a showy cascade from a hanging valley and for a pretty cascade on Walker Creek itself. The trail soon grows very steep again until, at a little over 2.25 miles, it crosses an aspen-covered bench opposite the hanging valley noted earlier.

Swing west-southwest across the bench, below a headwall, to cross the stream at 2.5 miles and climb again toward a lodgepole-covered outcrop to the northwest. Next, switchback up the southeast side of that outcrop, with the creek cascading down the headwall to your left. At 3 miles gain the next bench, which is dotted with stunted trees and backed by a glacially polished headwall to the southwest. A stream escapes below a rounded, gray formation on the right side of the headwall to flow down an aspen-lined channel that you soon curve west to cross. Resume ascending steeply, now across a scree slope, before curving through a slot on the west side of the gray formation to gain the next bench. Veer south below a cliff while climbing moderately and twice crossing a fork of Lower Sardine Lake's outlet at 3.5 miles.

Reach the northeast shore of clear Lower Sardine Lake at just over 3.5 miles and 9888 feet. The lake fills a barren, rocky cirque north-northeast of Peak 11619T. From here there are fabulous views of Mono Lake to the northeast, Mt. Gibbs to the northwest, and Mt. Lewis to the south-southeast. A broad swath of willows northwest of the lake marks the course of an inlet from Mt. Gibbs's southeast slopes.

Return the way you came.

33 Walker Lake

Place	Total Distance	Elevation	Difficulty Level	Type
Trailhead		7400		
Walker Lake (northeast end)	4	7942	MS	O&B
Walker Lake (head)	6	7942	MS	O&B

Best Time Early July–mid-October

Topos *Mount Dana, Koip Peak 7.5'*

Where to Stay

Mountain: Convict Lake Resort, Crystal Crag Lodge, Lundy Lake Resort, Tamarack Lodge and Resort, Wildyrie Lodge, Woods Lodge

Other: Double Eagle Resort and Spa, Mammoth Mountain Chalets, Mammoth Mountain Inn, McGee Creek Lodge, Mono Sierra Lodge, Sierra Gables Motel, Silver Lake Resort, Tioga Lodge, Tioga Pass Resort, Whispering Pines Resort

Towns and Agencies: June Lake Chamber of Commerce, Lee Vining Chamber of Commerce, Mammoth Lakes Visitors Bureau

HIGHLIGHTS There are two trails to the eastern Sierra's lovely Walker Lake. Trip 32 documents the southern one that reaches all the way to the Sardine Lakes and Mono Pass. The northern trail, described here, is one of the last to be closed by snow in winter and often the first to open in spring. Even when snow cloaks the slopes above 8500 feet, this route may be open.

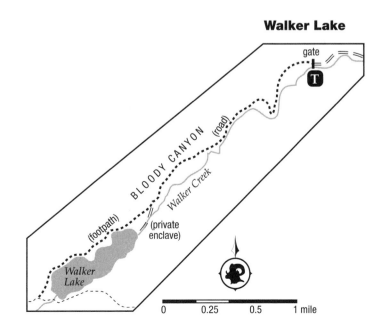

HOW TO GET TO THE TRAILHEAD From the northern junction of U.S. Highway 395 and State Route 158 (the June Lakes Loop) turn west, toward the Sierra and follow State Route 158 1.4 miles to a signed turnoff onto dirt roads to Parker and Walker lakes. (There are actually three turnoffs here within 0.1 mile; take any of them. By the end of summer, they may look like one, huge, dusty turnoff.) Turn right here and follow the road 0.5 mile more to another junction. Turn right and continue, taking the right fork at all junctions except for the one that goes through a ranch's fence—there, go left. Continue on the main road north toward Walker Lake past turnoffs to a couple of Los Angeles Department of Water and Power (LADWP) ponds on the left. The unseen second pond has an impressive roadside cascade. After passing that cascade, turn left (southwest) into the mouth of Bloody Canyon at the next dirt road with a LADWP NO CAMPING sign. Parallel Walker Creek and an impressive aspen grove for another 0.5 mile to reach a semicircular parking area on the left (south) side of the road.

ON THE TRAIL Start walking generally southwest up the road. At about 100 feet there is a gate that bars most—but not all—cars. People going to the private enclave at Walker Lake's outlet have keys to this gate and can (and do) drive beyond it.

Hemmed in by chaparral-covered moraines, the sandy road rises gently past aspens as views open gradually ahead of (right to left) Mt. Gibbs, Mt. Lewis, and Parker Peak. At a Y-junction between 0.5 and 0.6 mile, stay on the main road as it hooks right up a moderate grade. Go right again almost immediately to stay on the main road at the next Y-junction. Near the top of this short climb there are good views ahead to Mt. Dana and east to Mono Lake, low Panum Crater, and the north end of the otherworldly Mono Craters.

The road curves southwest again as it dips into patchy forest and then levels out, briefly meeting the creek. Around 1 mile, the forest gives way to a long meadow splashed with blue iris in spring, tinted vivid green in summer, and brushed with muted gold in fall. The road skirts the meadow's north edge for most of the next mile, offering excellent views of historic Bloody Canyon up to Mono Pass on Yosemite's border, the saddle between Mts. Gibbs and Lewis, and part of a major trade route across the Sierra used by Native Americans and pioneers.

Just beyond the meadow's southwest end a large sign points to the LI'L WALKER LAKE TRAIL on the right. Another sign forbids you to go farther on the road, as the enclave is ahead. Turn right onto the broad, sandy trail in the shade of fragrant Jeffrey pines. On this trail, presently top a low rise and parallel a fence with a hiker's pass-through at 2 miles. The lake's sparkling blue water is visible leftward through the pines. Optionally, toddle down to the shore (7935 feet) to end your hike.

To go farther, pick up the trail on the other side of the fence; the needle-covered path is very faint here. Occasional views of the lake across its deeply meadowed shoreline are sure to inspire oohs and aahs. Use trails angle toward the lake, but the main trail continues ahead, roughly tracing the lakeshore.

The trail ducks into a strip of lakeside aspens and reaches one of Walker Lake's several inlets. Step across on logs and into the huge aspen grove at the lake's head—a spectacular sight in its autumn glory! The trail may be very faint under fallen leaves as it begins to curve deeper into Bloody Canyon. The trail presently arrives at a signed junction with the trail over Mono Pass and from Walker Lake's south side. At about 3 miles, this junction makes a good turnaround point.

Retrace your steps.

34 Gibbs Lake

Place	Total Distance	Elevation	Difficulty Level	Type
Trailhead		7927		
Gibbs Lake	6.5	9530	S	O&B

Best Time   Early July–mid-October
Topo   *Mount Dana* 7.5'
Where to Stay

Mountain: Convict Lake Resort, Crystal Crag Lodge, Lundy Lake Resort, Tamarack Lodge and Resort, Tuolumne Meadows Lodge, Virginia Lakes Resort, Wildyrie Lodge, Woods Lodge

Other: Double Eagle Resort and Spa, Mammoth Mountain Chalets, Mammoth Mountain Inn, McGee Creek Lodge, Mono Sierra Lodge, Sierra Gables Motel, Silver Lake Resort, Tioga Lodge, Tioga Pass Resort, Whispering Pines Resort

Towns and Agencies: June Lake Chamber of Commerce, Lee Vining Chamber of Commerce, Mammoth Lakes Visitors Bureau

HIGHLIGHTS   Lovely Gibbs Lake, set in a deep canyon below 12,000- and 13,000-foot peaks, is ample reward for the stiff hike required to reach it.

HOW TO GET TO THE TRAILHEAD
You'll need a high-clearance vehicle for the road to the trailhead and a high-clearance, four-wheel-drive vehicle to get all the way to the trailhead parking. The turnoff to the Gibbs Lake Trailhead is on U.S. Highway 395 3.1 miles north of the northern junction of 395 and State Route 158 (the June

Mt. Gibbs from the ruins of the Ella Bloss Mine (Trip 72)

Gibbs Lake

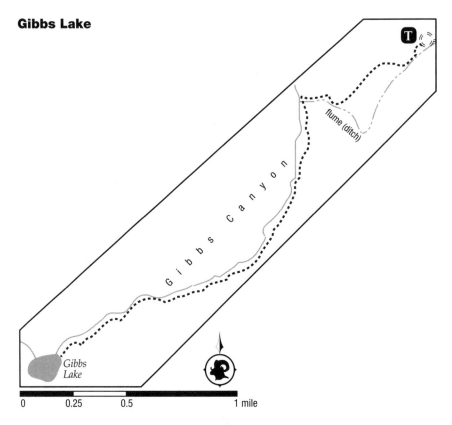

Lakes Loop) and 1.2 miles south of the junction of 395 and westbound State Route 120 (the Tioga Road), seemingly in a crease in the east face of prominent Williams Butte. There are turnoff signs on both sides of the highway, but the road is otherwise unsigned. Turn west onto this road (Horse Meadows Road) and follow it up to pretty Lower Horse Meadow, avoiding any turnoffs. Beyond Lower Horse Meadow, the road may become impassable to ordinary passenger vehicles; walk the rest of the way. Those with sturdier vehicles and nerves can continue to lovely Upper Horse Meadow, at the far (west) end of which there's a trailhead parking area under trees, 3.3 miles or less, depending on how far you can drive.

ON THE TRAIL Mileages given below are from the trailhead parking area. The trail—really a dusty, gated road—leaves from the right side of a trailhead information sign. Squeeze between the fence and gate and start climbing steeply up the trail. Forest cover permitting, enjoy fine over-the-shoulder views to Mono Lake at rest stops.

Around 0.75 mile the trail levels out briefly near some lovely cascades on Gibbs Creek. Beyond, the trail climbs again before leveling out near the ruins of a flume. Cross the flume on the pipe the water once flowed through and curve left as the road ends to the right. Now on a footpath, climb to a ridge above the creek. Moving off the ridge, trudge up a dry wash lined with stunted aspens. At nearly 1.6 miles, level out on a dry shoulder above the creek, from which Mts. Gibbs and

Dana are ahead to the west-southwest. Next, dip into forest cover, more or less paralleling Gibbs Creek.

At 2.5 miles enter Ansel Adams Wilderness near Gibbs Creek. Here, the beautiful creek meanders between grassy banks made colorful by currant, fragrant red heather, and Labrador tea. The ascent is gradual to moderate until, just before the lake, there's a brief, moderate to steep climb to the outlet of Gibbs Lake at 3.25 miles and 9530 feet. Use trails lead left and right; take one to find a great lunch spot.

Retrace your steps.

35 May Lundy Mine and Oneida Lake

Place	Total Distance	Elevation	Difficulty Level	Type
Trailhead		7803		
Blue Lake	5.75	9460	S	O&B
May Lundy Mine ruins	6+	9500	S	O&B
Oneida Lake	6.6	9656	S	O&B

Best Time   Early July–mid-October
Topos   *Lundy, Mount Dana* 7.5'
Where to Stay

Mountain: Convict Lake Resort, Crystal Crag Lodge, Lundy Lake Resort, Tamarack Lodge and Resort, Tuolumne Meadows Lodge, Virginia Lakes Resort, Wildyrie Lodge, Woods Lodge

Oneida Lake

May Lundy Mine and Oneida Lake

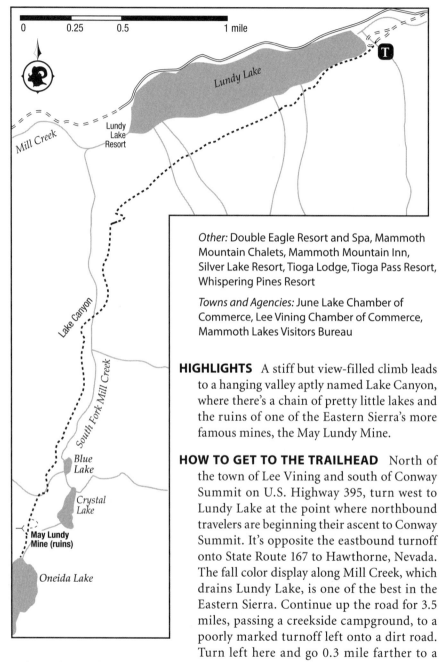

Other: Double Eagle Resort and Spa, Mammoth Mountain Chalets, Mammoth Mountain Inn, Silver Lake Resort, Tioga Lodge, Tioga Pass Resort, Whispering Pines Resort

Towns and Agencies: June Lake Chamber of Commerce, Lee Vining Chamber of Commerce, Mammoth Lakes Visitors Bureau

HIGHLIGHTS A stiff but view-filled climb leads to a hanging valley aptly named Lake Canyon, where there's a chain of pretty little lakes and the ruins of one of the Eastern Sierra's more famous mines, the May Lundy Mine.

HOW TO GET TO THE TRAILHEAD North of the town of Lee Vining and south of Conway Summit on U.S. Highway 395, turn west to Lundy Lake at the point where northbound travelers are beginning their ascent to Conway Summit. It's opposite the eastbound turnoff onto State Route 167 to Hawthorne, Nevada. The fall color display along Mill Creek, which drains Lundy Lake, is one of the best in the Eastern Sierra. Continue up the road for 3.5 miles, passing a creekside campground, to a poorly marked turnoff left onto a dirt road. Turn left here and go 0.3 mile farther to a large, dirt parking area at 3.8 miles. The trailhead is on the south side of Lundy Lake's dam by a locked gate.

ON THE TRAIL Get an early start, for the first leg of this trip can be very hot. Circumvent the gate on the dam's south side and follow a rocky and dusty road west along the lake's south shore. The road forks almost immediately; go left to begin a moderate to steep climb of this sunstruck south wall of Lundy Canyon. The meadow at the lake's west end and Lundy Lake Resort come into view as you rise, and the uphill side of the road becomes defined by low, rocky out-crops. Both sides of the road presently become hemmed in by willows, and ice may linger on the road in large patches after a sub-freezing night. Around 0.75 mile, pass an old road covered by rockfall that seems to have come up from the head of Lundy Lake. Continue climbing, crossing a pair of small streams, one in a culvert, and negotiating some marshy stretches.

At a little beyond 1.3 miles, enter forest cover as the road veers generally south into the hanging valley called Lake Canyon, from which South Fork Mill Creek cascades in a handsome waterfall. Ahead are the striking Doré Cliffs, named for the 19th-century artist Gustave Doré. The climb eases around 2 miles with views of Gilcrest Peak to the east, Peak 9148T to the west. Cross South Fork Mill Creek where it runs under the road through a culvert and then curve southeast through willow thickets at the base of a talus slope. After a short, steep climb, pass through patches of forest and soon come abreast of grassy Blue Lake at a little over 2.75 miles and 9460 feet. Ahead, a semicircle of handsome peaks defines the head of the cirque, and the Tioga Crest is on the right (west). Approaching a low, north-east-trending ridgelet, the road forks at 3 miles.

Go right (south-southwest) along the base of the ridgelet and then begin climbing moderately toward the head of the cirque. Passing the ridgelet, there's a good view east to the head of Crystal Lake and the ruins south of it—collapsing buildings and toppling telegraph poles of the May Lundy Mine. Ahead, perched on a tailings heap, are more May Lundy Mine ruins at just over 3 miles and 9500 feet; the tracks of its tramway are especially striking. Beginning with the discovery of ore in 1879, the May Lundy Mine yielded about $2 million in gold, and its tailings were reworked as late as 1937, according to *Mammoth Lakes Sierra*. Cross the stream and veer left onto the tailings heap for another look down on the ruined mine buildings, where boilers, engines, cables, and timbers lie strewn across the meadow south of Crystal Lake. The wind seems to carry echoes of the steam whistles, clanging machinery, and cursing miners that must have made this a lively, noisy place.

Back on the trail, cross the tramway tracks just before they head over ruined trestles into thin air. Picking up the trail on the other side, wind through more debris before making a short climb to an unmapped junction. Go right (south, ahead) to another unmapped junction where you see the blue expanse of Oneida Lake ahead. At this junction, the right fork (southwest) curves around to a ruined stone building and the left (south) descends a rocky footpath past a sign marking the Hoover Wilderness boundary to Oneida Lake's pretty north shore. Pick your way down to the shore of Oneida Lake at 3.3 miles and 9656 feet.

Return the way you came.

36 Lundy Canyon

Place	Total Distance	Elevation	Difficulty Level	Type
Trailhead		8200		
Base of first big cascade	1.3	8200	E	O&B
Base of canyon's headwall	5	8800	M	O&B

Best Time Late May–mid-October
Topo *Dunderberg Peak 7.5'*
Where to Stay

Mountain: Convict Lake Resort, Crystal Crag Lodge, Lundy Lake Resort, Tamarack Lodge and Resort, Tuolumne Meadows Lodge, Virginia Lakes Resort, Wildyrie Lodge, Woods Lodge

Other: Double Eagle Resort and Spa, Mammoth Mountain Chalets, Mammoth Mountain Inn, Silver Lake Resort, Tioga Lodge, Tioga Pass Resort, Whispering Pines Resort

Towns and Agencies: June Lake Chamber of Commerce, Lee Vining Chamber of Commerce, Mammoth Lakes Visitors Bureau

HIGHLIGHTS Beautiful Lundy Canyon is full of waterfalls in springtime, thanks mainly to Mill Creek, which runs down-canyon over a series of benches. Near the canyon's head are the stairstep cascades called Lundy Falls on upper Mill Creek, which connects Lake Helen at 10,107 feet in 20 Lakes Basin with upper Lundy Canyon at 8600 feet—1500-plus feet of splash and spray! Nameless white

Lundy Canyon

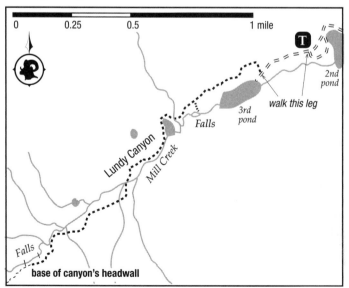

ribbons, tributaries of Mill Creek, streak the canyon's high walls. In autumn, Lundy Canyon's aspens put on one of the Eastern Sierra's best fall-color displays.

HOW TO GET TO THE TRAILHEAD You'll need a high-clearance vehicle. North of the town of Lee Vining and south of Conway Summit on U.S. Highway 395, turn west to Lundy Lake at the point where northbound travelers are beginning their ascent to Conway Summit. It's opposite the eastbound turnoff onto State Route 167 to Hawthorne, Nevada. The fall color display along Mill Creek, which drains Lundy Lake, is one of the best in the Eastern Sierra. Continue up the road for 3.5 miles, passing a creekside campground. Continue ahead along Lundy Lake and then to and through Lundy Lake Resort at 5.1 miles from U.S. Highway 395, beyond which the road is unpaved and rough. Pass a couple of charming beaver ponds and a large, whimsically painted rock. Continue another 1.4 miles to a trailhead parking loop with a restroom at 6.5 miles. The trailhead is near the upper, or northern, end of the loop.

ON THE TRAIL From the trailhead, walk up the narrow, rocky ruins of a spur road between aspens until, a little shy of 0.25 mile, there's an obvious ("marked trail on the right where the spur road curves left to a beaver pond ("3rd pond" on the book's map). Veer right onto the trail, which becomes open, rocky, and steep. From a rocky shoulder, enjoy a good view of Lundy Canyon's first big cascade ahead, part of Lundy Falls far ahead, and, over your shoulder, back to Lundy Lake. This is the best view of Lundy Falls from the trail.

Descend a little to enter Hoover Wilderness just before 0.6 mile, bottoming out at a junction with a use trail branching left to the base of this showiest of the falls on lower Mill Creek. Stroll over to the base of this first big cascade at 0.6 mile and 8200 feet (labeled "Falls" on the book's map); if it's a hot day, you'll enjoy the falls' cooling spray. Back on the main trail, climb to cross multiple channels of Mill Creek above the falls; the flowers here are splendid. Skirt a lovely little beaver pond, cross another stream, and note that high on the north-northwest wall of the canyon there's a long waterfall beneath some unnamed crags. Cross Mill Creek again below another dashing cascade to parallel and then cross a seasonal, usually dry streambed. The aspen forest here is particularly delightful in the fall.

Veering southeast, pass the ruins of a log cabin at 1.25 miles and emerge at an area of avalanche-downed trees. Look for cascades ahead and, seasonally, from the canyon walls on either side. Meet the creek again as the trail reenters forest and passes a pond. At a junction where a use trail comes in from the left, continue ahead (southwest) to cross an open, flowery slope while climbing.

At the next junction with another use trail, go left, and at a little over 2 miles, climb steeply on a rocky trail through mountain hemlock to the next bench in this canyon. Ascend the bench beside a steep meadow golden with butterweed in season, and then cross a scree slope before beginning to switchback steeply up a talus slope from whose lower part you glimpse Lundy Falls dropping through a steep slot in the canyon's headwall.

Continuing beyond here requires ascending the very tough trail between Lundy Canyon and Lake Helen in 20 Lakes Basin, which is briefly described in

Trip 70. So turn around here, at the base of the canyon's headwall at about 2.5 miles and 8800 feet.

Retrace your steps.

37 Virginia Lakes

Place	Total Distance	Elevation	Difficulty Level	Type
Trailhead		9860		
Blue Lake	0.6+	9886	E	O&B
Cooney Lake	2.5	10,246	M	O&B
Frog Lakes	2.75+	10,370	M	O&B
Unnamed pass/ viewpoint	6+	11,120+	S	O&B

Best Time   Early July–mid-October
Topo   *Dunderberg Peak 7.5'*
Where to Stay
   Mountain: Annett's Mono Village, Doc and Al's Robinson Creek Resort, Hunewill Guest Ranch, Lundy Lake Resort, Tuolumne Meadows Lodge, Twin Lakes Resort, Virginia Lakes Resort

   Other: Double Eagle Resort and Spa, Silver Lake Resort, Tioga Lodge, Tioga Pass Resort, Virginia Creek Settlement, Whispering Pines Resort

   Towns and Agencies: Bridgeport Chamber of Commerce, June Lake Chamber of Commerce, Lee Vining Chamber of Commerce

HIGHLIGHTS   Wander up a wonderfully scenic chain of lakes to a high viewpoint overlooking breathtaking backcountry scenery on the boundary of northern Yosemite National Park. The drive to the trailhead offers excellent fall color.

HOW TO GET TO THE TRAILHEAD   The road to Virginia Lakes strikes west from Conway Summit, which, at 8138 feet, is the highest point on U.S. Highway 395 and is between Lee Vining and Bridgeport. Turn west onto Virginia Lakes Road and follow it past side roads, one of which leads to Virginia Lakes Resort and a large parking area, with restrooms and water, at the roadend at 6.2 miles.

ON THE TRAIL   Head west from an information sign at the trailhead, which is next to the restroom, crossing an open slope and ignoring use trails on the left to the shore of upper Virginia Lake. The colorful slopes around the lake are part of a subrange sometimes called the Dunderberg Range that was "carved" from a roof pendant (see Trip 15). Curve north around a patch of forest, meeting a stock trail that comes in on the right (east). Continue ahead here, curving west, passing a couple of ponds, and enter Hoover Wilderness around 0.3 mile.

   The trail begins to trace the shoreline of pretty Blue Lake at a little more than 0.3 mile and 9886 feet. The lake's inlet cascades dramatically down the steep slope

Virginia Lakes

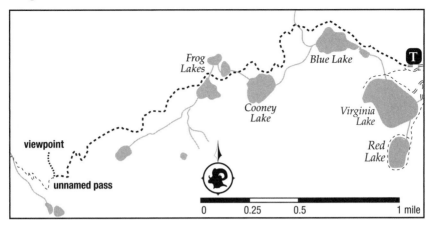

between Cooney and Blue lakes. Paralleling Blue Lake but leaving its shoreline behind, begin climbing moderately to steeply on a rocky and dusty trail across the slope northwest of the lake. In spite of its apparent barrenness, the slope supports quite a flower display, especially near the top of the climb.

At 0.75 mile cross unseen, higher Moat Lake's outlet stream and then curve south through a flowery hillside meadow before entering forest cover. At 1 mile, pass a tiny old cabin that's remarkably well preserved. Brush past another hillside meadow as the trail curves northwest and then south over a rocky, open slope. Beautiful, peak-ringed Cooney Lake at almost 1.25 miles and 10,246 feet soon comes into view.

A steep switchback climbs above Cooney Lake to a pretty bench where the trail crosses Cooney's inlet stream and reaches the lowest of the Frog Lakes at about 1.3 miles and 10,370 feet. The three delightful little Frog Lakes nestle together on this bench all at almost the same elevation, and a stop at one is almost irresistible. In very early season, these lakes' boggy shores are bright with white marsh marigold. Continuing, splash across the stream linking two of the Frog Lakes and soon leave the lakes behind. Follow the trail up a series of rocky, increasingly barren little benches, passing above an unnamed pond.

Make a final, steep, rocky attack on the crest that's plainly ahead, to stand atop an unnamed pass at a little more than 3 miles and at 11,120 feet. The view east, back over the Virginia Lakes, is simply astounding. But the view west is obscured by the terrain, so trek some 400 yards northwest over barren, shattered, metamorphic rock to an outcrop with awe-inspiring views northwest to Summit Lake on the eastern edge of northern Yosemite, to the Sierra Crest just west of Summit Lake, and the Hoover Lakes around the corner to the northeast. The rock colors here are amazing—gray, gray-green, brown, rust, cream, and very-nearly-blue, and the rocks are splashed with lichens in brilliant rusts and chartreuses. Tiny alpine flowers find shelter among these broken stones.

Retrace your steps.

38 Green, East, and West Lakes

Place	Total Distance	Elevation	Difficulty Level	Type
Trailhead		7900		
Green Lake	6	8945	M	O&B
East Lake	8.25	9458	S	O&B
West Lake	9.3	9870	S	O&B

Best Time   Early July–mid-October
Topo   *Dunderberg Peak 7.5'*
Where to Stay
  Mountain: Annett's Mono Village, Doc and Al's Robinson Creek Resort, Hunewill Guest Ranch, Lundy Lake Resort, Twin Lakes Resort, Virginia Lakes Resort
  Other: Tioga Lodge, Virginia Creek Settlement
  Towns and Agencies: Bridgeport Chamber of Commerce, Lee Vining Chamber of Commerce

HIGHLIGHTS   Trailside flower gardens brighten the stroll to picturesque Green Lake. From there, choose to visit beautiful East Lake or the rugged basin of pretty West Lake.

HOW TO GET TO THE TRAILHEAD   The turnoff to Green Creek Trailhead from U.S. Highway 395 is just north of State Route 270 (the eastbound road to Bodie State Historical Park) and south of Bridgeport. Turn west onto marked Green Creek Road. Go left at a junction with the Summit Meadows Road at 1 mile. Continue another 2.5 miles and go right at a junction with a spur road southbound to Virginia Lakes. Continue another 5.2 miles, veering right to a parking loop, with restrooms and water, at the trailhead, 8.7 miles from Highway 395.

ON THE TRAIL   Head southwest away from the marked trailhead on a dusty trail through a patchy to moderate Jeffrey pine forest, bobbing along high above Green Creek and crossing a creeklet beyond 0.25 mile. Clearings offer glimpses of Kavanaugh Ridge to

East Lake

Green, East, and West Lakes

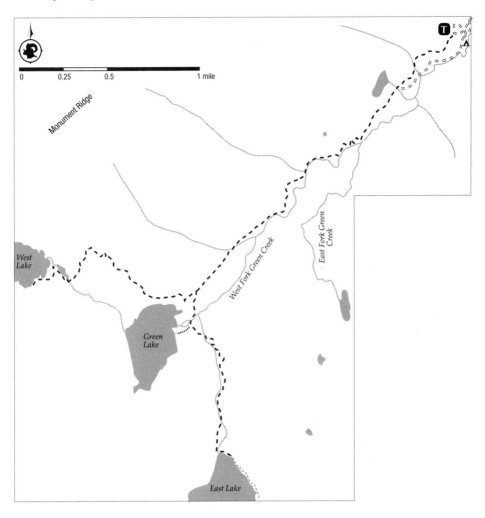

the south and Epidote Peak ahead to the southwest. At about 0.5 mile, descend to meet a road coming in on the left, from the campground, and at 0.6 mile meet Green Creek on the left, near the former trailhead.

Continuing southwest, ignore an unmapped, gated spur road on the right at a little more than 0.75 mile and shortly ford a creek, beyond which the trail dwindles to a footpath. Ascend moderately to steeply to an open ridgetop, and then descend, meeting the creek at nearly 1.25 miles. Veering away from the creek, begin switchbacking on a moderate grade up a lightly forested slope, and then ascend gradually to moderately above the cascading creek.

Cross a stream from Monument Ridge high above to the northwest and reach a marker for Hoover Wilderness at about 1.5 miles. Beginning in this area, there are wonderful flower displays along the trail, particularly in a marshy section around 1.6 to 1.75 miles. Around 2.25 miles, cross a dry wash and begin a moderate ascent southwest of an open ridge beneath Dunderberg, Epidote, and Gabbro peaks. At 2.6 miles reach the Green-West junction.

To go to Green and East lakes, go left at the Green-West junction, dipping to ford Green Lake's outlet at about 2.75 miles. On the other side, use trails branch southwest; take one to Green Lake at nearly 3 miles and 8945 feet. Green Lake is exceptionally scenic; its flower- and forest-lined shores are backed by pretty Glines Canyon, which lies below Virginia Pass across the lake.

Returning to the main trail to East Lake, turn southeast to ford East Lake's outlet for the first time, between two dashing cascades. Resume climbing, generally south, on small switchbacks through one dazzling patch of flowers after another. Cross the outlet again at 3.5 miles, continue climbing on switchbacks, skirt a forested meadow, and cross two strands of the outlet one after another just below East Lake. Reach the shore above big, beautiful East Lake at a little more than 4 miles and 9458 feet. Gabbro, Page, and Epidote peaks rise above East Lake's west shore. Find yourself a picnic spot and enjoy this splendid place at leisure.

If you want to go to West Lake and not East Lake, I recommend you follow the directions above to see Green Lake first and then return to the Green-West junction. Second, from the Green-West, junction go southwest (right if you don't go to Green Lake; left when returning from Green Lake). Follow the moderate to steep, dry, open, dusty trail through tobacco brush, junipers, and mule ears. Ahead there are cascades on West Lake's outlet. In a little less than 0.5 mile from the junction, begin working your way through a seasonally spectacular hillside meadow, crossing a little stream as you brush past larkspur, sweet cicely, willow, lupine, stickseed, mariposa lily, and purple-flowered wild onion.

Beyond the meadow the trail climbs steeply through a patchy forest of lodgepole, occasionally skirting a meadow, and rises into a subalpine world of stunted trees, shattered rock, and wide-ranging views. Crossing seasonal trickles, the track curves around a switchback leg with heart-stopping views of Green Lake below. At a little more than 1.3 miles from the junction, the trail tops out at 9880 feet near a spartan campsite off-trail to the east.

From here, descend quickly to a pond below West Lake under stunted lodgepoles. Crossing the outlet on a low dam, begin zigzagging up the now-faint trail high above the pond until the route drops abruptly to the shore of dramatic West Lake. The lake sits beneath the jagged peaks of Monument Ridge, 1.6 miles from the junction and at 9870 feet. This is a good place to stop; from here there's little more than a rough angler's path leading across steep slopes high above the water.

Retrace your steps.

39 Barney Lake

Place	Total Distance	Elevation	Difficulty Level	Type
Trailhead		7090		
Barney Lake	6	8300	S	O&B

Best Time   Early July–mid-October
Topo   *Buckeye Ridge 7.5'*
Where to Stay

Mountain: Annett's Mono Village, Doc and Al's Robinson Creek Resort, Hunewill Guest Ranch, Lundy Lake Resort, Silver Lake Resort, Twin Lakes Resort, Virginia Lakes Resort

Other: Tioga Lodge, Virginia Creek Settlement

Towns and Agencies: Bridgeport Chamber of Commerce, Lee Vining Chamber of Commerce

HIGHLIGHTS   A leisurely and lengthy walk through woods and flower-blessed meadows, followed by a short, scenic climb, leads to beautiful Barney Lake. The route can be sunny and very hot, so take plenty of water.

HOW TO GET TO THE TRAILHEAD   The road to the trailhead, Twin Lakes Road, branches west off U.S. Highway 395 on the northern edge of Bridgeport. Turn west onto signed Twin Lakes Road and follow it past three of the four Bridgeport area resorts and past the beautiful Twin Lakes, right into the fourth resort, Annett's Mono Village, at the head of upper Twin Lake, 13.5 miles from 395. There is limited, free public parking, which is poorly marked, so ask the person in the check-in kiosk where to park. There are restrooms and water, as well as a café and a store, at the parking area.

ON THE TRAIL   From the parking lot near the launching ramp, walk southwest between the signed boat house/workshop, entrance kiosk, and ice house. A sign on a telephone pole next to the ice house points the way to Barney Lake, as do several other signs as you follow dirt roads through the campground, generally west toward a meadow below a quartet of handsome little peaks. In less than 0.25 mile, walk around the road closure at the campground's west end and continue on the road, skirting the meadow (on the left) and avoiding a use trail going left into the meadow. A little short of Robinson Creek, the Barney Lake Trail bears right (northwest) off the road; follow it. Robinson Creek bubbles along on the left.

Pass granite outcrops on the right before beginning a gradual climb to a wilderness information display at 0.6 mile. Beyond, the trail climbs gradually to moderately as it curves around a flowery meadow and crosses a small stream. At nearly 1.25 miles, emerge at a broad valley whose floor is a huge, flowery meadow in season. The meadow sits in a beautiful amphitheater of peaks, including Robinson, Victoria, and Hunewill peaks. Ignore use trails branching left to Robinson

Creek and continue generally west-southwest toward the farther peaks through some amazing flower gardens. The scenery makes up for the heat and dustiness of this stretch.

Pass through a couple of stands of spindly aspens before reaching the wilderness boundary at a little over 2 miles, near which there's a magnificent view southward to the raw peaks around Little Slide Canyon. Approaching 2.3 miles, leave the meadow for the damp banks of Robinson Creek and then veer away to begin climbing gradually on switchbacks.

Crossing several streams, continue up the long switchbacks, enjoying splendid flower gardens here and there. At 2.6 miles leave the flower gardens briefly for a short, hot climb up a low, light-colored cliff before veering back to a shadier streambank, where the grade eases back to gradual. Cross the stream and presently reach the sandy northeast shore of big, beautiful Barney Lake at nearly 3 miles and 8300 feet. The lake's other shores are bounded by picturesque cliffs and peaks, including Cirque Mountain, Kettle Peak, and, especially, cleft Crown Point.

Retrace your steps.

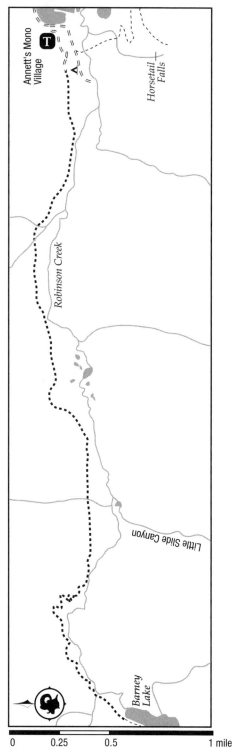

Barney Lake

0   0.25   0.5   1 mile

Crown Point over Barney Lake

Sequoia and Kings Canyon National Parks

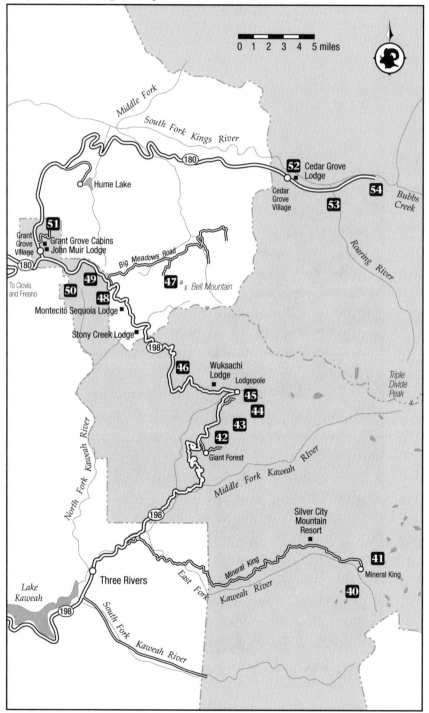

CHAPTER 4

Sequoia and Kings Canyon National Parks

The Western Sierra is where you'll find some of the range's most famous sights: huge trees, huge valleys, and huge waterfalls. This part of the range has been deemed most worthy of protection as national parks: Sequoia, Kings Canyon, and Yosemite. Here are the world's largest trees, the giant sequoias; immense, glacier-sculpted valleys of breathtaking splendor—Kings Canyon, Yosemite, and Hetch Hetchy; and great waterfalls, including Yosemite (one of the world's highest), Nevada, Vernal, Bridalveil, Tueeulala, and Wapama. Tucked in among all these immense wonders are smaller marvels: little jewels of lakes, gems of meadows, tumbling cascades, and lesser "yosemites" (as John Muir called glacier-sculpted valleys other than Yosemite Valley). Delightful lodgings beckon hikers to stay a while.

People came to the foothills of the Western Sierra in the 19th century to seek gold. In the 21st century, people come to seek the lasting "gold" of the range: the grand vistas, the many opportunities for outdoor recreation, and the renewing experience of being in the presence of so much beauty.

The Western Sierra hikes in this book begin in Sequoia National Park's Mineral King district, a high, beautiful valley reached by a long, difficult drive—and worth the trouble. The next hikes are those off the General's Highway, which runs through Sequoia National Park's Giant Forest district north through Sequoia National Forest and Giant Sequoia National Monument and into Kings Canyon National Park's Grant Grove district. The latter are the best places in this book to see giant sequoias. Finally, the trips dip down into the immense valley known as Kings Canyon—less famous but far deeper than Yosemite Valley to the north.

Recommended Maps

In addition to those listed in the trip write-ups, your library of maps should include the following. Get the latest edition/revision you can find. They're widely available, certainly at any of the local ranger stations.

- *Sequoia National Forest, Sierra National Forest, Stanislaus National Forest,* and *A Guide to the John Muir Wilderness and the Sequoia-Kings Canyon Wilderness.* U.S. Forest Service and U.S. Department of Agriculture.

- *Sequoia and Kings Canyon National Parks Guide Map.* Automobile Club of California.

- *Sequoia and Kings Canyon National Parks Recreation Map.* Tom Harrison Maps.

- *Trails of Mineral King, Trails of Giant Forest, Trails of Lodgepole, Trails of Grant Grove,* and *Trails of Cedar Grove.* Sequoia Natural History Association.

Individual Lodgings

Name	Nearest Community	Type	Facilities	Price Range	Contact Information	Website and Email Address
Cedar Grove Lodge	Cedar Grove Village	Other	Rooms	$$	Phone: 866-522-6966	www.sequoia-kingscanyon.com/cedargrovelodge.html
Grant Grove Cabins	Grant Grove Village	Mountain	Cabins, tent cabins	$–$$	Phone: 866-522-6966	www.sequoia-kingscanyon.com/cabins.html
John Muir Lodge	Grant Grove Village	Mountain	Rooms	$–$$	Phone: 866-522-6966	www.sequoia-kingscanyon.com/johnmuirlodge.html
Montecito Sequoia Lodge	Grant Grove Village	Mountain	Rooms, cabins	$$	2225 Grant Rd., Ste. 1 Los Altos, CA 94024 Phone: 800-227-9900 or 650-967-8612	www.montecitosequoia.com
Silver City Mountain Resort	None	Mountain	Cabins	$–$$$	*Summer:* P.O. Box 56 Three Rivers, CA 93271 Phone: 559-561-3223 *Winter:* 3101 Cielo Grande Atascadero, CA 93422 Phone: 805-461-3223	www.silvercityresort.com silvercity@thegrid.net
Stony Creek Lodge	Grant Grove Village	Mountain	Rooms	$$	Phone: 866-522-6966	www.sequoia-kingscanyon.com/stonycreeklodge.html
Wuksachi Lodge	Wuksachi Village	Mountain	Rooms	$$–$$$	Phone: 888-252-5757	

Towns and Agencies

Name	Nearest Community	Type	Contact Information	Website and Email Address
National Park Service: Accommodations Outside and Between Sequoia and Kings Canyon Parks		National Park Service		www.nps.gov/archive/seki/lodg_out.htm
Recreation.gov		Agency	Phone: 877-444-6777	www.recreation.gov
The Reservation Centre	Three Rivers	Agency	Phone: 866-561-0410	www.rescentre.com/sequoia.htm
Sequoia Foothills Chamber of Commerce	Three Rivers	Chamber of Commerce	P.O. Box 818 Three Rivers, CA 93271 Phone: 877-530-3300	www.threerivers.com

Note: Recreation.gov includes coverage of lodgings that are former lookout towers and guard stations, some of which are near the hikes.

40 Eagle or Lower Mosquito Lake

Place	Total Distance	Elevation	Difficulty Level	Type
Trailhead		7830		
Eagle Lake	7.6	10,010	S	O&B
Mosquito Lake	7	9060	S U	O&B

Best Time   Early July–mid-October
Topos   *Mineral King 7.5'; Mineral King* by Sequoia Natural History Association
Where to Stay
   Mountain: Silver City Mountain Resort

   Other: None

   Towns and Agencies: National Park Service: Accommodations Outside and Between
   Sequoia and Kings Canyon Parks

HIGHLIGHTS   This stiff hike, to one of two lovely lakes high on the ridge that
bounds Mineral King valley on the south, offers superb views over the valley
to the Great Western Divide, the glorious subrange that bounds the valley on
the north and east. Flower gardens brighten your climb, and a curious feature
called Eagle Sinkhole is sure to leave you puzzled.

HOW TO GET TO THE TRAILHEAD   From the junction of State Route 198 and
Mineral King Road in the community of Three Rivers, it's 21.1 slow and twisting miles, which takes about 1.5 hours, on narrow, partly paved Mineral King
Road to get to Silver City Mountain Resort, the only lodging within range of
Mineral King. Don't even think about trying to take a day trip to Mineral King
from Three Rivers! From Silver City, continue east on Mineral King Road,
past Cold Springs Ranger Station at 2.5 more miles. Continue east and then
south, passing the parking lot for the trail to Timber Gap, Monarch Lakes, and
Sawtooth Pass, to a fork.

ON THE TRAIL   Pause to read the trailhead information sign and then head southwest on the trail, ignoring a use trail that almost immediately darts right and
up to a private cabin (don't disturb any of the cabins). The rocky, dusty, and
gradually climbing trail is well-forested uphill but is broad enough and lightly
forested enough downhill that it can be quite hot at midday. Pass another cabin
and at 0.25 mile cross a footbridge over the stream below Tufa Falls, which is
not visible from here. A little beyond 0.3 mile, disregard an unmapped use trail
that descends steeply to the river on the left.
   Around 0.75 mile, begin to enjoy excellent views of the long, showy cascades
on Crystal Creek eastward across the valley and of Farewell Gap far ahead to the
southeast. Shortly dip into a cool nook and ford a creek; emerging, look for the
cascades of Franklin Creek ahead across the valley. At a junction a little beyond 1
mile, go right (west-northwest) to Eagle and Mosquito lakes.

Eagle or Lower Mosquito Lake and Lower Monarch Lake

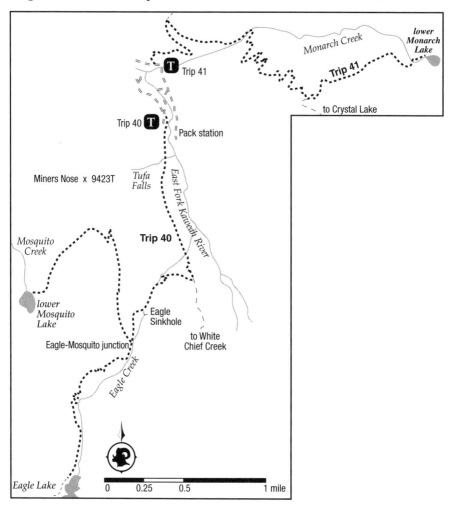

Begin a steep, switchbacking climb in patchy forest. Around 1.5 miles, switchback through a wet and wonderfully flowery hillside meadow, leveling out briefly near the top of the meadow to enjoy over-the-shoulder views up the Crystal Creek drainage to Mineral Peak, Glacier Pass, and Empire Mountain. Climb steeply again, veering away from the valley views to level out in moderate forest. The creekbed adjacent to the trail is strangely dry, just a channel of shattered metamorphic rock—where's the water? One mystery is solved and another posed when, just shy of 2 miles, the trail dips slightly to pass Eagle Sinkhole, where bubbling Eagle Creek simply disappears into a funnel of broken rock. Maybe it reappears as the spring that nourishes the hillside meadow you traversed earlier—or maybe not. Expert opinions differ.

At the Eagle-Mosquito junction, a little beyond 2 miles, you will need to choose which lake to visit. The mileage to visit both is about 10.5 miles, which is within the range of sturdy hikers who get an early start.

To go to Eagle Lake, bear left (south) at the Eagle-Mosquito junction, at first walking more or less near the creek on a level track soon climbing on a worn old trail up tiny, rocky, and steep switchbacks. Level off briefly at a meadowed bench and then begin climbing up the head of the bench through talus, which gets very rough at times. At the head of this bench, Eagle Creek slips down a steep granite wall; rest stops amid the sunstruck talus offer views of the peaks and streams on the Great Western Divide.

At the top of this climb, the trail levels out on another meadowy bench only to begin a gradual climb up another series of tiny benches. Keep your eyes peeled for the trail, as it is faint in places. Climb southward through granite boulders to a point abreast of a little dam on the left that raises Eagle Lake's level slightly. Several of Mineral King's lakes have been dammed as part of a hydroelectric project dating from the early 20th century; they're still maintained by Southern California Edison.

At Eagle Lake's dam, find the first good view of lightly forested, beautiful but overused Eagle Lake at a little less than 4 miles and 10,010 feet. Another few steps bring you to a junction with a use trail that climbs uphill on the right to an outhouse, while the main trail continues around the lake on the left. The lake's real size—it fills this little cirque—is camouflaged by a peninsula and some rocky islets.

To go to Lower Mosquito Lake, turn right (west) at the Eagle-Mosquito junction. Cross a patch of damp woods before beginning a hot ascent up a dry, meadowed slope. The loose, dusty trail levels out before descending to cross some rockslides; there are fine views across the valley to the Great Western Divide here. Now begin a long ascent, traversing the slopes south of Miners Nose in forest. Top the ridge at a saddle at 9360 feet a little south of Miners Nose at almost 3 miles, and then begin a moderate to steep descent to pretty lower Mosquito Lake at almost 3.5 miles and 9060 feet. In midseason the lake's forest- and meadow-lined shores may be plagued by mosquitoes; in late season, they may be abuzz with dragonflies. Shattered white cliffs rise across the lake, serving as a dramatic backdrop.

Whichever lake you choose to visit, eventually retrace your steps to the Eagle-Mosquito junction and then to your car.

41 Lower Monarch Lake

Place	Total Distance	Elevation	Difficulty Level	Type
Trailhead		7820		
Lower Monarch Lake	9+	10,380	S	O&B

Best Time   Early July–mid-October

Topos   *Mineral King* 7.5′; Sequoia Natural History Association *Mineral King*

Where to Stay

    Mountain: Silver City Mountain Resort

    Other: None

See map on page 120

Towns and Agencies: National Park Service: Accommodations Outside and Between Sequoia and Kings Canyon Parks

HIGHLIGHTS A long ascent leads through glorious flower gardens and past numerous viewpoints to beautiful lower Monarch Lake in a breathtaking cirque right under Sawtooth Peak. Since the first leg of the hike, to the ford of Monarch Creek, is steep, shadeless, and very hot by midday, be sure to get an early start.

HOW TO GET TO THE TRAILHEAD From the junction of State Route 198 and Mineral King Road in the community of Three Rivers, it's 21.1 slow and twisting miles, which takes about 1.5 hours, on narrow, partly paved Mineral King Road to get to Silver City Mountain Resort, the only lodging within range of Mineral King. Don't even think about trying to take a day trip to Mineral King from Three Rivers! Continue east on Mineral King Road to the parking lot for the trail to Timber Gap, Monarch Lakes, and Sawtooth Pass at 3.3 miles. There is parking with restrooms on either side of the road; the trail leaves from the lot on the north side.

Lower Monarch Lake

ON THE TRAIL Check out the trailhead information sign before heading northwest on the rocky and dusty trail on a grade that's gradual at first but soon grows steep. Just beyond 0.7 mile turn left (north-northeast) at a junction with the trail to Timber Gap.

The trail presently curves into the drainage of Monarch Creek and climbs steeply to moderately again, beetling high above Monarch Creek, on whose opposite bank a spring bursts forth in a pretty cascade at 1.3 miles. The trail is hot, steep, loose, and airy here, so watch your footing. A little farther on, turn right (southeast) at another junction.

Cross a small meadow, ford Monarch Creek at nearly 1.5 miles, and find the welcome shade of a fir grove. Traverse a slope with good views of the valley and begin a long ascent that winds up seemingly endless, gradually graded switchbacks. At 2.75 miles where a use trail darts left at a switchback turn, stay on the main trail. At about 3 miles, curve around a ridgelet and get a fine view of White Chief canyon and Eagle Creek's drainage across the way (see Trip 40), and of Vandever Mountain at the head of Farewell Canyon.

In the shade of sparse foxtail pines, go left (northwest) at another junction at nearly 3.5 miles. Negotiate one more switchback before swinging back over the ridgelet to overlook Monarch Creek. Ahead are the steep alpine meadows lining Monarch Creek's beautiful cascades as they pour out of lower Monarch Lake. Even more exciting, there's a glimpse northwest clear over Timber Gap to the high ridge that includes Alta Peak. Closer at hand, note Empire Mountain, Glacier Pass, aptly named Sawtooth Peak, and Sawtooth Pass. Westward views extend all the way to the bleached foothills around the Central Valley.

Upper Monarch Lake

Hikers with Class-2 scrambling experience who want to see upper Monarch Lake will find a number of airy routes to that high, delightfully barren, dammed lake. A route from the north side of the lower lake, its start mostly hidden in the willows, offers a discernible track with fine views back down to the lower lake. The obvious route that starts as a deep rut near the cascading stream that connects the lakes quickly leads out onto steep, water-slick slabs—not recommended.

Aiming at Sawtooth Peak, resume your hike on the gradual, rocky trailbed, slowly curving into the cirque that holds lower Monarch Lake. Snowmelt supports a handsome flower display in spite of the porous, thin soil. The fantastic cockscomb of Mineral Peak comes into view as the trail crosses a pair of briskly flowing outlet streams before ascending to an overlook of lower Monarch Lake. Across the sparkling lake, the stream connecting it to upper Monarch Lake spills steeply down high granite slabs in splendid cascades. Descend slightly to the shore of lower Monarch Lake at a little over 4.5 miles and 10,380 feet. There's a dilapidated pit toilet in the rocks above and northwest of the lake.

Retrace your steps to the trailhead.

42 Giant Forest Sequoia Loop

Place	Total Distance	Elevation	Difficulty Level	Type
Trailhead		7060		
Congress Trail loop	2.6	7040	M	Semi
Entire loop	6.7	7350	S	Semi

Best Time   Late May–mid-October

Topos   *Giant Forest, Lodgepole* 7.5′; *Giant Forest* by Sequoia Natural History Association (Note that this last map is currently misleading with respect to the trails on the ground, especially in the much-altered area around the General Sherman Tree. Also, the Lodgepole and Sherman Tree Trail that it shows as intersecting the first leg of this trip does not do so.)

Where to Stay

Mountain: Grant Grove Cabins, John Muir Lodge, Montecito Sequoia Lodge, Stony Creek Lodge, Wuksachi Lodge

Other: None

Towns and Agencies: National Park Service: Accommodations Outside and Between Sequoia and Kings Canyon Parks, Recreation.gov, The Reservation Centre, Sequoia Foothills Chamber of Commerce

HIGHLIGHTS This hike visits numerous giant sequoias, including the famed General Sherman Tree, in an area that attracts thousands of visitors. But this hike also includes time away from the throngs, in quiet nooks among the great, cinnamon-barked trees that are the largest living things on Earth (by volume and mass).

HOW TO GET TO THE TRAILHEAD Check to see if the free shuttle service is still available between this trailhead, Lodgepole, and other destinations in the Giant Forest area. This is the best way to get to this trailhead. If you must drive, then from Giant Forest Museum, drive 2.6 miles north on the Generals Highway to the junction with Wolverton Road. On the way, bypass the *former* turnoff, parking lot, and trailhead for the General Sherman Tree, where this hike used to start. Regulations now forbid the use of this lot and trailhead by able-bodied people except when the new trailhead off Wolverton Road is closed for some reason, such as snow. Otherwise, the former trailhead is reserved exclusively for the use of the handicapped.

Able-bodied hikers turn right (west) onto Wolverton Road. At the *second* turnoff along this spur road, 0.6 mile from the Generals Highway, turn right (south) and go another 0.7 mile to parking for the new General Sherman Tree trailhead, which has restrooms and water. The trail begins under an obvious, rustic archway lined with interpretive signs.

ON THE TRAIL From the parking lot, walk through the archway on the paved trail and curve around a huge boulder. Descend this very scenic path to a marvelous overlook of the giant General Sherman Tree. Note the full-sized mosaic of the Sherman Tree's cross-section in the pavement here.

After taking in the view, continue downhill to a major junction 0.4 mile from the parking lot. Here, the Congress Trail branches left (northeast, then south) and the General Sherman Tree is 0.1 mile more to the right (west). Detour to take in the General Sherman Tree at 0.5 mile. There are several paved, fenced side trails around the Sherman Tree worth exploring, including one around the great tree itself, but these side trails aren't part of this trip. The fences around the sequoias keep people off the most vulnerable parts of their shallow root systems. Mature giant sequoias have no taproots and depend instead upon a huge network of relatively shallow roots that may be damaged when the soil around them is compacted too much (for example, from years of human feet trampling on them). Walk

Giant Forest Sequoia Loop

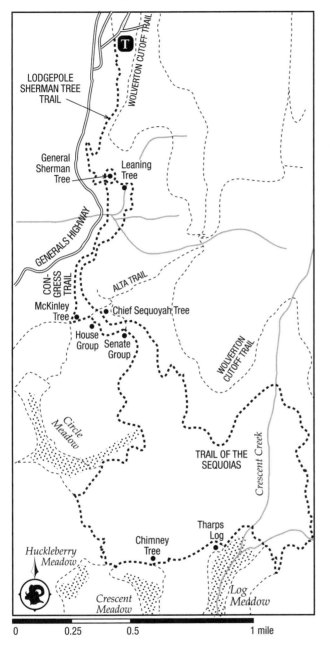

around the tree, which is believed to be the most massive living thing on Earth. It's estimated to be between 2300 and 2700 years old and is still growing vigorously.

Return to the junction with the Congress Trail, now having gone 0.6 mile. Here, begin the loop part of this trip by taking the signed CONGRESS TRAIL, which gets its name from a couple of dense clumps of giant sequoias along it, the House Group and the Senate Group. The Congress Trail is a narrow, irregular loop oriented roughly north-south and thus with east and west "sides." Go ahead (slightly northeast) at this junction, onto the east side of the Congress Trail, which sits high on a steep slope above the highway, unseen but audible below. Shortly curve left toward the Leaning Tree, a tilting giant sequoia growing out of a gully crossed on a footbridge. The paved trail, which now bears generally south, is covered with a light scattering of forest debris, and in spite of the crowds, shade and silence prevail. The west side of the Congress Trail is visible below. Presently cross another footbridge beside a mossy spring and then under a fallen giant sequoia that's been slightly hollowed out so hikers can pass through.

At 1.1 miles go left (south) at a junction for the full Congress Trail, climbing gradually. (The spur trail here is an unmapped shortcut to the Congress Trail's west side.) Continuing, stay on the paved Congress Trail at a poorly signed ju'nction with the dirt Alta Trail on the left, which cuts through this area. The next brief leg of this trail is the combined Congress and Alta trails. Soon reach a junction where the Alta and Congress trails part; turn left (south) on the paved Congress Trail toward the signed President Tree. The trail soon passes that very impressive giant.

In a few more steps, reach a signed junction with the dirt Trail of the Sequoias to the Chief Sequoyah Tree. (If you're hiking only the Congress Trail, stay on it and follow signs around its west side back to the General Sherman Tree; then retrace your steps to the trailhead.) For the full hike, hook left on the Trail of the Sequoias toward the Chief Sequoyah Tree.

Almost immediately, just before that tree and at an unsigned junction, a trail darts right (east) and uphill. Take it; it's the next leg of the Trail of the Sequoias, which wanders generally southward in long, indirect meanders. Here, the trip leaves the crowds behind for a hushed, beautiful forest not only of sequoias (whose cones are ridiculously little, egg-shaped, egg-sized, and tightly closed) but also of white firs, sugar pines (parents of the largest cones among the many littering the understory), Ponderosa pines, and a variety of wildflowers. (Let's hope that signage in the confusing Chief Sequoyah Tree area will be improved in the future. If it is, follow the signs to get onto and stay on the Trail of the Sequoias.)

A little beyond 2.25 miles, reach the hike's high point on a dry, boulder-strewn shoulder. Cross over this ridge and descend through burnt-over forest, tracing a deep gully's west edge. At 2.6 miles cross Crescent Creek at the gully's head and shortly curve through the shattered trunk of an immense, fallen sequoia. Step across a few trickling streams and, nearing 3.6 miles, reach another junction. Make a hard right turn (north) to Tharps Log, leaving the Trail of the Sequoias. Curl steeply down a slope to a T-junction on the edge of lovely Log Meadow. Here and at the next junction, go right (north) for Tharps Log, fording a stream at 3.6 miles and crossing another on a footbridge shortly thereafter. Continue around the meadow, staying in its forested edge, and finally descend at just over 3.8 miles to the hollowed-out giant sequoia log that served rancher Hale Tharp as a summer home while his cattle grazed the meadow, from 1861 to 1890.

Leaving Tharps Log and Log Meadow, take the trail from the "root" end instead of the paved one near the "door" end, quickly hooking northwest on a moderate climb and then descending over a fallen tree. Pass above Log Meadow to meet the spur trail right to the fragile shell of the Chimney Tree at 4.1 miles. Continue ahead and go right at the next two junctions, which come up almost immediately.

Heading generally north now, work back toward the General Sherman Tree, following the signs that point to features to aim for: the General Sherman Tree, the Congress Trail, the Senate Group, the House Group, and so on. At 4.5 miles reach a junction and turn right (northeast) toward the Congress Trail. Shortly reach a junction with the Alta Trail and go right (east) toward the Senate Group on the Congress Trail. Make a long, beautiful curve along Circle Meadow's east lobe, with a steep scramble over a rocky outcrop. Ford a meadow-feeding streamlet at 5.4 miles, and at about 5.9 miles, curve through an exceptionally fine stand of mature giant sequoias, the Senate Group, to an obscure junction with the paved *west* side of the Congress Trail (earlier, the trip took the trail's east side).

Go ahead (west) and soon pass the House Group of giant sequoias. Just beyond 6 miles, reach a five-way junction (including the Alta Trail) and take a wide right (north) on the Congress Trail to pass the McKinley Tree. Avoid any spur trails on this leg. Beyond the unsigned but obvious McKinley Tree, the trail bears north-northeast, traversing the slope high above the noisy highway.

At last begin a moderate to gradual descent, passing through a cut in another toppled giant. At nearly 6.3 miles, bear right at a junction to pass between a "matched" pair of sequoias and reach the signed General Sherman Tree-Congress Trail junction where the loop part of this trip began.

Retrace your steps another 0.4 mile to the parking lot on the steadily climbing trail to end this trip at 6.7 miles.

43 Panther Gap

Place	Total Distance	Elevation	Difficulty Level	Type
Trailhead		7340		
Panther Gap	5+	8520	M	O&B

Best Time Late May–mid-October

Topos *Lodgepole* 7.5'; *Lodgepole/Wolverton* by Sequoia Natural History Association

Where to Stay

Mountain: Grant Grove Cabins, John Muir Lodge, Montecito Sequoia Lodge, Stony Creek Lodge, Wuksachi Lodge

Other: None

Towns and Agencies: National Park Service: Accommodations Outside and Between Sequoia and Kings Canyon Parks, Recreation.gov

HIGHLIGHTS The superb views from Panther Gap over the Middle Fork Kaweah River to the Great Western Divide justify this hike, and the wonderful flower gardens on the way make getting to Panther Gap a joy.

HOW TO GET TO THE TRAILHEAD From Giant Forest Museum, drive 2.7 miles north on the Generals Highway and turn east toward Wolverton/General Sherman Tree. Bypass the right turn to the General Sherman Tree, and continue for 1.5 more miles from the highway to a very large, two-level parking loop, which has restrooms and water. The trailhead for the Lakes Trail, where this trip starts, is on the upper level of the parking loop. Store any bear-attracting foods or toiletries in the bear boxes adjacent to the trailhead, not in your car.

Panther Gap and Heather Lake

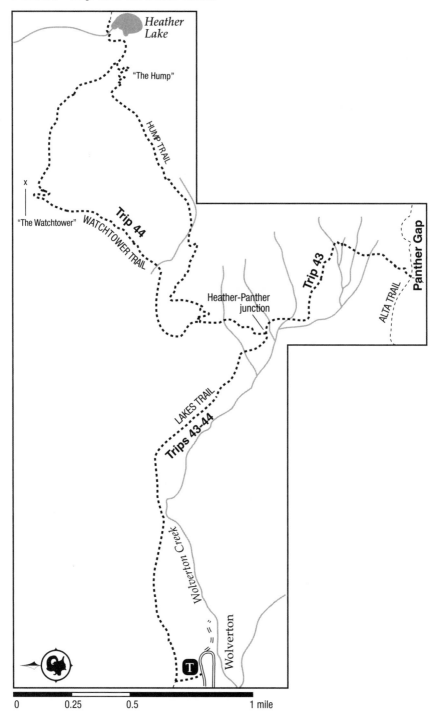

ON THE TRAIL Climb concrete steps leading generally north from the well-marked trailhead and from the upper leg of the parking lot. Ascend moderately to steeply on the duff Lakes Trail through a moderate to dense fir forest, shortly passing a dusty stock trail coming in from the left and then a spur going left. At both of these junctions go right, staying on the Lakes Trail. The trail gradually works its way up and then along a forested ridge, where breaks in the forest offer glimpses of peaks and granite domes to the north. At 0.75 mile traverse above musical little Wolverton Creek, and then descend to the meadow along the creek for a welcome and flowery break from the dense forest. At 1 mile the trail hooks right (southeast), and dry openings in the forest provide an abundant flower display. The grade steepens around 1.5 miles, and you soon ford a stream.

At 1.6 miles go right (east-southeast) at the Heather-Panther junction. The trail to Panther Gap ascends gradually to moderately through hillside meadows and across creeklets and springs and from one glorious flower garden through a patch of dense forest to the next garden. At 2.3 miles cross the final stream and meadow; ahead, blue sky appears over the rim of a ridge.

Climb moderate to steep switchbacks toward that sliver of sky; the last switchback is very steep. Near the top, meet the Alta Trail high above the Middle Fork Kaweah River. Use trails lead away from this junction to viewpoints. I suggest you go left on the Alta Trail very briefly, until it breaks out on the ridgetop at Panther Gap at a little more than 2.5 miles and 8520 feet. Pick a use trail leading south toward any open spot, from which the view will surely be sublime: across the Middle Fork Kaweah River to the granite domes of Castle Rocks; the jagged, light-colored peaks of the Great Western Divide, notably Empire Mountain, Sawtooth Peak, and Needham Mountain to the southeast and east, and Mt. Stewart and Eagle Scout Peak around Kaweah Gap to the east.

Retrace your steps.

44 Heather Lake

Place	Total Distance	Elevation	Difficulty Level	Type
Trailhead		7340		
Heather Lake	8	9260	S	Semi

Best Time Early July–mid-October

Topos *Lodgepole 7.5'; Lodgepole/Wolverton* by Sequoia Natural History Association

See map on page 128

Where to Stay

Mountain: Grant Grove Cabins, John Muir Lodge, Montecito Sequoia Lodge, Stony Creek Lodge, Wuksachi Lodge

Other: None

Towns and Agencies: National Park Service: Accommodations Outside and Between Sequoia and Kings Canyon Parks, Recreation.gov

HIGHLIGHTS Dramatic views over beautiful Tokopah Valley and a visit to pretty Heather Lake are rewards on this hike. Caution: Acrophobics beware! The final leg of the Watchtower Trail is extremely exposed above Tokopah Valley as it approaches Heather Lake. Although it has great views, it also has a potential 2000-foot fall down a steep granite cliff from a narrow, rocky trail. People with even mild cases of acrophobia will be better off taking the other branch, the steeper but less exposed Hump Trail, both ways, turning the trip into an out-and-back instead of a semiloop. The branches are about equidistant, but the Hump Trail climbs higher (to about 9500 feet).

HOW TO GET TO THE TRAILHEAD From Giant Forest Museum, drive 2.7 miles north on the Generals Highway and turn east toward Wolverton and the General Sherman Tree. Bypass the right turn to the General Sherman Tree, and continue for 1.5 more miles from the highway to a very large, two-level parking loop, which has restrooms and water. The trailhead for the Lakes Trail, where this trip starts, is on the upper level of the parking loop. Store any bear-attracting foods or toiletries in the bear boxes adjacent to the trailhead, not in your car.

ON THE TRAIL Climb concrete steps leading generally north from the well-marked trailhead and from the upper leg of the parking lot. Ascend moderately to steeply on the duff Lakes Trail through a moderate to dense fir forest, shortly passing a dusty stock trail coming in from the left and then a spur going left. At both of these junctions go right, staying on the Lakes Trail. The trail gradually works its way up and then along a forested ridge, where breaks in the forest offer glimpses of peaks and granite domes to the north. At 0.75 mile traverse above musical little Wolverton Creek, and then descend to the meadow along the creek for a welcome and flowery break from the dense forest. At 1 mile the trail hooks right (southeast), and dry openings in the forest provide an abundant flower display. The grade steepens around 1.5 miles, and you soon ford a stream.

At 1.6 miles go left (north) at the Heather-Panther junction. Climb moderately to steeply away from the junction, recrossing the stream, and reach another junction at 2 miles. To follow this hike's semiloop format—out to Heather Lake on the Watchtower Trail and back to the Heather-Panther junction on the Hump Trail—go left on the Watchtower Trail. The grade eases considerably as the path traverses a ridge. At a little more than 2.3 miles cross a multistranded stream that nourishes a steep hillside meadow. Near the granite monolith called The Watchtower, which bulges away from Tokopah Valley's south wall, the trail's downslope side grows steeper. Open spots permit views westward to granite domes and beyond them to the Central Valley. Begin a series of moderate to steep switchbacks on decomposed granite sand, reaching an airy overlook of Tokopah Falls at 3.25 miles. At a fork, go right, staying on the main trail. Shortly pass behind The Watchtower, whose summit stands free of the valley walls. More switchbacks carry hikers to a narrow, exposed leg on an exposed track blasted out of the cliff face. The track's downslope edge sits on an extremely steep drop down long granite slabs that sweep far, far down into Tokopah Valley. There are views over the valley and of Silver Peak and the Silliman Crest beyond.

The airy stretch ends a little before the next junction at 4 miles, where the Watchtower and Hump trails rejoin in a sparse lodgepole forest. Descend very slightly to pass a couple of junctions where use trails go left to the Heather Lake pit toilet. Staying on the main trail, pass overlooks above Heather Lake before descending a little more to cross the Heather outlet at a little more than 4 miles and 9260. The lake is set in a forested, granite cirque, which is a hanging valley high above Tokopah Valley.

Return to the last junction of the Watchtower and Hump trails, now with almost 4.3 miles on your boots. Go left (west-northwest) on the Hump Trail, ascending steep, sandy switchbacks to a 9500-foot saddle at 4.5 miles, just south of The Hump, a high point west of Heather Lake. There are fine over-the-shoulder views of Tokopah Valley on this climb. Now begin a very steep descent on loose terrain, eventually coming alongside a pretty, meadowed creek. At 5.3 miles cross the creek in a beautiful meadow and then resume descending in moderate forest, till the grade eases and the trail passes through another lovely little meadow at a little more than 5.75 miles. A few more steep switchbacks bring you to the lower junction of the Hump and Watchtower trails at nearly 6 miles.

A much more moderate descent leads to the Heather-Panther junction at almost 6.3 miles. Turn right here to retrace your steps to the Wolverton parking area at a little less than 8 miles.

45 Tokopah Falls

Place	Total Distance	Elevation	Difficulty Level	Type
Trailhead		6740		
Tokopah Falls viewpoint	3.5	7360	M	O&B

Best Time   Late May–mid-October

Topos   *Lodgepole 7.5'*; *Lodgepole/Wolverton* by Sequoia Natural History Association

Where to Stay

Mountain: Grant Grove Cabins, John Muir Lodge, Montecito Sequoia Lodge, Stony Creek Lodge, Wuksachi Lodge

Other: None

Towns and Agencies: National Park Service: Accommodations Outside and Between Sequoia and Kings Canyon Parks, Recreation.gov

HIGHLIGHTS Beautiful Tokopah Valley is a perfect example of a "yosemite," as John Muir called them, steep-sided, granite-walled, glacier-carved valleys other than Yosemite Valley. At Tokopah Valley's head, the long, showy cascades called Tokopah Falls crash down the granite slabs. Be prepared for midday crowds because this is a very popular hike.

Tokopah Falls

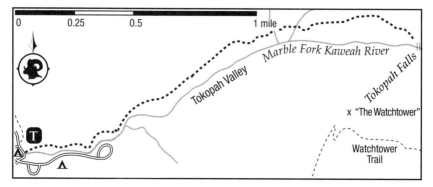

HOW TO GET TO THE TRAILHEAD From Giant Forest Museum, drive north on the Generals Highway for 4.4 miles and turn east to Lodgepole Visitor Center. There are also other visitor facilities at Lodgepole, like a gas station, a snack bar, and an ice cream parlor. Continue for another 0.6 mile beyond the visitor center parking through the Lodgepole Campground entrance station, where you may need to check in, to the trailhead parking lot near a bridge over the Marble Fork Kaweah River at 5 miles. The campground has both restrooms and water.

ON THE TRAIL The Tokopah Valley Trailhead is on the north side of the bridge. From there, the trail heads generally east, gradually ascending along the young Marble Fork Kaweah River, splashing along over picturesque slabs and around granite boulders. There are many use trails descending to the riverbank from the dusty main trail, which generally parallels the river. Nearing 0.6 mile, look for a 1600-foot monolith aptly named "The Watchtower" standing out from Tokopah Valley's sheer granite south wall (see Trip 44 to find out how to get a closer look at The Watchtower). A little beyond 1 mile, cross three flower-lined stream channels in quick succession on footbridges.

Lovely Tokopah Falls is in view by now, and the trail ascends moderately on a rocky track blasted through huge chunks of fallen rock. The trail ends at a viewpoint of Tokopah Falls at 1.75 miles and 7360 feet. In the fall, you may spot bears preparing for hibernation by gorging on the fruit of the many, aptly named bitter-cherry bushes that grow along the last leg of this trip.

Return the way you came.

46 Little Baldy

Place	Total Distance	Elevation	Difficulty Level	Type
Trailhead		7340		
Little Baldy's summit	3.3	8044	M	O&B

Best Time Early July–mid-October
Topos *Giant Forest, Muir Grove* 7.5'
Where to Stay:

> *Mountain:* Grant Grove Cabins, John Muir Lodge, Montecito Sequoia Lodge, Stony Creek Lodge, Wuksachi Lodge

> *Other:* None

> *Towns and Agencies:* National Park Service: Accommodations Outside and Between Sequoia and Kings Canyon Parks, Recreation.gov

HIGHLIGHTS Of the three hikes along the Generals Highway to summits with outstanding views, Little Baldy offers the best views east into the backcountry of Sequoia and Kings Canyon national parks.

HOW TO GET TO THE TRAILHEAD From Giant Forest Museum, drive 11 miles north on the Generals Highway, to Little Baldy Saddle. There is parking on both sides of the road; the trailhead is on the east side.

ON THE TRAIL From the marked trailhead on the east side of the road, start up the dusty duff trail through dense forest, climbing moderately to steeply at first. The grade soon eases to gradual as you negotiate a series of long, leisurely switchbacks; at the first and second switchback turns, be careful not to veer off onto use trails. The forest soon becomes patchy, and the open spots support a wide variety of flowers. A little beyond 1 mile, reach a forested ridgetop and shortly enjoy a brief, level stroll. Then climb briefly to a more open area where there are fine views southeast to Castle Rocks and Sawtooth Peak. Pass some granite outcrops and slabs and then make a moderate drop to the saddle below Little Baldy's summit.

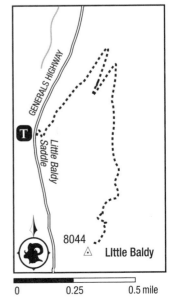

Little Baldy

The final ascent is moderate to steep and sometimes rocky. Near the top, the trail seems to peter out. Meander a few steps more to the old brass benchmark hammered into the broad, bare summit at 1.6 miles and 8044 feet. It's obvious why there used to be a lookout on this summit; there are spectacular views in all directions—Castle Rocks; the Great Western Divide, including Sawtooth and Eagle Scout peaks; Kaweah Peaks Ridge, including Black Kaweah, Red Kaweah, and Mt. Kaweah; Alta Peak; upper Tokopah Valley (Trip 45); Silliman Crest; Buck Rock; and Shell Mountain in the Jennie Lakes Wilderness (Trip 47).

Retrace your steps.

47 Weaver Lake

Place	Total Distance	Elevation	Difficulty Level	Type
Trailhead		7880		
Weaver Lake	3.75	8707	M	O&B

Best Time   Late May–mid-October

Topos   *Muir Grove 7.5'*; *Monarch Wilderness & Jennie Lakes Wilderness* by the U.S. Department of Agriculture and U.S. Forest Service

Where to Stay

Mountain: Grant Grove Cabins, John Muir Lodge, Montecito Sequoia Lodge, Stony Creek Lodge, Wuksachi Lodge

Other: None

Towns and Agencies: National Park Service: Accommodations Outside and Between Sequoia and Kings Canyon Parks, Recreation.gov

HIGHLIGHTS   Few wilderness lakes are readily accessible from the Generals Highway, but charming Weaver Lake, tucked under Shell Mountain, is a delightful, short hike away from a road. A new, unmapped but official trail that

Weaver Lake

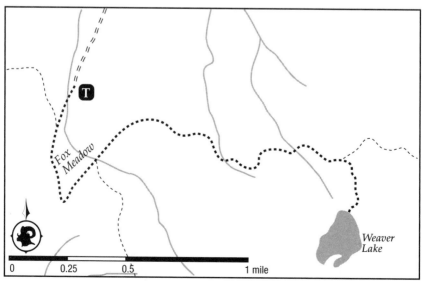

begins a little north of Fox Meadow saves a lot of hiking as compared to the Big Meadows Trailhead shown on the topo.

HOW TO GET TO THE TRAILHEAD This trailhead is unmapped and requires a high-clearance vehicle. From the junction of State Route 180 and the turnoff to Grant Grove visitor center, drive 1.5 miles south to The Wye (where State Route 180 meets the Generals Highway). Go south on the Generals Highway 6.8 more miles to the turnoff east onto Big Meadows Road. Follow this beautiful road generally east past the marked Big Meadows Trailhead and primitive Big Meadows Campground on the road's south side. Beyond here, the road becomes quite narrow and crosses a bridge over Big Meadows Creek. Take the first right turn after the bridge, onto a dirt road that climbs quickly. Following this dirt road, find two junctions; go left at the first junction and right at the next. These junctions are so close together that they may look like one big three-way junction.

Your goal—the roadend at about 7880 feet, just east of Fox Creek and north of Fox Meadow—is on the topo even if the trailhead isn't. Park at the wide turnaround at the roadend at 1.4 miles from Big Meadows Road and 15.2 miles from Grant Grove Visitor Center. The informally marked trailhead is at the south end of the turnaround.

ON THE TRAIL The trail heads generally south, almost immediately veering right to ford the red-fir-lined creek that drains Fox Meadow at a wonderfully flowery spot. Curving south again, the trail makes a gradual to moderate ascent roughly paralleling the creek. Meet the main trail coming up from the Big Meadows Trailhead a little before 0.25 mile. Note this obscure junction for the return, as it could be easy to miss. Turn left (south-southeast) on the sandy and dusty main trail, ascending through dense forest past Fox Meadow. A moderate ascent leads to a saddle, where the trail curves northeast without having crossed over the saddle. Breaks in the forest offer glimpses of Fox Meadow far below.

Reach a junction just before crossing the creek that feeds Fox Meadow. Go left (northeast) to Weaver Lake, fording the creek and climbing rather steeply onto a ridge where, at 0.75 mile, the trail crosses into Jennie Lakes Wilderness. Curve generally east along the ridge through patchy and then moderate forest. A little beyond 1 mile, wind across a lovely meadow with a tiny stream as the route continues generally eastward, climbing gradually to moderately. At 1.5 miles cross a seasonal stream, and just past 1.6 miles go right (east, then south) at a junction. Ascend gradually to beautiful, sparkling Weaver Lake at a little more than 1.75 miles and 8707 feet. The setting under slabby, gray Shell Mountain is delightful, with red heather, rosy spiraea, and shooting stars.

Retrace your steps.

48 Big Baldy

Place	Total Distance	Elevation	Difficulty Level	Type
Trailhead		7560		
Big Baldy's summit	4	8209	M	O&B

Best Time   Early July–mid-October
Topo   *General Grant Grove 7.5'*
Where to Stay

Mountain: Grant Grove Cabins, John Muir Lodge, Montecito Sequoia Lodge, Stony Creek Lodge, Wuksachi Lodge

Other: None

Towns and Agencies: National Park Service: Accommodations Outside and Between Sequoia and Kings Canyon Parks, Recreation.gov

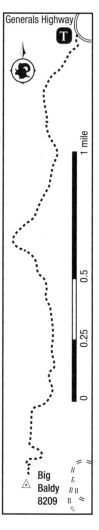

Big Baldy

HIGHLIGHTS A beautifully woodsy hike leads to fine views from the top of Big Baldy peak. Of the three superb view hikes off the Generals Highway, Big Baldy has the best views westward.

HOW TO GET TO THE TRAILHEAD From the junction of State Route 180 and the turnoff to Grant Grove visitor center, drive to The Wye and pick up the Generals Highway southbound to a small turnout near the apex of a near-hairpin curve, on the south side of the road and marked for Big Baldy. Park here, 8.2 miles from Grant Grove. The trailhead is right next to the turnout.

ON THE TRAIL The trail heads generally south and southwest on a duff surface, through moderate fir forest cover. Ignore a use trail that shortly darts off to the left. Shortly step into Kings Canyon National Park at a marked boundary and begin a moderate to steep climb on the northwest side of a forested ridge. Views to the west and northwest are excellent where breaks in the foliage permit, and the flower display is amazing for an area as well-forested as this one is. At an open, rocky area, pause to note that downhill to the right is Redwood Canyon and beyond it Redwood Mountain, Trip 50—together they are the home of the world's largest giant sequoia grove. The tops of most of the visible pine and fir trees have a marked taper; the more-rounded crowns of the giant sequoias stand out in that crowd like giant broccoli heads scattered among the tips of asparagus spears.

The grade eases and the trail settles down for a rolling ridgetop traverse, often but not always along the ridgeline. Soon it's back in moderate to dense forest broken by flowery patches. At the next forest opening, the rocky summit of Big Baldy is plainly visible ahead to the south. The next forested stretch is followed by a rocky, airy traverse above Redwood Canyon. Now it's time for the final climb on a winding, rocky, moderately graded trail. At Big Baldy's summit at 2 miles and 8209 feet, views are superb in every direction, although nearby ridges block long views to the east and south. Shell Mountain (Trip 47) rises to the east and the peaks of the Monarch Divide to the northeast, along with Buck Rock, named for the hawk-nosed "profile" of a face that imaginative viewers can make out from this perspective. To the west, beyond Redwood Canyon, the wrinkled, pale, heat-seared foothills bear dark patches of trees as well as what seem to be black scars of brushfires—mute testimony to the fiery, dry Central Valley summers and to human activity there.

Retrace your steps.

49 Buena Vista Peak

Place	Total Distance	Elevation	Difficulty Level	Type
Trailhead		7360		
Buena Vista Peak's summit	1.6	7605	E	O&B

Best Time   Late May–mid-October
Topo   *General Grant Grove 7.5'*
Where to Stay

Mountain: Grant Grove Cabins, John Muir Lodge, Montecito Sequoia Lodge, Stony Creek Lodge, Wuksachi Lodge

Other: None

Towns and Agencies: National Park Service: Accommodations Outside and Between Sequoia and Kings Canyon Parks, Recreation.gov

HIGHLIGHTS Of the three view hikes off the Generals Highway, the pretty stroll to Buena Vista Peak is the easiest—though it's by no means trivial—and offers surprisingly good views for such a short walk.

HOW TO GET TO THE TRAILHEAD From the junction of State Route 180 and the turnoff to Grant Grove visitor center, drive to The Wye and take the Generals Highway southwest. Be sure to stop at the wonderful Kings Canyon Overlook on the north side, which you will pass. Around the next curve in

Buena Vista Peak

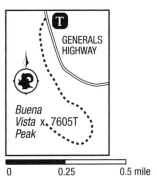

the road after that, park in a wide, dusty turnout on the west side of the highway by the trailhead, at a total of 4.7 miles.

ON THE TRAIL Head west-northwest away from the parking area, at first through open forest where granite slabs and boulders line the trail. The climb is moderate to steep on a dusty trail that shortly curves south and levels out amid immense, glacier-deposited boulders—"erratics"—and then toddles gradually along the east side of a ridge, just below the ridgeline. The trail winds through rocks and chaparral, over slabs, and up crude stone "stairs," on a nearly treeless slope from which there are occasional great views eastward. Between 0.6 and 0.75 miles, nearing the ridgetop, the dusty trail curves west and then northwest through boulders as it climbs moderately to steeply, traversing the east side of the summit knob to a tiny saddle.

From here, make a very short ascent on some trailless slabs toward two stunted Jeffrey pines on the still-higher knob that is Buena Vista Peak's open summit at a little more than 0.75 mile and 7605 feet. This is indeed *una buena vista*! To the southeast is Big Baldy (Trip 48); to the southwest, Redwood Mountain and Redwood Canyon (Trip 50); to the north, the Monarch Divide; to the northeast, Buck Rock; and to the east-southeast, the Silliman Crest. From this summit more than from the other trips with views off the Generals Highway (Trips 46 and 48) you can appreciate how much of this country is glacially-polished granite domes—less spectacular than Yosemite's but still remarkable.

Retrace your steps.

50 Redwood Mountain

Place	Total Distance	Elevation	Difficulty Level	Type
Trailhead		6220		
Redwood Mountain high point	4	6960	M	O&B
Entire loop	6	5520	S U	Loop

Best Time   Late May–mid-October
Topo   *General Grant Grove* 7.5'
Where to Stay

Mountain: Grant Grove Cabins, John Muir Lodge, Montecito Sequoia Lodge, Stony Creek Lodge, Wuksachi Lodge

Other: None

Towns and Agencies: National Park Service: Accommodations Outside and Between Sequoia and Kings Canyon Parks, Recreation.gov

HIGHLIGHTS The grove of giant sequoias that covers Redwood Mountain and fills Redwood Canyon is recognized by many authorities as the largest in the world.

Oddly, and fortunately, it's little-visited because it lies at the end of a rough dirt road and is outside both parks' main visitor areas. Most casual visitors to the giant sequoias are down south in the other huge grove, easily accessible Giant Forest in Sequoia National Park (see Trip 42). Come to Redwood Mountain Grove to enjoy its magnificent trees, hushed remoteness, and awe-inspiring beauty as you climb Redwood Mountain and return through Redwood Canyon via a "nursery" of baby sequoias.

HOW TO GET TO THE TRAILHEAD A high-clearance vehicle is necessary. From the junction of State Route 180 and the turnoff to Grant Grove visitor center, drive to The Wye and head 5 miles southwest on the Generals Highway to a an ill-signed turnoff southeastward, for Redwood Mountain Grove. (It's near a well-signed turnoff northward for Hume Lake at Quail Flat.) Follow this rough, winding dirt road for 1.9 more miles; go left at a Y-junction at a structure 0.1 mile more to parking on Redwood Saddle at a well-signed trailhead, which has a restroom, in the dense shade of numerous giant sequoias at a total of 7 miles.

ON THE TRAIL Begin with some orientation: Face the trailhead information sign and from there notice two trails leaving the parking area. To begin the hike, take the ascending trail (the descending one if the return route) and head generally southwest on a wiggly track. Climb moderately to steeply through this quiet forest of giant sequoias, sugar pines, red firs, and white firs. Ascend Redwood Mountain by stages: a steep haul up, then a longer, more gradual stretch on which to enjoy these beautiful trees. The drier sections have incense cedars, black oaks, and willows, too.

At 1 mile pass the Burnt Grove with its many standing but burnt trees. Beyond, zigzag up to an opening from which you have views eastward and where the forest is briefly dominated by live oaks and ponderosas, with a fragrant understory of kit-kit-dizze. Below, in Redwood Canyon, note the dozens—maybe hundreds—of giant sequoia crowns. Reach the trail's high point on Redwood Mountain at almost 2 miles and 6960 feet, just below the knob that is its actual summit. Take in the view of Redwood Canyon here before continuing. Those wanting a shorter hike can retrace their steps from here.

Young Sequoias

Young sequoias are unknown in mature groves that have been protected from fire for decades (a 20th-century practice now known to lead to unhealthy forests). Young sequoias were so rare then that some authorities once believed that giant sequoias no longer reproduced. Surprise: What was missing from the sequoias' life cycle was an absolutely necessary event—fire. These young trees are the beneficiaries of the National Park Service's new policy of conducting controlled burns. These burns clear the forest floor for seedlings, produce the mineral soil that sequoia seedlings require, and allow sequoia cones (the shape and size of chicken eggs) to open so their oatmeal-flake-sized seeds can disperse. Very young giant sequoias have the slender, tapering shape more typical of conifers than is the blunt-crowned shape of older giant sequoias—the product of hundreds, even thousands, of years of growth.

Those hikers continuing to Redwood Canyon begin a moderate descent that switches over to the west side of the long ridge that is Redwood Mountain, through moist woods full of giant trees. The trail suddenly veers back to the drier east slope, bringing an abrupt change in vegetation. You leave the giant sequoias behind for now but get to enjoy incense cedars, black and live oaks, kit-kit-dizze, and other chaparral species. Begin a long descent down Redwood Mountain's east slope, where the forest remains dry and the giant sequoias absent until, around 3.5 miles, the path crosses a creeklet and near 3.6 miles passes above a couple of giant sequoias. In just a few more steps, you reach a stand of very young sequoias, most less than 5 feet high, some barely 1 foot high—bonsai-sized by giant sequoia standards.

At 4 miles and nearly 5520 feet, in Redwood Canyon, admire a very handsome group of giant sequoias at a junction and then go left (northwest) to return to the parking lot. The canyon floor is lush with low-altitude growth: dogwood, rose, ginger, raspberry, blackberry, strawberry, and selfheal. Pass young incense cedars and firs as you begin a gradual to moderate climb up Redwood Canyon paralleling Redwood Creek.

Redwood Mountain

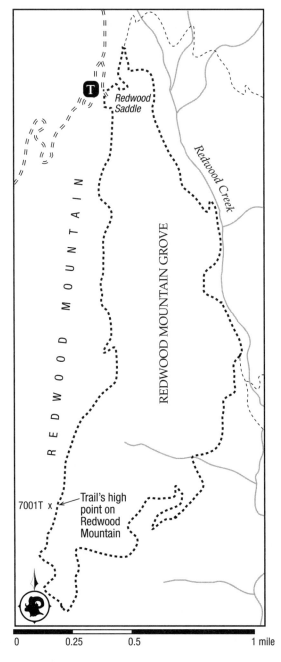

Nearing 4.6 miles, leave the creek behind and switchback once up Redwood Canyon's west slope. Continue uphill, presently walking through the shattered trunk of a huge, fallen sequoia. The state of this trunk demonstrates one reason the timber industry hasn't stripped the mountains of their giant sequoias: Giant sequoia wood is weak and brittle, making it commercially unprofitable. Soon the path climbs up and around another fallen monster, reaching a junction guarded by a particularly huge sequoia at 5.5 miles. Go left (south), switchbacking up to the parking lot, passing many fine, mature giant sequoias, and closing this unforgettable loop at 6 miles.

51 Park Ridge Loop

Place	Total Distance	Elevation	Difficulty Level	Type
Trailhead		7420		
Panoramic Point	0.3	7520	E	O&B
Entire loop	4.25+	7761	M	Loop

Best Time Late May–mid-October

Topos *General Grant Grove, Hume 7.5'; Grant Grove* by Sequoia Natural History Association

Where to Stay

Mountain: Grant Grove Cabins, John Muir Lodge, Montecito Sequoia Lodge, Stony Creek Lodge, Wuksachi Lodge

Other: None

Towns and Agencies: National Park Service: Accommodations Outside and Between Sequoia and Kings Canyon Parks, Recreation.gov

HIGHLIGHTS The Park Ridge Loop is worthwhile for its outstanding views. The entire loop is really a double loop—on the map, it looks like a lumpy figure-eight.

HOW TO GET TO THE TRAILHEAD From the junction of State Route 180 and the turnoff to Grant Grove visitor center, continue east on the road that separates the visitor center from Grant Grove Village's restaurant, lodge check-in, and gift shop, away from 180. Curve left past the first set of Grant Grove Cabins and then bear right at a marked Y-junction onto Panoramic Point Road. Follow this narrow road, paved until near its end, passing lovely Summit Meadow and, on the right, a gated-off dirt road that will be part of your trail. The parking area, which has restrooms and picnic tables, is in a fir grove at 2.4 miles.

ON THE TRAIL The marked trailhead is on the east side of the parking area, from which the path switchbacks up a moderate grade on a paved trail to a spectacular viewpoint with benches and interpretive signs. This is Panoramic Point at less than 0.2 mile and 7520 feet, a worthwhile destination in itself. The breathtaking view eastward sweeps from Mt. McGee in the north to Eagle Scout Peak in the south, and the interpretive signs identify many features in between as well as nearer. Even people who don't like hiking should at least visit Panoramic Point.

If you're continuing on the loop, pick up a gradual dirt path where the paved trail ends. Numerous use trails dart left to airy viewpoints. Stick to the main trail, which stays high on the ridge and slightly back from its edge, undulating over low knobs. After savoring eastward views, enter moderate, viewless forest cover before crossing the ridgeline to enjoy some views west at an open spot. Back in the forest, follow the gradually to moderately ascending dusty duff trail through a variety of flowering shrubs and plants.

A little beyond 1 mile reach the hike's high point, where there's not much to see because of the forest cover. After a moderate descent, meet the park's fire road at a poorly marked junction on a long saddle at a little less than 1.5 miles—"the first saddle." (From the first saddle, you can cut the loop short by turning right, northwest, on the fire road and returning to Panoramic Point Road.)

To continue on the full hike, turn left (south-southeast) on the fire road. The next trail junction is very hard to spot from the first saddle, so stay on the fire road for now and plan to pick up the trail again on the return from Park Ridge Fire Lookout, which is the next destination.

The fire road, lined with handsome firs, climbs gradually as it passes an area logged many, many years ago and then dips to pass around the head of a pretty meadow. The road gradually ascends and at a little over 2 miles approaches a small saddle where it veers southwest

Park Ridge Loop

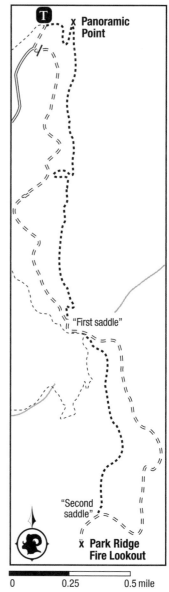

and a footpath comes in sharply from the right (north-northeast)—call this "the second saddle." Note the footpath; it's part of the return route and is unmarked except for red metal tags pounded into the occasional tree trunk. Staying on the road for now, head southwest toward the building, antennas, and power and telephone lines ahead; they're at the lookout. Reach Park Ridge Fire Lookout at 2.25 miles and 7540 feet, where there are nice views westward. There are no public facilities here except for a rickety picnic table. The lookout tower is someone's home, so be sure to ask permission before ascending the tower for even better views.

Return to the second saddle. At 2.3 miles, go left (north-northeast) on the footpath noted earlier. Ascend steeply through sparse forest to a little summit where the sometimes indistinct trail continues on the west side of the ridge (left when you face away from the lookout tower). The trail undulates moderately on this steep west slope, fairly near and occasionally crossing over the ridgeline. At an area of slabs, where the trail is very faint, continue ahead a short distance to find the trail again.

Descend to the first saddle at about 3 miles and reach a junction from which the fire road is visible about 25 feet away to the right. The junction's own trail markers are so low that they're all but invisible from the fire road. To the left (west), a spur leads to a junction with the Manzanita and Azalea trails. With the fire road in sight, turn right to meet the road and then turn left (northwest) onto the road. Shortly pass the poorly-marked junction where the trail reached the first saddle when coming from Panoramic Point.

Continue on the road, gradually ascending through a pleasant but viewless forest. At 3.5 miles, an open stretch offers fine views westward over Grant Grove. Eventually the path reenters forest and at a little more than 3.6 miles curves along a delightfully flowery meadow. Presently begin a gradual descent, passing above Summit Meadow, and reach a gate at about 4 miles. Beyond the gate you meet Panoramic Point Road, on which you drove up. Turn right (northeast) onto the road for a brief uphill stretch to close the loop at the parking lot, a little more than 4.25 miles.

52 Cedar Grove Overlook

Place	Total Distance	Elevation	Difficulty Level	Type
Trailhead		4680		
Overlook	5.6	6086	S	O&B
Entire loop	7	6220	S	Loop

Best Time   Late May–mid-October

Topos   *Cedar Grove* 7.5'; *Cedar Grove* by Sequoia Natural History Association

Where to Stay

Mountain: Grant Grove Cabins, John Muir Lodge, Montecito Sequoia Lodge

Other: Cedar Grove Lodge

Towns and Agencies: National Park Service: Accommodations Outside and Between Sequoia and Kings Canyon Parks, Recreation.gov

HIGHLIGHTS The spectacular views up, down, and over Kings Canyon from Cedar Grove Overlook are this hike's rewards, and there are other splendid viewpoints

Cedar Grove Overlook

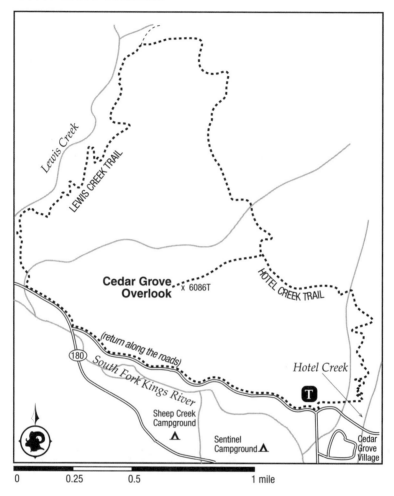

along the way. Get an early start because the ascent above Hotel Creek is mostly exposed and can be very hot.

HOW TO GET TO THE TRAILHEAD From the junction of State Route 180 and the turnoff to Grant Grove visitor center, continue east on 180 and wind down into Kings Canyon. Take the signed turnoff to Cedar Grove Village and Cedar Grove Lodge.

ON THE TRAIL From Cedar Grove Lodge, walk to the access road that brought you into the lodge's parking lot and turn right (north), away from State Route 180. A sign reading RANGER STATION/CAMPGROUND points left, but your route heads right. At less than 0.2 mile reach a junction with the pack station road; turn right (east) toward the pack station and almost immediately find the official trailhead on the left (north) at 0.2 mile. Of the two trails here, take the one on the right that heads east—it's the start of the Hotel Creek Trail.

Head uphill on the hot, sandy Hotel Creek Trail. Soon it begins a series of switchbacks upward, high above Hotel Creek's west bank. From early switchbacks there are views of the Sheep Creek drainage to the south, across Kings Canyon. Climbing higher opens up inspiring views of the high peaks to the east. Most signs of civilization, except road noise, soon disappear, hidden by the valley floor's substantial forest.

At nearly 2.5 miles on the nose of a ponderosa-clad ridge, reach a junction with a spur trail to Cedar Grove Overlook. There are glimpses of the Monarch Divide to the north and northwest from here. Go left to dip across a saddle and then ascend to spectacular Cedar Grove Overlook at a little more than 2.75 miles and 6086 feet. To the west, deep in Kings Canyon, the South Fork Kings River rolls toward its confluence with the Middle Fork; below is Cedar Grove Village; across the canyon is Lookout Peak; to the east are Buck Peak and Glacier Monument; to the north are Lewis Creek's canyon and the Monarch Divide; to the northwest is Stag Dome; and to the northeast is Comb Spur.

Return to Hotel Creek Trail, now at a little less than 3.25 miles. At the junction, those taking the out-and-back trip should turn right and return to Cedar Grove Village, while those continuing on the loop turn hard left toward Lewis Creek. Continuing on the loop, begin a north-northwest descent through a scorched, open forest. Cross an unnamed creek with a pleasant flower garden before angling gradually northwest up the next ridge. From this ridge, which is the hike's high point, there are fine views of the Monarch Divide. Beyond, the dusty trail descends and curves westward almost toward Stag Dome on a fire-scarred slope.

Meet the Lewis Creek Trail at almost 4.5 miles. Turn left (southwest) here and begin zigzagging down a series of longish, moderate to gradual switchbacks on a dusty trail with little shade. Shortly before reaching the road back to Cedar Grove Village, go right (ahead, south) at a junction by a ditch to the Lewis Creek Trailhead. In a few more steps, turn left (east) along the shoulder of the highway, facing traffic.

The road soon forks. Go left on what turns out to be a pleasant secondary road back to Cedar Grove Village, and follow the shoulder under incense cedars. Close the loop at the spur road that leads right to Cedar Grove Lodge at almost 6.75 miles. From here, turn right and retrace your steps to the lodge's parking lot for a total of almost 7 adventurous miles.

53 Roaring River Falls and Zumwalt Meadows

Place	Total Distance	Elevation	Difficulty Level	Type
Trailhead		4860		
Roaring River Falls	0.5	5000	E	O&B
Entire semiloop	4+	5010	M	Semi

Roaring River Falls and Zumwalt Meadows

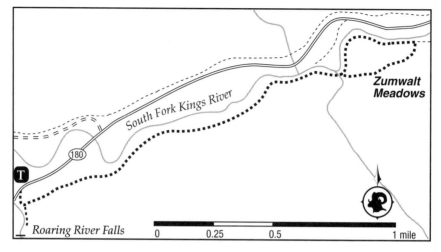

Best Time   Late May–mid-October

Topos   *The Sphinx* 7.5'; *Cedar Grove* by the Sequoia Natural History Association

Where to Stay

Mountain: Grant Grove Cabins, John Muir Lodge, Montecito Sequoia Lodge

Other: Cedar Grove Lodge

Towns and Agencies: National Park Service: Accommodations Outside and Between Sequoia and Kings Canyon Parks, Recreation.gov

HIGHLIGHTS   Deep in Kings Canyon, Roaring River crashes down through a slot in the steep south wall, giving visitors a chance to see its last few cascades—Roaring River Falls—before it joins South Fork Kings River. Up-canyon, the placid river meanders by idyllic Zumwalt Meadows.

HOW TO GET TO THE TRAILHEAD   From the junction of State Route 180 and the turnoff to Grant Grove visitor center, continue east on 180 and wind down into Kings Canyon. Stay on 180 past the turnoff to Cedar Grove Village and continue to marked parking for Roaring River Falls at 2.8 miles past the Cedar Grove Village turnoff.

ON THE TRAIL   Head south on a paved trail, bypassing for now a trail that takes off left for Zumwalt Meadows, and ascend to a large viewing area for Roaring River Falls at less than 0.25 mile and 5000 feet. Most of the upper cascades are hidden by the deep, convoluted slot through which Roaring River drops, but the lowest cascades make a fine spectacle as they thunder through huge boulders. The cascades are short on height, but in early season they make up for that in volume: their roar is deafening, and you may be drenched by their chilly spray.

Retrace your steps to the Zumwalt Meadows junction bypassed earlier, now at about 0.3 mile. Turn right (east) and follow the trail under incense cedar and live oak as it swings disconcertingly near the highway and then mercifully away to climb over a moraine. The floor of Kings Canyon is full of nested moraines, left by successively smaller glaciers.

Beyond the moraine, briefly meet the river and then skirt a half-meadowed, half-forested area damp enough to support an understory of bracken and horsetail. The river is always within hearing if not within sight as the trail winds through waist-high bracken and under black oaks and pines. At 1.3 miles puff your way over the next moraine and meet the Zumwalt Meadows trail at a bridge at almost 1.6 miles. At this junction, a trail goes left over the bridge to Zumwalt Meadows' own parking lot, while the trail to the meadows goes ahead (right). Without crossing the bridge, continue ahead, over an unnamed creek, to meet the loop trail around Zumwalt Meadows at 1.6 miles and 4880 feet. The right branch keeps to the forest edge, while the left heads for the beautiful meadow, which lies entirely on the south side of the river. Arbitrarily, take the right branch for now, passing huge glacial erratics and climbing over a rockfall opposite imposing North Dome. Willows and box elders block most of the meadow view from here but add fall color.

At a little more than 2 miles turn left (north) at a junction to curve around Zumwalt Meadows' north end and head generally west, first in forest and then at the meadow's edge, where the placid South Fork Kings River curls picturesquely between its sandy banks. Close the loop part of this trip and head back to Roaring River Falls. At the junction by the footbridge, now at a little more than 2.5 miles, continue ahead (west) to return to Roaring River Falls's parking lot, a little more than 4 miles.

54 Mist Falls

Place	Total Distance	Elevation	Difficulty Level	Type
Trailhead		5040		
Mist Falls	7.3	5800	S	O&B

Best Time Late May–early July
Topos *The Sphinx* 7.5'; *Cedar Grove* by Sequoia Natural History Association
Where to Stay

Mountain: Grant Grove Cabins, John Muir Lodge, Montecito Sequoia Lodge

Other: Cedar Grove Lodge

Towns and Agencies: National Park Service: Accommodations Outside and Between Sequoia and Kings Canyon Parks, Recreation.gov

HIGHLIGHTS Lovely Mist Falls is a favorite destination for visitors to Kings Canyon. Although its volume diminishes considerably over the season, it remains a pleasant spot to visit. On the way, there are beautiful views of the South Fork Kings River and spectacular over-the-shoulder views toward the curious formation called The Sphinx on Kings Canyon's south wall.

HOW TO GET TO THE TRAILHEAD   From the junction of State Route 180 and the turnoff to Grant Grove visitor center, continue east on 180 and wind down into Kings Canyon. Stay on 180 past the turnoff to Cedar Grove Village and continue 5.6 miles to park at the large roadend loop. The trailhead is near the north end of the loop, and there are restrooms, water, and a summer ranger station.

ON THE TRAIL   Three trails leave from this trailhead: On the far left, a footpath heads west down the valley floor; on the left, the steep Copper Creek Trail claws its way up Kings Canyon's north wall; and on the right, the Paradise Valley Trail heads generally east.

Take the latter past the information sign and the ranger station, enjoying the forest's woodsy fragrance. Cross two streams while passing the site of long-gone Kanawyers (kah-NOY-ers) Camp. The trail is sandy, sometimes shady, and sometimes exposed and hot. Twine down into a damp area thick with horsetails and bracken ferns, curving north along the west side of the South Fork Kings River, here flowing north to south away from Paradise Valley. At 1.5 miles turn left (northeast) at a junction and begin a gradual climb paralleling the river, sometimes climbing over or through rockfalls. Near 2.6 miles, reach a pleasant area of lunch-worthy rocks overlooking some beautiful pools and cascades. Beyond, ascend granite slabs still bearing patches of polish, the work of long-gone glaciers. Check the opposite canyon wall occasionally for the seasonally showy cascades of Glacier Creek. Pause often to look back at the strange "horns" of The Sphinx, high on the opposite side of Kings Canyon.

At 3.5 miles reach a signed overlook of beautiful Mist Falls, where, in season, the spray rising in the narrow, shady canyon explains the falls' name. Use trails lead to the base of the falls here, and many people brave the slippery scramble to get closer to the crashing water. Either stop here or head farther up the Paradise Valley Trail until you're opposite the top of Mist Falls at 3.6 miles and 5800 feet, for a different view.

Retrace your steps.

Mist Falls

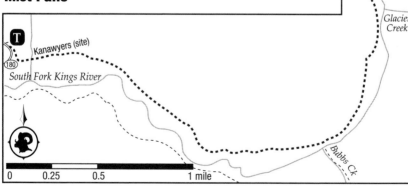
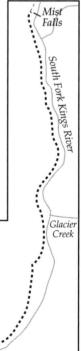

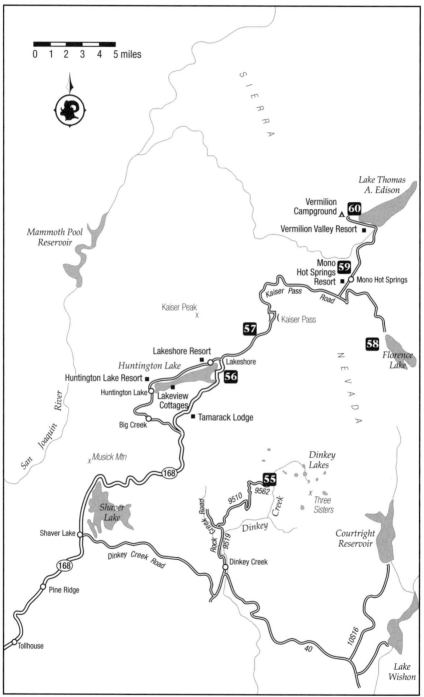

0 1 2 3 4 5 miles

SIERRA

Lake Thomas
A. Edison

Vermilion
Campground ▲ **60**
Vermilion Valley Resort ■

Mammoth Pool
Reservoir

Mono
Hot Springs **59**
Resort ■ ○ Mono Hot Springs

Kaiser Pass Road

Kaiser Peak
×

57
(Kaiser Pass

NEVADA

58

Florence
Lake

Lakeshore Resort ■
Huntington Lake ○ Lakeshore
Huntington Lake Resort ■ **56**
Huntington Lake ○ Lakeview
Cottages
■ Tamarack Lodge
Big Creek ○

San Joaquin River

× Musick Mtn

168

Dinkey
Lakes

9510 9562 **55**

Dinkey Creek

× Three
Sisters

Courtright
Reservoir

Shaver
Lake

Shaver Lake ○

168

Dinkey Creek Road

Rock Creek Road

9519

Dinkey ○ Dinkey Creek

Pine Ridge ○

Tollhouse ○

10S16

40

Lake
Wishon

CHAPTER 5

Between the Parks

Between Sequoia-Kings Canyon and Yosemite national parks lies a varied and beautiful landscape of peaks, valleys, and lakes that invites visitors to explore. Hikes in this surprising treat of an area are all accessed via State Highway 168 west out of Fresno and Clovis. The first major community of interest is Shaver Lake: Follow 168 north and east out of Clovis, up and down through foothills and then finally into Shaver Lake, where the area of interest begins. Other than that, driving directions in this section don't share a common point of origin. Consider Kaiser Pass a barrier to dayhiking in the Florence Lake-Lake Edison region when staying in the Shaver Lake-Huntington Lake region, and vice versa.

A gigantic hydroelectric project in the early 20th century, the Big Creek Project, paved the way almost literally. It created many of the roads that make visits here easier, and it also created the larger lakes (reservoirs) that this book uses as jumping-off points. (*The Story of Big Creek* by David H. Redinger et al. is an entertaining introduction to the project's challenging engineering and fascinating history.) There's a monument at the high point on the drive, Kaiser Pass, to one of the Alaskan dog-team huskies, Babe, who served this project so well during two bitter winters.

Recommended Maps

In addition to those listed in the trip write-ups, your library of maps should include the following. Get the latest edition/revision you can find. They're widely available, certainly at any of the local ranger stations.

■ *Sequoia National Forest, Sierra National Forest,* and *A Guide to the John Muir Wilderness and the Sequoia-Kings Canyon Wilderness.* U.S. Forest Service and U.S. Department of Agriculture.

■ *Sequoia and Kings Canyon National Parks Recreation Map* and *Dinkey Lakes Wilderness.* Tom Harrison Maps.

Individual Lodgings

Name	Nearest Community	Type	Facilities	Price Range	Contact Information	Website and Email Address
Huntington Lake Resort	Lakeshore	Mountain	Cabins	$$	Phone: 559-893-6750	www.huntingtonresort.com
Lakeshore Resort	Lakeshore	Other	Cabins	$–$$	Phone: 559-893-3193 Fax: 559-893-2193	www.lakeshoreresort.com reservations@lakeshoreresort.com
Lakeview Cottages	Lakeshore	Mountain	Cabins	$–$$	*Summer:* P.O. Box 177 Lakeshore, CA 93634 Phone: 559-893-2330 *Winter:* 7081 N. Marks, #104-371 Fresno, CA 93711 Phone: 559- 553-3550	www.lakeviewcottages.net
Mono Hot Springs Resort	Lakeshore	Mountain	Cabins, tent cabins	$–$$	*Summer:* General Delivery Mono Hot Springs, CA 93642 Phone: 559-325-1710 *Winter:* P.O. Box 215 Lakeshore, CA 93634 Phone: 559-325-1710	www.monohotsprings.com
Tamarack Lodge	Lakeshore	Mountain	Rooms	$	P.O. Box 175 Lakeshore, CA 93634 Phone: 888-268-0274 or 559-893-3244	www.tamarackmotorlodge.com gere@netptc.net
Vermilion Valley Resort	Lakeshore	Mountain	Rooms, tent cabins	$	Edison Lake P.O. Box 258 Lakeshore, CA 93634 Phone: 559-259-4000	www.edisonlake.com info@edisonlake.com

Towns and Agencies

Name	Nearest Community	Type	Contact Information	Website and Email Address
K&K Property Management	Lakeshore	Agency	P.O. Box 252 Shaver Lake, CA 93667 Phone: 800-987-7368	www.huntingtonlake.com condorentals@huntingtonlake.com
Shaver Lake Chamber of Commerce	Shaver Lake	Chamber of Commerce	P.O. Box 58 Shaver Lake, CA 93664 Phone: 559-841-3350 or 866-500-3350	www.shaverlakechamber.com shaverchamber@psnw.com

55 Dinkey Lakes

Place	Total Distance	Elevation	Difficulty Level	Type
Trailhead		8620		
First Dinkey Lake	5+	9239	M	O&B
Mystery Lake	3	8963	M	O&B
Entire semiloop	6.5+	9380	S	Semi

Best Time   Early July–mid-September

Topos   *Dogtooth Peak 7.5'*; *Dinkey Lakes Wilderness* by U.S. Department of Agriculture and U.S. Forest Service

Where to Stay

  Note: A variety of hotels are available in Shaver Lake.

  Mountain: None

  Other: None

  Towns and Agencies: Shaver Lake Chamber of Commerce

HIGHLIGHTS   Dinkey Lakes Wilderness is spectacularly beautiful—lakes, meadows, and peaks—but the drive to it is hair-raising. Nevertheless, the Dinkey Lakes are worth the trouble.

HOW TO GET TO THE TRAILHEAD

Look on this drive as an adventure. A sturdy, stable, high-clearance vehicle is essential; four-wheel-drive is desirable, even if only as a security blanket. This is a very long drive that takes more than an hour one way and is extremely rough near the end; it would have disqualified a less-attractive hike. From the town of Shaver Lake, turn east off 168 and onto Dinkey Creek Road. Follow two-lane, paved Dinkey Creek Road 9.2 miles to a junction with paved Rock Creek Road. Turn left onto scenic, one-lane Rock Creek Road (Forest Road 9S09) and follow it 6 miles as it gets progressively narrower and rougher, to a T-junction with Forest Road 9S10.

Swede Lake

Dinkey Lakes

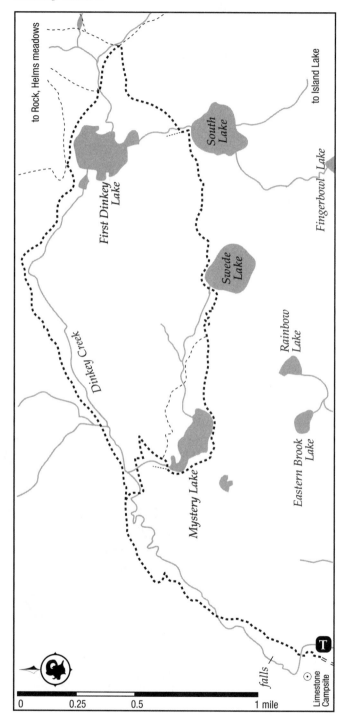

Go right onto partly paved Forest Road 9S10 and bounce along to the first major junction at 4.7 more miles, where you make a hard right onto unmarked Forest Road 9S62 to begin the last and worst 2.2 miles. Ascend the pothole-plagued road to a shoulder from which you make a heart-in-mouth descent that passes a couple of forks to the right. Go left, staying on the "main" road, at each fork; they lead to/from an off-road-vehicle trailhead. Beyond them, jounce fairly levelly through a sandy-floored forest to a large trailhead parking area. Park here, 22.1 nerve-racking miles from Highway 168 and not far from the spot labeled on the topo as "Limestone Campsite."

ON THE TRAIL Note that the USGS topo predates the wilderness area's designation. Head northeast down a rocky slope, past a TRAIL sign and into a forest of spindly lodgepoles, where Dinkey Creek splashes past gray limestone cliffs on the right. Use trails may be confusing here; the route dips almost immediately down to the creek, fords it, and goes right (east-northeast) at a junction with a use trail. Climb moderately away from the creek, cross an intermittent watercourse, and ascend moderately into dense, mature forest.

The sandy trail's grade soon eases, and the path presently comes alongside Dinkey Creek. A little before 0.5 mile, dip to cross the creek again and shortly enter Dinkey Lakes Wilderness. Now traverse through snow-bent trees, past a meadow, and between steep slopes of light and dark granites. Wind moderately up a rocky slope through glacier-polished slabs and then veer off to the northwest side of a widening valley to avoid the valley's soggy, meadowy floor. Through breaks in the dense forest, look for beautiful granite walls soaring on the left.

The pleasant, sandy trail rolls on and on through forest and meadow, where patches of dwarf bilberry in the understory make a brilliant show in fall. At a little more than 1 mile reach a junction: The left (east-northeast) branch heads to First Dinkey Lake, and the right (southeast) goes to Mystery Lake. Hikers going only to pretty Mystery Lake on an out-and-back should go right here.

Those going to First Dinkey Lake, perhaps the loveliest on this trip, go left here. Soon you meet Dinkey Creek again on a gradual climb through a "garden" of erratics. At about 1.6 miles cross a tributary, beyond which the ascent becomes more noticeable. The beautiful valley widens, and the trail curves right (east) to cross an unmapped creeklet below the steep cliffs of Peak 9777. Continuing eastward, climb gradually to moderately to a bench and follow the trail up a long meadow past a pond. Shortly reach an overlook of breathtaking First Dinkey Lake at a little more than 2.5 miles and 9239 feet, splendidly set in a deep meadow and backed by the toothy ridge called Three Sisters. Numerous use trails lead to the pond and to the lake on the right, while other use trails lead to campsites on the left.

Back on the main trail, pass an obvious camping area and reach a junction—the sign that marks it is on a tree some 35 yards farther on, on the left fork, and is hard to spot. Go right (southeast) to skirt the forested edge of First Dinkey Lake's meadow. At an unmarked junction near 3 miles, just before the lake's eastern inlet, go right, stepping across the inlet and making a lazy curve across an open area.

Reach another junction at a little more than 3 miles. and go right (west) in moderate forest on rocky terrain, curving around First Dinkey Lake and then climbing away from it. The trail grows faint in the deep duff; ducks and blazes may help. Step across a use trail paralleling a runoff channel and then cross the stream connecting First Dinkey and South lakes. At a T-junction just across the stream, continue on the left branch to reach South Lake at a little more than 3.5 miles and 9294 feet. The lake, backed by tall cliffs and fringed by mountain hemlocks, is perfectly charming.

Leaving South Lake, gradually ascend a moraine, passing immense erratics and topping out at 9380 feet at about 3.75 miles. Descend the moraine moderately to steeply, with views of lovely Swede Lake. Cliffs at its southeast end help create a dramatic setting. Squish through a marsh along the outlet of Swede Lake at a little more than 4 miles and 9224 feet and then ford the outlet.

From there, soon begin a steep, switchbacking descent to the bench holding Mystery Lake. Level out in a small meadow at a junction at 4.5 miles. Avoid the right (northwest) fork, since it leads to disgusting campsites above Mystery's north shore, and take the left (west) fork to spend more time beside Mystery Lake. The nearly level trail becomes muddy and rutted as it passes a small pond. The lake soon comes into view ahead, and presently the path traces the south shore of pretty Mystery Lake at 4.75 miles and 8963 feet. Near the west end of Mystery Lake, a use trail bears right to a knoll. Stay on the main trail, swinging north-northwest through the flowery meadow west of the knoll and then skirting the west tip of the lake.

Come alongside Mystery's outlet and reach a junction at a little more than 5 miles. Go right (northeast) to cross the outlet and almost immediately reach another junction. Avoid the right fork because it passes through depressingly filthy campsites near Mystery's north shore. Take the left branch north on a well-beaten track, curving north-northeast and then west on a gradual descent.

Cross Mystery Lake's outlet again, on big granite slabs, and find yourself once more down in the lovely valley below the lakes. Cross Dinkey Creek and curve north across the valley floor to return to the first junction you encountered on this hike, at 4.75 miles. Turn left and retrace your steps, a little more than 6.5 miles.

56 Rancheria Falls

Place	Total Distance	Elevation	Difficulty Level	Type
Trailhead		7560		
Rancheria Falls viewpoint	1.3	7530	E U	O&B

Best Time Late May–early July
Topos *Huntington Lake, Kaiser Peak 7.5'*
Where to Stay
  Mountain: Huntington Lake Resort, Lakeview Cottages, Tamarack Lodge
  Other: Lakeshore Resort
  Towns and Agencies: K&K Property Management, Shaver Lake Chamber of Commerce

HIGHLIGHTS An easy hike leads to a small canyon down whose headwall dash the seasonally high, showy cascades called Rancheria Falls.

HOW TO GET TO THE TRAILHEAD

The marked turnoff to Rancheria Falls is beyond Shaver Lake and almost to Huntington Lake. Look for the Rancheria Falls turnoff 0.5 mile south of Huntington Lake. Here, turn east on a road that almost immediately becomes dirt, and follow it to a junction in another 0.5 mile. Turn right to find the marked trailhead at a hairpin turn in another 0.8 mile. Park along the shoulder.

Rancheria Falls

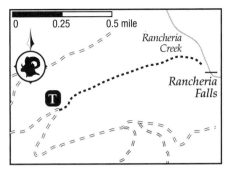

ON THE TRAIL Note that the topos don't show the trail or the falls. The trail is narrow in places and traverses very steep terrain; parents should keep a tight rein on children. The path immediately cross a tiny footbridge over a roadside runoff channel and then heads northeast on a broad, dusty trail. There's a good flower display along this trail. Climbing moderately to steeply, soon cross another footbridge and then curve east, high above Rancheria Creek. Big old stumps dot the steep hillside, evidence of former logging. By 0.3 mile the grade has eased considerably.

A little before 0.6 mile, the track abruptly begins a rocky, moderate to steep descent toward the noise of falling water, curving right (southeast) into a steep-walled, rocky little canyon. Visible ahead are the long, beautiful cascades of Rancheria Falls. The terrain is very steep here, so watch your step as the grade eases to gradual. The trail peters out at a viewpoint for Rancheria Falls at a little over 0.6 mile and 7530 feet, in clumps of creambush. The upper cascades leap over a succession of thin, rocky shelves, while the lower cascades crash through boulders, finally roaring away down the stony creekbed far below. The loose rock around here, which fills much of this handsome amphitheater, makes scrambling any closer to the falls a dicey proposition.

Retrace your steps.

57 Twin Lakes

Place	Total Distance	Elevation	Difficulty Level	Type
Trailhead		8300		
Potter Pass	4	8980	M	O&B
Lower Twin Lake	5.75	8603	S U	O&B
Upper Twin Lake	6.25	8601	S U	O&B

Best Time   Early July–mid-October

Topos   *Mt. Givens, Kaiser Peak 7.5'; Kaiser Wilderness* by U.S. Department of
Agriculture and U.S. Forest Service

Where to Stay

Mountain: Huntington Lake Resort, Lakeview Cottages, Tamarack Lodge

Other: Lakeshore Resort

Towns and Agencies: K&K Property Management, Shaver Lake Chamber of Commerce

HIGHLIGHTS   An attractive, well-graded trail leads past flower-filled meadows to
wonderful views at Potter Pass and to two pretty lakes in Kaiser Wilderness.

HOW TO GET TO THE TRAILHEAD   At the end of State Route 168, the left fork
heads west to Huntington Lake and the community of Lakeshore, and the right
fork, Kaiser Pass Road, heads northeast to Kaiser Pass. Turn right and drive
northeast on Kaiser Pass Road 4.8 miles to a poorly marked, large parking
turnout on the southeast (right) side of the road. The equally poorly marked
trailhead is across the road.

ON THE TRAIL   Head west on a sandy and dusty trail in dense lodgepole forest,
passing an information sign and soon curving north across a sandy, boulder-
studded, moderate slope. Patches of forest and chaparral alternate as the track
switchbacks upward to top a small rise, beyond which a very gradual descent
rounds a little meadow and crosses a couple of streamlets that feed it.

Resume a gradual to moderate ascent, passing a heap of huge boulders, and
at 0.6 mile cross a footbridge over a trickling stream and its narrow, wildflower-
filled hillside meadow. At 0.75 mile cross another streamlet and soon ford Midge
Creek, which supports a fine, flowery meadow. The trail then climbs away from
Midge Creek, and, nearing 1.25 mile, crosses a saddle and contours northwest
through meadows and streams. Beyond, the path breaks out into the open with a
view of rocky, unnamed peaks ahead to the west.

Near 1.5 miles begin climbing again, crossing a tributary of Potter Creek on
a footbridge in a willow-choked meadow. In a few more steps, find an opening in
the forest that permits fine views of Huntington Lake to the southwest, as well as

Upper Twin Lake

Twin Lakes

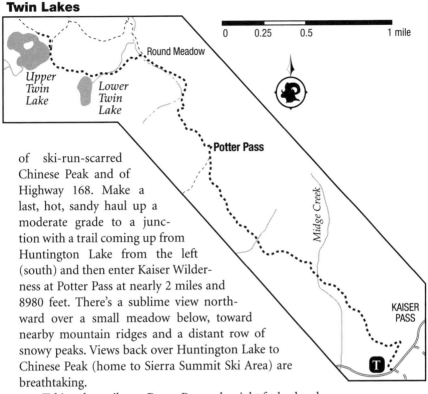

of ski-run-scarred Chinese Peak and of Highway 168. Make a last, hot, sandy haul up a moderate grade to a junction with a trail coming up from Huntington Lake from the left (south) and then enter Kaiser Wilderness at Potter Pass at nearly 2 miles and 8980 feet. There's a sublime view northward over a small meadow below, toward nearby mountain ridges and a distant row of snowy peaks. Views back over Huntington Lake to Chinese Peak (home to Sierra Summit Ski Area) are breathtaking.

Taking the trail over Potter Pass—the right fork, ahead and north—descend moderately to steeply on sandy switchbacks, crossing a streamlet that feeds a blossoming hillside meadow. The trail levels out as it brushes past the southwest end of the small meadow below the pass and then curves generally north as it descends gradually to moderately into dense forest. After crossing an intermittent stream, climb a little while traversing a dry meadow from which there's a good view of Kaiser Peak to the west.

Soon the trail returns to forest, skirting a meadow and then making a short, steep descent to a junction. Go left (west-southwest) to cross a stream and pass below a striking outcrop of white rock. An open traverse above Round Meadow offers more of those wonderful views of distant peaks, and stands of aspen in this area offer good fall color.

Beyond a wooded stretch, find pleasant Lower Twin Lake at a little more than 2.75 miles and 8603 feet, tucked below a peak of white rock. Leaving Lower Twin Lake, make an easy ascent of a low saddle, pass a pond, and shortly spot Upper Twin Lake. Make a short, steep descent toward the lake to discover that the main trail skirts above the lake while use trails lead down to its edge. Pick a use trail and reach the east shore of Upper Twin Lake at a little more than 3 miles and 8601 feet. (Officially, Upper Twin Lake is lower than Lower Twin Lake.) Most of the lake is bound by low, rocky cliffs that, together with Kaiser Peak, give this beautiful lake an especially picturesque setting.

Retrace your steps.

58 Dutch Lake

Place	Total Distance	Elevation	Difficulty Level	Type
Trailhead		7380		
Dutch Lake	6.25	9100	S	O&B

Best Time Early July–mid-October
Topo *Florence Lake 7.5'*
Where to Stay
  Mountain: Mono Hot Springs Resort, Vermilion Valley Resort
  Other: None
  Towns and Agencies: None

HIGHLIGHTS An often-steep hike earns rave reviews when it deposits visitors at lovely Dutch Lake.

HOW TO GET TO THE TRAILHEAD Don't even think about trying to daytrip from Huntington Lake to this trailhead or to those of Trips 59 or 60. Kaiser Pass Road grows so narrow and tortuous that it makes the drive long and exhausting. Even though this may be the worst drive to get to a resort in this book, it's worth it. Be sure to monitor your fuel level as there is no reliable source of gasoline beyond Lakeshore village at Huntington Lake. Sometimes there's gas at Mono Hot Springs Resort, but don't count on it.

Viewpoint above Florence Lake

The Kaiser Pass Road snakes from Huntington Lake up past the Potter Pass Trailhead (Trip 57) before turning into a twisting, often-steep, one-lane road. The road crawls painfully over Kaiser Pass and then winds down exposed cliffsides and through breathtaking scenery—but don't take your eyes off the road. At a seasonal High Sierra Ranger Station partway down there's information and some stupendous views. Farther on, you reach a signed junction: The left branch heads to Mono Hot Springs

Resort, Lake Edison, and Vermilion Valley Resort and the right proceeds to Florence Lake.

Turn east for Florence Lake and follow this twisting, pothole-plagued, sometimes unpaved road for 6 miles to a large, two-tiered parking area, which has a restroom. The upper tier is for overnight and overflow parking, and the lower tier is for day-use parking. If the area's scenery hasn't already made your heart go pitty-pat, the view over Florence Lake to Mt. Shinn and Ward Mountain certainly will. The nearby, seasonal Florence Lake Store operates a ferry service (for a fee) across the lake in the summer.

ON THE TRAIL The trailhead is at the right side of the lower parking tier, just beyond the gate that bars the public's vehicles from the road to Florence Lake's dam, and high above the lake's surface. It's signed DUTCH AND HIDDEN LAKE TRAIL. Pick up the rocky and dusty trail, which makes a switchback before reaching

Dutch Lake

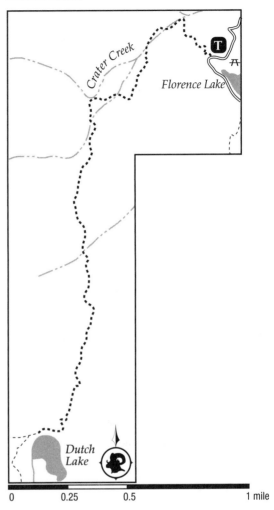

an information sign and trail register box; sign in. In about 0.2 mile enter John Muir Wilderness as the trail winds generally northwest, ascending moderately through an interesting mix of chaparral, sparse forest, and granite slabs. There are excellent views over Florence Lake as the trail grows steeper. Nearing 0.5 mile, climb while paralleling a seasonally dry creekbed and lose the views when the trail angles across the creekbed. Climb steeply, taking a breather when the trail levels briefly at the next creek crossing. Climbing again, follow lines of rocks and the occasional duck where the trail crosses huge granite slabs. Heavy stock use leaves the trail full of loose rocks and deep dust by late season.

Nearing 1 mile, the grade eases to moderate as it winds through handsome, rounded, granite outcrops. Beyond a stand of white fir and lodgepole, the climb grows very steep again. A little beyond 1.25 miles, the grade eases once in a while as the path begins traversing through patches of white fir. Around 1.75 miles, pause at a viewpoint that's partially obscured by trees to pick out features like The Tombstone, with Florence Lake far below it; the peaks of the Mono Divide; Ward Mountain; and Mt. Shinn.

At 2 miles cross a meadowy area, pleasantly cool and flowery, and step over multiple, seasonal streamlets. Now curve across an open, slabby, sandy area into a stand of lodgepole and soon cross another stream. Beyond the stream, head generally south across a broad area of water-stained slabs, which can be slippery going in early season. The track fades out on the rock, but ducks, plus occasional piles of horse poop, help hikers navigate the slabs, which are interlaced with meadowy strips fed by seeps and supporting a wonderful array of flowers.

Beyond the slabs, the trail returns to forest and then thrashes through muddy thickets of alder before curving west-southwest to climb steeply to moderately up the rocky lip of a moraine to the shallow bowl that holds forest- and meadow-ringed Dutch Lake at a little more than 3 miles and 9100 feet. Cliffs to the west are outliers of Mt. Ian Campbell, which is itself out of sight. Fall brings glowing patches of color—from subdued to vibrant reds—to the lake's shores.

Return the way you came.

59 Doris and Tule Lakes

Place	Total Distance	Elevation	Difficulty Level	Type
Trailhead		6540		
Doris Lake	1.5	6823	E	O&B
Both lakes	3+	6780	M U	O&B

Best Time Early July–mid-October
Topos *Mt. Givens* 7.5'; *Ansel Adams Wilderness* by U.S. Department of Agriculture and U.S. Forest Service
Where to Stay
  Mountain: Mono Hot Springs Resort, Vermilion Valley Resort
  Other: None
  Towns and Agencies: None

HIGHLIGHTS Mostly easy hiking on uninteresting trails leads to two very pretty little lakes.

HOW TO GET TO THE TRAILHEAD Hikers staying at Mono Hot Springs Resort can start from the cabin door. Otherwise, from the signed junction between Mono Hot Springs and Florence Lake junction on the Kaiser Pass Road, go north for Mono Hot Springs and descend very steeply to cross South Fork San Joaquin River on a one-lane bridge. Just over the bridge, at 1.7 miles, take the spur road marked for Mono Hot Springs Resort 0.25 mile more to parking in a signed day-use area in the midst of the resort's cabins, store, and café.

This hike starts between the westernmost cabin and the westernmost loop of Mono Hot Springs Campground, where dirt Forest Road 7S10 angles right (northwest) past a huge, dark, lichen-spotted boulder. The official trailhead is near the end of Forest Road 7S10, but the road is truly dreadful and the walk from the resort is short.

ON THE TRAIL Follow dusty, rutted Forest Road 7S10 northwest, past signed, fenced Mono Tourist Pasture. Stay on the road as it passes a signed spur trail left to the campground's amphitheater, visible to the left. Shortly pass a capped but leaking spring, ascend moderately, and reach an unmapped fork where either branch will do, as they shortly rejoin.

At 0.25 mile, where the road widens to form a turnaround and parking area, veer left (north) and soon pick up a foot trail in granite outcrops by an information sign. The open, sandy, and rocky trail begins a moderate to gradual ascent in a sparse, dry forest of Jeffrey pines. A little beyond 0.3 mile meet a trail coming up a sandy slope on the right and joining your

Doris and Tule Lakes

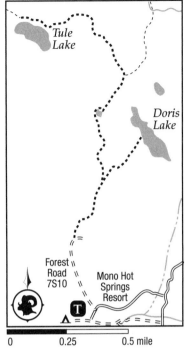

trail. Continue ahead (left) on the main trail, shortly entering Ansel Adams Wilderness. Continue the rocky ascent generally north over a parched landscape that seems more like the scorched foothills below Shaver Lake than the Sierra. Occasional damp spots along the trail support wildflowers.

At a junction at a little more than 0.5 mile go right (northeast) to Doris Lake for now. After a short level stretch, climb steeply through boulders to top out on a tiny saddle before descending steeply to curve north over the tops of boulders—watch your footing here. Next, gradually ascend a seasonally damp draw, passing a stand of reeds, and reach the shore of beautiful little Doris Lake at 0.75 mile and 6823 feet. A use trail leads around and then up the large outcrop just to the left; the top is a marvelous viewpoint, featuring not only the wonderful cliff-lined lake but handsome peaks to the east and southeast.

Now retrace your steps to the junction you passed earlier and turn right to continue to Tule Lake. Immediately begin a steep, loose, rocky climb that presently eases to a sandy trail with a moderate to gradual grade, topping out among boulders at 6920 feet. Now descend moderately, leveling out to pass some seasonal ponds. At 1.5 miles all told, reach another junction. Go left (north-northwest), following the trail as it wanders up and down through forlorn, dry, Jeffrey pine forest until it passes a huge stand of tules on the left and then crosses a low saddle to sparkling, reed-rimmed Tule Lake ahead. Dark cliffs across the lake help frame the lily-pad-spangled sheet of water at a little more than 1.6 miles and 6780 feet.

Retrace your steps past both junctions to the south end of Forest Road 7S10 to end the hike at a little more than 3 miles.

60 Along Lake Edison

Place	Total Distance	Elevation	Difficulty Level	Type
Trailhead		7660		
Slabs near head of Lake Edison	9	7650	S	O&B

Best Time Early July–mid-October
Topos *Sharktooth Peak, Graveyard Peak 7.5'*
Where to Stay
 Mountain: Mono Hot Springs Resort, Vermilion Valley Resort
 Other: None
 Towns and Agencies: None

HIGHLIGHTS A pleasant trail leads through forest to excellent views over the big, beautiful reservoir called Lake Edison and beyond it, eastward, into the High Sierra. Dense aspen groves near the lake's east end provide dramatic fall color.

HOW TO GET TO THE TRAILHEAD From the signed junction between Mono Hot Springs and Florence Lake junction on the Kaiser Pass Road, take the left fork and bypass the turnoff to Mono Hot Springs Resort. Follow the winding, partly paved road to Lake Edison, eventually curving below the lake's hulking dam before ascending to the turnoff to Vermilion Valley Resort, which is just off the road. The trailhead is farther on, but a stop to visit the resort's store and café is a treat. In season, as long as the lake's level permits, you can cut the hike nearly in half by taking the seasonal, resort-operated ferry (for a fee) to or from the head of Lake Edison. To experience the whole hike, continue past the resort

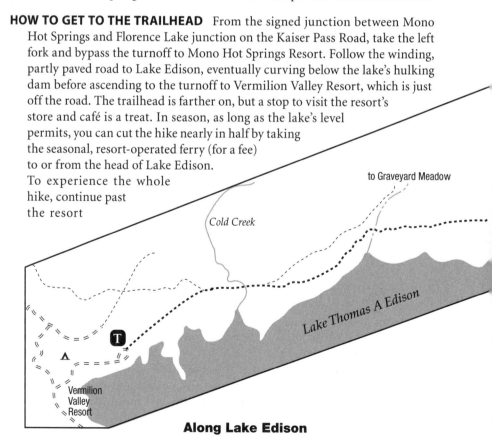

Along Lake Edison

and toward the campground. Pass the first campground turnoff and then the pack station turnoff. Follow the road to a parking area bounded by huge logs at the farthest end of the campground loop that's the farthest to the east. Start the hike at a trailhead that isn't on the 1982 topo, 0.8 mile past the turnoff to Vermilion Valley Resort and 8.8 miles from the Mono-Florence junction. Hikers staying at Vermilion Valley Resort can follow use trails tracing the lakeshore into the campground on foot and pick up this hike at the easternmost campground loop's far end.

ON THE TRAIL Go through an opening in a huge fallen log and head east toward an information sign and a trail sign directing hikers toward Goodale Pass, the Pacific Crest Trail/John Muir Trail (PCT/JMT), and Mono Creek. Follow the sandy trail through a moderate Jeffrey pine forest, enjoying the flowers scattered through the understory. Note that this hike skirts but doesn't enter the adjacent wilderness areas.

The trail winds gradually through viewless forest, passing a junction just shy of 0.5 mile where a stock-worn trail comes in on the left. Continuing

slabs at head of Lake Edison

Lake Thomas A Edison

| 0 | 0.25 | 0.5 | 1 mile |

ahead, descend slightly to a junction at a little more than 0.5 mile. Turn left (northeast) to cross Cold Creek on an unusually handsome footbridge, and then turn right on the other side to join the unbridged right (southeast) fork.

Turning left (east) on the reunited trail, reach another junction at a little more than 0.75 mile. Go right (east-southeast, lakeward), with brief lake views around 1 mile as the trail veers near the water. The forest closes in again, but its dreariness is soon relieved by a flower-lined, seasonal creek small enough to hop across. Leaving the creek, climb a low, rocky ridge offering some lake views, though the lake is now far below the trail. Climbing some more, pass a treeless knob on the right from which there's a nice view southwest across Lake Edison to its dam and beach and beyond it into the Kaiser Pass country. More viewpoints follow as the path climbs gradually, till it tops out at a rocky point with a view of Bear Ridge across the lake and of the shapely white summits of Sierra peaks due east.

The views become obscured as the trail descends moderately through patchy forest to the lake's shore where tiny beaches between granite slabs may beckon, depending on the water level, at a little more than 2.5 miles. The shoreline is steep and rocky, and the trail rolls up and down as it negotiates one shoreline obstacle after another. At a little over 2.75 miles pass through a stand of aspens. Beyond, zigzag steeply up an outcrop dotted with deciduous oaks, beginning a rocky but view-filled ascent that's partly blasted out of the granite. Topping out at the hike's high point at 3.3 miles and 7920 feet, note glacier-polished granite surfaces on Bear Ridge opposite, the head of the lake and the rust-tinted Vermilion Cliffs to the east-northeast, and huge gray cliffs beyond them.

Now descend high "steps" in the trail, cross a couple of granite slabs, and enter the shade of a grove of large aspens whose round, fluttering leaves are fresh green in summer, clear yellow to orange and red in fall. Cross a tiny, seasonal channel and climb over some big boulders before reaching a junction at about 4.3 miles with the trail to the seasonal ferry landing near the lake's east end (right, southeast). The junction is unsigned when the ferry isn't running, but the heap of rocks used to prop up the sign is still pretty obvious.

Turn right onto this spur trail and follow it down past boulders to slabs near the head of Lake Edison at 4.5 miles and 7650 feet. In addition to being the ferry landing, these slabs provide great views west across the lake, whose true head is normally farther east—exactly where depends on the lake's level.

Retrace your steps.

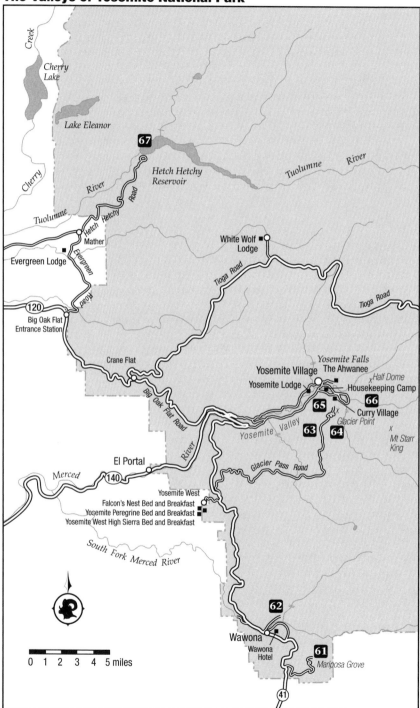

CHAPTER 6

The Valleys of
Yosemite National Park

Great chasms and spectacular waterfalls characterize Yosemite National Park's wonderful valleys. The southernmost of these is Wawona, the valley of South Fork Merced River. Wawona is the home of Yosemite's best giant-sequoia grove. The next hikes are in the park's stunning Glacier Point Road district north of Wawona and high above Yosemite Valley. The next valley to the north is famed Yosemite Valley itself, carved by the main Merced River and its glacier. There's one hike that originates in Yosemite Valley but zips out of the Valley as fast as it can. This book doesn't have hikes in Yosemite Valley proper: Early in the morning and late in the evening, Yosemite Valley can be sublimely beautiful. But at midday, the Valley is hot, dusty, crowded, and noisy. The best way to enjoy Yosemite National Park then is to be somewhere else. (For another, completely different Yosemite district, see the hikes from State Route 120 in the next chapter.) Continuing north, there's a wonderful waterfall hike in the peaceful Hetch Hetchy district. Hetch Hetchy was once another great chasm, but it has been drowned by a reservoir. John Muir himself regarded Hetch Hetchy Valley as being as worthy of preservation as Yosemite Valley. Some believe that the loss of Hetch Hetchy Valley broke John Muir's heart and led to his death.

Recommended Maps

In addition to those listed in the trip write-ups, your library of maps should include the following. Get the latest edition/revision you can find. They're widely available, certainly at any of the local ranger stations.

- *Humboldt-Toiyabe National Forest, Inyo National Forest, Sierra National Forest,* and *Stanislaus National Forest.* U.S. Forest Service and U.S. Department of Agriculture.

- *Yosemite National Park Guide Map* and *Sierra Nevada Yosemite Area.* Automobile Club of Southern California.

- *Map and Guide to Yosemite Valley* and *Map and Guide to Wawona and the Mariposa Grove.* Rufus Graphics in cooperation with the Yosemite Association.

- *Yosemite National Park Recreation Map* and *Yosemite Valley.* Tom Harrison Maps.

Individual Lodgings

Name	Nearest Community	Type	Facilities	Price Range	Contact Information	Website and Email Address
The Ahwahnee	Yosemite Village	Other	Rooms, cabins	$$$	Phone: 559-253-5635	http://www.yosemitepark.com/Accommodations_TheAhwahnee.aspx
Curry Village	Yosemite Village	Other	Rooms, cabins, tent cabins	$–$$	Phone: 559-253-5635	http://www.yosemitepark.com/Accommodations_CurryVillage.aspx
Evergreen Lodge	Groveland	Other	Cabins	$–$$	33160 Evergreen Road Groveland, CA 95321 Phone: 209-379-2606	www.evergreenlodge.com info@evergreenlodge.com
Falcon's Nest Bed and Breakfast	Yosemite West	Mountain	Rooms	$$	7507 Henness Circle Yosemite West, CA 95389 Phone: 209-372-8517 Fax: 209-372-4241	www.yosemitewest.com/falconbb.htm
Housekeeping Camp	Yosemite Village	Other	Tent cabin	$	Phone: 559-253-5635	http://www.yosemitepark.com/Accommodations_HousekeepingCamp.aspx
Wawona Hotel	Wawona	Other	Rooms	$$	Phone: 559-253-5635	www.yosemitepark.com
Yosemite Lodge	Yosemite Village	Other	Rooms	$$	Phone: 559-253-5635	www.yosemitepark.com
Yosemite Peregrine Bed and Breakfast	Yosemite West	Mountain	Rooms	$$–$$$	7507 Henness Circle Yosemite West, CA 95389 Phone: 209-372-8517 Fax: 209-372-4241	www.yosemitewest.com/peregrin.htm
Yosemite West High Sierra Bed and Breakfast	Yosemite West	Mountain	Rooms	$$	7460 Henness Ridge Road Yosemite, CA 95389 Phone: 209-372-4808	www.yosemitewest.com/hsierra.htm

Towns and Agencies

Name	Nearest Community	Type	Contact Information	Website and Email Address
Mariposa County Chamber of Commerce	Represents communities west of Yosemite Valley	Chamber of Commerce	P.O. Box 425 Mariposa, CA 95338 Phone: 209-966-2456	www.mariposachamber.org
The Redwoods	Wawona	Agency	P.O. Box 2085 Wawona Station Yosemite National Park, CA 95389 Phone: 209-375-6666	www.redwoodsinyosemite.com info@redwoodsinyosemite.com
Yosemite Lodging and Vacation Rentals	Wawona	Agency	P.O. Box 2172 Wawona Station Yosemite National Park, CA 95389 Phone: 800-732-4544	www.yosemiterentals.com
Yosemite Sierra Visitors Bureau	Represents communities south of Wawona	Visitors Bureau	Phone: 559-683-4636 Fax: 559-683-5697	www.yosemitethisyear.com ysvb@yosemitethisyear.com
Yosemite West Condominiums	Yosemite West	Agency	7421 Yosemite Park Way Yosemite, CA 95389 Phone: 888-296-7364 or 310-314-1580	http://www.yosemitewest.com/condos.html info@scenicwonders.com
Yosemite's Four Seasons	Yosemite West	Agency	7519 Henness Circle Yosemite National Park, CA 95389 Phone: 800-669-9300 or 209-372-9000 Fax: 209-372-8800	http://yosemitelodging.com
Yosemite's Scenic Wonders	Yosemite West	Agency	7403 Yosemite Park Way Yosemite National Park, CA 95389 Phone: 888-YOSEMITE or 888-967-3648	www.yosemitelodgingreservations.com info@scenicwonders.com

61 Mariposa Grove

Place	Total Distance	Elevation	Difficulty Level	Type
Trailhead		5600		
California Tree	1.3	5900	E	O&B
Museum semiloop	3.5+	6461	M	Semi
Entire semiloop	5.3	6810	M	Semi

Best Time   Late May–mid-October

Topos   *Mariposa Grove 7.5'; Map and Guide to Wawona and the Mariposa Grove of Big Trees* by Rufus Graphics in cooperation with the Yosemite Association

Where to Stay

Mountain: Falcon's Nest Bed and Breakfast, Yosemite Peregrine Bed and Breakfast, Yosemite West High Sierra Bed and Breakfast

Other: Wawona Hotel

Towns and Agencies: The Redwoods, Yosemite Lodging and Vacation Rentals, Yosemite Sierra Visitors Bureau, Yosemite West Condominiums, Yosemite's Four Seasons, Yosemite's Scenic Wonders

HIGHLIGHTS   This is the best and most accessible grove of giant sequoias in Yosemite National Park. At the hike's high point, there's a magnificent vista from Wawona Point. (However, Sequoia and Kings Canyon national parks offer far larger and more impressive giant sequoia groves than any in Yosemite. See Trips 42 and 50.)

HOW TO GET TO THE TRAILHEAD   Hikers staying in the Wawona area in the summer should take the free shuttle bus to the grove. Hikers staying elsewhere or visiting in spring, fall, or winter should take State Route 41 to Yosemite's South Entrance, between Fish Camp and Wawona. At the South Entrance, take the Mariposa Grove Road east—ahead if coming from Wawona, right if from Fish Camp—to a large parking area, which has restrooms, water, a ranger station, and a gift shop, under giant sequoias at the Mariposa Grove, 2.1 miles from the South Entrance Station. Get an early start; even in off-season, this lot may be jammed by midday. Tram tours of the grove are available.

ON THE TRAIL   The whole grove consists of lower and upper groves, the lower grove being the easier to see and the upper grove sporting the finer trees. Numerous footpaths crisscross through the groves. Beware because some trails marked on the maps may no longer exist, but the ones in this trip do.

From the far (northeast) end of the parking lot, follow a broad duff and sand trail northeast past interpretive displays and into the lower grove. A sequoia grove is far from consisting purely of giant sequoias; there are plenty of ponderosa pines, white firs, cedars, black oaks, and sugar pines. Giant sequoias, the largest living things on Earth, dominate by virtue of their size and longevity. They can live to be 3200 years old, maybe older, and never stop growing while they live.

In just a few steps, pass a toppled giant sequoia, The Fallen Monarch, and cross the tram road. At 0.25 mile find fallen giant sequoias sawed through, with signs explaining their annual rings. Shortly ascend a broad, low-stepped "staircase" to cross the tram road and meet a very handsome group of sequoias called The Bachelor and the Three Graces. Between 0.3 and 0.5 mile a series of interpretive signs explains the many specialized requirements sequoias have for natural reproduction. Around here, some sequoias have bark that's smooth on the side facing the trail, due to years of people stroking their shaggy red sides.

Cross a stringer on a footbridge and enter a burned-over area, the result of a prescribed burn to reduce debris and the number of unnaturally competing species and to help giant sequoias reproduce. A little beyond 0.5 mile, reach the Grizzly Giant Tree. Walk around it on either side and about halfway around, pick up the marked trail north to the California Tree and to the upper grove. The California Tree at 0.6 mile and 5900 feet is a walk-through tree, its pedestrian tunnel carved out for tourists in 1895. Those wanting to hike only the lower grove

Mariposa Grove

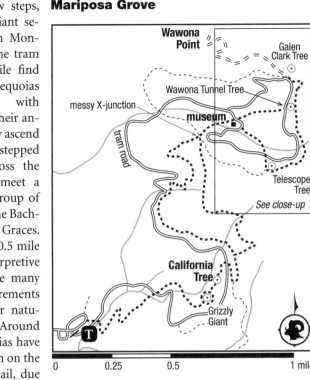

Close-up of Upper-Grove Roads and Trails

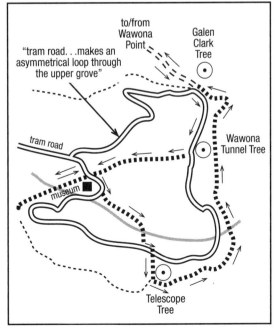

should retrace their steps from the California Tree.

To continue with the entire hike, wind uphill, roughly paralleling the tram road, on a less developed footpath than the one in the lower grove. A little beyond 0.75 mile cross the tram road and head toward the upper grove's museum. At a junction a little farther on, curve left (northeast) where the right fork heads south-southeast to Fish Camp. Climb past a particularly large tree on the left to another junction at almost 1 mile: both branches go to the museum.

> ## Gutted Giants
>
> Trees like the Telescope Tree are fragile, because the heartwood that was burnt away was its main supporting structure. (The heartwood is not living, growing tissue.) Such trees can topple at any time due to wind, snow loading, or other stresses. However, the layer of living, growing tissue is nearer the bark and remains alive, so the tree continues to grow and thrive.

Arbitrarily, to begin the first (lower) loop part of this hike, take the right branch here, pass above a spring, cross an area dotted with patches of cedar seedlings, and enter the oppressive silence of a white-fir forest. Now contouring across a hillside, dip through a small gully and resume climbing, reaching the upper grove at 1.6 miles at a sort of messy X-junction: ahead to the museum; right on the upper loop trail; left toward the Galen Clark Tree; and hard left to return to the lower grove and the parking lot via the Clothespin Tree and the Faithful Couple. The tram road, which makes a hairpin turn past this junction, makes an asymmetrical loop through the upper grove; this trip uses sections of it to hike the upper grove.

Take the branch that leads ahead to the museum, following the faint path through many immense, beautiful giant sequoias over ground thickly strewn with cones the size of chicken eggs. The area is full of confusing trails, but avoid confusion by heading for the museum, not the Mariposa Tree. At the next junction, go right to skirt the meadow below the museum and pass some restrooms. In a few more steps, reach another junction; turn left on a walkway across the meadow and toward the museum, now visible ahead. Reach the seasonally-open museum in the upper grove a little short of 2 miles and at 6461 feet and, if it's open, drop in for a visit. Tram tours stop here, too, and there are books for sale as well as exhibits. To cut the hike short now, skip to the fourth paragraph from the end of the trip description, which begins with "Continuing, retrace your steps past the museum . . ."

To continue the full hike, when leaving the museum, follow the walkway behind it to pick up the lower side of the tram-road loop briefly. On the road, bear right for now. (It's easier to follow this part of the hike on the "Close-up of upper-grove roads and trails" map in this book; the small arrows on the map show you this trip's direction in the upper grove.) At nearly 2 miles spot a signed junction with the trail to the Telescope Tree and turn left (east) to pick up that trail.

On this trail, soon pass the fallen Stable Tree, in whose side rangers once put mangers for their horses. Winding upward, pass one giant after another, and meet the road again. Turn left on the road and walk about 30 paces to the Telescope Tree, a still-living giant whose heartwood has been gutted by fire from top to bottom.

Turn right onto the trail that passes the tree, where there's an opening that allows hikers to stick their heads in and to look up at the sky through the hollowed trunk. Continuing up this same trail, at nearly 2.25 miles, meet the Outer Loop Trail. Turn left (east) on the Outer Loop Trail, just shy of a rightward-leaning giant. Near 2.5 miles pass above two giant sequoias fused together at the base and nearly fused with a third tree. Just downhill and soon visible is the shattered corpse of the Wawona Tunnel Tree, tree that people once drove automobiles through but that toppled during the winter of 1968–69.

The trail switchbacks down to meet the tram road at nearly 2.6 miles, passing by the Galen Clark Tree, at a junction. The left fork here is the tram road; the right fork, also a road, is now the "trail" to Wawona Point, which is accessible only on foot; and the middle fork is a foot trail that may be hard to spot—but you won't be taking it, anyway. Beginning an out-and-back segment, follow the right fork up to a former parking lot at Wawona Point at 3 miles and 6810 feet, from which there are magnificent views over the South Fork Merced River.

Galen Clark

Yosemite pioneer Galen Clark (1814–1910) came west for his health in the 1850s. He had expected to live only six more months but instead found healing and lived 43 more years, serving at various times as Yosemite's guardian. He "discovered" the Mariposa Grove, and many Yosemite features are named for him. He and John Muir became great friends and took three exploratory journeys together. One story about Clark says that when he was in his nineties, a visitor asked him how he got around Yosemite nowadays. He thought for a bit and then responded, "Slowly!"

Retrace your steps to the junction near the Galen Clark Tree and take the tram road left, toward the Wawona Tunnel Tree, at a little more than 3.3 miles total. Follow the road to the Wawona Tunnel Tree's root end, a little short of 3.5 miles. This is perhaps the best vantage point from which to appreciate the Wawona Tunnel Tree's size. Nearby on the right are some wooden steps leading downhill toward the museum; take the steps downhill to meet a trail and follow it toward the museum. Cross the lower side of the tram-road loop to pick up the museum walkway again.

Continuing, retrace your steps past the museum and down and across the meadow, passing the tallest tree in the grove, the 290-foot Columbia Tree, on the left. In this area with its many confusing trails, simplify things by following the signs that point toward the parking lot via the Clothespin Tree, not the Mariposa Tree. Head uphill of the restrooms, following signs for the Grizzly Giant Tree and the parking lot. Meeting the tram road, turn right on it for about 100 steps, to the point where the road makes a hairpin turn. Leave the road bearing right and downhill to return to the previously mentioned messy X-junction a little short of 4 miles. Take the westbound branch toward the Clothespin Tree and the Faithful Couple Tree.

Stay on this trail by veering left at a junction where another trail/road comes in on the right. Descend the hillside in long, lazy switchbacks. Stay on the trail when it approaches the road just downhill of the Clothespin Tree (turn around to enjoy an excellent view of this tree) by going left where a spur forks right leading to the road.

On the trail, continue the winding descent and meet the tram road again opposite the Faithful Couple Tree, a pair of giant sequoias fused together. Turn left (east) and walk down the road a few steps to pick up the marked trail to the Grizzly Giant Tree and the parking lot on the left side of the road. On this next trail segment, wander up and down, generally northeastward, dodging deadfalls in a spectral, burnt forest and roughly paralleling the tram road. Close the loop part of this hike at the second junction encountered on the way to the upper grove, now at nearly 4.6 miles. Reverse your steps from here, past the California Tree and the Grizzly Giant Tree, to reach the parking lot after nearly 5.3 rewarding miles.

62 Chilnualna Falls

Place	Total Distance	Elevation	Difficulty Level	Type
Trailhead		4200		
Upper Chilnualna Falls	8–8.3	6240–6400	S	O&B
Viewpoints above falls	8.5	6440	S	O&B

Best Time Late May–early July

Topos *Wawona, Mariposa Grove 7.5′*

Where to Stay

Mountain: Falcon's Nest Bed and Breakfast, Yosemite Peregrine Bed and Breakfast, Yosemite West High Sierra Bed and Breakfast

Other: Wawona Hotel

Towns and Agencies: The Redwoods, Yosemite Lodging and Vacation Rentals, Yosemite Sierra Visitors Bureau, Yosemite West Condominiums, Yosemite's Four Seasons, Yosemite's Scenic Wonders

HIGHLIGHTS Don't let the fact that you can't pronounce "Chilnualna" (chill-NWALL-nah) keep you away from these spectacular cascades and the lovely trail to them.

HOW TO GET TO THE TRAILHEAD From the junction of Highway 41 and the spur road to the Wawona Hotel, drive a little more than 0.3 mile northwest up Highway 41 toward Wawona Campground and Yosemite Valley, passing the Wawona gas station and store. Turn right (east) on Chilnualna Falls Road. Follow it past a turnoff to the Wawona Ranger Station and a number of turnoffs to private cabins and resorts. At the road's end, at a total of 2 miles, find a large dirt parking area on one side of the road and the trailhead, with an information sign, at the extreme east end of the road. Park here.

ON THE TRAIL From the trailhead the trail angles northward up through moderate
forest cover; stark Wawona
Dome is visible to the right.
In quick succession cross
a paved road, go left at an
unmapped fork, climb some
more, and go right at the next
fork (also unmapped) onto a
dirt road high above rushing
Chilnualna Creek. The spring
flower display along this trail
can be amazing, but beware of
poison oak. Climb moderately
to steeply as the forest thick-
ens, and just ahead spot dramatic cascades roaring down a
steep, rocky streambed.

Chilnualna Falls

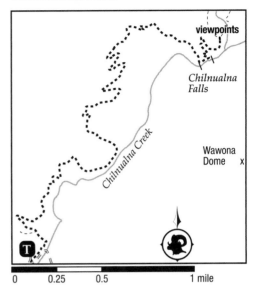

From here, the climb along
the creek is beautiful and exciting but so steep that at times there are stone stairs to
help! At 0.25 mile turn away from the creek to continue the steep climb through
live oak and kit-kit-dizze to a junction near 0.3 mile with a horse trail coming
in on the left (the spectacular, creekside section of trail is too steep and exposed
for equestrians). Now in Yosemite Wilderness, the grade eases as the leaf-littered
trail contours a slope clad in manzanita, incense cedar, and live and deciduous
oaks. Views southwest reveal the Chowchilla Mountains from some switchback
legs; on others, hikers seem almost nose-to-nose with Wawona Dome. The route
is sometimes near the creek and sometimes far, occasionally obliging you to hop
over seasonal seeps and tributary streams.

Near 2.5 miles the trail winds past a view of a striking torrent of water crashing down a sheer rock wall. It's an inspiring sight. A little beyond 3 miles cross
a stream on mossy rocks between its small cascades, gaining more views of the
falls ahead. Alas, these lower cascades, so showy from below, will turn out to be
inaccessible from the trail—but the upper cascades make up for that. Traverse
a gully full of wild azalea and blue ceanothus before beginning a leg that's been
blasted out of the cliff face the trail crosses. Swing into Chilnualna Creek's steep
channel at last and see that here, at upper Chilnualna Falls at 4-plus miles and
6240 to 6400 feet, the falls are a series of beautiful cascades separated by charming
stretches where the creek pools or glides over slabs.

This hike continues up to the next trail junction to allow hikers to wander
around and take in the outstanding views over the South Fork Merced River from
several nearby viewpoints above the falls at 4.25 miles and 6440 feet.

Retrace your steps.

63 Sentinel Dome and Taft Point

Place	Total Distance	Elevation	Difficulty Level	Type
Trailhead		7740		
Sentinel Dome only	2	8122	E	O&B
Taft Point only	2+	7503	E	O&B
Entire loop	4.5	8122	M	Loop

Best Time   Early July–mid-October

Topos   *Half Dome 7.5'*; *Map & Guide to Yosemite Valley* by Rufus Graphics in cooperation with the Yosemite Association

Where to Stay

Mountain: Falcon's Nest Bed and Breakfast, Yosemite Peregrine Bed and Breakfast, Yosemite West High Sierra Bed and Breakfast

Other: The Ahwahnee, Curry Village, Housekeeping Camp, Wawona Hotel, Yosemite Lodge

Towns and Agencies: Mariposa County Chamber of Commerce, The Redwoods, Yosemite Lodging and Vacation Rentals, Yosemite Sierra Visitors Bureau, Yosemite West Condominiums, Yosemite's Four Seasons, Yosemite's Scenic Wonders

HIGHLIGHTS This hike is a gem in every way: a beautiful trail offering wonderful contrasts and spectacular views, obtained by an exciting but surprisingly easy scramble to the top of one of Yosemite's famous granite domes—one of the park's must-see trips.

HOW TO GET TO THE TRAILHEAD Yosemite's Glacier Point Road winds generally northeast from its junction with State Route 41 at Chinquapin, which is between and about 2000 feet higher than Yosemite Valley and Wawona, and less than a mile from the turnoff for Yosemite West. Turn north onto the Glacier Point Road, pass Badger Pass Ski Area and Bridalveil Campground, and at 13.6 miles from Chinquapin turn into a large parking area, with restrooms, on the left (west) side of the road. If you get to Glacier Point, you have gone too far. Because this parking lot may be jammed by midday, get an early start.

ON THE TRAIL From the trailhead sign, head for the junction visible just ahead to the northwest. At the junction, it's left (south-southwest) for Taft Point and right (northeast) for Sentinel Dome. It's better to climb Sentinel Dome early in the hike, while you have more energy, so turn right here in an open red fir forest floored with coarse, light, decomposed-granite sand. Cross an unnamed, unmapped creeklet on a footbridge and climb a little over granite slabs. After a brief dip into forest, contour along a mostly open slope on the rocky and sandy trail, gaining a little altitude. Forest alternates with granite slabs, and rusty trail signs help keep hikers on track. Far-reaching views open down Yosemite Valley, and west to El Capitan, while Sentinel Dome looms ahead. At 0.6 mile pick up an old road and turn left (north) toward the dome, enjoying glimpses of Half Dome to the right while winding through the forest behind Sentinel Dome.

The road climbs moderately to steeply to a loop from whose west side, at a little more than 0.75 mile, begins the trailless but obvious ascent of Sentinel Dome. Treat the dome as a flight of stairs whose steps vary in height, and pick the route with the "step height" that suits you best, working back and forth across the slope, finding the most congenial route. Views get better and better the higher you go; even hikers unwilling to go all the way will enjoy going partway. Find yourself atop Sentinel Dome at about 1 mile and 8122 feet. The summit, though airy, is quite gentle and broad. At the top near a dead Jeffrey pine is a compass rose inscribed to help identify features in the magnificent scene all around.

Eventually retrace your steps to the loop's west side. Walk across it and pick up a signed spur trail to the Pohono Trail (which starts at Glacier Point) on the loop's east side. Turn left (northeast) onto the spur trail and follow it downslope rather steeply toward a radio facility, enjoying a terrific view of Half Dome and crossing the road a couple of times. Veer left, pass below the radio facility/cellphone site and find yourself on the northwest side of the ridge on which Sentinel Dome sits.

Soon reach a junction with the Pohono Trail at 1.5 miles; go left (southwest) to begin a one-switchback, descending traverse from which there are wonderful views of Yosemite Valley when the vegetation permits. At 2.25 miles ford Sentinel Creek; not far below, the creek plunges unseen over Yosemite Valley's wall as Sentinel Falls. A use trail along the creek's east side leads north to an airy viewpoint of the top of the falls as well as of Yosemite Valley.

Sentinel Dome and Taft Point

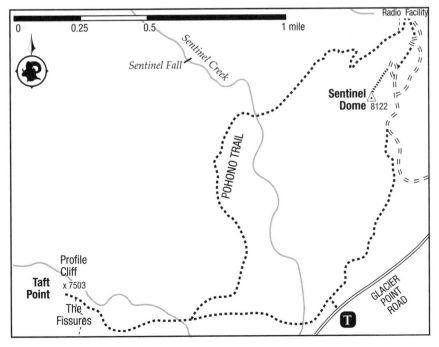

Climbing out of the creekbed, stroll briefly along the valley's edge to enjoy the magnificent views, and then veer into forest again. Presently emerge from forest to ascend a ridge above Sentinel Creek and catch over-the-shoulder views of Sentinel Dome. Still climbing, reach a junction at a little more than 3 miles: The left (east) branch returns to the parking area, and the right (west) continues to Taft Point.

Turn right for Taft Point and step across a trickle in a narrow, wet meadow. Head generally west to emerge from the forest onto a broad stone apron that's the edge of a large, rocky, chaparral-splattered bench. Use trails seem to splay every which way toward a cliff edge that's Yosemite Valley's south rim. The area is so open you don't really need a trail, so explore here and there to see The Fissures, deep vertical slashes in an even deeper gash in the Valley's rim, and to stand on railing-guarded Taft Point at 3.3 miles and 7503 feet (a little more than 1 mile if you're hiking out-and-back to Taft Point only). The views over Yosemite Valley are breathtaking as well as vertiginous.

When you're ready to return, look for the trail you came in on at the extreme left side of the broad stone apron at the edge of the forest. From there, retrace your steps to the previous junction at nearly 4 miles and go ahead (right) to Glacier Point Road. Bob over a pair of low, open ridges with views to the left of Sentinel Dome and ford Sentinel Creek in a gully near the road.

At a little more than 4.3 miles close the loop near the parking lot, turn right on the spur to the parking lot, and reach the lot at a little less than 4.5 miles.

64 To Yosemite Valley via Falls

Place	Total Distance	Elevation	Difficulty Level	Type
Trailhead		7214		
Happy Isles shuttle stop	7.75	4020	S	Shuttle

Best Time Late May–late August

Topos *Half Dome 7.5'; Map & Guide to Yosemite Valley* by Rufus Graphics in cooperation with Yosemite Association

Where to Stay

Mountain: Falcon's Nest Bed and Breakfast, Yosemite Peregrine Bed and Breakfast, Yosemite West High Sierra Bed and Breakfast

Other: The Ahwahnee, Curry Village, Housekeeping Camp, Wawona Hotel, Yosemite Lodge

Towns and Agencies: Mariposa County Chamber of Commerce, The Redwoods, Yosemite Lodging and Vacation Rentals, Yosemite Sierra Visitors Bureau, Yosemite West Condominiums, Yosemite's Four Seasons, Yosemite's Scenic Wonders

HIGHLIGHTS Like Trip 63, this is a Yosemite must-see hike. Spectacular views attend nearly every step past three of Yosemite's most famous waterfalls—three

Yosemite Valley and Vernal and Nevada Falls

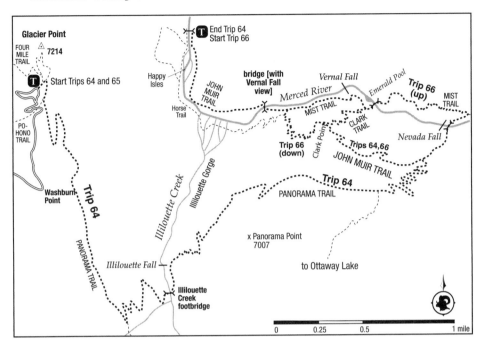

of them that are invisible from the Valley itself. Unless the day is extremely hot or it's late in the season, bring rain gear for the Mist Trail along Vernal Fall.

HOW TO GET TO THE TRAILHEAD No matter where you're coming from, the best way to take this shuttle trip is to get to Yosemite Valley and take the hiker's shuttlebus to Glacier Point. Leave your car parked at your Yosemite Valley lodgings or at a day-use lot in the Valley, and then buy your ticket and catch the shuttle at Yosemite Lodge. Be sure to take one of the earlier shuttlebuses to allow plenty of time for this hike. The bus ride from the last pickup point in the Valley to Glacier Point takes about an hour one way and is very beautiful. End the hike at the Happy Isles shuttle stop in Yosemite Valley, from which there's a free shuttlebus back to your lodgings or car. Glacier Point has restrooms, water, a telephone, and a snack/gift shop.

ON THE TRAIL Be sure to walk all around Glacier Point before leaving, as these are the finest Yosemite Valley views anywhere. In early season, you can even hear those huge waterfalls! This trip's trail, the Panorama Trail, begins behind—southeast from the bare edge of—the Glacier Point area and appears to head off in a completely wrong direction, roughly paralleling the parking area. Almost immediately, the trail swings into the forest and reaches a Y-junction.

Go left (southeast) on the Panorama Trail to begin a gradual descent through a forest of mostly burnt trees on chaparral-clad slopes. From these leisurely switchbacks, look for famous features such as Half Dome, Mt. Broderick, and Liberty Cap; see the John Muir Trail switchbacking down a slot on the east side of the Panorama Cliffs; and hear the roar of the great falls.

Waterfall Hazards

Take the NO SWIMMING signs at Yosemite's waterfalls seriously. Drowning is the most common cause of death in U.S. national parks and monuments. Every year, several people are killed when they ignore the signs, are caught in strong currents of numbingly cold water—remember, this is all snowmelt straight from Sierra peaks!—and are swept over one of the falls.

At a switchback turn at a little more than 1.3 miles, reach another junction. Go left to continue on the Panorama Trail, enjoying superb views of Half Dome, Panorama Point, and Mt. Starr King. At a little more than 1.75 miles cross a seasonal stream whose gully is filled with currant bushes, make a switchback turn, and near 2 miles reach a use trail that bears off left a few yards to the best, albeit vertiginous, viewpoint overlooking the top of 370-foot Illilouette (ill-lill-oo-ETTE) Fall. These cascades, very impressive in early season, are tucked into the side of a deep slot called Illilouette Gorge and are invisible from most of the typical tourist viewpoints. There's no railing at this viewpoint, the drop is very steep, and the footing may be poor because of decomposed granite, so be careful.

Back on the main trail, the forest grows denser and cooler as the trail crosses the currant-filled streambed a couple more times on its way down to the banks of Illilouette Creek, which makes a wonderfully picturesque dash over granite slabs here. A trestle footbridge over Illilouette Creek at 2.3 miles and 5900 feet conducts hikers safely over the creek. Swimming is dangerous here because of the water's swiftness and iciness and the area's proximity to Illilouette Fall.

From lovely Illilouette Creek, bear left (north) on the far (east) side of the footbridge and begin climbing through sparse forest and chaparral relieved by occasional dense patches of oaks. Zigzag moderately up some 760 feet, at times staring straight across Illilouette Gorge to the starting point at Glacier Point (look for sunlight glinting off the windshields of cars on the Glacier Point Road). At last, having risen high enough and gone far enough east, hikers can see beyond Glacier Point and into Yosemite Valley. Excellent views of North Dome, Basket Dome, Royal Arches, the Ahwahnee Hotel, and Washington Column enliven this leg of the ascent. Near 3.6 miles the trail becomes shadier and levels out atop Panorama Cliff, a wonderful viewpoint. Nevada Fall suddenly comes into heart-stopping view and hearing as the trail begins a gradual descent to a junction.

Go left (ahead, east) for Nevada Fall, switchbacking down a more pronounced grade. Cross and recross an unnamed, unmapped streamlet, and then play tag with another one as you brush up to it and veer away from it. There's a confusion of junctions approaching 5 miles and the south side of Nevada Fall; most are use-trail shortcuts between the area's major trails—the Mist Trail and the John Muir Trail. The major junction here is a T-junction where the Panorama Trail ends at the John Muir Trail. For now turn right to see Nevada Fall.

Any questions about which way to go at other junctions near Nevada Fall are resolved by the fall's roar, which is louder than a freight train here. Emerge from forest onto huge granite slabs—note this spot—on the south side of the Merced River at the top of 594-foot Nevada Fall at 5 miles and 5940 feet, opposite Liberty Cap. The trail vanishes on the open, sand-dusted slabs, so head for the bridge that crosses the river a little upstream of the fall. Exercise extreme care in approaching the sheer lip of this dangerous fall.

Cross the bridge to the fall's north side and look around the north rim for a steep staircase leading down to a railing-protected overlook of the canyon below and of the fall's white plumes. On the north side of Nevada Fall there's a day-use area and restrooms as well as the upper junction of the John Muir and Mist trails. Pause to decide whether the next leg of your hike will be on the Muir Trail or the Mist Trail. This description follows the Muir Trail for now and then switches to the Mist Trail later on.

After taking in the pleasures of Nevada Fall, return to the south side and back to the junction of the John Muir and Panorama Trails. Take the Muir Trail west (right) through forest, hopping over springs, avoiding use trails, and crossing slabs. Leaving the forest behind, the partly-paved trail traverses a dripping cliff face where it is partly protected on the steep downhill side by a stone wall. Over-the-shoulder views of Nevada Fall are amazing from this stretch. Beyond the damp traverse, long, sandy switchbacks lead generally west on a moderate grade down toward the Valley, and there are stunning views of Nevada Fall and Liberty Cap either ahead or over the shoulder at nearly every point.

One of the best views is at Clark Point, by the junction with the Clark Trail at a little more than 5.75 miles. Turn right onto the Clark Trail to begin descending steep, rocky, exposed switchbacks. The upper switchbacks afford excellent views of Nevada and Vernal falls, while an overlook about two-thirds of the way down, at a little more than 6 miles, offers a breathtaking view of Vernal Fall.

At nearly 6.3 miles reach a T-junction with the Mist Trail; go left to Emerald Pool and Vernal Fall, shortly passing deep and dangerous Emerald Pool and a spur trail left to a pit toilet. Soon you stand on the slabs, with railings, at the top of 317-foot Vernal Fall at a little more than 6.5 miles and 5000 feet, exhilarated by

Half Dome, Nevada Fall, and Vernal Fall as seen from the Panorama Trail

The Happy Isles

The Happy Isles are a pair of lovely, rocky, forested islets separated by picturesque branches of the Merced River, and many hikers enjoy a stop here on their way to or from the falls. Happy Isles' bigleaf maples and dogwoods provide welcome summer shade and glorious fall color. A wheelchair-accessible trail traverses the islets. Hikers can also visit the Happy Isles Nature Center, which is on the west side of the river here.

the noise and mist in spite of the crowds normally found here. Now veer left to walk steeply up slabs on the south side of Vernal Fall. Topping out, take a look at the descent the Mist Trail makes from here. Put on your rain gear now to avoid getting soaked by Vernal Fall's mist.

Between this point and the base of Vernal Fall, the Mist Trail is an extraordinarily steep series of high stone stairs, damp to soaking wet, rarely protected on the downhill side by railings. The trail clings to the side of the canyon next to the fall, often so close that you not only hear and see the fall but are practically in it. This segment has recently been reworked with new stones and with grooves in the stairsteps to help with traction and to carry away excess water. Take your time, pausing often to look back at the fall—and to allow the crowds working their way upward to pass. The grade eases at the base of Vernal Fall, and at a little less than 7 miles the route passes huge boulders that provide viewpoints of the fall just before the Mist Trail blends back into the John Muir Trail.

Continue ahead (right, west, downhill) onto the John Muir Trail, shortly passing a spur trail to restrooms on the left and then a drinking fountain on the right as the path veers right to cross the river on a footbridge. Pause on the bridge at 7 miles and 4400 feet to enjoy a wonderful view upstream to Vernal Fall, framed by sheer stone walls and nearby branches. Across the bridge, on the north side of the river, the trail curves west again to descend steeply past the mouth of Illilouette Gorge; you may be able to spot the fall one last time. Beyond Illilouette Gorge, the trail curves northward as it continues its steep descent.

Near Happy Isles, a trail branches left down stone steps toward the isles. To finish this hike, continue ahead (right) to the road that loops past Happy Isles and the trail to Mirror Lake. Cross left over the Merced on a large bridge at 7.6 miles, and follow signs past restrooms to the Happy Isles stop for the free Yosemite Valley shuttlebus at 7.75 miles and 4020 feet, the end of this hike. Catch the next shuttlebus back to your lodgings or car.

65 Four Mile Trail

Place	Total Distance	Elevation	Difficulty Level	Type
Trailhead		7214		
Yosemite Lodge shuttle stop	5.3+	3980	M	Shuttle

Best Time Late May–mid-October

Topos *Half Dome 7.5'; Map & Guide to Yosemite Valley* by Rufus Graphics in cooperation with the Yosemite Association

Where to Stay

Mountain: Falcon's Nest Bed and Breakfast, Yosemite Peregrine Bed and Breakfast, Yosemite West High Sierra Bed and Breakfast

Other: The Ahwahnee, Curry Village, Housekeeping Camp, Wawona Hotel, Yosemite Lodge

Towns and Agencies: Mariposa County Chamber of Commerce, The Redwoods, Yosemite Lodging and Vacation Rentals, Yosemite Sierra Visitors Bureau, Yosemite West Condominiums, Yosemite's Four Seasons, Yosemite's Scenic Wonders

HIGHLIGHTS Amazing views over Yosemite Valley attend the descent of the Four Mile Trail from scenic Glacier Point to the Valley floor. A stroll across the floor of Yosemite Valley to a shuttle stop completes the trip.

HOW TO GET TO THE TRAILHEAD No matter where you're coming from, the best way to take this shuttle trip is to get to Yosemite Valley and take the hiker's

Four Mile Trail

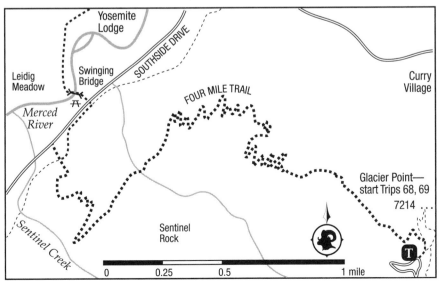

shuttlebus to Glacier Point. Leave your car parked at your Yosemite Valley lodgings or at a day-use lot in the Valley, and then buy your ticket and catch the shuttle at Yosemite Lodge. Take one of the earlier shuttlebuses to allow plenty of time for this hike. The bus ride from the last pickup point in the Valley to Glacier Point takes about an hour and is very beautiful. End the hike at the Happy Isles shuttle stop in Yosemite Valley, from which there's a free shuttlebus back to your lodgings or car. Glacier Point has restrooms, water, a telephone, and a snack/gift shop.

Cathedral Rocks (left) and El Capitan as seen from Four Mile Trail

ON THE TRAIL Be sure to walk all around Glacier Point before leaving, as these are the finest Yosemite Valley views anywhere. In early season, you can even hear those huge waterfalls! To begin this hike, find the trailhead behind the snack/souvenir building. Forks to the right lead to Glacier Point; for the Four Mile Trail, bear left to descend through a moderate to dense forest on the duff trail, now longer than 4 miles thanks to reworking. Shortly pass a large boulder with a trail rules sign and then cross a seasonal stringer. Curving through a gully, glimpse the north wall of Yosemite Valley ahead. A little past 0.25 mile, reach a point where there's a view toward North Dome and Basket Dome, with Mt. Hoffman behind them; toward Mt. Watkins, with Tenaya (ten-EYE-ah) Peak behind it; toward Tenaya Canyon and Clouds Rest; and toward Half Dome. Farther on, the remnant of Mirror Lake—quickly transforming into Mirror Meadow—is visible. Next, Yosemite Point and Upper Yosemite Fall come into view—a truly breathtaking sight. The gradual descent briefly shifts to a slight climb, and soon you spot Lower Yosemite Fall and the Middle Cascades between the falls.

Resuming the descent, traverse exposed rock faces where the downhill side of the trail is a sheer drop to the Valley floor. At 0.6 mile reach the first switchback

Surviving the Gnats

Like most live-oak woods at this altitude, this one is apt to be full of tiny flying insects whose goal, it seems, is to commit suicide by flying into your eyes, up your nose, or down your throat. To foil most of them, keep your sunglasses on and tie a bandana bandit-style over your nose and mouth, or pick up a fallen brush of twigs and leaves with which to fan the critters away.

turn at a fine view of Sentinel Rock, as well as a view westward down the Valley to El Capitan. The descent becomes steeper and more switchbacking. Traverse another rock face at 1.5 miles and then negotiate a gully whose loose rock demands that the downhill side of the trail be propped up in places. Swing out of the gully to enjoy excellent views of Yosemite Falls and then zigzag down through another gully. Handsome Douglas big-cone spruce trees (*Pseudotsuga macrocarpa*) shade the trail here and there. The trail surface, which is made up mostly of rocks and coarse sand, becomes looser, and the grade becomes steeper. The exposure on the downhill side continues to be nerve-racking, but the views more than compensate for the steep, exposed going.

At nearly 3.5 miles cross a pretty but unnamed stream, enter a viewless forest of live oak, and make a long traverse downward.

Nearing 4 miles, road noise rises from the Valley floor. At about 4.25 miles pass a trailhead sign as the trail becomes paved and veers left. Follow the paved path across the intersecting Valley floor footpath that roughly parallels the road; reach the road at a little more than 4.3 miles and 3980 feet, the end of the Four Mile Trail.

To pick up a shuttlebus to your car or lodgings, go back a few steps to that last intersection and pick up the Valley floor footpath. Turn northeast on it (left if coming back from the main road, right if turning onto it directly from the descent of the Four Mile Trail). It's roughly 1 mile more to the nearest shuttlebus stop, at Yosemite Lodge. Follow the Valley floor footpath till roughly opposite Swinging Bridge, near a picnic area with restrooms. Cross the road, traverse the picnic area, cross Swinging Bridge over the Merced River, and follow the footpath across Leidig Meadow to the outbuildings of Yosemite Lodge. Pick up the lodge's road system here and follow it generally northeast to the shuttlebus stop at Yosemite Lodge, to end this hike at about 5.3 miles.

66 Vernal and Nevada Falls

Place	Total Distance	Elevation	Difficulty Level	Type
Trailhead		4020		
Bridge only	1.5	4400	M	O&B
Top of Vernal Fall only	2.5	5000	S	O&B
Entire semiloop	6	5940	S	Semi

Best Time Late May–late August

Topos *Half Dome 7.5'; Map & Guide to Yosemite Valley* by Rufus Graphics in cooperation with the Yosemite Association

See map on page 181

Where to Stay

Mountain: Falcon's Nest Bed and Breakfast, Yosemite Peregrine Bed and Breakfast, Yosemite West High Sierra Bed and Breakfast

Other: The Ahwahnee, Curry Village, Housekeeping Camp, Yosemite Lodge

Towns and Agencies: Mariposa County Chamber of Commerce, Yosemite West Condominiums, Yosemite's Four Seasons, Yosemite's Scenic Wonders

HIGHLIGHTS On this steep, spectacular trip hikers visit two beautiful and famous Yosemite waterfalls, Vernal and Nevada falls, from the Valley floor. As noted in Trip 64, it's a good idea to take rain gear for the Mist Trail leg beside Vernal Fall.

HOW TO GET TO THE TRAILHEAD From lodgings in the Valley or from a day-use parking lot, take the Valley's free shuttlebus to the Happy Isles stop, which has restrooms, water, and a snack stand, as well as the nearby Happy Isles Nature Center. (The public's cars are banned from the road necessary to get to that stop.)

ON THE TRAIL Cross the Merced River on the bridge east of the Happy Isles shuttlebus stop. Beyond the bridge, leave the sidewalk and descend to a broad footpath along the Merced. Head south on this trail, passing an information sign that marks this as the northern terminus of the John Muir Trail. Abreast of the Happy Isles, a pair of rocky islets in the Merced, bypass a turnoff and bridge to the islets, and continue south, climbing steadily up the Merced's deep granite gorge. As the trail begins curving east, look west (right) occasionally

for a glimpse of Illilouette (ill-lill-oo-ETTE) Fall crashing down Illilouette Gorge on the far side of the Merced. (The Happy Isles are an ideal destination for a very short and wheelchair-accessible hike. If you want to do such a trip, don't cross the road bridge but instead head south from the stop, pass the restrooms, and follow signs.)

Still climbing on the John Muir Trail, at about 0.6 mile, reach a bridge across the river from which there's a magnificent view of Vernal Fall upstream. It's a fine destination for a shorter hike. On the other side of the bridge, find water and restrooms. Stay on the John Muir Trail to the next signed junction at 0.75 miles, veer left (east-southeast) off the John Muir Trail and onto the Mist Trail. Almost immediately spot a junction with a signed HORSE TRAIL returning to Yosemite Valley, a trail that you should avoid.

Stay on the Mist Trail and wind

Fall foliage on the Merced River past huge boulders before reaching a feature for which the Mist Trail is well known: a long series of extraordinarily high, steep, exposed rock "steps" leading up toward 317-foot Vernal Fall. In early and sometimes even midseason, this is the place to don rain gear in order to avoid being soaked by Vernal's dense mist. Climb carefully: The perpetual mist can make the stairs wet and slippery, there are no railings, and the falling water creates a strong breeze. There are sure to be steady streams of hikers going up to and down from the fall.

The steps actually climb above the fall's lip, to a huge granite slab on Vernal's south side. Railings along the exposed edge allow views of the fall with a little protection, at about 1.1 miles into the hike. This is a good turnaround point for hikers wanting a shorter hike.

To continue, friction-walk the slab down and away from the fall to pick up the nearly level path again by deep, dangerous Emerald Pool. Shortly begin traversing slabs while following a line of boulders. There's a spur trail to a pit toilet near here. Soon, the Mist Trail reaches its junction with the steep and scenic Clark Trail (right, southeast; it connects the lower Mist and higher John Muir trails). Stay on the Mist Trail.

Near 1.6 miles, cross the Merced River on a footbridge, beyond which the trail angles northeast toward Mt. Broderick and Liberty Cap, climbing gradually in a thicket of live oak plagued by bugs. Veer away from, and then back toward, the river and through a day-use area in a cool grove of incense cedars.

As the moderate climb resumes, the roar of Nevada Fall makes hikers' ears perk up, and at 2 miles hikers are abreast of the base of Nevada Fall. Trees interfere with the view from the trail, so work over to the water's edge to take in this heart-stopping spectacle. Back on the trail, zigzag steeply up smooth, sand-dusted, rock "steps" through a jumble of boulders, enjoying occasional, excellent views of the fall. The climb becomes steeper and steeper, and the switchbacks tighter and tighter, as the trail veers into a rocky chute between the canyon's north wall and an outcrop on Nevada Fall's north side, where there are no views of the fall.

At the top of this exhausting climb, you reach another day-use area, this one with toilets, and also with a T-junction (the upper junction) with the John Muir Trail. Here, it's left to Little Yosemite Valley, and right to Nevada Fall and to return to Yosemite Valley on the John Muir Trail. Take the right fork and curve west on a gradual, sandy-rocky tread to reach the Muir Trail and a footbridge over the Merced River just upstream of Nevada Fall at 2.75 miles and 5940 feet. Explore both sides of the fall, being careful to stay out of the water. As mentioned in Trip 64, there's a steep access route to an overlook area on the extreme north side of the fall and bounded by railings. From that overlook there's a vertiginous view of the fall and the canyon below.

Leaving Nevada Fall, head across the slabs on its south side to the junction of the John Muir and Panorama Trails. The junction isn't obvious and there are lots of use trails in the area, but keep your eyes peeled for the Muir Trail headed back down toward Yosemite Valley. Take the John Muir Trail west through forest, hopping over springs, avoiding use trails, and crossing slabs. Leaving the forest behind, the trail traverses a dripping cliff face where it is partly protected on the steep downhill side by a stone wall. Over-the-shoulder views of Nevada Fall are amazing from this stretch. Beyond the damp traverse, long, sandy switchbacks lead generally west on a moderate grade down toward the Valley, and there are stunning views of Nevada Fall and Liberty Cap either ahead or over the shoulder at nearly every point.

One of the best views is at Clark Point, by the junction with the Clark Trail at a little more than 5.75 miles. Stay (left) on the John Muir Trail, enjoying the winding, sometimes view-filled descent along Panorama Cliff's east face. There's wonderful fall color on this leg from bigleaf maple trees in season. There may also be lots of gnats; foil them by keeping your sunglasses on and tying a bandana bandit-style over your nose and mouth. Zigzag down past the signed HORSE TRAIL on the left just before closing the loop part of this trip at the lower junction with the Mist Trail at 5.25 miles.

From this lower John Muir Trail-Mist Trail junction, retrace your steps to Happy Isles at 6 miles to complete this eye-popping hike.

67 Tueeulala and Wapama Falls

Place	Total Distance	Elevation	Difficulty Level	Type
Trailhead		3813		
Tueeulala Fall	3	4020	E	O&B
Wapama Fall	4	3880	M	O&B

Best Time   Late May–early July
Topos   WP *Hetch Hetchy Reservoir* 15'; *Lake Eleanor* 7.5'
Where to Stay
  Mountain: None
  Other: Evergreen Lodge
  Towns and Agencies: None

HIGHLIGHTS   Flooded or not, Hetch Hetchy Valley remains a beautiful place to visit. This trip to two of Hetch Hetchy's waterfalls, Tueeulala ("twee-LAH-lah") and Wapama, is also unforgettable because of its wildflowers.

HOW TO GET TO THE TRAILHEAD   The reference point for drives in the Hetch Hetchy district is its one lodging, Evergreen Lodge. To find Evergreen Lodge, take State Route 120 toward Yosemite's Big Oak Flat entrance station. Your goal is the junction of State Route 120 and the Evergreen Road. This junction is outside of Yosemite's boundary, about a mile north of the Big Oak Flat entrance station. (You've overshot this junction if you get to Big Oak Flat entrance station while eastbound or go more than a mile west of the entrance station while westbound.) Follow Evergreen Road east and then north about 6.6 miles to Evergreen Lodge.

From Evergreen Lodge, follow Evergreen Road north to the junction with Hetch Hetchy Road by Camp Mather, which is private. Bear right on Hetch Hetchy Road to the boundary of Yosemite National Park and Mather Ranger Station,

Tueeulala and Wapama Falls

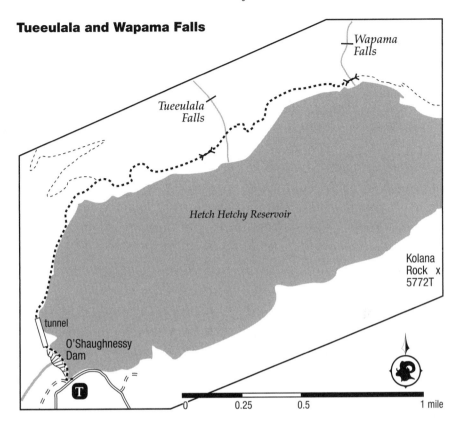

1.9 miles. Continue on this winding, narrow road down to a very large, one-way roadend loop with a day-use-only parking area at the bottom, at O'Shaughnessy Dam, 9.5 miles. There are restrooms with water a little before the parking area.

ON THE TRAIL Head north-northwest across the dam, pausing to enjoy the wonderful views over Hetch Hetchy Reservoir, especially eastward: Tueeulala and Wapama falls and Hetch Hetchy Dome to the left (north) and Kolana Rock to the right (south). Soon curve through a poorly lighted tunnel and emerge on a broad trail along the reservoir's shore. In season, hikers can already hear the falls as well as see both of them ahead. At 0.3 mile begin a gentle climb through bigleaf maple, and then dip into a ferny nook where cottonwoods crowd a tiny stream and wild grapevines drape the trees. At 0.5 mile cross a stream on a footbridge as water cascades down the rock face on your left, and the wildflower display in season is exquisite.

At 0.6 mile go right (toward the reservoir) at a junction and around a point, and soon begin descending through a meadow and then oak woodland. Ford one streamlet and then, at a little more than 1 mile, ford another stream that splashes down from the cliffs above to glide over granite slabs—a double line of rocks defines the trail here.

Beyond the slabs find the beaten path again, with Tueeulala Falls visible ahead. On this leg of the hike, some cascades on Rancheria Creek are visible in the

About Hetch Hetchy

John Muir regarded Hetch Hetchy Valley as the equal of Yosemite Valley, and old photographs tend to confirm his judgment. He was horrified when, in 1901, San Francisco proposed damming and using Hetch Hetchy as the city's reservoir. Muir and the infant Sierra Club fought the plan for many years but finally lost in 1913. Some believe a broken heart over this loss contributed to Muir's death in 1914. The reservoir here, behind O'Shaughnessy Dam (completed in 1923 and raised in 1938), drowns Hetch Hetchy Valley, from which drinking water is still piped to San Francisco.

On the other hand, Yosemite Valley sees millions of visitors and is badly shopworn and over-commercialized. Hetch Hetchy Valley, largely inaccessible because it is flooded (boating is prohibited) has remained little-known and relatively little-visited. Which valley has suffered the worse fate?

While at Hetch Hetchy, visitors may be asked by volunteer groups to sign petitions to restore the valley. Some proposals consider damming the Tuolumne farther downstream in order to provide water to San Francisco. Most restoration plans envision banning cars and commercialization from the restored valley proper in the hope of not turning the renewed Hetch Hetchy into another Yosemite Valley.

distance, next to Le Conte Point. Continuing, make an exposed, rocky climb into a bit of forest, top out at 4060 feet, and then make a stony descent to a bridged crossing of a rockfall. Pass below delicate, seasonal, 1000-foot Tueeulala Falls at a little more than 1.5 miles and 4020 feet, shortly making a rocky ford of the fall's unnamed stream.

One final, long, rocky, steep, switchbacking descent leads to the base of two-tiered, 1400-foot Wapama Falls at about 2 miles and 3880 feet, in season a raging monster of snowy foam and bright rainbows that leaves visitors drenched in seconds. Looking up Wapama Falls to see its full drop is nearly impossible because you're blinded by spray. It takes five footbridges to span the boulder-choked stream, Falls Creek, that forms Wapama Falls. The creek can be so high in early season that it's unsafe to cross the bridges. If it's safe, walk over the footbridges and back to take in the full spectacle.

Retrace your steps.

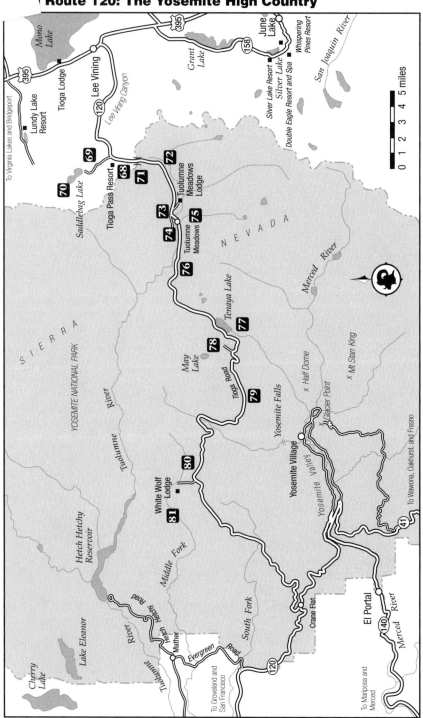

Note: Virginia Lakes Resort is shown on map on p. 86.

CHAPTER 7

State Route 120: The Yosemite High Country

Yosemite National Park's most famous scenery may lie in Yosemite Valley (Chapter 6), but its grandest scenery is along State Route 120, the Tioga Road. The road crosses the Sierra Crest, topping out at 9945-foot Tioga Pass. Granite peaks, glacier-carved lake basins, mine ruins, fabulous Valley views from one of Yosemite's famed granite domes: They're all along the Tioga Road.

Some of the best hikes included in this chapter are just east of the park's boundary in an area that should have been part of the park but instead was left out to satisfy mining interests. Mining is what first brought people to the Tioga Pass region. Because the region is a contact zone (see Trip 15), prospectors expected to find precious ores way up here. (On these next hikes, you'll visit the ruins of some of these ventures.) Alas, there are no precious ores along the Tioga Road, but there are riches aplenty in these satisfying hikes, in order from east to west off the Tioga Road.

Recommended Maps

In addition to those listed in the trip write-ups, your library of maps should include the following. Get the latest edition/revision you can find. They're widely available, certainly at any of the local ranger stations.

- *Yosemite National Park. No. 206.* Trails Illustrated/National Geographic.
- *Yosemite National Park and Vicinity.* Wilderness Press.
- *Yosemite National Park Recreation Map* and *Yosemite High Country Trail Map.* Tom Harrison Maps.
- *Guide to Yosemite National Park.* Automobile Club of Southern California.
- *Hoover Wilderness Region Trail Map.* Tom Harrison Maps.

Individual Lodgings

Name	Nearest Community	Type	Facilities	Price Range	Contact Information	Website and Email Address
Double Eagle Resort and Spa	June Lake	Other	Cabins, rooms	$$–$$$	P.O. Box 736 June Lake, CA 93529 Phone: 760-648-7004	www.doubleeagle.com cblack@doubleagle.com
Lundy Lake Resort	Lee Vining	Mountain	Cabins, trailers	$	P.O. Box 550 Lee Vining, CA 93541 Phone: 626-309-0415	None
Silver Lake Resort	June Lake	Other	Cabins	$$–$$$	P.O. Box 116 June Lake, CA 93529 Phone: 760-648-7525	www.silverlakeresort.net
Tioga Lodge	Lee Vining	Other	Rooms, cabins	$–$$	P.O. Box 580 Lee Vining, CA 93541 Phone: 760-647-6423 Fax: 760-647-6074	www.tiogalodge.com lodging@tiogalodge.com
Tioga Pass Resort	Lee Vining	Other	Cabins, rooms	$$–$$$	P.O. Box 7 Lee Vining, CA 93541	www.tiogapassresort.com reservations@tiogapassresort.com
Tuolumne Meadows Lodge	Lee Vining	Mountain	Tent cabins	$	P.O. Box 578 Yosemite National Park, CA 95389 Phone: 559-253-5635	www.yosemitepark.com/Accommodations_TuolumneMeadowsLodge.aspx
Virginia Lakes Resort	Lee Vining and Bridgeport	Mountain	Cabins	$–$$$	HC 62, Box 1065 Bridgeport, CA 93517 Phone and Fax: 760-647-6484	www.virginialakesresort.com
Whispering Pines Resort	June Lake	Other	Rooms, cabins	$–$$$	18 Nevada St. June Lake, CA 93529 Phone (in CA): 800-648-7762 Phone (outside CA): 760-872-6828 Fax: 760-748-7589	www.discoverwhisperingpines.com
White Wolf Lodge	Yosemite Village	Mountain	Cabins, tent cabins	$–$$	P.O. Box 578 Yosemite National Park, CA 95389 Phone: 559-253-5635	www.yosemitepark.com/Accommodations_WhiteWolfLodge_LodgingDetails.aspx

Note: Several lodgings, towns, and agencies near State Route 120 are also listed in the previous chapters on the east and west sides of the southern Sierra.

Towns and Agencies

Name	Nearest Community	Type	Contact Information	Website and Email Address
June Lake Chamber of Commerce	June Lake	Community	P.O. Box 2 June Lake, CA 93529 Phone: 760-648-7584	www.junelakechamber.org
Lee Vining Chamber of Commerce	Lee Vining	Community	Phone: 760-647-6629	www.leevining.com info@leevining.com

68 Bennettville Site and Lakes

Place	Total Distance	Elevation	Difficulty Level	Type
Trailhead		9520		
Bennettville site	1.5	9800	E	O&B
Shell Lake	2	9842	E	O&B
Fantail Lake	3.3–3.75	9891	M	O&B

Best Time Early July–mid-October

Topos *Tioga Pass, Mount Dana 7.5'*

Where to Stay

Mountain: Lundy Lake Resort, Tuolumne Meadows Lodge, Virginia Lakes Resort

Other: Double Eagle Resort and Spa, Silver Lake Resort, Tioga Lodge, Tioga Pass Resort, Whispering Pines Resort

Towns and Agencies: June Lake Chamber of Commerce, Lee Vining Chamber of Commerce

HIGHLIGHTS Near Tioga Pass, the picturesque remains of the 19th-century mining town of Bennettville will have shutterbugs scrambling to record the mellow colors and striking terrain. Beyond, a chain of pretty lakes leads into a magnificent cirque in Hall Research Natural Area, between Yosemite and Hoover Wilderness.

HOW TO GET TO THE TRAILHEAD Only 2.2 miles east of Tioga Pass and just past Tioga Pass Resort is a junction with a road going north to Saddlebag Lake. (The turnoff is between Tioga Pass to the west and Ellery Lake to the east.) Turn north here and almost immediately turn left into the parking area next to the entrance to Junction Campground, 2.3 miles from Tioga Pass. The trailhead is inside the campground, which has restroom facilities.

ON THE TRAIL Pause at the parking area to read the story of Bennettville and the Great Sierra Mine (Trip 71) on the marker here. Then walk about 50 yards into

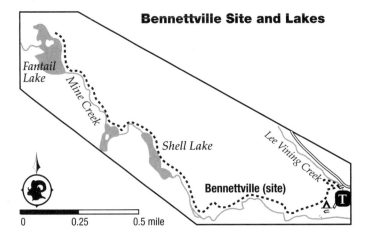

Bennettville Site and Lakes

Junction Campground, crossing Lee Vining Creek on a bridge and heading for an information sign on the right, near the streambank. The trail here is faint, but it's marked by a row of rocks.

Turn right onto the trail, briefly paralleling the creek to a Y-junction: The right trail (ahead) is a use trail along the creek. Go left (northwest) toward Bennettville, making a short, steep climb to traverse above the campground and enjoy a view of Mt. Dana's west face. Shortly climb again, this time moderately, before making a wide turn northwest above Mine Creek. Then make a switchback turn as you descend to cross an unnamed tributary of Mine Creek.

Heading southwest now, come out above Mine Creek's deep, rocky channel, where the creek makes a gooseneck and forms a handsome little waterfall. Trace the streambank, which is surprisingly flowery for such a rocky region, before skirting a small meadow, crossing a streamlet, and switchbacking up a little ridge overlooking Mine Creek. At a Y-junction, take either fork; they soon meet again.

Curving around the base of a knob, hikers presently see a tailings heap on the slopes ahead and buildings upslope on the right. Make a short, steep climb to the buildings, which are the reconstructed remains of Bennettville, at 0.75 mile and 9800 feet. The two standing buildings are the barn/bunkhouse to the south and the assay office to the north. Their soft, weathered colors against the rust-colored rock and the deep blue sky are a photographer's delight. Explore both, but watch out for soft floors and questionable stairways; look but don't damage or remove anything. Distinctive artifacts of the early days here are flat-sided, hand-wrought nails, a few rusty examples of which may be strewn about.

From Bennettville the trail heads southwest past a sign concerning the wilderness and natural areas on this trip. Now curve up and over an outcrop to another Y-junction: Two sets of tracks, neither seeming more than a use trail, diverge here, one descending to the banks of Mine Creek, the other staying higher on the outcrop. The higher trail is easier going. Take either; they converge and diverge several times. Just stay within sight of the creek and lakes.

Reach the east side of lovely Shell Lake at a little over 1 mile and 9842 feet, where beautiful White Mountain rises to the west-northwest. As the trail traces Shell Lake's shore, the valley holding these little lakes begins to open ahead, re-

Bennettville

vealing views up the valley to majestic Mount Conness. The next lake, with a tiny grassy islet, is unnamed.

Enter Hall Research Natural Area at 1.5 miles and touch the southeast shore of charming Fantail Lake at 1.6 miles and 9891 feet. It's surely the prettiest lake in this chain, and in the prettiest setting: surrounded by a flower-spangled meadow, backdropped by White Mountain and the Sierra Crest. At nearly 2 miles, a low, broad outcrop of light-colored rock on Fantail's northeast shore provides views of cascades from the crest glaciers and from higher Spuller Lake.

Return the way you came.

69 Gardisky Lake

Place	Total Distance	Elevation	Difficulty Level	Type
Trailhead		9720		
Gardisky Lake	2+	10,483	M	O&B

Best Time Early July–mid-October

Topos *Tioga Pass, Mount Dana 7.5'*; *Map & Guide to Tuolumne Meadows* by Rufus Graphics in cooperation with the Yosemite Association

Where to Stay

Mountain: Lundy Lake Resort, Tuolumne Meadows Lodge, Virginia Lakes Resort

Other: Double Eagle Resort and Spa, Silver Lake Resort, Tioga Lodge, Tioga Pass Resort, Whispering Pines Resort

Towns and Agencies: June Lake Chamber of Commerce, Lee Vining Chamber of Commerce

Gardisky Lake

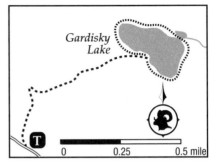

HIGHLIGHTS The short, steep climb to Gardisky Lake leads to a gem of an alpine lake in a jewel of a meadow.

HOW TO GET TO THE TRAILHEAD

Just 2.2 miles east of Tioga Pass, turn north on the road to Saddlebag Lake. Continue up the Saddlebag Lake road, which is largely unpaved and sometimes quite rough. At 3.4 miles spot a small parking lot on the left (west) side of the road; this lot is *before* Saddlebag Lake. The trailhead is across the road.

ON THE TRAIL Begin a deceptively moderate ascent northwest up a west-facing slope. The going soon becomes steeper, and the trail crosses a flower-lined creek (not on the topo or on the book's map). As the trail becomes steeper yet, short switchbacks help tame the climb. The higher the path rises, the better the views are over Lee Vining Creek to the Sierra Crest, including White Mountain and Mt. Conness.

One last steep pull ends at a bench with a flowery meadow flanked by white-bark pines. The grade eases to gentle, and soon the small ponds below Gardisky Lake come into view. The trail fades out as it approaches Gardisky. Head for the lake proper, as opposed to the ponds, by bearing slightly left to reach it at a little more than 1 mile and 10,483 feet. The lake's setting is treeless, but the broad meadow around the lake supports a wonderful flower garden. The ground is spongy with ground-squirrel burrows; bare, red-brown Tioga Peak towers over the lake's south shore; and the rusty rocks around the lakeshore are spattered with chartreuse and red lichens.

This hike ends here. Optionally, walk around the lake on an angler's trail, faint in places, which circles it. Follow the trail to the lake's east bay, which is cut off from the rest of the lake by a dense band of willows, and work your way to the lake's outlet. Gardisky's outlet plunges down the steep cliffs here, allowing hikers to stare straight down the outlet to the Tioga Road, down Lee Vining Canyon, and across Mono Basin to Mono Craters and the distant White Mountains—a spectacular view. Now work your way around the lake's other side.

Retrace your steps.

70 20 Lakes Basin

Place	Total Distance	Elevation	Difficulty Level	Type
Trailhead		10,080		
Greenstone Lake	2.5	10,120	E	O&B
Steelhead Lake	4.6	10,270	M	O&B
Hummingbird Lake	3.75+	10,230	M	O&B
Single loop, taking ferry both ways	4.5	10,360	M	Loop
Entire double loop, without ferry	7.5	10,360	S	Loop

Best Time   Early July–mid-October

Topos   *Tioga Pass, Dunderberg Peak 7.5'; Map & Guide to Tuolumne Meadows* by Rufus Graphics in cooperation with the Yosemite Association

Where to Stay

Mountain: Lundy Lake Resort, Tuolumne Meadows Lodge, Virginia Lakes Resort

Other: Double Eagle Resort and Spa, Silver Lake Resort, Tioga Lodge, Tioga Pass Resort, Whispering Pines Resort

Towns and Agencies: June Lake Chamber of Commerce, Lee Vining Chamber of Commerce

HIGHLIGHTS   Imagine a rugged, near-timberline basin set among majestic peaks and full of pretty lakes, yet so near a trailhead that you could visit nearly all those lakes on a dayhike. And what if, in spite of the rugged setting, the trail stayed on gentle to moderate terrain? Does it sound too good to be true? Well, it is true—and this is it.

HOW TO GET TO THE TRAILHEAD   Just 2.2 miles east of Tioga Pass is the junction with the road to Saddlebag Lake. Follow the road to its end at 4.8 miles, where, on the edge of huge Saddlebag Lake, it suddenly turns into a parking lot. There's a café, store, and ferry service (fee) across Saddlebag Lake at adjacent Saddlebag Lake Resort, which has restroom facilities and water. There are also restrooms in the parking lot.

OPTIONS   This trip is a double loop—a figure-eight—one loop around Saddlebag Lake and the other within 20 Lakes Basin. Taking the ferry ride would change the hiking distances by eliminating one or more of these legs: west (left) side of Saddlebag Lake, 1.25 miles, and east (right) side of Saddlebag Lake, a little less than 1.75 miles. Taking the ferry both ways can therefore save nearly 3 miles. The best part of the trip is within 20 Lakes Basin, so you won't miss much by taking the ferry. The following describes the entire route from Saddlebag Lake's west side, circling through 20 Lakes Basin from west to east (Greenstone Lake to Hummingbird Lake), and returning on Saddlebag's east side.

ON THE TRAIL Find the trailhead a few steps south of the dam, where the trail begins as an old road that dips down below the face of the dam. (Don't cross on the dam.) Climbing up on the other side, the road becomes a footpath north-northwest along Saddlebag Lake's west side. Occasional use trails doodle down to the water.

Mimulus

The trail wanders over shattered rocks in rust, brown, gray, and cream colors, and through a surprising array of flowers in season. The splendid peaks around the head of 20 Lakes Basin come into view, with granite North Peak and reddish, metamorphic Mt. Scowden particularly striking. The trail changes from rocky to dusty as it approaches the lake's head at a little over a mile, and then fades out as it reaches the stream that's the outlet of Greenstone Lake and an inlet of Saddlebag Lake.

Continue across the stream to pick up the trail coming from the ferry landing at Saddlebag's head. A spur trail curves a short distance around Greenstone's south shore. Greenstone Lake at 1.25 miles and 10,120 feet is very beautiful—and is a starting point for a cross-country scramble to the Conness Lakes, which is not part of this trip.

Soon the trail meets a use trail coming up from the ferry landing. Stay on the main trail, bearing west and entering Hoover Wilderness at a little more than 1.3 miles. Skirt the east end of Greenstone Lake as the route begins a gradual to moderate climb on this wide, dusty trail that was once a road to a now-defunct mine deep in the basin. Traverse above skinny, rock-rimmed Wasco Lake and an unnamed companion, crossing a divide: behind you, streams drain southeast through Saddlebag Lake and Lee Vining Creek, and ahead, streams drain north into Mill Creek through Lundy Canyon.

Now descend a little, passing Wasco's head and the ponds along its outlet, to reach lovely Steelhead Lake at a little over 2.3 miles and 10,270 feet. The stream from higher, unseen Cascade Lake spills noisily into Steelhead's southwest side. (A use trail here leads west into Cascade's basin—an optional but recommended detour.) As the trail approaches Steelhead's north end, it swings east, descends a little, veers north past tarns and a pretty lakelet on the east, and crosses Steelhead's outlet to reach a signed trail junction at 2.75 miles.

Go right, climbing steeply but briefly up a knob north of the lakelet. North of the lakelet, pass a seasonal tarn before descending through a flowery meadow past another charming lakelet. Reach islet-filled Shamrock Lake at just over 3 miles and 10,250 feet. Now climb up and over a talus slope on Shamrock's north side, and then descend a little before climbing a knob east of Shamrock. Atop the

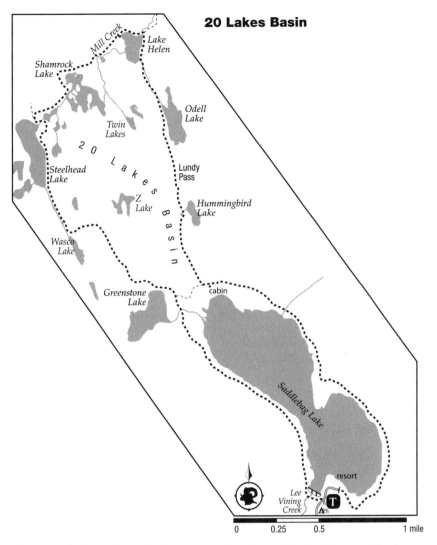

20 Lakes Basin

knob, the trail may be indistinct—rows of rocks and ducks help—as it leads to an overlook of beautiful Lake Helen, Lundy Canyon, and Great Basin peaks far to the east. The meadow south of Lake Helen is a gem. On the east side of Lake Helen, note the return trail.

Keep your eyes peeled here. The route to Lake Helen from this overlook curves right (northeast) and descends the knob's north face—look for more rows of rocks—rather than swinging left (east) onto the obvious slopes above Lake Helen. Descend short, rocky switchbacks to the knob's base, and then continue down an obvious path past the lovely cascades and ponds southwest of Lake Helen. The stony trail bobs over a couple of rocky ridgelets to skirt the lake's northwest bay, touching down at last at Lake Helen's outlet at 4 miles and 10,107 feet.

Ford the outlet to find a junction: Left (northeast) heads to Lundy Canyon, and right (south) goes to Odell Lake and back to Saddlebag Lake. There are lovely views over Lundy Canyon and its waterfalls about five minutes down the left-hand fork. But the route for this hike lies on the right-hand fork, which begins with a short, steep climb to circumvent a low cliff. Trace the east shore of Lake Helen on a rocky path before climbing moderately southeast up a rocky draw through which Odell Lake's outlet flows into Lake Helen. In season, there is a fine flower display along this little stream.

The climb tops out above handsome Odell Lake at 4.75 miles and 10,267 feet. Stay above the lake as the path climbs gradually to a high point just south of Odell. This high point is unsigned Lundy Pass at 10,320 feet, where there are fine views of the surrounding peaks. Now begin a gradual descent to Saddlebag Lake, crossing the outlet of little Hummingbird Lake at just over 5 miles and 10,230 feet—veer left (east) up the tiny stream for a few steps to visit Hummingbird.

At nearly 5.3 miles, leave Hoover Wilderness, and at almost 5.75 miles reach a junction: To the right (west) is a spur that meets the main trail near Greenstone Lake; ahead is a use trail to the ferry landing; and the left (east) fork traverses Saddlebag Lake's east side.

For this trip, turn left into forest cover and pass a private cabin at 5.6 miles—don't disturb the resident(s). On an old road above the lakeshore, stroll through an open lodgepole forest, climbing a little on a gradual grade. The forest vanishes as the trail crosses above the peninsula that juts south into the lake. Runoff on the steep slopes above the lake supports long, narrow, flowery meadows, and there are fine over-the-shoulder views back into 20 Lakes Basin.

Trees reappear near the south end of the lake, and signs warn hikers out of the meadow below the trail: WILDLIFE HABITAT AREA . . . CLOSED TO FOOT TRAFFIC. The old road curves around the meadow, rising slightly to a gate that separates the trail from the parking lot where, at nearly 7.5 miles, the loop ends by the restrooms.

71 Gaylor Lakes and Great Sierra Mine Ruins

Place	Total Distance	Elevation	Difficulty Level	Type
Trailhead		9943		
Middle Gaylor Lake	2+	10,334	M U	O&B
Upper Gaylor Lake	3.3	10,510	M U	O&B
Great Sierra Mine ruins	4	10,760+	S U	O&B

Best Time   Early July–mid-October

Topos   *Tioga Pass* 7.5'; *Map & Guide to Tuolumne Meadows* by Rufus Graphics in cooperation with the Yosemite Association

Where to Stay

Mountain: Lundy Lake Resort, Tuolumne Meadows Lodge, Virginia Lakes Resort

Other: Double Eagle Resort and Spa, Silver Lake Resort, Tioga Lodge, Tioga Pass Resort, Whispering Pines Resort

Towns and Agencies: June Lake Chamber of Commerce, Lee Vining Chamber of Commerce

HIGHLIGHTS The steep initial climb leads to two lovely alpine lakes, and the sight of Yosemite's Cathedral Range reflected in middle Gaylor Lake on a peaceful morning is guaranteed to stop hikers in their tracks. Beyond upper Gaylor Lake, the ruins of the Great Sierra mine beckon, and views from the mine are spectacular.

HOW TO GET TO THE TRAILHEAD This trailhead is right at 9945-foot Tioga Pass on State Route 120 (Tioga Road). The parking lot is on the north side of the road immediately west of Yosemite National Park's entrance station and therefore just inside the park.

ON THE TRAIL Head steeply northwest up a multi-rutted trail through a mix of forest and meadow. A little beyond 0.3 mile step across a seasonal trickle and traverse a sloping meadow. The rocky-dusty trail gradually inches north as it continues its steep climb. At a little over 0.75 mile, it emerges on an open saddle at 10,540 feet with fabulous views: to the north, the gray rock of Gaylor Peak; to the east, Mts. Dana and Gibbs soar above blue ponds in Dana Meadows; and to the south and southeast, rounded Mammoth Peak and the jagged Kuna Crest pierce the sky. Just a few steps farther north, below the saddle, lies big, blue middle Gaylor Lake—it seems as if you could take a running jump into it—and the Cathedral Range, with Cathedral Peak easily identifiable, to the south.

About 50 feet below the saddle on its north side, a use trail branches left and this trip bears right (north-northwest) to complete a steep, rocky, loose descent to the shore of middle Gaylor Lake at a little over 1 mile and 10,334 feet. At 1.25 miles step across the stream linking middle and upper Gaylor lakes and reach a junction: left on a use trail around middle Gaylor Lake, right (north) to upper Gaylor Lake. Turn right to follow the linking stream gradually up a broad, flower-sprinkled alpine meadow strewn with glacial erratics. Following this path and hopping over tributary streams in the meadow, reach the shore of shimmering upper Gaylor Lake at nearly 1.6 miles and 10,510 feet. The lake is flanked by narrow meadows and cupped in rocky knolls, graced by only a scattering of stunted trees. Graceful

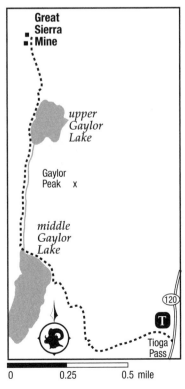

Gaylor Lakes and Great Sierra Mine Ruins

Great Sierra Mine

upper Gaylor Lake

Gaylor Peak x

middle Gaylor Lake

120

Tioga Pass

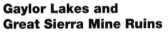

0   0.25   0.5 mile

Around Upper Gaylor Lake

While this hike turns right to the mine ruins, adventurous hikers may want to follow the use trail around to the low point on the northeast side of the lake, where they can work their way cross-country up a shallow draw and past a couple of seasonal tarns to an eye-popping overlook of Tioga and Ellery lakes, State Route 120, Tioga Peak on the Tioga Crest, Lee Vining Peak, and Mts. Dana and Gibbs.

Gaylor Peak, with a permanent snowfield low on its north face, rises abruptly from the lake's south shore.

The stony trail continues along upper Gaylor Lake's west shore to an un-mapped runoff stream from a permanent snowfield high in a steep draw north of the lake. Avoid a use trail that tempts visitors to head up the draw on the draw's west (nearer) side but that soon peters out. Just over (east of) the runoff stream, find an indistinct junction: right (north) up the draw to the ruins of the Great Sierra Mine, left on a use trail to continue circling the lake.

Meanwhile, back on this hike's route, turn north up the steep draw for 0.3 mile more of very steep climbing to a ruined stone building with yard-thick, un-mortared walls and a still-standing chimney. This is one of several ruined structures left by the unsuccessful Great Sierra Mine (also called the Tioga Mine) at 2 miles and 10,760 feet, most of whose workers lived in Bennettville (unseen and far below and visited in Trip 68). There are more ruins scattered over the slopes above this first, most impressive ruin. Walk around to explore them all, but watch out for the vertical mineshafts. There may be no precious ores here, but it is an El Dorado of Sierra views: The view over upper Gaylor Lake, Gaylor Peak, and middle Gaylor Lake and of the Sierra peaks beyond is breathtaking.

Retrace your steps.

72 Summit and Spillway Lakes

Place	Total Distance	Elevation	Difficulty Level	Type
Trailhead		9689		
Mono Pass and Summit Lake	7	10,604	S	O&B
Spillway Lake	7+	10,450	S	O&B
Entire trip	8.5	10,640	S	O&B

Best Time   Early July–mid-October

Topos   *Tioga Pass, Mount Dana, Koip Peak 7.5'*

Where to Stay

Mountain: Lundy Lake Resort, Tuolumne Meadows Lodge, Virginia Lakes Resort

Other: Double Eagle Resort and Spa, Silver Lake Resort, Tioga Lodge, Tioga Pass Resort, Whispering Pines Resort

Towns and Agencies: June Lake Chamber of Commerce, Lee Vining Chamber of Commerce

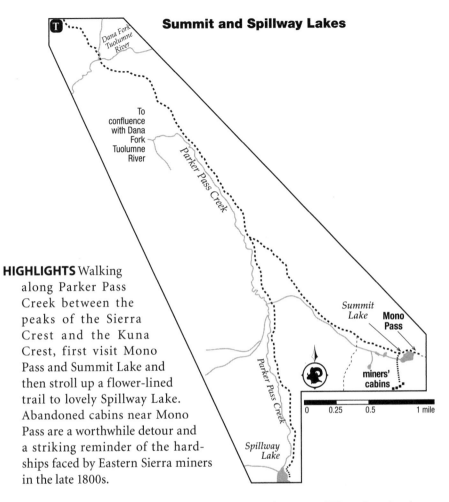

Summit and Spillway Lakes

HIGHLIGHTS Walking along Parker Pass Creek between the peaks of the Sierra Crest and the Kuna Crest, first visit Mono Pass and Summit Lake and then stroll up a flower-lined trail to lovely Spillway Lake. Abandoned cabins near Mono Pass are a worthwhile detour and a striking reminder of the hardships faced by Eastern Sierra miners in the late 1800s.

HOW TO GET TO THE TRAILHEAD   About 1.5 miles west of Tioga Pass is a large turnout and parking area (with a restroom) on the south side of the road, marked as the Mono Pass Trailhead. (The trailhead lies between Tioga Pass on the east and Tuolumne Meadows on the west.)

ON THE TRAIL   Pick up the trail from the parking lot and head south-southeast gradually downhill on an old road now closed to vehicles, soon leaving moderate to dense forest behind for a meadow in the shadows of Mts. Dana and Gibbs. Forest and meadow alternate as the track reaches the Dana Fork of the Tuolumne River. Just before the river, a footpath branches left and that's the track to take. Soon reach the river and cross two branches of it. Climb a low ridge, veering east, and then descend to skirt another meadow before ascending the next ridge.

   A little beyond 1 mile, there's a beautiful view of Mt. Gibbs over the creek below to the southwest, Parker Pass Creek. A few more steps lead to a ruined cabin left of the trail and then to a large clearing with a tremendous view south-southeast of the Kuna Crest. The trail begins a long, gradual climb, and a little beyond

Mono Pass Trail and Bloody Canyon

This trip officially stops at Summit Lake, but there are better eastward views available a little over 0.3 mile more down the Mono Pass Trail. From there, hikers can take in Mono Lake and the otherworldly Mono Craters. This detour gives hikers a better appreciation of the jagged walls and sharp, reddish hornfels rock that make up this canyon. It was named Bloody Canyon because those rocks cut the legs of horses and mules traveling the canyon, causing bloody splatters. The shrinkage of Mono Lake due to Los Angeles's water diversions is very evident from this viewpoint.

1.75 miles fords a tributary of Parker Pass Creek just before reaching a junction. Here, the options are left (southeast) to Mono Pass or right (south) to Spillway Lake. If you must choose, the visit to Mono Pass, uninteresting Summit Lake, and the miners' cabins offers better views and a tangible slice of local history, but Spillway Lake is certainly the more beautiful spot.

Arbitrarily, this trip goes left to Mono Pass to find that the trail grows rockier as the climb turns from moderate to steep and the forest closes in. Patches of flowers brighten open spots on the slopes, and the climb eases as the path crosses a talus slope below a dark outcrop. At 2.75 miles, with a large meadow apparent downslope on the right, pass a collapsed cabin and leave the forest behind. Skirt the large meadow, which is surrounded by peaks: Mt. Gibbs immediately on the left; Mt. Lewis ahead (southeast); and Peaks 12060, 12664, and 12462 to the south. At an unmarked junction a little shy of 3.25 miles, the trail to Parker Pass diverges right (south) while this trip goes left (southeast) for Mono Pass.

At the next junction, bypass a use trail branching right (south) just above a little pond and stay on the main trail (left, east-southeast) to reach Mono Pass and Summit Lake at 3.25 miles and 10,604 feet on the Yosemite National Park-Ansel Adams Wilderness boundary. From Mono Pass, the Mono Pass Trail winds down Bloody Canyon past Upper and Lower Sardine Lakes to Walker Lake.

Parker Pass Creek

Backtrack to the junction west of Mono Pass with the use trail above a little pond. Take this trail left (south) across the meadow and ascend a small ridge to find a cluster of well-preserved but long-abandoned miners' cabins at 3.5 miles and 10,640 feet. They are remains of the Ella Bloss Mine—one more Eastern Sierra non-bonanza, according to *Mammoth Lakes Sierra*. Views of Mt. Gibbs from the cabins' doorways are thrilling sights for today's hikers who have cozy rooms to return to by car, but chilling reminders of how hard and lonely life must have been in this remote, barren, windswept landscape in the late 1870s and early 1880s.

Retrace your steps to the Mono Pass Trail from here and turn left, now at 3.75 miles total, back to the junction with the trail to Spillway Lake at 4.5 miles total. Turn left (south) to Spillway Lake and gradually ascend the long meadow that Parker Pass Creek nourishes, occasionally fording seasonal tributaries. There are excellent views north to Gaylor Peak and the Sierra and Tioga crests, over your shoulder.

At 5.5 miles the trail pulls alongside noisy cascades on Parker Pass Creek. Soon, hemmed in by willows, the trail gets a bit steeper as it climbs toward a great open bowl below the three 12,000-foot peaks noted earlier. Reach Spillway Lake at nearly 6 miles and 10,450 feet, splendidly set below the peaks and ringed with flower-spangled meadows.

The scenery ahead to the north when leaving Spillway Lake almost makes up for having to retrace your steps to the trailhead, for a total of 8.5 wonderful miles for the whole trip.

73 Dog Lake and Dog Dome

Place	Total Distance	Elevation	Difficulty Level	Type
Trailhead		8584		
Dog Lake	2.5	9170	E	O&B
Entire semiloop	3.6	9300	M	Semi

Best Time   Early July–mid-October

Topos   *Tioga Pass* 7.5'; *Map & Guide to Tuolumne Meadows* by Rufus Graphics in cooperation with the Yosemite Association

Where to Stay

Mountain: Lundy Lake Resort, Tuolumne Meadows Lodge, Virginia Lakes Resort

Other: Double Eagle Resort and Spa, Silver Lake Resort, Tioga Lodge, Tioga Pass Resort, Whispering Pines Resort

Towns and Agencies: June Lake Chamber of Commerce, Lee Vining Chamber of Commerce

HIGHLIGHTS From the east edge of exquisite Tuolumne Meadows, at the foot of awe-inspiring Lembert Dome, follow trails to pretty Dog Lake and then to the back sides of Lembert Dome and its unnamed neighboring dome to the north,

Dog Lake, Dog Dome, and Tuolumne Meadows Loop

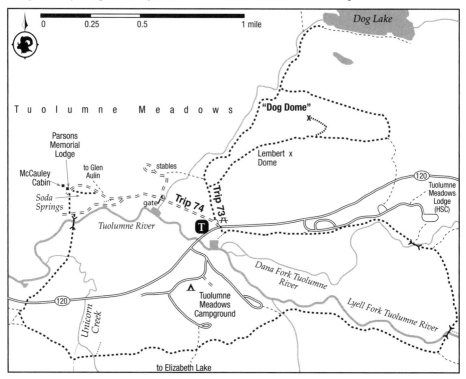

unofficially known as "Dog Dome." A scramble onto Dog Dome's summit offers panoramic views over Tuolumne Meadows; bouldering skills are helpful.

HOW TO GET TO THE TRAILHEAD Just 7 miles southwest of Tioga Pass is a turnoff signed for Lembert Dome and Soda Springs, just before the highway crosses the Tuolumne River. Turn northwest into a large parking area, which has restrooms and picnic tables, on the north side of the road. If the lot is full, as it often is by midday, look for parking farther along the spur road. A modest store, a snack shop, and a gas station(all seasonal) are a little farther west on the highway.

ON THE TRAIL From the restrooms, follow the trail northwest through spindly lodgepole, skirting the base of massive Lembert Dome. The trail is broad and sandy at first and then crosses granite slabs between parallel rows of rocks. A few steps beyond the slabs, reach a junction. The right fork is the return trail for this trip.

Take the left fork, beginning a moderate climb and bypassing a spur trail on the left signed for stable parking. Continue ahead (right) and in a few steps bypass yet another spur (unmapped) to the stables on the left. Continue on the main trail under Lembert Dome's sheer west face and then below a low dome north of Lembert, which is Dog Dome.

The trail becomes very steep and rough as it ascends a forested draw to the bench on which Dog Lake sits. Dog Lake's outlet stream splashes down the draw on the left. The grade eases around 0.75 mile, just below the bench, and at nearly 1 mile the path reaches another junction. The right (southeast) trail heads to Lembert Dome, parking for Dog Lake, and Tuolumne Meadows Lodge, but you go left to Dog Lake.

At 1 mile reach another junction: Left (north) heads to Young Lakes. Head right (northeast) to gain your first view of big, blue Dog Lake at just under 1.25 miles and 9170 feet, where the trail curves right and down to the lakeshore. As lovely as the lake is, the sight of the Sierra Crest beyond the lake's east end is its most striking feature. Walking around the lake is highly recommended.

Reluctantly leaving Dog Lake, return to the next-to-last junction passed on the way to Dog Lake, the one at nearly 1 mile. Pause to consider whether the ascent of Dog Dome's back (east) side and the subsequent steep descent between the domes, which may require a little bouldering, is for you. If not, retrace your steps to the Lembert Dome parking area from here.

Otherwise, to continue, turn left to Lembert Dome at 1.5 miles total. Pass a seasonal pond tucked hard under Dog Dome's north face while ascending gradually, presently swinging south to top out at nearly 2 miles on a forested ridge on the east side of both domes, which are all but invisible through the trees. From here the main trail begins descending and almost immediately reaches a junction; the left trail heads to parking for Dog Lake (your car is at Lembert Dome parking).

Turn right toward the domes, and follow the track west nearly 0.5 mile to a saddle between Lembert and Dog domes at almost 3 miles. Lembert Dome's summit, massive and steep, is on your left; Dog Dome's flatter, easier summit is on the right. From here, it's a short cross-country stroll onto Dog Dome's summit at 9400-plus feet following the route of your choice (the mileage for this final ascent isn't included in distances given herein). From the summit there are breathtaking views over Tuolumne Meadows to the west, into Yosemite's backcountry to the north, of the Sierra Crest to the east, and of the Cathedral Range to the south, with only Lembert Dome in the way. (Bouldering-savvy hikers may also wish to tackle Lembert Dome.)

Back on the saddle between the domes, continue west and shortly begin a very steep descent on a beaten track between the domes, along which a low rock ledge may call for a little boulder-scrambling—nothing serious. This track is a return trail for those who have climbed the difficult Class-5 routes on the faces of Lembert and Dog domes. Cross an unmapped seasonal stream draining the area between the domes on the way down.

At the bottom, close the loop part of this trip at 3.5 miles at the junction just beyond the granite slabs. Turn left and retrace your steps to the parking area at 3.6 miles.

74 Tuolumne Meadows Loop

Place	Total Distance	Elevation	Difficulty Level	Type
Trailhead		8584		˙
Entire loop	4.6	8740	M	Loop

Best Time   Late May–mid-October

Topos   *Tioga Pass, Vogelsang Peak 7.5'; Map & Guide to Tuolumne Meadows* by Rufus Graphics in cooperation with the Yosemite Association

See map on page 210

Where to Stay

Mountain: Lundy Lake Resort, Tuolumne Meadows Lodge, Virginia Lakes Resort

Other: Double Eagle Resort and Spa, Silver Lake Resort, Tioga Lodge, Tioga Pass Resort, Whispering Pines Resort

Towns and Agencies: June Lake Chamber of Commerce, Lee Vining Chamber of Commerce

HIGHLIGHTS   Maybe steep climbs to alpine lakes or airy scrambles onto granite domes just aren't your thing. But nearly everyone will find strolling through beautiful Tuolumne Meadows and along the tumbling Tuolumne River to be richly rewarding.

HOW TO GET TO THE TRAILHEAD   Just 7 miles southwest of Tioga Pass is a turn-off signed for Lembert Dome and Soda Springs, just before the highway crosses the Tuolumne River. Turn northwest into a large parking area, with restrooms and picnic tables. If the lot is full, as it often is by midday, look for parking farther along the spur road. A modest store, a snack shop, and a gas station (all seasonal) are a little farther west on the highway.

ON THE TRAIL   From the Lembert Dome parking lot, take the dusty spur road west-northwest, avoiding the turnoff right to the stables. Beyond the gate across the spur road at 0.2 mile, continue out into Tuolumne Meadows' east edge, where Lembert Dome is back to the northeast and Unicorn and Cathedral peaks are to the southwest—not to mention the wonderful array of granite domes surrounding the meadow.

    The road curves west, and interpretive signs along the way explain the area's history and ecology. There are lots of official and unofficial trails in this very popular area, but here's an overview of this trip: In general, stroll west through Tuolumne Meadows on the *north* side of Highway 120. Then curve south to cross the Tuolumne River and the highway and work generally east through the meadow's forested edge on the *south* side of the highway, and then northwest back to Lembert Dome. To stay on course, pause to familiarize yourself with the local landmarks before setting out.

    At a Y-junction at 0.5 mile, take the signed right fork (west-southwest) slightly uphill toward Parsons Memorial Lodge and go right again at the next junction.

Lyell Fork of the Tuolumne River

At the signed junction with the trail to Glen Aulin, go left and then left again at the next junction to pass a reconstructed "cabin" with some natural soda springs bubbling up through rust-colored earth.

Meeting an old road at nearly 0.6 mile, turn left and continue toward the lodge, which once belonged to the Sierra Club and now is used for park functions. Pause to admire the lodge's stonework and the log-work of adjacent McCauley Cabin, but don't go in unless they're open for visitors. There's a restroom near McCauley Cabin.

From the front of Parsons Memorial Lodge, a trail signed VISITOR CENTER heads southeast toward the sparkling Tuolumne River. Take it downhill to meet another old road; turn left and follow it as it curves toward Lembert Dome to shortly meet a trail that crosses the river on a footbridge as it heads for the visitor center. (Routes around the Parsons Lodge area are approximated on the book's map. If you find the tangle of roads, trails, and use trails in this area confusing, it's not a problem; the lodge and the footbridge are clearly visible from the junction with the trail to Glen Aulin. Head for the lodge and then for the footbridge on whichever route pleases you.)

Go right, cross the river, and follow this trail through the meadow. Heading toward the highway, cross two streamlets that pass under the trail through culverts (the streamlets appear as one stream on the map), and then cross the highway at a little more than 1 mile to pick up the trail on the other side of the asphalt.

Here, the trail bears right (west), signed for Tuolumne Meadows Lodge—the signs actually say H S C, for "High Sierra Camp," instead of "Lodge"—seemingly in the wrong direction because that lodge is farther east, toward Tioga Pass. It's just circumventing a little obstacle. At almost 1.25 miles find a junction and take the left fork southeast toward Tuolumne Meadows Campground and Elizabeth Lake. Soon the path reaches another junction; take the left fork ahead (southeast) toward the campground.

On this leg, south of the highway, the sandy and dusty trail rolls up and down through moderate-to-sparse lodgepole with a flower-speckled understory. At 1.5 miles dip across Unicorn Creek on a footbridge and meet yet another junction; the left route goes to the campground. Go right (ahead), presently cross a pair of big runoff channels, and ramble along until, just past a third runoff channel, step across the trail from Tuolumne Meadows Campground to Elizabeth Lake. The main trail continues ahead to a junction at a little over 2.5 miles; the left (northwest) trail goes to the campground. Go ahead, toward Tuolumne Meadows Lodge, cross a creek, enter Yosemite Wilderness, and cross yet another (unmapped) creek. Look for glimpses of Lyell Fork Tuolumne River with its inviting slabs, pools, and low cascades as the track continues east, roughly paralleling the river. Use trails lead to the river's charming banks.

At a junction near 3.25 miles, it's left (northeast) over the river to Tuolumne Meadows Lodge or right (southeast) to Donohue Pass on the John Muir Trail. Go left and cross the river on a pair of footbridges—shown as a single bridge on the book's map. On the other side, curve left on the well-worn, sandy trail where a use trail leads right, farther along the riverbank. At the next junction, at a little over 3.6 miles, beside Dana Fork Tuolumne River, go left to parallel the smaller, prettily forested Dana Fork on its south bank for a few yards. Turn right to cross the fork on a footbridge to another junction, and turn left (west) here to continue paralleling the Dana Fork on its north bank, rather than going to Tuolumne Meadows Lodge.

Bypass a couple of use trails back to the lodge and then a couple of spur trails to the Dog Lake parking area at nearly 4 miles. Paralleling a service road, continue west past employee residences, the Tuolumne Meadows Ranger Station, and a parking area for people getting wilderness permits. Ignore any use trails branching left along this stretch.

The trail widens and the forest retreats as the route begins to parallel the highway. It's apparent that Tuolumne Meadows is opening up ahead, to the west. At a fork at 4.5 miles, go right to cross the highway toward prominent Lembert Dome and reach the Lembert Dome parking lot at 4.6 miles to close the loop.

75 Elizabeth Lake

Place	Total Distance	Elevation	Difficulty Level	Type
Trailhead		8680		
Elizabeth Lake	4	9487	M	O&B

Best Time   Early July–mid-October

Topos   *Vogelsang Peak* 7.5'; *Map & Guide to Tuolumne Meadows* by Rufus Graphics in cooperation with the Yosemite Association

Where to Stay

Mountain: Lundy Lake Resort, Tuolumne Meadows Lodge, Virginia Lakes Resort

Other: Double Eagle Resort and Spa, Silver Lake Resort, Tioga Lodge, Tioga Pass Resort, Whispering Pines Resort

Towns and Agencies: June Lake Chamber of Commerce, Lee Vining Chamber of Commerce

HIGHLIGHTS Elizabeth Lake's alpine setting under rugged granite peaks is a wonderful sight any time but gains added charm late in the year from dashes of fall color.

HOW TO GET TO THE TRAILHEAD

Just 7.2 miles southwest of Tioga Pass is the entrance to Tuolumne Meadows Campground. Turn south into the campground, stop at the entrance station to get permission to go to the Elizabeth Lake Trailhead, and then follow road signs toward the group-campground loop. The trailhead is off the spur road to the loop, which is the second paved turnoff left from the main campground road. Follow the spur to a gate just before the signed Horse Camp; the trailhead is here, 0.4 mile from the highway. Park in the adjacent lot. There are toilets and water available in the campground when it's open. If the campground is closed, park near the entrance and walk through the campground.

Elizabeth Lake

ON THE TRAIL Head generally south through moderate-to-dense lodgepole forest, climbing moderately up a moraine on a rocky-dusty trail, and soon reaching a junction. Go ahead (south) and continue uphill. As the forest thins near 0.6 mile, there is an over-the-shoulder glimpse of handsome peaks to the north and northwest. At a little over 1 mile cross an unmapped seasonal trickle as the path approaches a level area on the moraine. Swing a little southwest toward Unicorn Creek and ford a seasonal tributary of the creek; notice the bare slopes of Unicorn peeping through the thinning forest. Ahead glimpse the lake, but keep your eyes on the trail, which is studded with rocks and crisscrossed by thick roots.

At an unmapped junction at a little over 1.75 miles, the right fork is a use trail branching toward the lake's north end, while the official trail continues left along the lake's east side. At the next fork (also unmapped), take the official trail (the right fork) toward the lake, crossing a tributary of Unicorn Creek (the left fork is another use trail). Shortly discover pretty Elizabeth Lake at 2 miles and 9487 feet, in a dramatic cirque bounded by cliffs and Unicorn Peak to the west and south, and by Johnson Peak to the east. Use trails dart off to the lakeshore, so follow one to a welcoming log or rock.

Return the way you came.

76 Cathedral Lakes

Place	Total Distance	Elevation	Difficulty Level	Type
Trailhead		8570		
Lower Cathedral Lake	6.6	9288	S U	O&B
Upper Cathedral Lake	7	9570	S	O&B
Entire trip	7.4	9570	S	O&B

Best Time   Early July–mid-October

Topos   *Tenaya Lake 7.5'; Map & Guide to Tuolumne Meadows* by Rufus Graphics in cooperation with the Yosemite Association

Where to Stay

Mountain: Lundy Lake Resort, Tuolumne Meadows Lodge, Virginia Lakes Resort

Other: Double Eagle Resort and Spa, Silver Lake Resort, Tioga Lodge, Tioga Pass Resort, Whispering Pines Resort

Towns and Agencies: June Lake Chamber of Commerce, Lee Vining Chamber of Commerce

HIGHLIGHTS Lower Cathedral Lake, with its broad, stream-threaded meadow, is a joy to discover; upper Cathedral Lake is a gem set among sculpted peaks. Sturdy hikers will have no trouble visiting both. They're especially lovely when their shared showpiece, delicate Cathedral Peak, is reflected in the lakes' still surfaces.

HOW TO GET TO THE TRAILHEAD Just 8.3 miles southwest of Tioga Pass on State Route 120, and west of the turnoff to Tuolumne Meadows visitor center, find parking for the signed Cathedral Lakes Trailhead on either side of the road. There are restrooms and water at the nearby visitor center.

Cathedral Lakes

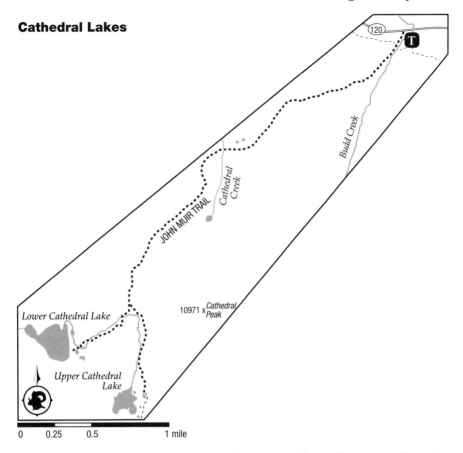

ON THE TRAIL The rocky and sandy trail leads generally southwest away from the highway, almost immediately reaching a junction. The right (west) trail leads to May Lake and Tenaya Lake, and the left (east) goes to Tuolumne Meadows Lodge. Continue ahead, now on the John Muir Trail, climbing gradually through a mixed conifer forest. The trail's grade soon eases to the point where it feels almost level. At about 1 mile, the forest thins to reveal Cathedral Peak's outliers ahead on the left and massive Medlicott Dome, glimpsed through the trees, ahead on the right.

The trail curves south through a meadowy area at a little over 1.25 miles, where the west face of an outlier of Cathedral Peak looms over you. Wind through some rocks, cross another meadow, and, coming abreast of a spring, begin a more noticeable ascent. The climb tops out at a little more than 2 miles and 9560 feet on a broad, sandy, lightly forested saddle below Cathedral Peak. Medlicott and Mariuolumne domes are on the right, Echo Peaks is ahead, and Cathedral Peak is on the left. Leaving the saddle, twine gradually down through forest to a Y-junction at 2.75 miles. The right fork leads to Lower Cathedral Lake, the left (the John Muir Trail) to Upper Cathedral Lake.

To visit Lower Cathedral Lake, head right, curving downhill, swinging through a meadowy area and across a creek and then descending steeply on a rocky track booby-trapped with tree roots. Level out on the east edge of the meadow that surrounds Lower Cathedral Lake on two sides. Multiple tracks make ruts across the meadow among the granite slabs that dot it. Ford the streams threading the meadow several times, finally reaching the granite slabs that ring Lower Cathedral Lake at nearly 3.3 miles and 9288 feet. Talk about acres of glacial polish! Optionally, go around the lake's north side to an overlook of Tenaya Lake, toward which Lower Cathedral Lake's outlet flows down a very steep channel past Pywiack Dome.

To visit Upper Cathedral Lake, follow the left fork at the junction at 2.75 miles and go generally southeast. Climb gradually on the sandy trail below the chiseled spire of Cathedral Peak, now through moderate forest, now in the open, before descending slightly toward a tarn east of Upper Cathedral Lake. Just before the tarn, a use trail darts over granite slabs to the lake proper, which sits in a beautiful, open, gently sloping bowl bounded by Cathedral, Tressider, and Echo peaks—a truly wonderful setting.

Retrace your steps.

77 Lower Sunrise Lake

Place	Total Distance	Elevation	Difficulty Level	Type
Trailhead		8170		
Lower Sunrise Lake	6.5	9166	S	O&B

Best Time   Early July–mid-October

Topos   *Tenaya Lake 7.5'; Map & Guide to Tuolumne Meadows* by Rufus Graphics in cooperation with the Yosemite Association

Where to Stay

Mountain: Tuolumne Meadows Lodge, White Wolf Lodge

Other: Tioga Pass Resort

Towns and Agencies: None

HIGHLIGHTS Views from the trail that climbs Sunrise Mountain help make up for the steep ascent, and attractive lower Sunrise Lake is worthy of hikers' efforts.

HOW TO GET TO THE TRAILHEAD Just 15.8 miles west of Tioga Pass is a signed trailhead on the south (Tenaya Lake) side of the road at a turnout with a small parking area and restroom. (The trailhead lies between Tenaya Lake on the east and Olmsted Point on the west.)

ON THE TRAIL As you face the restroom building, the trailhead is just to the left at a closed, gated road. Walk about 150 feet down the road to a marked trail on the right, turn right, walk briefly to the edge of a flowery meadow, and find a junction. Go left (east) to Sunrise Lakes, soon crossing Tenaya Lake's outlet and curving right (south) at a sign. Enter a lodgepole forest and reach another junction at 0.2 mile. Here, go right (south-southwest) to Sunrise High Sierra Camp.

Lower Sunrise Lake

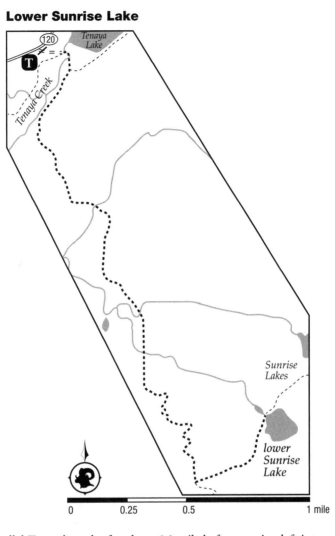

Tenaya Lake

120

T

Tenaya Creek

Sunrise Lakes

lower Sunrise Lake

| 0 | 0.25 | 0.5 | 1 mile |

Parallel Tenaya's outlet for about 0.3 mile before veering left into an area of slabs. Around 0.5 mile begin a gradual to moderate, rocky climb that leads to a viewpoint of Sunrise Mountain, Clouds Rest, and granite domes. Descend again, crossing a boulder-strewn wash, top another low rise, and then cross the multi-stranded outlet of Mildred Lake at nearly 1.25 miles. Beyond this ford, begin a moderate-to-steep ascent in forest, fording several more streams (not all on the book's map) before beginning the steepest part of the hike, a hot slog up Sunrise Mountain's slabby sides through a sparse forest. The tough climb rewards hikers with increasingly expansive views west and north, including landmarks like Tuolumne Peak and Mt. Hoffmann. The going gets steeper, and eventually mountain hemlocks close in, restricting views but offering welcome shade.

After nearly 2.5 miles, puff up to a junction on a saddle at 9270 feet in a mixed, dry forest. A use trail near this junction leads southwest about 300 feet to a spectacular view of Clouds Rest, Half Dome, Mt. Watkins, and Glacier Point. Take the left fork (east-northeast) toward Sunrise Lake. Contour along a slope, climb over a small saddle, and descend steeply to lower Sunrise Lake at 3.25 miles and 9166 feet. People throng to this pretty lake, which is set off by a beautiful exfoliating granite shoulder to the east.

Retrace your steps to the trailhead.

78 May Lake

Place	Total Distance	Elevation	Difficulty Level	Type
Trailhead		8846		
May Lake	2+	9329	E	O&B

Best Time   Early July–mid-October
Topos   *Tenaya Lake 7.5'; Map & Guide to Tuolumne Meadows* by Rufus Graphics in cooperation with the Yosemite Association
Where to Stay
   Mountain: Tuolumne Meadows Lodge, White Wolf Lodge
   Other: Tioga Pass Resort
   Towns and Agencies: None

HIGHLIGHTS   A rather easy trail offers excellent views as it leads to a lovely lake. Next to the lake, a small, easily climbed granite dome offers sweeping views.

May Lake

HOW TO GET TO THE TRAILHEAD Just 19.5 miles west of Tioga Pass on State Route 120 is the turnoff to the May Lake Trailhead. (The trailhead is between Olmsted Point on the east and Porcupine Flat on the west.) Turn right (north), through a small parking area, and drive 1.8 winding, sometimes steep miles up this one-lane road to a large parking area by a tarn. (In very early or late season, when May Lake High Sierra Camp is closed, this spur road may be closed and gated. In that case, park in the small lot at the turnoff and hike up the road.)

May Lake

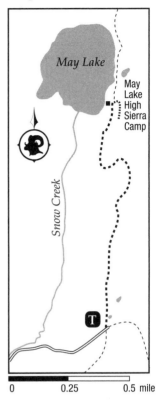

0   0.25   0.5 mile

ON THE TRAIL There are three trails leading away from this parking area: To the southeast, a trail leads back to Tenaya Lake and Sunrise High Sierra Camp; from the south end of the tarn, the May Lake Trail leads north; and a third trail is a continuation of the road. Take the wide, sandy path that follows the west shore of the tarn through a mixed conifer forest. There's a view of Mt. Hoffmann to the northwest. Presently climb a little through granite outcrops. The grade eventually eases as it traverses granite slabs, where the route is shown by rocks.

As the route ascends through boulders, spectacular views open up to the east, and hikers can plainly see the cascading outlet of Lower Cathedral Lake (Trip 76) splashing down between Pywiack Dome and Tenaya Peak on its way to Tenaya Lake. Look for the Cathedral Range to the east, Mt. Lyell far away to the southeast, and Half Dome and Liberty Cap to the south.

Switchback up the east side of a small dome, with the views getting better and better, till the path curves around the dome's west side to a tiny saddle from which the white tents of May Lake High Sierra Camp are visible below in season, by the lakeside. At a junction near a pit toilet, the right fork leads into the camp, while the left leads directly to the lake.

Reach the shore of lovely May Lake at a little more than 1 mile and 9329 feet. On the other side of the lake, the white cliffs of Mt. Hoffmann soar into a deep blue sky. When the camp is operating, noise from it may be distracting. A scramble up the low dome just east of the camp, perhaps requiring a little friction walking and maybe a handhold or two, is more a must than an option. The views from its top include not only those listed above but the Tioga Crest to the northeast, Tenaya Lake, many granite domes, and the Kuna Crest.

Retrace your steps.

79 North Dome

Place	Total Distance	Elevation	Difficulty Level	Type
Trailhead		8140		
North Dome's summit	8	7542	S U	O&B

Best Time   Early July–mid-October
Topos   *Yosemite Falls* 7.5′
Where to Stay
   Mountain: Tuolumne Meadows Lodge, White Wolf Lodge
   Other: Tioga Pass Resort
   Towns and Agencies: None

HIGHLIGHTS North Dome, whose south face is alarmingly steep when seen from Glacier Point and Yosemite Valley, has an easy, broad, walk-up north slope. At the dome's summit, views over Yosemite Valley are truly breathtaking. An optional side trip to Indian Rock includes a close-up look at a natural arch, a feature that's extremely rare in the Sierra.

HOW TO GET TO THE TRAILHEAD Just 22.1 miles west of Tioga Pass are a large turnout and a parking area on the south side of the road, an area that's often filled by midday. The turnout is marked for the Porcupine Creek Trail. (The trailhead lies between Olmsted Point on the east and Yosemite Creek on the west.)

ON THE TRAIL From the marked trailhead, go south through moderate to dense forest dominated by red fir. Descend rather steeply at first and soon meet a paved road. Temporarily pick up the road to continue the descent, as advised by a rusty sign, and follow it until it becomes blocked by fallen trees; then take an obvious footpath to avoid the deadfalls, unless they've been cleared. Near 0.5 mile ford a flower-lined stream, a tributary of Porcupine Creek, leaving the road behind.

   Shortly cross Porcupine Creek and then climb a little. In season, there is a remarkable display of flowers scattered through this forest. Resume the descent a little past 0.6 mile, ford another creek at almost 1 mile, and presently traverse a small, grassy meadow.

   After a level stretch, climb to a saddle and find a junction at just over 1.3 miles. The left (northeast) trail goes to Yosemite Valley, but this hike continues right (southwest). Almost immediately there's another junction: Take the left (southeast) fork for North Dome, soon curving south-southwest and climbing moderately through thinning forest.

   Near 1.6 miles emerge behind a ridge. About 60 feet along this ridge, you'll find a nice view over Yosemite Valley (which is itself invisible) to Sentinel Dome off Glacier Point Road. Back on the main trail, climb again into forest; openings in the canopy on the downhill side afford glimpses of the glacially sculpted ridge across the canyons of Lehamite and Indian Canyon creeks.

At a little more than 2 miles ford an unnamed, unmapped stream just below a narrow, flower-filled meadow, and then begin ascending a switchback moderately to steeply through an open to moderate forest. Near the top of this climb meet a spur trail left (north) to Indian Rock.

Otherwise, go right to stay on the main trail and continue toward North Dome. Make an undulating traverse of the ridgeline of open, hot, sandy Indian Ridge. As the trail descends gradually toward the end of Indian Ridge, reach a faint trail junction with good views of Half Dome and Mt. Watkins, views that are even better a little farther out onto the ridge-nose following a spur trail (the right fork at the faint junction). North Dome is visible from here, below and to the left. The severely acrophobic may prefer to enjoy the view here and then retrace their steps.

Continuing on the main trail—the left fork at the faint junction—descend the east side of Indian Ridge very steeply at first. The grade eases as you reenter forest, and the trail crosses over Indian Ridge, growing faint (ducks may help). After a rocky, open descent, reach a trail junction at 3.3 miles. Go left to North Dome. Use trails lead to viewpoints, but keep to the main route, heading for North Dome. Make an airy descent of the east side of the ridge, a descent that grows steep, rocky, and exposed.

North Dome

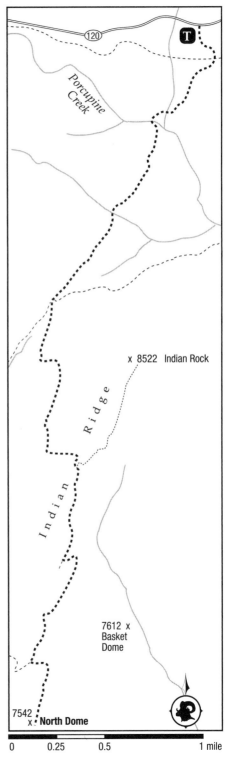

Spot the forested saddle just below and north of North Dome, but before it, hikers must negotiate perhaps the worst few feet of this trail—a steep friction walk across a section of granite slab. Reach the saddle at last and shortly find a sandy path that climbs moderately up the north side of North Dome. On North Dome's top (at 4 miles

---

Detour to Indian Rock

This optional side trip is a steep scramble up a beaten track on a sparsely timbered, sandy slope to Yosemite National Park's one and only natural arch, 8522-foot Indian Rock. It's an out-and-back detour of 0.6 miles and 402 feet, not included in the figures at the beginning of this write-up.

---

and 7542 feet), discover that the best views are a little beyond the summit, where there are some hiker-sized potholes that make good, secure spots for taking in the incredible scene. From here, there's a hawk's-eye view of the floor of Yosemite Valley, some 3500 feet below the perch. Notable points above and around the great valley include Sentinel Dome, Glacier Point, Illilouette Fall, Half Dome, Mt. Broderick and Liberty Cap, and Clouds Rest. Half Dome seems so near you could reach out and touch it.

Retrace your steps.

80 Lukens Lake

Place	Total Distance	Elevation	Difficulty Level	Type
Trailhead		7875		
Lukens Lake	4+	8230	M	O&B

Best Time   Late May–mid-October

Topos   WP *Hetch Hetchy Reservoir* 15′; *Tamarack Flat, Yosemite Falls* 7.5′

Where to Stay

Mountain: Tuolumne Meadows Lodge, White Wolf Lodge

Other: None

Towns and Agencies: None

HIGHLIGHTS   A pleasant forest stroll leads to quiet Lukens Lake where, pretty as the lake is, the big attraction is the magnificent, blooming meadow at its east end.

HOW TO GET TO THE TRAILHEAD   Just 32.3 miles west of Tioga Pass is the marked turnoff to White Wolf Lodge, on the north side of the road. The turnoff lies between Porcupine Flat on the east and Crane Flat on the west. Follow the spur road to White Wolf 1.1 more miles to parking at White Wolf Lodge, just before the entrance to White Wolf Campground, for a total of 33.4 miles. There are restrooms, water, a store, and lodging at the trailhead. (There's another trailhead to Lukens Lake on Highway 120, 2 miles east of the turnoff to White

Lukens Lake

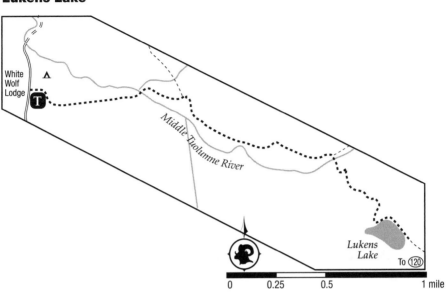

Wolf. Parking is on the opposite side of the highway from the ill-signed trailhead. See the sidebar below for this trip description.)

ON THE TRAIL Starting from White Wolf, head generally east from the signed trailhead on the east side of the parking lot, briefly skirting the campground and avoiding the many use trails by following the broader, main trail. (If starting from the alternate trailhead on 120, see the sidebar below.)

Ascend very gradually through moderate to dense lodgepole forest. The trail provides an opening in the forest and is lined with flowers taking advantage of that extra bit of sunshine. Boulders add variety to the route. At 0.5 mile descend slightly and ford Middle Tuolumne River, which is only a creek here.

Resuming the gradual ascent, soon traverse a series of meadows and at 0.6 mile reach a junction. The left (northwest) trail leads to Harden Lake, but this hike goes right (ahead, east) to Lukens Lake. The trail can be boggy and buggy here, but press on to meet Middle Tuolumne River again and parallel it for a while. The trail grade increases to moderate and leaves the meadows behind.

Veering away from the river, the trail levels out and enters another meadowy, mucky section interrupted by a sandy rise. Reach a junction at nearly 1.5 miles. The left (northwest) branch heads to Ten Lakes. Go right to ford Middle

To Lukens Lake from the Trailhead on State Route 120

Cross the highway to the signed trailhead at 8180 feet and ascend north-northeast through dense forest to a saddle at 8340 feet. Descend on a northwestward curve to the lake's east-end meadow, and brush through growth that may be more than shoulder-high to find the lake's edge at 0.6 mile. The best picnic spots are at the other, north end of the lake. Retrace your steps.

Tuolumne River again, which may be dry by late season—and beyond it find that the trail abruptly becomes moderate to steep as well as rocky as it climbs into a mixed red fir/lodgepole forest.

Soon the path skirts a pretty hillside meadow above whose head there's a rocky, forested rim. In a few more minutes, top that rim to reach little Lukens Lake at 2 miles and 8230 feet. The peaceful lake is ringed by trees except for the meadow at its east end. What a meadow that is in season—flowers, flowers, and more flowers! Follow the trail around the north side of the lake to walk through this wonderfully varied, natural garden, 2.3 miles to the far end of the meadow. The better picnic spots, however, are along the lake's north side.

Retrace your steps.

81 Harden Lake

Place	Total Distance	Elevation	Difficulty Level	Type
Trailhead		7875		
Harden Lake	4+	7484	M U	O&B

Best Time   Late May–late August

Topos   WP *Hetch Hetchy Reservoir* 15'; *Tamarack Flat, Hetch Hetchy Reservoir* 7.5'

Where to Stay

Mountain: Tuolumne Meadows Lodge, White Wolf Lodge

Other: None

Towns and Agencies: None

HIGHLIGHTS It's a pleasant, easy walk to surprisingly pretty Harden Lake, a shallow, blue pond that may dry up late in a dry year but is mighty nice when there's water in it.

HOW TO GET TO THE TRAILHEAD Just 32.3 miles west of Tioga Pass is the marked turnoff to White Wolf Lodge, on the north side of the road. The turnoff lies between Porcupine Flat on the east and Crane Flat on the west. Follow the spur road to White Wolf 1.1 miles to parking at White Wolf Lodge, just before the entrance to White Wolf Campground, for a total of 33.4 miles. There are restrooms, water, a store, and lodgings at the trailhead.

ON THE TRAIL On foot, continue north along the road you drove in on, passing the White Wolf Campground entrance and then employee residences, beyond which the road is closed to the public's cars. Circumvent a gate; just beyond, the road meets Middle Tuolumne River, which is creek-sized here. Cross the river on a bridge to continue strolling along the sandy-rocky, gradually descending road, which now swings near, now swings away from the river. Keep one eye peeled for Park Service vehicles on the road, the other eye alert for flowers dotting the roadside.

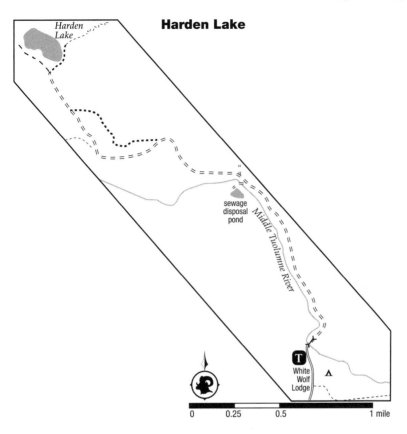

Harden Lake

Nearing 1 mile a spur road veers left to a sewage pond; stay on the main road. Beyond this fork, the road rises gradually to a junction at a little past 1 mile with a road on the right; stay left, on the main road. There are fence posts along the right side of the road on the next stretch, along with signs announcing DO NOT DRINK WATER/SEWAGE DISPOSAL AREA.

The road begins to descend again and the forest becomes quite dense. At the base of a huge red-fir tree at a little over 1.25 miles, a signed foot trail branches right (west), a shortcut as compared to staying on the road. Go right on the foot trail, climbing gradually on duff and sand, through a mixed forest with a bracken understory. At nearly 1.5 miles a use trail comes in from the right; note this for the return, to avoid going off on the use trail.

Continue west until the trail levels out and then swings north to begin a moderate descent through the forest and gradually curve west. Approaching 2 miles, meet the road again as the foot trail ends. Turn right (northwest) on the road, and soon pass a little meadow that offers a welcome break from the forest. At the next junction, at nearly 2 miles, the road continues left (northwest), while a footpath veers right (northeast) to Harden Lake.

Go right to emerge above Harden Lake at just over 2 miles and 7484 feet, where use trails lead off to its boulder-dotted shore. Harden Lake is so shallow that it may dry up late in a dry year, but with water in it, it's surprisingly pretty.

Retrace your steps.

State Route 108: Sonora Pass Country

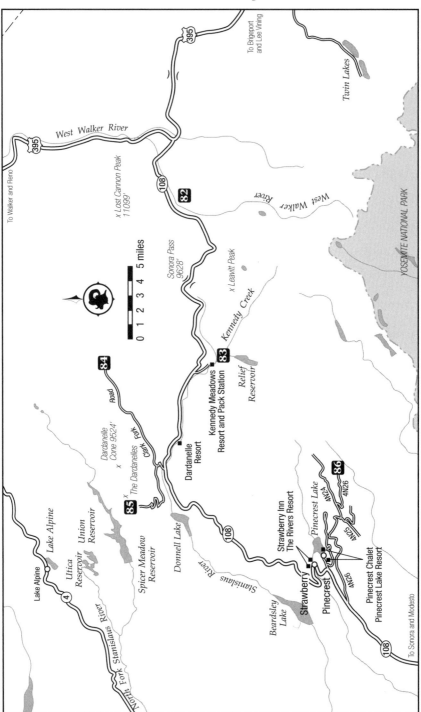

CHAPTER 8

State Route 108: Sonora Pass Country

State Route 108, the Sonora Pass Road, tops out at 9628-foot Sonora Pass. It's the first road north of State Route 120, the Tioga Road (Chapter 7) that crosses the Sierra. South of State Route 108 lie Hoover and Emigrant wildernesses. North of it lies Carson-Iceberg Wilderness. It's a land where some of the granite grandeur of the southern Sierra begins to give way to the fantastic volcanic shapes more characteristic of the northern Sierra.

Mountain men came here looking for furs, and then miners came looking for gold. Now, visitors come looking for enjoyment in this tranquil region—compared to bustling Sierra regions like Tioga Pass Road or Lake Tahoe. Visitors come away with treasure aplenty in cherished memories from these hikes.

Recommended Maps

The following maps might be helpful for this region:

- *Stanislaus National Forest.* U.S. Department of Agriculture and U.S. Forest Service.
- *Yosemite National Park Recreation Map, Hoover Wilderness Region Trail Map,* and *Emigrant Wilderness Trail Map.* Tom Harrison Maps.

Individual Lodgings

Name	Nearest Community	Type	Facilities	Price Range	Contact Information	Website and Email Address
Dardanelle Resort	Dardanelle	Other	Rooms, cabins	$–$$	Sonora Pass, Hwy. 108 Dardanelle, CA 95314 Phone: 209-965-4205	www.dardanelleresort.com dardanelleresort@aol.com
Kennedy Meadows Resort and Pack Station	Kennedy Meadows	Mountain	Cabins	$–$$	P.O. Box 4010 Sonora, CA 95370 Phone (Summer): 209-965-3911 or -3900 Phone (Winter): 209-965-3900	www.kennedymeadows.com
Pinecrest Chalet	Pinecrest	Other	Cabins	$–$$$	500 Dodge Ridge Rd. Pinecrest, CA 95364 Phone: 209-965-3276	www.pinecrestchalet.com pchalet@mlode.com
Pinecrest Lake Resort	Pinecrest	Other	Rooms, cabins	$–$$$	P.O. Box 1216 Pinecrest, CA 95364 Phone: 209-935-3411	www.pinecrestlakeresort.com frontdesk@pinecrestlakeresort.com
The Rivers Resort	Strawberry	Other	Cabins	$$–$$$	P.O. Box 81 Strawberry, CA 95375 Phone: 800-514-6777 or 209-965-3278	www.gorrr.com mweathers@mlode.com
Strawberry Inn	Strawberry	Other	Rooms	$$	P.O. Box 61 Strawberry, CA 95375 Phone: 800-965-3662 or 209-965-3662	www.strawberryinns.com sbinn@sonnet.com

Towns and Agencies

Name	Nearest Community	Type	Contact Information	Website and Email Address
Bridgeport Chamber of Commerce	Bridgeport	Community	P.O. Box 541 Bridgeport, CA 93517 Phone: 760-932-7500	www.bridgeportcalifornia.com bridgeportcalifornia@bridgeportcalifornia.com
Tuolumne County Visitors Bureau	Sonora	Visitors Bureau	P.O. Box 4020 Sonora, CA 95370 Phone: 800-446-1333 or 209-533-4420	www.thegreatunfenced.com tcvbinfo@mlode.com

82 Leavitt Meadow Loop

Place	Total Distance	Elevation	Difficulty Level	Type
Trailhead		7140		
Roosevelt and Lane lakes only	5.3	7260	M	O&B
Entire semiloop	6+	7780	S	Semi

Best Time Early July–mid-October
Topos WP *Emigrant Wilderness; Pickel Meadow* 7.5'
Where to Stay
   Mountain: Dardanelle Resort, Kennedy Meadows Resort and Pack Station
   Other: None
   Towns and Agencies: Bridgeport Chamber of Commerce

HIGHLIGHTS Broad Leavitt Meadow, ringed by impressive peaks and divided by the wide, meandering West Walker River, is one of the Sierra's prettiest meadows. The huge aspen grove on its west side puts on the region's best fall-color display. This hike begins along the meadow's east side. Visit three very charming lakes and then return high on a ridge overlooking Leavitt Meadow and its magnificent setting.

HOW TO GET TO THE TRAILHEAD Just 7.8 miles east of Sonora Pass on State Route 108, turn into Leavitt Meadows Campground. (This turnoff is west of the entrance to the U.S. Marine Corps facility at Pickel Meadow and east of Sonora Pass.) The trailhead is on the lower campground road, just above the river at a small day-use parking area. When the campground is open, there are restrooms and water. When it's closed, park off the highway and walk the short distance downhill to the trailhead.

ON THE TRAIL From the day-use parking lot in the campground, descend to the footbridge over the West Walker River; there's beautiful fall color here thanks to the aspens along the river. On the other side of the river, climb steeply to a lichen-splattered outcrop before descending slightly onto a wooded flat. Shortly reach a junction where the loop begins. For this trip, go right (west) toward the West Walker River Trail and find views of cliffs and peaks opening ahead. Descend to a junction with a mess of forks: use trails, once-official but now-closed footpaths, and horse trails. Before continuing, hikers may wish to follow a use trail down to the rocky riverbank for great views.)

Take the leftmost fork to meet the West Walker River Trail. It makes an open, undulating traverse of the lower west side of the ridge east of Leavitt Meadow. Views across the meadow and of the surrounding mountains are more than enough to make up for the rough, dusty trail. Nearing 1 mile, cross a willow-lined seep, and around 1.5 miles enter a sparse forest. Ascend to a low saddle, and then make a short, steep climb to traverse granite slabs. The grade eases as the path traverses a dry, rocky slope, climbing gradually to moderately. Leavitt Meadow is occasionally visible.

At a little over 1.75 miles reach a junction on a little saddle. For now, go right (ahead, south-southeast) to Roosevelt and Lane lakes. Continue ahead to Roosevelt and Lane lakes to an unmarked junction where the main trail goes ahead (left, south-southeast) while another trail dives downhill to the right (northwest). Staying on the main trail, climb a little into a narrow valley whose floor may be filled by seasonal ponds. Cross a low saddle and, at a little over 2 miles, find a historical marker explaining that the route was once part of the West Walker-Sonora Road, a wagon "road" of the early 1850s, so difficult it was soon abandoned.

Continue, twining steeply down into a tiny valley full of evergreens and aspens. The descent moderates as it approaches lovely Roosevelt Lake at nearly 2.5 miles and 7260 feet; the scenery southeastward over the lake is stunning. The trail winds along the west side of the little lake to reach the next gem, Lane Lake at just over 2.6 miles and 7260 feet, where the setting is also an eye-popper.

Next, return to the junction with the trail to Secret and Poore lakes and, at a little over 3.3 miles total, go right (north-northeast). Climb quickly to a junction with the trail to Poore Lake; go left (north-northwest) to Secret. Wind moderately up onto the ridge whose lower west slopes the path traversed at the start of this trip. Pass a seasonal tarn and then descend into a pretty, forested swale with a pond or two.

Beyond the swale, climb to a low saddle and reach a junction at just over 3.75 miles. Go right to pic-

Leavitt Meadow Loop

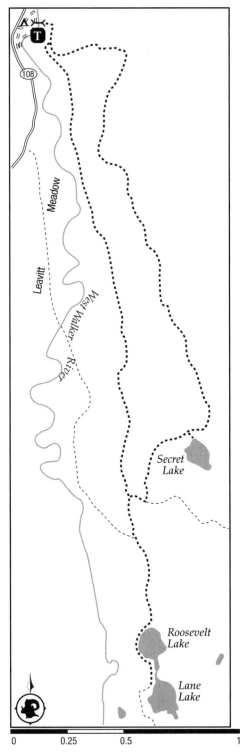

turesque Secret Lake at just over 3.75 miles and 7500 feet—another gem but, to judge from the trampled shoreline, no secret. Next, retrace your steps to the last junction, and turn right onto the main trail, which undulates past Secret Lake's north end at 4 miles.

Now begin a moderate to steep climb on the open slope above large Poore Lake, marveling at the colorful slopes to the east. Views at the 7780-foot summit of this climb are spectacular: the Sweetwater Mountains to the east, Mt. Emma to the southeast over Poore Lake, the Sierra Crest beyond Leavitt Meadow to the west, and the Sierra Nevada and the Sweetwater Mountains' meeting to the north. A few more steps lead to an overlook of the U.S. Marine Corps winter training facility at Pickel Meadow.

Continuing, the rocky trail undulates past more fine viewpoints and traverses a flat covered with sagebrush and mountain mahogany before dropping steeply through a wooded pocket, across a little meadow, down sagebrush slopes, and past a line of aspens. The trail then hooks sharply west across a meadow at nearly 5.6 miles. There's a faint, unmarked, messy junction in the middle of the iris-dotted meadow, with use trails leading north toward Millie Lake, which isn't worth the trouble, and south—avoid both. Go ahead over a low ridge, and reach another unmarked, unmapped, use-trail junction to the left. Avoid that one, too, and continue northwest to close the loop part of this hike at nearly 6 miles at the junction with the new West Walker River Trail.

Turn right to retrace your steps, just over 6 miles.

83 Relief Reservoir Overlook

Place	Total Distance	Elevation	Difficulty Level	Type
Trailhead		6320		
Relief Reservoir viewpoint	6.25	7520	S	O&B

Best Time Early July–mid-October
Topos WP *Emigrant Wilderness; Sonora Pass 7.5',* USDA/USFS *Emigrant Wilderness*
Where to Stay
   Mountain: Dardanelle Resort, Kennedy Meadows Resort and Pack Station
   Other: None
   Towns and Agencies: Tuolumne County Visitors Bureau

HIGHLIGHTS A strikingly lovely hike leads to a big, beautiful backcountry reservoir in a splendid setting.

HOW TO GET TO THE TRAILHEAD Just 9.1 miles west of Sonora Pass on State Route 108 is a marked turnoff for Kennedy Meadows on the south side of the road, east of Dardanelle Resort. Turn off here and follow the spur road 1 mile past campground turnoffs to Kennedy Meadows Resort. There's additional parking 0.5 mile back toward the highway, on the east side of the road, for overnighters. Dayhikers not staying at the resort may still park at the resort after getting the resort's permission. A fire in October 2007 destroyed the main lodge building and a few of the cabins, but the resort reopened as usual in 2008 with cabin rentals, horseback rides, and a temporary store. They expect to open their new lodge building soon. The resort has restrooms, water, a store, and lodgings, and will have food service when the lodge building reopens.

ON THE TRAIL The route begins as an old road at the south end of the resort; the road is closed to the public's vehicles beyond here. Stroll away from the resort under incense cedar and white fir and between granite cliffs on the left and the river on the right. Soon climb away from the river, uphill past a water tank and through a stock fence. Pass the signed NIGHT CAP TRAIL on the left (a rough, unmapped route to aptly named Night Cap Peak)

Relief Reservoir Overlook

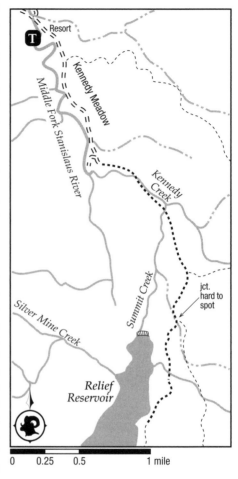

and continue ahead (southeast) to top the rise. Beyond, descend to level out at Kennedy Meadow's south lobe, with a stunning view of Leavitt Peak. In season, the meadow is a grazing allotment, and you may find cattle here along with unpleasant quantities of dung in late season.

After skirting the meadow's far side and ignoring a spur road branching to the river, head into forest to reach the signed HUCKLEBERRY TRAIL. It's this hike's route and a continuation of the old road, and so rocky that it's impassable to cars. Entering Emigrant Wilderness at a little over 0.75 mile, parallel tumbling Kennedy Creek to cross the creek at just over 1 mile on a stout footbridge. On the other side of the bridge, use trails branch right, while the main trail curves left. (Note that beyond here, the trails on the ground are considerably different from those shown on the 7.5′ topo; see one of the other maps.) A use trail merges on the right; continue ahead here, noting this junction for the return.

Soon begin climbing moderately to steeply on a wide, rocky, and dusty trail blasted out of the local rock formations. The narrow walls of Kennedy Creek's

Above Relief Reservoir

canyon close in, adding drama to this scenic ascent. Near 1.5 miles cross another stout footbridge high above the creek, which roars down the rocky canyon. At a junction at 1.5 miles, not on the book's map, the left fork appears to be a ruined, older track, while the right is more gradual, less rocky, and in better shape (they'll rejoin). Take the right fork; at 1.6 miles the tracks rejoin. Continue ahead (south-southeast) as Summit Creek comes rushing in from Relief Reservoir.

Veer left through a steep, dry, rocky slot, emerging into a sort of natural amphitheater cupped in handsome cliffs. At a little over 2 miles reach a junction with the trail to Kennedy Lake; go right (ahead) to Relief Reservoir. Ford a seasonal rill, pass the signed PG&E relief cabin, and wind moderately uphill onto a rocky, open outcrop, where a pair of tracks diverge and soon converge by an old boiler. Beyond the boiler, there's an open bench covered with sagebrush and rabbitbrush. An unsigned junction with an unmaintained, secondary trail in this area may be hard to spot; if you note it, take the right fork.

Cross a couple of boulder-filled washes and, approaching a granite outcrop on the right and a line of aspens near 3 miles, look down to the right to see Relief Reservoir's dam. A noisy creek splashes down cliffs to the east, and hikers soon ford it in the shade of white firs. An optional, 0.5-mile, out-and-back detour to the outcrop offers excellent views over the reservoir and to the peaks around it.

Pass above the line of aspens—a gloriously colorful sight in the fall—and, as the trail begins a slight descent, take advantage of several opportunities to step off it at viewpoints overlooking the water below. Particularly from a viewpoint above a peninsula at a little over 3 miles and 7520 feet, there are wide-ranging views over Relief Reservoir: south, deep into Emigrant Wilderness; north, beyond State Route 108 (invisible) and into Carson-Iceberg Wilderness.

This trip turns around here, so retrace your steps to Kennedy Meadows Resort.

84 Boulder Creek and Lake

Place	Total Distance	Elevation	Difficulty Level	Type
Trailhead		6440		
Boulder Creek	4.6+	6920	M	O&B
Boulder Lake	8.6+	8120	S	O&B

Best Time   Early July–mid-October
Topos   *Disaster Peak 7.5'*; USDA/USFS *Carson-Iceberg Wilderness*
Where to Stay
  Mountain: Dardanelle Resort, Kennedy Meadows Resort and Pack Station
  Other: The Rivers Resort, Pinecrest Chalet, Pinecrest Lake Resort, Strawberry Inn
  Towns and Agencies: Tuolumne County Visitors Bureau

HIGHLIGHTS A generally easy stroll along the pretty Clark Fork Stanislaus River—good fall color—gives way near the river's confluence with Boulder Creek to a steep, interesting ascent to likeable little Boulder Lake.

HOW TO GET TO THE TRAILHEAD Just 17.1 miles west of Sonora Pass on State Route 108 is the junction with the paved but ill-marked Clark Fork Road. The turnoff is between Dardanelle Resort on the east and Donnels Reservoir vista on the west. Turn northeast onto the Clark Fork Road; stay on this narrow, paved road past campgrounds and junctions with dirt roads, to reach the abrupt roadend at Iceberg Meadow 9.2 miles from the highway. Park off the road.

Boulder Lake

Boulder Creek and Lake

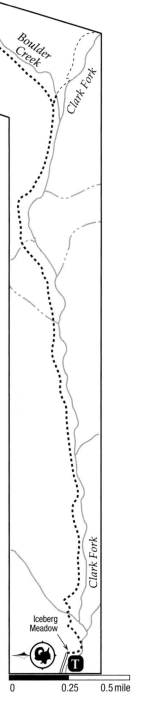

Boulder Lake

Boulder Creek

Clark Fork

ON THE TRAIL Face Iceberg Meadow; the trailhead is on the right (south) side of the road. The Clark Fork flows nearby, and the stark peak called The Iceberg rises above it. The track is quite faint as it heads across an unmapped trickle and enters Carson-Iceberg Wilderness on a duff trail. Curve between the meadow's fence and a creeklet, heading east-northeast to ford the creeklet and pass a trail sign. Then zigzag up into an area of large boulders. At the top, at a little past 0.3 mile, there's a nice view of the Iceberg and of the surrounding hills and cliffs.

Make a gradual descent to the Clark Fork's banks and enjoy a long, leisurely, near-streamside stroll through beautiful woods—good fall color. At a little over 2 miles, finally veer uphill, away from the stream, and at a little over 2.3 miles reach a junction and take the left (northeast) fork to Boulder Creek and Boulder Lake. (Those wishing to stop at the creek should scamper down the right trail fork as far as Boulder Creek's waterside a few steps below at a little over about 2.3 miles and about 6920 feet and then retrace their steps from there.)

To continue to Boulder Lake, go left (ahead) to begin a moderate to steep climb paralleling boulder-choked Boulder Creek. Veering away from the stream at 2.75 miles, the trail heads very steeply up and generally northward on switchbacks too short to show up on the book's map. At a little over 3 miles the grade eases as the trail meets the stream again and curves north toward a gap between two peaks. The soil is sandy, and the forest is open, and soon the path crosses a small meadow seasonally bright with the big yellow flowers of mule ears.

Ford the creek near a seasonal tributary to pick up duff trail in moderate forest. The trail may be very faint here. Almost immediately cross the tributary and head northeast past huge boulders on the left, roughly paralleling Boulder Creek a short distance away. Curve back to the tributary, but instead of crossing it, swing uphill alongside it, through rocks, on an indistinct track flanked

Clark Fork

Iceberg Meadow

T

0   0.25   0.5 mile

by junipers, firs, and pines. At 3.5 miles the trail curves north-northwest, back toward Boulder Creek and across the tributary. The track continues uphill and generally north toward light-colored cliffs visible through the trees.

Veer north-northwest on a chaparral-covered slope just below the cliffs, beginning a very steep, loose ascent where splashes of blue and white paint on the slope's boulders help mark the sandy trail. Multiple paths diverge and converge as the track struggles up through manzanita and mountain mahogany.

After leveling out in open forest on a narrow bench beside Boulder Creek, the trail climbs away from the bench and curves across a rocky gully. At a little over 4 miles, where an obvious use trail drops left to the creek, note a spot of paint on a boulder to the right. Keep right on the main trail. Climb steeply up the rocky track past lodgepole and juniper till it levels out on a sandy shelf. In a few more steps enter a wooded basin with Boulder Peak's impressive cliffs to the northeast. Shortly the trail reaches an unsigned junction where the main trail continues left (east) up the basin and a use trail drops right (south) to small, lodgepole-ringed Boulder Lake at a little over 4.3 miles and 8120 feet.

Return the way you came.

85 Sword Lake

Place	Total Distance	Elevation	Difficulty Level	Type
Trailhead		7180		
Sword Lake	4.75	6859	M U	O&B

Best Time   Early July–mid-October

Topos   *Spicer Meadow Reservoir* 7.5'; USDA/USFS *Carson-Iceberg Wilderness*

Where to Stay

Mountain: Dardanelle Resort, Kennedy Meadows Resort and Pack Station

Other: The Rivers Resort, Pinecrest Chalet, Pinecrest Lake Resort, Strawberry Inn

Towns and Agencies: Tuolumne County Visitors Bureau

HIGHLIGHTS   Sword Lake and the little ponds near it, set in forested knolls and separated by glacially polished granite slabs, are simply beautiful and well worth the trip.

HOW TO GET TO THE TRAILHEAD   Just 17.1 miles west of Sonora Pass on State Route 108 is the junction with the paved but ill-marked Clark Fork Road. The turnoff is between Dardanelle Resort on the east and Donnels Reservoir vista on the west. Turn northeast on Clark Fork Road and go 0.4 more miles to a junction past the second bridge; turn left onto this winding, sometimes extremely rocky and dusty dirt road. Follow it to its end at a large, dusty parking area 6.4 more miles. Get an early start; the trail is very popular, and the parking area is apt to be packed with cars by midday on a weekend.

The Dardanelles

This stunning formation is a remnant of an ancient volcanic flow down a long-vanished canyon whose walls and surrounding terrain have eroded away. That left the Dardanelles and similar features standing hundreds of feet above the rest of the present landscape. The name comes from their resemblance to similar formations along the Dardanelles, the strait between the Aegean Sea and the Sea of Marmara that separates what are now European and Asian southwestern Turkey. In ancient times, this strait was called the Hellespont.

ON THE TRAIL Head generally north into an open, mixed conifer forest with big patches of scrub. Almost immediately reach a fork. Go left on the County Line Trail to begin a very steep climb on a very dusty trail. At 0.25 mile the grade eases briefly before the trail makes an even steeper attack on the slope. Then top out, gasping, at a little over 0.3 mile and 7540 feet, and enter Carson-Iceberg Wilderness. There's a nice view over Spicer Meadow Reservoir from a rocky knoll just left of the trail.

Now begin an undulating traverse of a forested slope, skirting a small, mule-ears-splashed meadow downslope to the left. At about 0.75 mile pass through a gate in a barbed-wire fence; close the gate behind you. At 0.75 mile reach a junction and go left (north-northwest) to Sword Lake.

Ahead is a valley dotted with small aspens and willows that give it fall color. Soon begin a moderate to steep descent next to a damp meadow, crossing its little stream as the grade eases. Near 1 mile a granite outcrop offers views northwest over huge Spicer Meadow Reservoir, while a glance up and to the right reveals the "pillars" of the Dardanelles.

Continue down steeply, crossing an alder-lined fork of Dardanelles Creek and then winding through rocky knolls. Near 2 miles reach a junction and go right (north) to Sword Lake, soon passing a tiny pond. Find another junction at nearly 2.25 miles and go left, ascending slightly. Soon the

Sword Lake

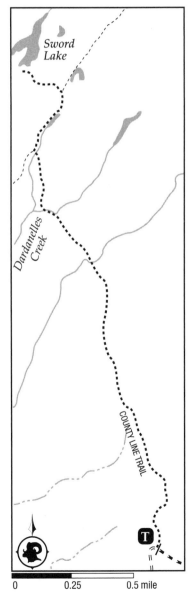

0   0.25   0.5 mile

path descends to serene, rockbound, enchanting Sword Lake at a little over 2.3 miles and 6859 feet. The fact that this charmer is very busy on weekends doesn't detract much from its beauty. Contrary to what the topo shows, there is no maintained trail to Lost Lake. To find that lake, scramble west over granite slabs, passing a couple of attractive ponds.

Return the way you came.

86 Camp Lake

Place	Total Distance	Elevation	Difficulty Level	Type
Trailhead		7152		
Camp Lake	5	7590	E	O&B

Best Time Late May–mid-October
Topos WP *Emigrant Wilderness; Pinecrest* 7.5′; USDA/USFS *Emigrant Wilderness*
Where to Stay
  Mountain: None
  Other: The Rivers Resort, Pinecrest Chalet, Pinecrest Lake Resort, Strawberry Inn
  Towns and Agencies: Tuolumne County Visitors Bureau

HIGHLIGHTS A pretty hike leads to the dramatic setting of little Camp Lake. Granite slabs south of the lake provide fun, easy scrambling and fine views.

HOW TO GET TO THE TRAILHEAD Summit Ranger Station is located at a road junction known as "the Pinecrest Y," between State Route 108 and Pinecrest Lake Road. The ranger station is easier to spot than the junction, and both are about 35.1 miles west and south of Sonora Pass, between Strawberry and Long Barn. Turn east, toward Pinecrest Lake, at the junction. Drive 0.3 mile to a junction with Dodge Ridge Road. Turn left onto Dodge Ridge Road, and go 2.9 more miles to a junction signed for the CRABTREE CAMP and GIANELLI CABIN TRAILHEADS. Turn right, toward the trailheads, and go 0.5 mile to a T-junction. Turn left to the trailheads, and drive 1.6 miles to the Bell Meadow junction. Go ahead; the pavement ends temporarily as the road passes through Aspen Meadows Pack Station. Beyond the pack station, find pavement again and continue, staying on the paved road at any junctions. The pavement ends again 1.2 miles from the Bell Meadow junction, and the road gets rough.

At 2.7 miles from the Bell Meadow junction, turn right at a junction where the road to the Gianelli Cabin Trailhead goes left. Drive another 0.5 mile to the main parking lot for Crabtree Camp, a one-night backpackers' campground, and the trailhead. The signed trailhead and its information displays are at the main parking lot's east end. Nearby there are water and restrooms.

ON THE TRAIL Head east on the duff trail and almost immediately cross Bell Creek on a stout footbridge. Just beyond the bridge, angle right (south) to climb

Camp Lake

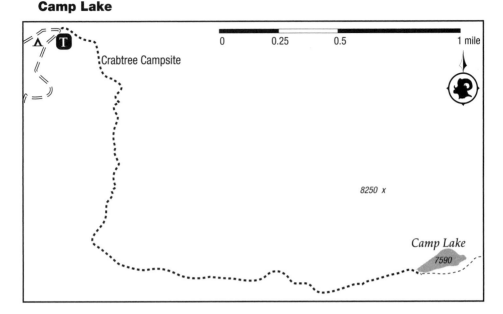

moderate to steep switchbacks before leveling out. The track passes an EMI-GRANT WILDERNESS sign early on, but the true wilderness boundary lies much farther east. Ford a couple of small streams and settle down for a long, pleasant, undulating traverse through a fir forest.

After fording another small stream, make an abrupt switchback and begin a steady southeastward climb above the stream on a steep to moderate grade. The grade eases near a small, flowery meadow. Ford the stream again and then curve east on a gradually ascending path through patchy ponderosa pine and fir, enjoying the groundsel, stickseed, lungwort (bluebells), and larkspur that seasonally brighten this stretch. Beyond a seasonal stream, find the signed CAMP LAKE/PINE VALLEY junction at 1.4 miles. Bear left (east-southeast) toward Camp Lake.

Continue the ascent to an overlook of granitic Pine Valley, far below. Next, descend a little and then resume the gradual climb through a display of showy penstemon, yarrow, and the yellow brodiaea called "pretty face." Briefly head south to skirt a large pond. Beyond, curve eastward through patchy forest punctuated by flowery meadows and striking outcrops.

After fording a small creek, reach an obscure sign probably marking Emigrant Wilderness's true boundary. Continue generally east, soon reaching the rocky southwestern tip of little Camp Lake at about 2.5 miles. This is a good stopping point; beyond, the trail climbs high above the lake before descending near, but not to, its east shore. By midsummer, Camp Lake offers cool but not icy swimming and very easy boulder-scrambling to the south.

Retrace your steps.

State Route 4: Ebbetts Pass Country

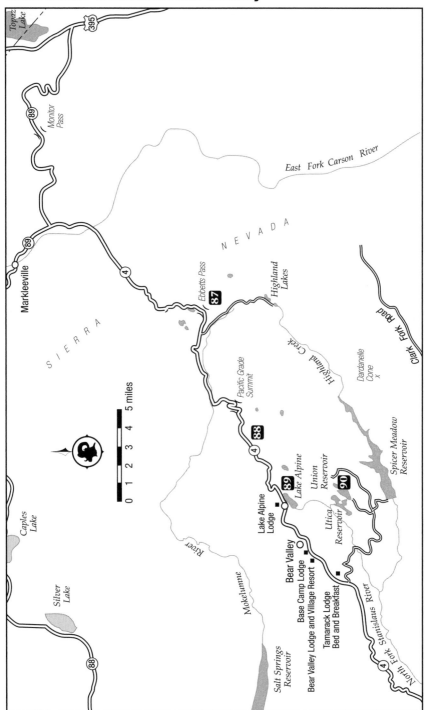

CHAPTER 9

State Route 4: Ebbetts Pass Country

S tate Route 4, the Ebbetts Pass Road, crosses the crest at 8732-foot Ebbetts Pass. This highway is the next highway north of State Route 108, the Sonora Pass Road (Chapter 8) that crosses the Sierra. Carson-Iceberg Wilderness lies south of State Route 4, and Mokelumne Wilderness lies north of it. The region is a fascinating mix of granitic and volcanic landscapes. Unlike much of State Route 108, State Route 4 isn't in a river canyon, and the scenery from the road is often breathtaking. Down in the western foothills (outside the geographical range of this book) there's a grove of giant sequoias at Calaveras Big Trees State Park, east of the little town of Arnold.

State Route 4 is a steep, one-lane, twisting road from a little west of Lake Alpine, 17 miles west of Ebbetts Pass, to about the 7000-foot marker some 11–12 miles east of Ebbetts Pass. Daunting though that road may be, once visitors learn what the region has to offer, they come back often.

The eponymous Major Ebbetts apparently thought the pass would make the perfect emigrant route across the northern Sierra, but other routes received far greater use. Happily, the most scenic part of State Route 4 remains largely undeveloped.

Recommended Maps

The only recommended map for this region is *Stanislaus National Forest,* published by the U.S. Department of Agriculture and U.S. Forest Service.

Individual Lodgings

Name	Nearest Community	Type	Facilities	Price Range	Contact Information	Website and Email Address
Base Camp Lodge	Bear Valley	Other	Rooms	$	P.O. Box 5450 Bear Valley, CA 95223 Phone: 209-753-6556	www.basecamplodge.com mail@basecamplodge.com
Bear Valley Lodge and Village Resort	Bear Valley	Other	Rooms	$–$$$	P.O. Box 5440 Bear Valley, CA 95223 Phone: 209-753-2327	www.bearvalleylodge.com info@bearvalleylodge.com
Lake Alpine Lodge	Bear Valley	Other	Cabins, tent cabins	$–$$$	*Summer:* P.O. Box 5300 Bear Valley, CA 95223 Phone: 209-753-6358 *Winter:* P.O. Box 579 Big Sur, CA 93920 Phone: 623-266-3714	www.lakealpinelodge.com info@lakealpinelodge.com
Tamarack Lodge Bed and Breakfast	Bear Valley	Other	Rooms	$–$$$	P.O. Box 5039 Bear Valley, CA 95223 Phone: 888-753-2038 or 209-753-2038	www.tamarackholiday.com innkeeper@tamarackholiday.com

Towns and Agencies

Name	Nearest Community	Type	Contact Information	Website and Email Address
Bear Valley Vacation Rentals	Bear Valley	Agency	P.O. Box 5250 Bear Valley, CA 95223 Phone: 877-897-8828 or 209-753-2334	www.bearvalleyvacationrentals.com forfun@bearvalleyrealestate.com

87 Noble Lake

Place	Total Distance	Elevation	Difficulty Level	Type
Trailhead		8732		
Flower-gardens-in-gullies	3.5–5	8400–8320	M U	O&B
Noble Lake	7.6	8870	S U	O&B

Best Time   Late May–mid-October
Topos   *Ebbetts Pass 7.5'*; USDA/USFS *Carson-Iceberg Wilderness*
Where to Stay
   Mountain: None
   Other: Base Camp Lodge, Bear Valley Lodge and Village Resort, Lake Alpine Lodge, Tamarack Lodge Bed and Breakfast
   Towns and Agencies: Bear Valley Vacation Rentals

HIGHLIGHTS This hike offers one beauty spot after another en route, while the destination that anchors the far end of the trip is just "okay." In season there are flowers galore along the trail, particularly in a series of lovely flower-gardens-in-gullies between 1.75 and 2.5 miles on the way to Noble Lake.

HOW TO GET TO THE TRAILHEAD Parking is at Ebbetts Pass, on the south side of the road, in a grassy pullout. Two trailheads, both for the Pacific Crest Trail (PCT), which crosses State Route 4 here, are a couple minutes' walk east down the road. (If the grassy pullout is full, try the PCT parking lot 0.4 mile farther east. Take the spur trail to the southbound PCT and pick up the hiking directions with the second paragraph.)

ON THE TRAIL From the pass, carefully walk downhill east on State Route 4's shoulder to the ill-marked trailheads on either side of the road. Pick up the PCT on the southeast side of the road; the marker here is a bare post. Skirt between a knoll on the right and a tiny meadow on the left; the flower display here, while modest, is attractive. Curve around the meadow's head and begin a moderate to gradual ascent with over-the-shoulder glimpses of Ebbetts Peak.

At a little over about 0.25 mile meet a spur from the PCT parking lot 0.4 mile farther east on State Route 4, coming in on the left (north). Go right (east), staying on the PCT, and soon passing the eroding edges of some ancient volcanic mudflows. At a little before 0.5 mile top out on a knob at 8860 feet in an open spot dotted with cheery yellow mule ears and with a view of Highland Peak ahead.

Now descend moderately to gradually, curving around the head of an unnamed drainage and crossing several runoff channels full of stones from the ancient mudflow above. For a while there's little to do except to enjoy a rolling traverse through patches rich with fragrant flowers and herbs (lupine, wallflower, and mugwort, among others).

Noble Lake

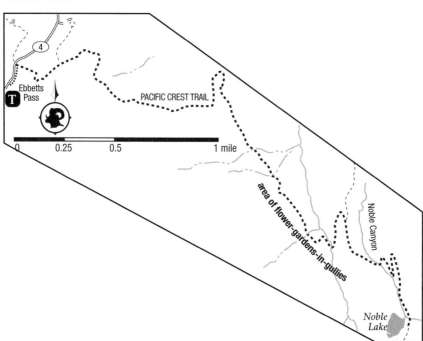

At 1 mile enter an open forest below some granite outcrops. There are some really huge mountain hemlocks as the path crosses an unmapped, intermittent stream and winds moderately up the little ridge adjacent to the stream. Near the unmapped tarn/meadow that's the source of the stream, cross the ridge and make a long northward traverse. Then curve around the ridge's nose on a gradual to moderate descent across steep, sandy, lightly forested slopes pleated by occasional runoff channels.

At 1.5 miles, as the track rounds a small prominence, enjoy a view south toward Tryon Peak and far over Noble Canyon, deep into the drainage of Noble Lake. The next leg, though hot and exposed, nevertheless puts on a brave show of flowers thanks to numerous seeps. At 1.75 miles begin crossing a series of streams, fed by springs high above the trail, that have sculpted interesting gullies out of the mudflows, gullies in which seasonally cascading water supports dazzling but seasonal flower gardens. Any of these flower-gardens-in-gullies between 1.75 and 2.5 miles makes a wonderful interim destination for those who don't care to go all the way to Noble Lake. The last garden, the low point of this hike at 8320 feet, is tucked deep into a side canyon in the mudflow walls of Noble Canyon.

After fording that canyon's stream, the trail begins a moderate-to-steep climb up a loose, open slope, leveling off a little as it rounds a small ridge. Climb again, this time gradually to moderately, gaining over-the-shoulder views north down Noble Canyon. At 2.6 miles meet a trail that goes left (north) down into Noble Canyon; go right (ahead, south-southeast), staying on the PCT. In moderate forest now, contour deep into the head of Noble Canyon until, at the canyon's head, the forest abruptly gives way to sunstruck, crumbling slopes. At nearly 3 miles ford Noble Lake's outlet and begin a series of switchbacks that rise gradually to moderately up the rough, rocky slope. The views, improve as the trail climbs, especially those of Reynolds and Raymond peaks and the peaks around Blue Lakes to the northwest (off State Route 88). These slopes erode quickly, so be aware that the trail tread may be very narrow and loose.

At a little over 3.5 miles cross an unmapped streamlet near the top of the last switchback before coming alongside the lake's meadowy outlet. After another loose, rocky stretch, squish upward through a marshy section, gain Noble Lake's bench and spy the lake to the right. Cross the outlet of the lakelet above Noble Lake, and just beyond 3.75 miles find use trails down to Noble Lake's overused shore. The lake's setting is volcanic, with no hint of the Sierra's granite grandeur, almost as if it were in another range altogether.

Retrace your steps.

88 Heiser and Bull Run Lakes

Place	Total Distance	Elevation	Difficulty Level	Type
Trailhead		8060		
Heiser Lake only	4	8340	M U	O&B
Bull Run Lake	9	8333	S U	O&B

Best Time   Early July–mid-October
Topos   *Pacific Valley, Spicer Meadow Reservoir 7.5'*; USDA/USFS *Carson-Iceberg Wilderness*
Where to Stay
Mountain: None
Other: Base Camp Lodge, Bear Valley Lodge and Village Resort, Lake Alpine Lodge, Tamarack Lodge Bed and Breakfast
Towns and Agencies: Bear Valley Vacation Rentals

HIGHLIGHTS   A beautiful, undulating trail leads from Mosquito Lake on State Route 4 to two very lovely lakes, each of which is an ample reward for the significant ups and downs required to get to it.

HOW TO GET TO THE TRAILHEAD   About 8.2 miles west of Ebbetts Pass on State Route 4 is shallow Mosquito Lake, one lake in early season and two ponds when it's drying up by late season, on the south side of the road is west of Ebbetts Pass and east of Lake Alpine. There is a small parking lot just west of the lake at the trailhead, and Mosquito Lake Campground across the highway has restrooms.

ON THE TRAIL   Head briefly south on the marked Heiser Lake Trail, almost immediately meeting a junction. The right (west) branch goes to Lake Alpine on the Emigrant Trail. Go left (south), curving around Mosquito Lake before veering south to begin a steep climb up the moraine south of the lake in moderate to sparse forest. Gaining the ridge at last, veer a few steps to the left to the ridgetop, from which there are fine views northeast to Raymond and Reynolds peaks.

Back on the main trail, begin a descent on a sandy trail and enter Carson-Iceberg Wilderness at nearly 0.5 mile. Continue, generally south-southeast, through forest relieved by a couple of small meadows and then, at a little over 0.75 mile, climb up the next moraine. From the rocky summit at 1 mile and 8360 feet, there are views of Henry and Bull Run peaks. Now make a sometimes-steep descent through a forest interrupted by beautiful granite formations. Bottom out in a forested nook with a seasonal stream near 8160 feet and soon begin climbing again.

At 1.5 miles reach the Heiser-Bull Run junction. Go left (east) to Heiser Lake, beginning a gradual to moderate ascent and topping out on another moraine, above Heiser Lake, visible through the forest to the south. A moderate to steep descent leads to a bench that holds slim, sparkling Heiser Lake at 2 miles and 8340 feet.

Return to the Heiser-Bull Run junction and, to continue to Bull Run Lake, turn left at 2.5 miles total. Heading southwest, enjoy a short, level segment in the forest before plunging steeply down a loose, open, rocky slope to a series of forested benches. The grade eases and the trail crosses a couple of intermittent streams.

Heiser and Bull Run Lakes

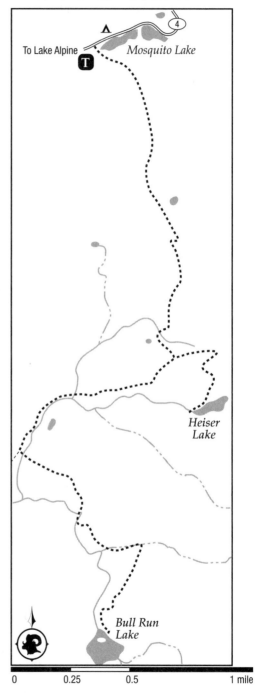

At nearly 3.25 miles, reach a junction. The right (southwest) branch returns to a different trailhead west of Mosquito Lake on State Route 4. Go left (east) to cross the boulder-choked outlet of Heiser Lake and continue a gradual descent through moderate forest, bottoming out near 7820 feet. Having crossed an unnamed intermittent stream, begin following a gradual to moderate, circuitous, rocky, sometimes-faint track through granite outcrops.

Work up the narrowing, rockbound gully around Bull Run Lake's outlet, passing a lovely tarn on the right at a little over 4 miles. At a little over 4.3 miles, meet Bull Run Lake's outlet and turn south-southeast along it. This path is so ill-maintained that it's little better than a use trail and requires some very easy friction-walking up granite slabs. Look for Bull Run Lake on the right at 4.5 miles and 8333 feet in an amphitheater of granite cliffs, ringed by forest and meadow.

Retrace your steps.

89 Duck Lake

Place	Total Distance	Elevation	Difficulty Level	Type
Trailhead		7380		
Entire semiloop	3.3+	7540	M	Semi

Best Time Early July–mid-October

Topos *Spicer Meadow Reservoir* 7.5'; USDA/USFS *Carson-Iceberg Wilderness* (Since the *Spicer Meadow Reservoir* topo doesn't show all the trails for this loop, the one of Carson-Iceberg Wilderness is better for this hike.)

Where to Stay

Mountain: None

Other: Base Camp Lodge, Bear Valley Lodge and Village Resort, Lake Alpine Lodge, Tamarack Lodge Bed and Breakfast

Towns and Agencies: Bear Valley Vacation Rentals

HIGHLIGHTS So leisurely that it's almost "easy" instead of "moderate," this hike includes a visit to charming Duck Lake.

HOW TO GET TO THE TRAILHEAD Just 16.4 miles west of Ebbetts Pass on State Route 4 is the East Shore Road turnoff. (You have overshot the turnoff if you

Duck Lake

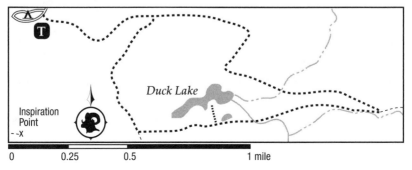

get to Mosquito Lake while eastbound or Lake Alpine while westbound.) Turn south here and drive 0.4 mile more to the Silver Valley/Highland Creek Trailhead, where the East Shore Road elbows west, 16.8 miles. There's no lot; park on the shoulders.

ON THE TRAIL From the trailhead, hike southeast past an information sign on the Highland Creek Trail through a moderate forest whose understory is dotted with wildflowers. Begin a gradual to moderate ascent, passing an unmarked trail on the right and then another on the left. Ignoring both trails, continue ahead (east-southeast) on the broad, dusty track, passing another information sign and entering Carson-Iceberg Wilderness.

The trail veers east-northeast along a pleasant ridgetop, soon using a hiker's pass-through to negotiate a wire fence. Top out at a little over 0.3 mile at 7340 feet after a gradual climb and then descend to a junction at a little under 0.5 mile: left (east) to Rock Lake, right (south) to Duck Lake. This is the start of the loop part of this hike, and, arbitrarily, go left for now, on the leg that's not on the 7.5′ topo.

Descend a dry slope where Jeffrey pines provide sparse shade for a chaparral understory. Nearing 0.75 mile, turn south past a huge, four-trunked juniper and presently veer generally southeast to east where patches of duff-floored forest alternate with areas of granite slabs and outcrops rising from a sandy floor. At a little over 1.25 miles skirt a seasonal tarn and a meadow on the right while passing some very handsome outcrops on the left. Just beyond 1.5 miles cross an intermittent stream and reach a junction.

Go right (southwest) toward Duck Lake along an unmapped streambed and then in it—fortunately, the streambed is usually dry. At 1.6 miles exit the streambed on its left side, following blazes on the trees because the trail is extremely faint

Duck Lake

and ill-maintained through here. While passing a meadow on the right a little beyond 1.75 miles, the trail begins to curve northwest, becoming more distinct as it enters a patch of damp forest. Cross an intermittent stream at nearly 2 miles, and then emerge at a tiny, seasonal pond (unmapped) and its little meadow. First skirt the meadow and then, where the trail fades out, swing left to cross the meadow, ford the stream, and pick up the tread on the other side in the forest edge (blazes on the trees may help).

Now heading west on the south side of the meadow, pass a shallow, seasonal pond, wind through some granite outcrops, spot a sheet of water to the right (north), and take any of several use trails down to the shore of meadow-ringed Duck Lake at 2.25 miles and 7180 feet. It may not be spectacular but it's mighty pretty, set off by a handsome granite dome to the northeast (Point 7766) and by Inspiration Point, an intriguing mudflow monument to the west.

Leaving Duck Lake, return to the trail, continue west, and reach a junction at nearly 2.5 miles. Go right, enjoying the view east over Duck Lake as the path heads for the ridge north of the lake. Spot Bull Run Peak over Duck Lake and then reach the forest edge. Begin climbing moderately to steeply on a wide, dusty and sandy trail, angling northeast on a big switchback. The grade soon eases, and at almost 3 miles the trail reaches a junction—the one where the loop part of this trip began. Turn left to return to the trailhead at a little more than 3.3 miles.

90 Three Lakes Loop

Place	Total Distance	Elevation	Difficulty Level	Type
Trailhead		6940		
Elephant Rock Lake	Negligible	6922	E	O&B
Entire loop	4.6	7315	M	Loop

Best Time Late May–mid-October
Topos *Spicer Meadow Reservoir* 7.5'; USDA/USFS *Carson-Iceberg Wilderness*
Where to Stay
   Mountain: None

   Other: Base Camp Lodge, Bear Valley Lodge and Village Resort, Lake Alpine Lodge, Tamarack Lodge Bed and Breakfast

   Towns and Agencies: Bear Valley Vacation Rentals

HIGHLIGHTS A leisurely loop carries hikers past three pretty lakes, two of which are real stunners.

HOW TO GET TO THE TRAILHEAD Just 22.6 miles west of Ebbetts Pass on State Route 4 is the turnoff for Spicer Meadow Reservoir. It's west of the Bear Valley turnoff and east of the community of Dorrington. Turn south and go 8.1 miles to a turnoff east onto dirt Forest Road 7N01. This turnoff is before the reservoir.

Three Lakes Loop

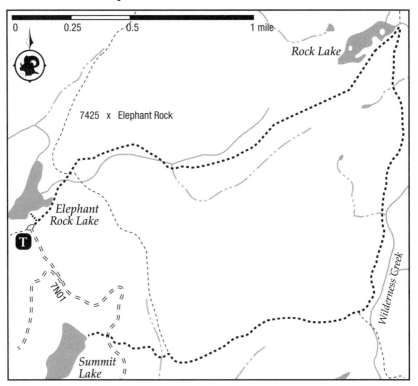

Follow 7N01 4.1 miles past the turnout/trailhead for Summit Lake and past a side road that hooks left, to reach the dusty roadend parking for Elephant Rock Lake.

ON THE TRAIL At least two very obvious paths lead northeast from the parking lot. Take the left trail, which heads to Rock and Duck lakes but isn't signed. It begins in dense forest and shortly crosses a marked mountain-biking trail. (The mountain-biking trail isn't on this book's map.) By a sign that reads LAKESIDE ZONE, reach a junction with a use trail. Scoot down the left fork to see Elephant Rock over beautiful Elephant Rock Lake (day use only) at a negligible distance from the trailhead and 6922 feet. Then return to the main trail and turn left (northeast) on it.

    Cross a runoff channel, skirt the meadowed east bay of Elephant Rock Lake, and pass a low granite dome on the right. While crossing Elephant Rock Lake's inlet, hikers may hear and smell the small herd of cattle that grazes here in season. Shortly reach a junction by the boundary of Carson-Iceberg Wilderness. Go ahead (north) for Rock Lake, entering the wilderness and curving around Elephant Rock. At 0.5 mile dip across a runoff channel and come abreast of Elephant Rock Lake's east tributary.

After paralleling the tributary for a while, cross it and make a brief climb over a little rocky ridge. Around 0.75 mile hop over another stream and, heading generally east-northeast, begin winding gradually up another rocky ridge, this one with an unmapped streamlet creasing its ridgeline. The trail crosses the stream to continue ascending the ridge on its easier northwest side. Twine through a maze of rocks and chaparral that threatens to choke off the trail at any moment—but a well-trod track does exist. Nevertheless, the occasional duck or blaze is helpful as the path heads gradually to moderately up to cross the streambed once more at nearly 1.25 miles.

Leaving the stream behind, continue ascending on a gentle, sandy, forested slope. Cross a secondary ridgeline almost imperceptibly at 1.5 miles before descending to the shore of beautiful Rock Lake at nearly 1.6 miles and 7315 feet. At an apparent junction at 1.75 miles go either way because the forks rejoin shortly, and reach a real junction in a few more steps. Go right (south) toward Highland Lakes on a sandy trail through moderate to open forest, level at first and then descending as it curves southwest. At a junction at a little over 2.75 miles, go right (west) toward Summit Lake and begin a moderate to steep climb up a ridge. Once up the ridge, the trail's grade eases as it curves west-northwest. Exit Carson-Iceberg Wilderness at a little over 3.3 miles. Veering northwest, ascend to a junction at 3.6 miles.

Go left (west) for Summit Lake, meeting Forest Road 7N01 a little short of 4 miles at the signed Summit Lake Trailhead, where there's a small parking area. Cross the road and pick up the trail to Summit Lake. In a few steps spot the lake and then reach its shore. Summit Lake (day use only) at nearly 4 miles and 7068 feet is good-sized, attractive, and has densely forested shores.

Back at the road, turn left (north) to follow the road to the Elephant Rock Lake Trailhead, descending very gradually. Close the loop at nearly 4.6 miles back at the roadend parking lot for Elephant Rock Lake.

State Routes 88 and 89: Wildflower Country

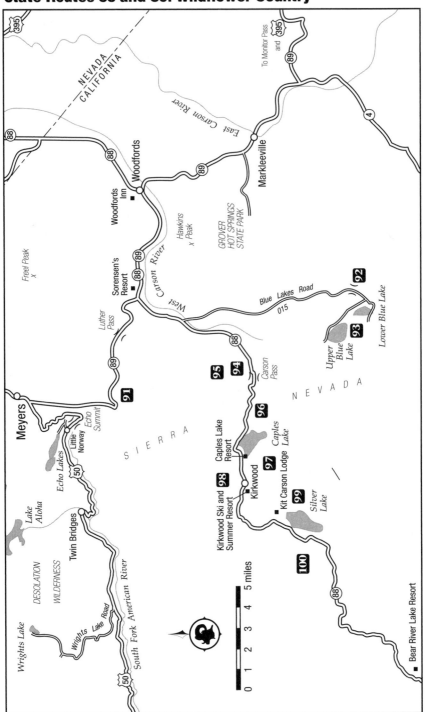

CHAPTER 10

State Routes 88 and 89: Wildflower Country

S outh of Lake Tahoe, State Route 89 swoops west from U.S. Highway 395 over Monitor Pass in the Pine Nut Mountains to meet State Route 4 near Markleeville and then State Route 88 from Nevada, near Woodfords, where State Route 4 ends. State Routes 89 and 88 briefly roll west together before parting company. State Route 89 goes north over Luther Pass to Lake Tahoe, while State Route 88 continues west over Carson Pass to meet State Route 49 at Jackson, in the Gold Country.

The Carson Pass region is famed for its flower displays, in season grander in variety and sheer abundance than those in almost any other region of the Sierra. South of 88 lies Mokelumne Wilderness, a wonderland of rolling volcanic terrain. North of 88 and around 89 lies a similar region that's not official wilderness but should be. It's often called the Dardanelles Roadless Area.

Recommended Maps

In addition to those listed in the trip write-ups, your library of maps should include the following. Get the latest edition/revision you can find. They're widely available, certainly at any of the local ranger stations.

- *El Dorado National Forest.* U.S. Department of Agriculture and U.S. Forest Service.
- *Toiyabe National Forest.* Carson Ranger District. U.S. Department of Agriculture and U.S. Forest Service.

Individual Lodgings

Name	Nearest Community	Type	Facilities	Price Range	Contact Information	Website and Email Address
Caples Lake Resort	Kirkwood	Other	Rooms, cabins	$–$$$	P.O. Box 88 Kirkwood, CA 95646 Phone: 209-258-8888	www.capleslakeresort.com caples@volcano.net
Kirkwood Ski and Summer Resort	Kirkwood	Other	Hotel rooms, condominiums, private homes	$–$$$	P.O. Box 1 Kirkwood, CA 95646 Phone: 800-967-7500	www.kirkwood.com
Kit Carson Lodge	Kirkwood	Mountain	Rooms, cabins	$$–$$$	*Winter:* Kit Carson, CA 95644 Phone: 530-676-1370 *Summer:* 4521 Holiday Hill Court Shingle Springs, CA 95682 Phone: 209-258-8500	www.kitcarsonlodge.com
Sorensen's Resort	Kirkwood	Other	Cabins	$$–$$$	14255 Highway 88 Hope Valley, CA 96120 Phone: 800-423-9949 or 530-694-2203	www.sorensensresort.com info@sorensensresort.com
Woodfords Inn	Woodfords	Other	Rooms	$	20960 Hwy 89 Markleeville, CA 96120 Phone: 530-694-2410	www.woodfordsinn.net info@woodfordsinn.net

Towns and Agencies

Name	Nearest Community	Type	Contact Information	Website and Email Address
Alpine County Chamber of Commerce (represents Markleeville, Woodfords, etc.)	Markleeville	Chamber of Commerce	P.O. Box 265 Markleeville, CA 96120 Phone: 530-694-2475	www.alpinecounty.com info@alpinecounty.com
Amador County Chamber of Commerce and Visitors Bureau	Jackson	Chamber of Commerce and Visitors Bureau	P.O. Box 596 Jackson, CA 95642 Phone: 209-223-0350	www.amadorcounty chamber.com
Lake Tahoe Visitor Information (VirtualTahoe)	South Lake Tahoe	Agency	P.O. Box 7172 #173 Stateline, NV 89449-7172 Phone: 800-210-3459, 800-371-2620, or 530-544-5050	www.virtualtahoe.com contactus@virtualtahoe.com
South Lake Tahoe Chamber of Commerce	South Lake Tahoe	Chamber of Commerce	3066 Lake Tahoe Blvd. South Lake Tahoe, CA 96150 Phone: 530-541-5255	www.tahoeinfo.com sltcc@sierra.net

91 Dardanelles and Round Lakes

Place	Total Distance	Elevation	Difficulty Level	Type
Trailhead		7260		
Big Meadow	1	7500	E	O&B
Round Lake	6	8037	M	O&B
Dardanelles Lake	7.5	7740	S	O&B
Both lakes	9	8037	S	O&B

Best Time   Early July–mid-October
Topos   *Freel Peak, Echo Lake 7.5'*
Where to Stay

Mountain: Kit Carson Lodge

Other: Caples Lake Resort, Kirkwood Ski and Summer Resort, Sorensen's Resort, Woodfords Inn

Towns and Agencies: Alpine County Chamber of Commerce, Amador County Chamber of Commerce and Vistors Bureau, Lake Tahoe Visitor Information, South Lake Tahoe Chamber of Commerce

HIGHLIGHTS The Dardanelles Roadless Area, in which both of these lakes lie, offers wonderful scenery and a number of lakes. Dardanelles Lake is one of the prettiest and Round Lake one of the most interesting. One of this trip's legs uses a short stretch of the multiuse (foot, horse, and bike) Tahoe Rim Trail.

HOW TO GET TO THE TRAILHEAD Just 3.4 miles northwest of Luther Pass on State Route 89 is the Big Meadow Trailhead turnoff on the northeast side of the road (between Luther Pass on the south and the junction with U.S. Highway 50 on the north). Turn here onto a short spur road that leads to a T-junction, turn left, and go 0.1 mile to a parking loop that has restrooms and water, in season. The trail leaves from the far end of the parking loop at a poorly signed trailhead and looks very unpromising but gets better.

ON THE TRAIL From the far end of the parking lot, head south on a sandy trail marked TAHOE RIM TRAIL. In 0.1 mile reach State Route 89 and cross the highway carefully to pick up the trail again; it's well-signed here. Curve south-southwest when leaving the highway, climbing moderately to steeply on a dusty duff trail into dense conifer forest. At a little over 0.3 mile the grade eases and shortly passes through a fence. At nearly 0.5 mile reach a junction. Go right (south) to find the forest giving way to splendid Big Meadow at 0.5 mile and 7500 feet, crossing its stream on a footbridge. The meadow, cradled by handsome peaks, sports a wonderful variety of flowers in season.

The trail continues south-southeast across the meadow toward a ridge and reenters forest at 0.75 mile. Resume a gradual to moderate climb broken by a few short, steep hauls, where patches of dense forest alternate with bright, flowery

Luther Pass

Once known as Fay Canyon, Luther Canyon is a Nevada State Historical Landmark. In *Place Names of the Sierra Nevada,* Peter Browning writes, "Ira Manley Luther (1821–1890), a native of New York State, came to California in 1850. He discovered a pass from Hope Valley to Lake Valley in 1852 and took the first wagons across it in 1854." Browning explains that Luther operated a sawmill near the mouth of Fay Canyon in the early 1860s.

openings. Beginning at a little over 1.5 miles come abreast of a small stream that nourishes a long, narrow, flower-rich meadow. At a little over 1.6 miles, find another hiker's pass-through in a wood-and-barbed-wire fence and, as the trail angles up the east side of a ridge, head toward blue sky that you can see through the red firs atop the ridge. The trail tops out in a few more steps and then begins a gentle descent on the west side of the ridge. Soon there are views of volcanic mudflow formations and of a granite basin to the west. Unusual boulders full of smaller rocks dot the landscape near the bottom of this descent; the rocks have eroded from those ancient mudflows. At 2.25 miles and the bottom of the descent, reach another junction: the branch ahead (south) heads for Round Lake and the mudflow formations on the Tahoe Rim Trail, and the sharp right (northwest) branch proceeds to Dardanelles Lake and Christmas Valley.

To go to Dardanelles Lake first, turn right here, soon tracing a stream on the left (west). At an unmarked Y-junction, take the trail that heads left across the stream (southwest) toward Dardanelles Lake. Cross a wet meadow and pass north of a lily-pad-covered pond. The trail descends gradually to moderately to meet and parallel another stream. Stroll northwest for a while, and stay on the trail as it curves southwest to cross the stream. Now climb south gradually to moderately before abruptly swinging west to the trail's end on the shores of beautiful,

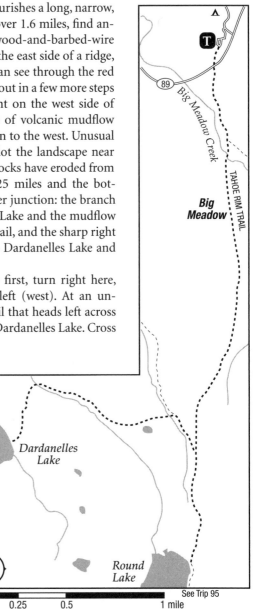

Dardanelles and Round Lakes

See Trip 95

0   0.25   0.5   1 mile

popular Dardanelles Lake at a little over 3.75 miles and 7740 feet. The lake is ringed by slabs offering many pleasant picnic sites as well as by handsome cliffs on its south side. Then return to the junction with the Tahoe Rim Trail.

To go to Round Lake, go ahead, staying on the Tahoe Rim Trail if you're coming from Big Meadow, or turn right onto the Tahoe Rim Trail if you're coming from Dardanelles Lake. Begin a series of short, steep ascents and descents. At an apparent but unmarked junction, take the left fork through a red fir forest full of those mudflow boulders. One more steep, dusty ascent and then a level stretch take hikers to a point slightly above the dusty north shore of Round Lake at a little over 3 miles and 8037 feet. A web of use trails spreads out from here, leading around the lake. The formation on the lake's east shore is a volcanic mudflow formation like the Dardanelles (see Trip 85) and looks rather like an Assyrian ziggurat.

Return to the junction with the trail to Dardanelles Lake and from there to the trailhead in 9 miles if you visited both lakes.

92 Lily Pad and Upper Sunset Lakes

Place	Total Distance	Elevation	Difficulty Level	Type
Trailhead		7960		
Lily Pad Lake	3.75+	7830	M U	O&B
Upper Sunset Lake	4.5	7830	M U	O&B

Best Time   Late May–mid-October

Topos   *Pacific Valley* 7.5'; USDA/USFS *Mokelumne Wilderness*

Where to Stay

Mountain: Kit Carson Lodge

Other: Caples Lake Resort, Kirkwood Ski and Summer Resort, Sorensen's Resort, Woodfords Inn

Towns and Agencies: Alpine County Chamber of Commerce, Amador County Chamber of Commerce and Visitors Bureau, Lake Tahoe Visitor Information, South Lake Tahoe Chamber of Commerce

HIGHLIGHTS   A great viewpoint, fine flowers, and two pretty lakes—one with a knockout flower display of its own in season—await hikers on this leg of the famed Pacific Crest Trail (PCT).

HOW TO GET TO THE TRAILHEAD   Just 6.3 miles east of Carson Pass on State Route 88 is the junction with the Blue Lakes Road. Turn left (south) onto the Blue Lakes Road and follow it up toward Blue Lakes as it grows rougher and the pavement ends, for 10.6 more miles to Forest Road 097 on the left. Turn left onto Forest Road 097, and almost immediately turn left again onto a very short

Lily Pad and Upper Sunset Lakes

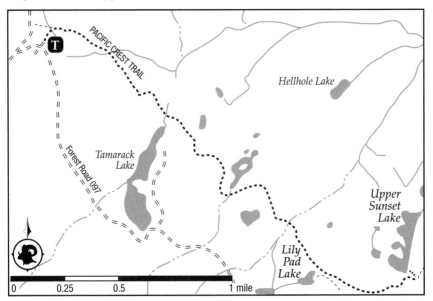

spur road to reach a large parking area in less than 0.1 mile. The parking area is marked for the Blue Lakes Trailhead of the PCT and has a restroom.

ON THE TRAIL The marked trail, which is really a spur to the PCT—itself slightly east of here—starts near the restroom. Go northwest in moderate lodgepole forest, enjoying the wealth of flowers surrounding the trail. Hop across a stream almost immediately, curve east-northeast around a meadow, and reach a junction with the PCT at 0.1 mile; go right. The sandy trail descends gradually to moderately to cross a couple of branches of a stream at 0.3 mile in another flower garden. Presently wind among outcrops and then, at 0.75 mile, ford another stream—the outlet of higher Tamarack Lake—and climb moderately to a saddle at 1 mile, from which there are excellent views of a handsome ridge of jagged peaks. The most striking are Raymond and Reynolds peaks—the latter looks like an enormous fang from here.

Leaving the saddle, descend the now rocky and dusty trail into forest, passing above an unnamed lake, and ford a stream at nearly 1.6 miles. Climb away from the stream to reach Lily Pad Lake at nearly 2 miles and 7830 feet, a very pretty spot with its forest fringe, surrounding granite slabs, and water lilies. Next, return to the main trail.

Continuing to Upper Sunset Lake, climb over a rocky ridge and then descend a little to cross Upper Sunset Lake's inlet in a densely flowered meadow. With all its flowers, this oddly shaped lake is extremely attractive.

Retrace your steps from here.

93 Blue Lakes to Granite Lake

Place	Total Distance	Elevation	Difficulty Level	Type
Trailhead		8140		
Granite Lake	3.5+	8700	M	O&B

Best Time   Early July–mid-October

Topos   *Carson Pass; Pacific Valley 7.5'; USDA/USFS Mokelumne Wilderness*

Where to Stay

Mountain: Kit Carson Lodge

Other: Caples Lake Resort, Kirkwood Ski and Summer Resort, Sorensen's Resort, Woodfords Inn

Towns and Agencies: Alpine County Chamber of Commerce, South Lake Tahoe Chamber of Commerce

HIGHLIGHTS   Reached by a pleasant trail, Granite Lake is short on size but long on beauty.

HOW TO GET TO THE TRAILHEAD   Just 6.3 miles east of Carson Pass on State Route 88 is the junction with the Blue Lakes Road. Turn left (south) onto the Blue Lakes Road and follow it up toward Blue Lakes as it grows rougher and the pavement ends, for 10.6 more miles past its junction with Forest Road 097. Continue around the "hook" in the Blue Lakes Road past Lower Blue Lake to a point past Middle Creek Campground and just below the dam on Upper Blue

Granite Lake

Blue Lakes to Granite Lake

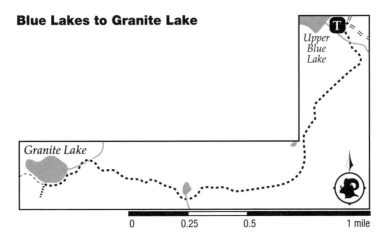

Lake. Park in the turnout on the left (southwest) side of the road for the Grouse Lake Trailhead, just below the spillway, on the edge of Upper Blue Lake's outlet.

ON THE TRAIL Head south-southwest to ford the stream from Upper Blue Lake's spillway, and then climb a little into a moderate forest of spindly lodgepoles. Curve southeast, soon crossing another stream that supports a modest but attractive flower garden. Ascend gradually to moderately to a ridge where the duff trail trends generally south. Traversing the ridge, climb very gradually to enter Mokelumne Wilderness at 0.75 mile on a now-sandy trail.

After a short climb, pass a beautiful lakelet at a little over 1 mile. The trail becomes confused and indistinct around here. To stay on track, follow the lakelet's east shore to its outlet, perhaps scrambling over some boulders. Then cross the outlet going northwest, and climb steeply up a sparsely shaded slope. The grade eases on a shoulder, and the path continues west through small meadows and past tarns. Climb again, top a small ridge, and then descend a little to follow a trail that curves west-southwest along Granite Lake's outlet, fording the outlet twice. Reach beautiful Granite Lake at a little over 1.75 miles and 8700 feet. An optional ascent of a draw about halfway around the lake leads to an overlook of Meadow, Rice, and Evergreen lakes and of the peaks surrounding the area.

Return the way you came.

94 Frog and Winnemucca Lakes

Place	Total Distance	Elevation	Difficulty Level	Type
Trailhead		8573		
Frog Lake	2	8860	E	O&B
Winnemucca Lake	4	8980	M	O&B

Best Time   Early July–mid-October
Topos   *Carson Pass* 7.5'; USDA/USFS *Mokelumne Wilderness*
Where to Stay

Mountain: Kit Carson Lodge

Other: Caples Lake Resort, Kirkwood Ski and Summer Resort, Sorensen's Resort, Woodfords Inn

Towns and Agencies: Alpine County Chamber of Commerce, Amador County Chamber of Commerce and Visitors Bureau, Lake Tahoe Visitor Information, South Lake Tahoe Chamber of Commerce

HIGHLIGHTS   The Carson Pass region is justly famed for its wildflower displays, and in season these are not just little gardens here and there or flowery strips along creeks but great carpets of blossoms. On this hike and the next two, visitors revel in these displays while visiting some wonderful lakes.

HOW TO GET TO THE TRAILHEAD   This trailhead is right at Carson Pass, next to a visitor center, where visitors can get good advice free and relevant maps and books at a price. The parking lot is often full by midday. The center has restrooms and a ranger station. Note that there are two parking lots at Carson Pass. The one at the Carson Pass visitor center, on the southwest side of the road, serves southbound trailheads. The other lot is 0.3 mile west of the pass proper, on the north side of the road, and serves northbound trailheads.

ON THE TRAIL   This trailhead is incorrectly shown on the *Carson Pass* 7.5' topo; it starts near the southeast side of the parking lot that's on the south side of State Route 88, between the visitor center and the restrooms. Head south-southwest on a dusty duff trail, descending gradually into a moderate conifer forest and passing an unmapped tarn and some granite outcrops. Curve around a meadow, cross a stream, and then enter Mokelumne Wilderness at just over 0.3 mile.

Now begin a moderate to gradual climb through a mix of tall grass and dryland flowers. The grade eases as the path crosses a shoulder to reveal a view of the odd peak named Elephants Back ahead (southeast). Round Top towers to the right (south) as the trail heads southeast. Make a lazy contour of an open, flowery slope, and nearing 1 mile reach an unsigned junction with the spur trail to Frog Lake. Go left to the lake at a little under 1 mile and 8860 feet. The lake sits on a little bench above the valleys to the east. There are excellent views eastward on the far side of the lake—follow a use trail around the lake and then across the meadow on the lake's east side to slabs overlooking Red Lake Peak, State Route 88 and Carson Pass, Red Lake, Hawkins Peak, Hope Valley, and Reynolds and Raymond peaks.

Back on the main trail, turn left to continue the hike and climb moderately toward Round Top to an overlook of Caples Lake. At a little over 1 mile reach a junction with the Pacific Crest Trail (PCT). Go right to stay on this trip's trail, passing Elephants Back and drifting into a dry meadow and then a very wet meadow offering combined seasonal displays of bistort, catchfly, columbine, elephant heads, green gentian, green orchids, hawkweed, knotweed, lungwort, lupine, marsh marigolds, meadow rue, mountain pride, onion, pearly everlasting, popcorn flower, Queen Anne's lace, threadstem phlox, valerian, white violet, and wild carrot.

At nearly 1.6 miles cross a stream lined by plants that love very wet environments. Shortly before 2 miles, top out and begin a brief descent to dramatically set Winnemucca Lake at 2 miles and 8980 feet. If the flowers haven't impressed you, the cliff-backed lake, right under Round Top peak, will. From the rise above the lake there are excellent views of Elephants Back and Round Top and across unseen Carson Pass to Red Lake Peak.

Frog and Winnemucca Lakes

About Carson Pass

In the 1840s, famed explorers John C. Frémont and the eponymous Christopher "Kit" Carson roamed the Sierra near Carson Pass. From 1856 to 1876, John A. "Snow-shoe" Thomson (Americanized as "Thompson") carried mail between California and Nevada in the winter, using Carson Pass. He traveled on heavy, homemade, 10-foot wooden skis crafted according to his memories of his boyhood skiing experiences in Norway. He carried 50–80 pounds of mail at a time but almost no special clothing for himself, relying on his exertion for warmth. His heroic feats have never been equaled, much less surpassed, by European Americans in the Sierra.

Optionally, traverse the lake's north shore to a junction with a trail northward to Woods Lake. A short way down this trail is another spectacular meadow (the mileage for this brief detour is not included in the summary information). Retrace your steps.

95 Meiss and Round Lakes

Place	Total Distance	Elevation	Difficulty Level	Type
Trailhead		8560		
Lakelet on saddle	2+	8780	E	O&B
Meiss Lake	6.3	8314	S U	O&B
Round Lake	8+	8037	S U	O&B
Both lakes	9.4–9.5	8790	S U	O&B

Best Time   Late May–mid-October
Topos   *Caples Lake, Carson Pass 7.5′*; USDA/USFS *Mokelumne Wilderness*
Where to Stay

Mountain: Kit Carson Lodge

Other: Caples Lake Resort, Kirkwood Ski and Summer Resort, Sorensen's Resort, Woodfords Inn

Towns and Agencies: Alpine County Chamber of Commerce, Amador County Chamber of Commerce and Visitors Bureau, Lake Tahoe Visitor Information, South Lake Tahoe Chamber of Commerce

Meiss Lake

HIGHLIGHTS The seasonal display of flowers along the first leg of this hike is breathtaking. Beyond, climb to a lovely, unnamed lakelet and descend through more flowers to the headwaters of the Upper Truckee River, marshy Meiss Lake, and interesting Round Lake.

HOW TO GET TO THE TRAILHEAD This trip starts from the Pacific Crest Trail (PCT) parking lot 0.3 mile west of Carson Pass, on the north side of the road. The south-side parking lot, which is 0.3 miles east, has restrooms, water, and a visitor center.

ON THE TRAIL Pick up the trail at the northwest corner of the lot. Amid dry-land flowers, head west over a seasonal trickle and past an information sign. The trail traverses between the highway to the left and juniper-crowned gray granite cliffs on the right. The sandy trail reaches a junction at a little over 0.25 mile; go left (southwest) on the PCT, still traversing above the highway and briefly aiming at the stark buttes beyond Caples Lake. Descend slightly as the track veers northwest to excellent views of Caples Lake from a trail bracketed by a fine display of blossoms and a small stand of conifers. At 0.6 mile the trail curves through a patchy lodgepole forest, and you emerge to a seasonally amazing—stupendous!—magnificent!—flower display: a steep hillside thickly carpeted with bright yellow, daisy-like mule ears and sky-blue lupine.

Continue, crossing a pair of unmapped, seasonal streams, and begin switchbacking up a slope, heading for an obvious low point just west of Red Lake Peak. The grade eases on a saddle with a lovely, unnamed lakelet at a little over 1 mile and 8780 feet, to the west of a fence with a hiker's pass-through. Double ruts lead away into a high meadow spangled with blue iris, and spectacular views open up as the route continues north, rising very gradually to a broad saddle. From here, you can see Lake Tahoe in the distance, peaks in Desolation Wilderness, granite slopes in Dardanelles Roadless Area, and the strange volcanic formation that towers over Round Lake.

The paired ruts depart the main trail, heading up to the right; stay on the PCT as it swings left, downhill. Numerous runoff channels crease these rocky, windswept slopes, and at nearly 1.5 miles the PCT crosses a stream bright with blossoms. Make a steep, rocky descent to the broad meadows visible below. The grade eases just before the path fords a fork of the Upper Truckee River at 1.6 miles.

The trail rolls across broad, flower-strewn Meiss Meadow, crossing the river again, before reaching an unmapped Y-junction at almost 2.25 miles. The left (west) branch heads to the picturesque cabins of a cow camp. Go right to continue on the PCT, passing through a ruined fence and shortly reaching a junction at nearly 2.3 miles with the trail to Round Lake: left (northwest) on the PCT to Showers and Meiss lakes, right (northeast) to Round Lake on the Tahoe Rim Trail.

To go to Meiss Lake, turn left and cross a low, forested ridge before approaching the Upper Truckee River again at 2.6 miles. Meiss Lake is visible from here, shimmering a short distance away, north down a branch of the meadow. Follow a use trail north toward the lake, picking your way through the meadow when the

Meiss and Round Lakes

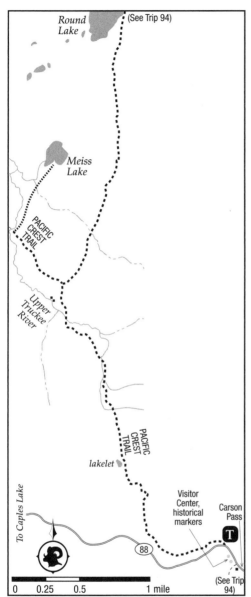

track peters out. Early in the season, much of the meadow around the lake is covered by standing water that's ankle- to calf-deep. A prominent, rocky "islet" on the lake's south edge offers dry ground and views over Meiss Lake at just over 3 miles and 8314 feet. Return to the PCT. Retrace your steps 0.7 mile to the junction with the Tahoe Rim Trail.

To go to Round Lake, turn northeast onto the dusty Tahoe Rim Trail to cross broad, forested knolls before abruptly descending to a stream crossing at 3 miles at the south edge of another, smaller, flowery meadow. Skirt an old log fence while crossing this boggy meadow and ascend the next knoll, atop which there are more meadows. After topping out, begin a long, gradual descent to the east edge of the meadow south of Round Lake, crossing the unmapped intermittent streams feeding the meadow. Reach Round Lake at a little over 4 miles and 8037 feet. There's a wonderful mudflow formation towering over Round Lake, the same ziggurat-like one seen from the saddle at 8790 and also on Trip 91. Retrace your steps 1.7 miles to the junction.

From the junction of the routes to Meiss and Round lakes, retrace your steps 2.3 miles to the trailhead. It's a total of 9.4 to 9.5 miles if you went to both lakes.

96 Woods Lake Loop

Place	Total Distance	Elevation	Difficulty Level	Type
Trailhead		8220		
Winnemucca Lake	2.6	8980	M	O&B
Entire loop	4+	9420	M	O&B

Best Time   Late May–mid-October

Topos   *Caples Lake, Carson Pass* 7.5'; USDA/USFS *Mokelumne Wilderness*

Where to Stay

Mountain: Kit Carson Lodge

Other: Caples Lake Resort, Kirkwood Ski and Summer Resort, Sorensen's Resort, Woodfords Inn

Towns and Agencies: Alpine County Chamber of Commerce, Amador County Chamber of Commerce and Visitors Bureau, Lake Tahoe Visitor Information, South Lake Tahoe Chamber of Commerce

HIGHLIGHTS   Exceptional flower displays line this looping route to two beautiful lakes in dramatic settings under Round Top Peak.

HOW TO GET TO THE TRAILHEAD   Just 1.9 miles west from Carson Pass on State Route 88 is the turnoff south for Woods Lake Recreation Area, west of Carson Pass and east of Caples Lake. Follow narrow, paved Woods Lake Road all the way to its end, past the turnoff into the Woods Lake Campground, to day-use parking at Woods Lake, 1.4 miles (3.3 miles from Carson Pass). The parking area has a picnic area, water, and restrooms. The trailhead is just before the picnic area and slightly past the campground entrance, on the opposite side of the road from that entrance, at a footbridge over Woods Lake's outlet. This is a very pretty, very popular area. If the day-use parking area is full, go back up the road and over the bridge to find day-use-only parking at a big dirt turnout next to the stream. (There is a small day-use parking area, which charges a fee, right across from the campground entrance.)

ON THE TRAIL   The trailhead is poorly marked on Woods Lake Road, but the footbridge is obvious. Head east over the footbridge and almost immediately begin winding gradually to moderately up a rocky outcrop in open forest. Round Top Peak soon comes into view, and the scattering of flowers along this first leg is a delightful appetizer for the floral feast to come.

A little beyond 0.5 mile pass the signed ruins of one of the many old mining operations around here. Continuing, the flower display grows more impressive until, starting about 0.6 mile, the trail emerges into an immense, gently sloping meadow below Winnemucca Lake, where flowers carpet the slope. Indian paintbrush in blazing hues dominates but is far from the whole show.

Woods Lake Loop

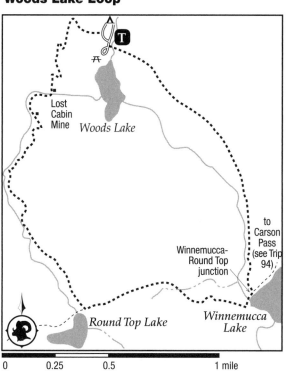

The trail traverses the meadow, ascending gradually, and near 1 mile enters Mokelumne Wilderness. Cross multiple runoff channels, one of which is likely to be the trail early in the season. Near the south end of the meadow, begin a steep climb toward Round Top, enjoying over-the-shoulder views of Red Lake Peak. At 1.3 miles reach the Winnemucca-Round Top junction. Follow use trails (ahead) for a few steps to the shore of beautiful Winnemucca Lake (8980 feet). Backtrack to the Winnemucca-Round Top junction and head initially southwest for Round Top Lake. Ford Winnemucca's flower-blessed outlet and climb through alpine meadows, curving westward through this cirque. The goal is a windy saddle dotted with whitebark pines and reached at a little over 2 miles and 9420 feet. Views include Hawkins Peak to the east as well as nearby, towering Round Top.

Views open to the west on the gradual descent to stark, lovely Round Top Lake at a little over 2.25 miles and 9340 feet under rugged Round Top and a jagged ridge called The Sisters. The topo shows a trail southeast to Round Top, but that's a use trail or a scramble at best.

From the junction at Round Top Lake, begin returning to Woods Lake by taking the right (northwest) fork, descending toward a view of Caples Lake on a rocky, moderate to steep trail paralleling Round Top Lake's outlet. Exit Mokelumne Wilderness at almost 3 miles and continue the descent on open, rocky slopes past a Land Survey Monument, leveling out briefly on benches. Cross a stream, pass the ruins of a stone cabin at almost 3.3 miles, brush the lake's outlet stream, and almost immediately veer right (north-northeast) past mine ruins on both sides of the stream. Be careful not to trespass; Lost Cabin Mine is still an active claim.

The trail heads over a low saddle before resuming its steep descent past more mine signs. Curving east-northeast, it offers views of the mine ruins and of Woods Lake below. Cross the outlet stream on a marked new trail, below more mine ruins, at nearly 3.5 miles. Meet a four-wheel-drive road in a few more steps and continue descending on it, being careful to stay out of the mining claim area.

Circumvent a gate and meet the road through Woods Lake Campground near Site 12 at just under 4 miles.

Turn right, toward Woods Lake, on the campground road, and shortly meet the Woods Lake Road near the trailhead and the day-use parking lot to close this loop at a little more than 4 miles.

97 Emigrant Lake

Place	Total Distance	Elevation	Difficulty Level	Type
Trailhead		7780		
Emigrant Lake	7.75+	8580	S	O&B

Best Time Early July–mid-October

Topos *Caples Lake 7.5'*; USDA/USFS *Mokelumne Wilderness*

Where to Stay

Mountain: Kit Carson Lodge

Other: Caples Lake Resort, Kirkwood Ski and Summer Resort, Sorensen's Resort, Woodfords Inn

Towns and Agencies: Alpine County Chamber of Commerce, Amador County Chamber of Commerce and Visitors Bureau, Lake Tahoe Visitor Information, South Lake Tahoe Chamber of Commerce

HIGHLIGHTS Beginning with a leisurely stroll along the west shore of big, blue Caples Lake, this trip then makes an interesting ascent to lovely Emigrant Lake, which has an impressive subalpine setting.

HOW TO GET TO THE TRAILHEAD From Carson Pass on State Route 88, head 4.9 miles west, pass the turnoff for Caples Lake Resort, and park in a lot beyond the dam at the western tip of Caples Lake. This parking area is west of Caples Lake Resort and east of Kirkwood Inn and has restroom facilities and water. The trailhead is near the restrooms.

ON THE TRAIL Head southeast through willows on the marked trail and climb up to the lake's level to begin a leisurely traverse of its scenic, forested shore on a well-worn, dusty, duff trail. Enter Mokelumne Wilderness almost immediately, and on the way between here and the start of the ascent to Emigrant Lake, cross a number of seasonal streams. The changing views of Red Lake Peak, Elephants Back, and Round Top across the lake, and of the lake itself, are the principal attractions on this stretch. At a little over 1 mile veer away from the lakeshore on a dry, gravelly slope with a scattering of lodgepoles—this is the short, wide peninsula that pooches northeast into the lake about halfway along its western-southwestern shore.

Cross
a trace of
the old Emi-
grant Road,
as marked on a
dead tree. Where
a junction sign indi-
cates that the old Emi-
grant Road is to the right,
continue on the left fork, going south-southeast. Soon dip
to the lakeshore again and then,
nearing the southeast end of Caples
Lake at a little over about 1.3 miles, begin
climbing. At an apparent Y-junction, either
fork will do; they soon rejoin.

At nearly 1.6 miles, heading almost south
now, top a rocky shoulder and descend to cross an
unmapped creeklet. With the south arm of the lake still
visible below, continue, now over rocky outcrops, now in
forest, now across a meadow. At a little over 2.25 miles, begin
climbing, sometimes steeply, beside a strand of multi-chan-
neled Emigrant Creek. Nearing 3 miles, pass an ill-marked
junction with an ill-maintained trail that goes right (west)
to Kirkwood Meadows. Continue ahead (left, south), cross
the creek strand, and pass some handsome cascades. Climb
gradually to moderately southward, working over to the next
strand of Emigrant Creek to the east. Cross that next strand
at nearly 3.25 miles, just below a beautiful little waterfall.

Now zigzag up, glimpsing more pretty cascades, until
a final level stretch brings hikers alongside Emigrant Lake's
outlet and then to the lake itself. Chilly but lovely Emigrant
Lake at nearly 4 miles and 8580 feet sits in a very stark cirque
under Covered Wagon Peak. The lake's shores are softened
by meadow grasses and dotted with flowers.

Retrace your steps.

Emigrant Lake

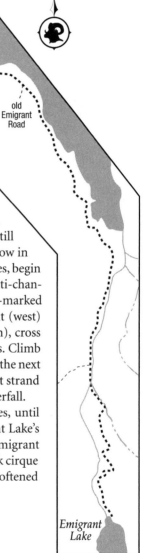

old
Emigrant
Road

Caples Lake

Emigrant
Lake

0   0.25   0.5   1 mile

98 Lake Margaret

Place	Total Distance	Elevation	Difficulty Level	Type
Trailhead		7660		
Lake Margaret	4.6	7540	M U	O&B

Best Time Early July–mid-October

Topos *Caples Lake 7.5'*; USDA/USFS *Mokelumne Wilderness*

Where to Stay

   Mountain: Kit Carson Lodge

   Other: Caples Lake Resort, Kirkwood Ski and Summer Resort, Sorensen's Resort, Woodfords Inn

   Towns and Agencies: Alpine County Chamber of Commerce, Amador County Chamber of Commerce and Visitors Bureau, Lake Tahoe Visitor Information, South Lake Tahoe Chamber of Commerce

HIGHLIGHTS A stroll through the beautiful meadows along Caples Creek precedes a scramble to pretty Lake Margaret. Near the end, hikers must friction-walk somewhat-steep slabs; bouldering skills will be helpful.

HOW TO GET TO THE TRAILHEAD Drive 5.2 miles west of Carson Pass on State Route 88. Pass the turnoff for Caples Lake Resort, and about 0.3 mile west of Caples Lake's west dam, turn onto a spur road headed north. The turnoff may or may not be marked. It's west of Caples Lake and east of Kirkwood Inn. Follow the rough spur road 0.1 mile to a small, rough parking area and a trailhead on a cliff's edge.

ON THE TRAIL Head generally north, at first on sparsely timbered slopes, descending into moderate forest and scattered flowers. At a little over 0.3 mile, ford a branch of Caples Creek; the ford ranges from difficult in early season to dry in late season. Get back on the main trail on the far side of the creek, and follow it northeast along the forested margin of the beautiful meadows that spread along Caples Creek.

    The trail strikes out across a meadow near 0.6 mile to cross another branch of Caples Creek on a footbridge that may be in pretty sad shape. Beyond, the trail winds over a rocky ridgelet, heading generally west. Nearing the top of the ridgelet, curve past an unmapped, lily-pad-dotted tarn on the left and head north again. At a little over 1 mile top the ridgelet and enter an area of granite slabs where the descending trail is a little hard to follow; carefully note your surroundings at the top of these slabs so you can locate the main trail on your return. Continue north, looking for ducks and blazes on trees and paralleling a runoff channel. The trail soon becomes distinct again as it reenters forest and curves northeast.

    At a little over 1.3 miles, pass a large pond on the right, ringed by rocks and alders. Trace its outlet—may be dry—along a long, narrow meadow before crossing it at 1.5 miles and then recrossing it. Nearing 2 miles, negotiate a boggy section along the sluggish creek. The route becomes hemmed in by high, wonderful flowers—look for giant larkspur here. At 2 miles ford the creek, a ford made somewhat difficult by the sheer density of the blooming plants here. Soon veer into a more open, drier area below a handsome, rocky outcrop and begin winding up into the rocks, friction-walking on the slabs at times.

Abruptly curve north onto a forested trail through the rocks and shortly reach the rocky shores of lovely Lake Margaret at 2.3 miles and 7540 feet. Picturesque rocky islets dot Lake Margaret, and rocky knolls around it add to its sense of seclusion.

Retrace your steps.

Lake Margaret

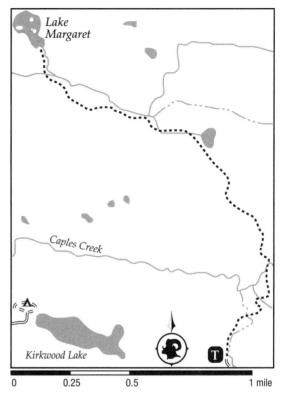

99 Silver Lake to Granite and Hidden Lakes

Place	Total Distance	Elevation	Difficulty Level	Type
Trailhead		7300		
Granite Lake only	2	7580	E	O&B
Hidden Lake	6	7700	M	O&B

Best Time   Early July–mid-October
Topos   *Caples Lake 7.5'*; USDA/USFS *Mokelumne Wilderness*

Where to Stay

Mountain: Kit Carson Lodge

Other: Caples Lake Resort, Kirkwood Ski and Summer Resort, Sorensen's Resort, Woodfords Inn

Towns and Agencies: Alpine County Chamber of Commerce, Amador County Chamber of Commerce and Visitors Bureau, Lake Tahoe Visitor Information, South Lake Tahoe Chamber of Commerce

HIGHLIGHTS Two surprisingly pretty lakes invite exploration beyond beautiful Silver Lake. There's no alpine grandeur at these lakes, but there is the quiet charm of the mid-elevation Sierra.

HOW TO GET TO THE TRAILHEAD Just 11.1 miles west of Carson Pass on State Route 88 is the turnoff south to Kit Carson Lodge, west of Kirkwood Inn and east of Silver Lake's on-highway shoreline. Follow signs through dense forest dotted by summer cabins toward Camp Minkalo; the road is very narrow and its surface poor beyond Kit Carson Lodge. Drive 0.5 mile past the lodge's turnoff to a fork; go left. In 0.2 mile go right at another fork. In 0.6 mile reach a dusty parking area beyond the trailhead and outside the Camp Minkalo gate.

ON THE TRAIL Find the trailhead where the road meets the parking area, which is on the right when you face back down the road. Head east-southeast between forest and granite slabs on a dusty trail with a sparse flower display. Briefly parallel a stream on the left, and then veer right (south-southeast) away from the stream and onto the slabs. Follow the dusty track between the slabs until, nearing 0.5 mile, the path crosses an unnamed, intermittent creek on a footbridge upstream of a very pretty little waterfall.

A little beyond the bridge, at 0.5 mile, reach a junction. The right (west) trail goes to Plasse's Resort, which doesn't have lodging. Go left (south), temporarily leaving the forest behind to ascend sunstruck slabs on a footpath worn be-

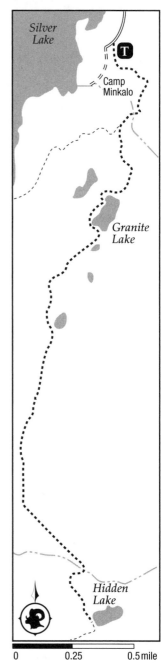

Silver Lake to Granite and Hidden Lakes

tween them. Occasional patches of forest offer needed shade, and a little before 1 mile the trail crosses a small patch of forest to reach the north shore of stunning Granite Lake at 7580 feet. Sky-mirroring waters fill a nearly rectangular hollow sculpted in handsome, light-colored granite. This spot is high on a ridge over-looking Silver Lake, and there are excellent views from the slabs west of Granite Lake.

This area is an extremely popular stop for equestrians, and, particularly at a junction at the lake's southwest end, the dust is deep and the poop is ripe. The fact that its shores are mostly granite rather than more-easily displaced dirt or sand probably helps keep Granite Lake from becoming a mud puddle. A smaller lake northwest of and below Granite, visible from the red-stained slabs on the west shore, may appeal to hikers who don't mind doing a little bushwhacking.

Round Granite Lake on its west side, and reach an unmapped junction at the lake's southwest corner. On the right is a well-horse-traveled use trail that drops off this ridge. Turn left around Granite's south end and then curve south to pass a pretty tarn on the left. There's plenty of equine company from here on; stand quietly off the trail when riders need to pass.

Next, stroll into patchy lodgepole forest, cross a seasonal stream, and skirt a long meadow full of corn lilies. At a little over 1.75 miles, reach a signed but un-mapped junction. Go left (south) through an open, dry forest on a dusty trail to reach an apparent three-way, unsigned junction at a little over 2 miles. Only the middle fork is blazed, so take it and stay on the blazed route, ignoring the many dusty use trails threading the area.

At 2.6 miles the trail begins to curve around the pretty valley of a nameless stream. Cross the stream a little past 2.75 miles to a spot just above Hidden Lake at 3 miles and 7700 feet. There's an unmapped junction near the lakeshore. The left branch rounds the lake on a use trail, and the right heads to Plasse's Resort. Hidden Lake, backed by granite cliffs and shaded by lodgepoles, is very pretty.

Retrace your steps.

100 Shealor Lake

Place	Total Distance	Elevation	Difficulty Level	Type
Trailhead		7440		
Shealor Lake	2.5	7180	M U	O&B

Best Time Early July–mid-October

Topos *Tragedy Spring* 7.5′, USDA/USFS *Mokelumne Wilderness*

Where to Stay

Mountain: Kit Carson Lodge

Other: Caples Lake Resort, Kirkwood Ski and Summer Resort, Sorensen's Resort, Woodfords Inn

Towns and Agencies: Alpine County Chamber of Commerce, Amador County Chamber of Commerce and Visitors Bureau, Lake Tahoe Visitor Information, South Lake Tahoe Chamber of Commerce

HIGHLIGHTS Shealor (pronounced *SHAY-ler*) Lake is one of the prettiest of the dozens of small lakes caught in the hollows glaciers left behind in the low, rolling, lightly forested country north of State Route 88 (Trip 98's Lake Margaret is another such lake). Climb the granite dome separating Shealor Lake from the highway, enjoying wonderful views along the way, and then descend to the lake.

Shealor Lake

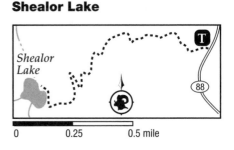

HOW TO GET TO THE TRAILHEAD Just 17.9 miles southwest of Carson Pass on State Route 88 is a tiny parking lot west of the highway, in an area where the road makes a pronounced curve between a couple granite domes. This ill-marked turnoff is west of Silver Lake and east of Plasse's Resort.

ON THE TRAIL Find the trail at the upper end of the parking lot, and bear right (north) away from the lot. At first the duff trail is in moderate forest, but it soon enters boulder-studded, patchy forest. Ascend gradually to moderately now, enjoying over-the-shoulder views of Thunder Mountain, to reach an area of granite slabs. Head northwest up the slabs without veering off into the dirt below the slabs; ducks are helpful here. Shortly pick up the dusty trail again and climb gradually to moderately, curving along the forest edge between slabs and meadow. Presently make a switchback turn and climb southwest up a small granite dome. Ducks are again helpful.

At the ridgeline at almost 0.5 mile, you are on a saddle between knobs at 7720-plus feet (on the 7.5′ topo, it's near the red number 6). There are beautiful views east toward Silver Lake (the lake itself is mostly obscured by forest) and of the peaks around it. Now head west down the other side of the dome, to a rolling, once-glaciated landscape where other bare domes beckon. Far ahead and below to the left, a pretty lake bound by cliffs, forest, and meadow sits on a steplike bench amid the domes. It's one of the Shealor Lakes, and the sight is inspiring. The other lakes come into view early on during the descent of this open, rocky, very loose trail; the footing is poor, so be careful. The trail is sometimes indistinct, too; the goal is to keep working safely down to that lake. While descending, steeply at times, and friction-walking a few slabs, notice bits of glacial polish glittering in the sun that strikes the granite cliffs around the lake.

At the bottom of the descent, level out briefly by a patch of forest south of the lake, and then veer right (north) through chaparral and onto the open slabs on the lake's east shore. Pick your way down to the shore of this little gem, Shealor Lake at 1.25 miles and 7180 feet, which is picturesquely rockbound on most sides.

Return the way you came.

U.S. Highway 50: South of Tahoe

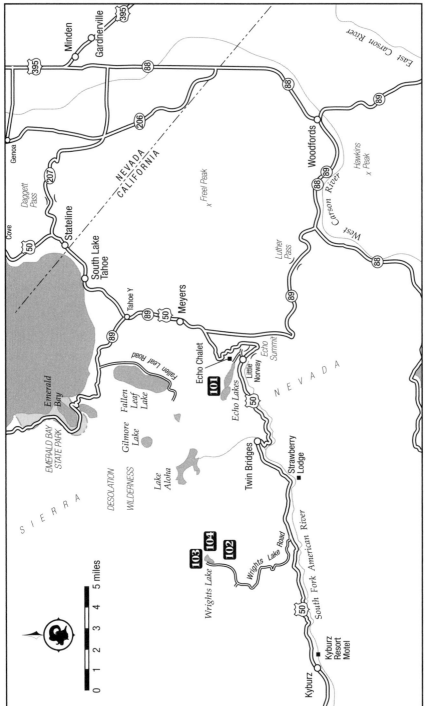

CHAPTER 11

U.S. Highway 50: South of Tahoe

North of State Route 88, U.S. Highway 50 descends the steep, forested canyon of the American River from Echo Summit westward. The scenery is excellent, but the dauntingly high canyon walls seem at first glance to offer few hiking opportunities. However, marvelous hiking lies just off the roads that branch north from the highway to trailheads in Desolation Wilderness.

Small, lake-filled Desolation Wilderness is the backcountry gem of the Tahoe Sierra. Desolation Wilderness's proximity to the San Francisco-Sacramento area and to crowded Lake Tahoe means the wilderness is very heavily used. As a result, dayhikers are required to have permits; all trailheads for Desolation Wilderness destinations in this book have self-issue stations.

Recommended Maps

In addition to those listed in the trip write-ups, your library of maps should include the following. Get the latest edition/revision you can find. They're widely available, certainly at any of the local ranger stations.

■ *El Dorado National Forest.* U.S. Department of Agriculture and U.S. Forest Service.

■ *Lake Tahoe Basin Management Unit.* U.S. Department of Agriculture and U.S. Forest Service.

■ *Desolation Wilderness and the South Lake Tahoe Basin.* Wilderness Press.

Individual Lodgings

Name	Nearest Community	Type	Facilities	Price Range	Contact Information	Website and Email Address
Echo Chalet	Kyburz	Mountain	Cabins	$–$$$	9900 Echo Lakes Road Echo Lake, CA 95721 Summer (phone): 530-659-7207 Winter (fax): 530-620-7207	www.echochalet.com echochalet-since1939@earthlink.net
Kyburz Resort Motel	Kyburz	Other	Rooms	$–$$	P.O. Box 27 Kyburz, CA 95720 Phone: 530-293-3382	http://kyburzresortmotel.com
Strawberry Lodge	Kyburz	Other	Rooms, cabins	$–$$$	17510 Highway 50 Kyburz, CA 95720 Phone: 530-659-7200	http://strawberry-lodge.com info@strawberrylodge.com

Towns and Agencies

Name	Nearest Community	Type	Contact Information	Website and Email Address
El Dorado County Visitors Authority (includes Kyburz)	Placerville	Chamber of Commerce	542 Main Street Placerville, CA 95667 Phone: 530-621-5885 or 800-457-6279	www.visiteldorado.com tourism@eldoradocounty.org
Lake Tahoe Visitor Information (VirtualTahoe)	South Lake Tahoe	Agency	P.O. Box 7172 #173 Stateline, NV 89449-7172 Phone: 800-210-3459, 800-371-2620, or 530-544-5050	www.virtualtahoe.com contactus@virtualtahoe.com
South Lake Tahoe Chamber of Commerce	South Lake Tahoe	Chamber of Commerce	3066 Lake Tahoe Blvd. South Lake Tahoe, CA 96150 Phone: 530-541-5255	www.tahoeinfo.com sltcc@sierra.net

101 Tamarack and Triangle Lakes

Place	Total Distance	Elevation	Difficulty Level	Type
Trailhead		7414		
Tamarack Lake	7+	7740	S	O&B
Entire semiloop	9.3	8360	S U	Semi

Note   A permit is required for day use; they are available at a self-issue station at the trailhead.

Best Time   Early July–mid-October

Topos   *Echo Lake* 7.5'; USDA/USFS *Desolation Wilderness*

Where to Stay

Mountain: Echo Chalet

Other: Kyburz Resort Motel, Strawberry Lodge

Towns and Agencies: El Dorado County Visitors Authority, Lake Tahoe Visitor Information, South Lake Tahoe Chamber of Commerce

HIGHLIGHTS This is a wonderfully scenic hike, and the pleasure starts right at the trailhead by Echo Chalet, beginning with a breathtaking view over Echo Lakes.

HOW TO GET TO THE TRAILHEAD Start from Echo Summit, the high point between South Lake Tahoe and Strawberry and on a hairpin turn. Head north-northwest on U.S. Highway 50 around the densely forested hairpin, as if toward Strawberry and the Central Valley. Pass the ruins of defunct resort Little Norway on the right and then reach a junction with Johnson Pass Road on the right, 1 mile from Echo Summit. Turn east (right) onto Johnson Pass Road and follow it 0.6 mile to a messy Y-junction with Echo Lakes Road.

Turn north (left) here and follow Echo Lakes Road 1 mile to a couple of large parking areas, before the road elbows down to Echo Lakes. Ignore turnoffs to summer camps and cabins on the way. There's a paved lot on the left, and a dirt lot visible on a spur to the right, where the Pacific Crest Trail (PCT) and Tahoe-Yosemite Trail (TYT) pass through this area. Echo Chalet's parking is reserved for their guests, so park here and walk steeply down the last 0.2 mile of the road to the trailhead or the water-taxi dock. Note that the hiking mileages given in the hike description are from the trailhead only. There are restrooms, water, a telephone, and a seasonal water-taxi service near the trailhead. If Echo Chalet is open, it operates a small store.

Taking the water-taxi across Lower and Upper Echo lakes can eliminate a lot of walking along the lakes' north shores—more than 2.3 miles if you take the water-taxi one way and 4.6 miles if you take it both ways.

ON THE TRAIL The trailhead for this hike, as well as for the combined PCT and TYT, is at Lower Echo Lake's dam, next to Echo Chalet. Walk across the dam and then wind up a knoll north of the dam to find nice views over South Lake

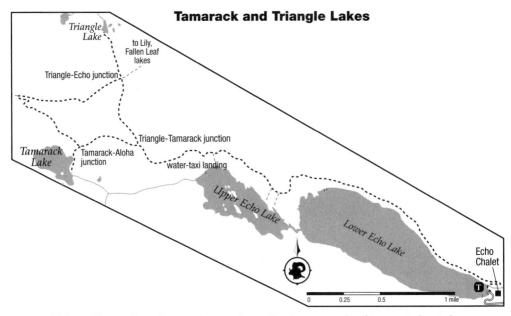

Tamarack and Triangle Lakes

Tahoe. The trail angles northwest along the slopes north of Lower Echo Lake, soon crossing angled slabs on an airy path that was blasted out of them. Views across Lower Echo Lake and of the lake itself lend interest to this leg, which can be very hot as the forest is sparse. The downhill slopes can be very steep.

Beyond the slabs, avoid turnoffs to the charming, privately owned lakeside cabins below on this up-and-down traverse. Pass beneath some low cliffs, and presently round the ridge that separates Lower Echo Lake from Upper Echo Lake except for a narrow channel. Now the forest cover is fuller and the going much cooler; paths dart off here and there to private, dollhouse cabins, but stay ahead on the main trail. At 2.3 miles reach a junction. The spur to the left (south) heads 0.1 mile downhill to the water-taxi landing at Upper Echo Lake, where there's a shack with a phone for calling for a return water-taxi.

Those who took the water-taxi can pick up the trip at this junction. Go ahead, continuing on the PCT and TYT. Cross a stream at 2.5 miles and soon climb in open country on another rocky trail segment blasted through granite—great over-the-shoulder views along this leg. Reach the Desolation Wilderness boundary at about a little over 3 miles and then the Triangle-Tamarack junction: The right (north) trail comes down from Triangle Lake and is your return route from the loop part of this trip, and the left (west-northwest) trail is the PCT and TYT toward the Tamarack Lake junction and Lake Aloha.

Continue toward Tamarack Lake, enjoying a surprising wildflower display despite the sandy, dry terrain. At 3.3 miles reach the Tamarack-Aloha junction. Scamper off to the left, descending toward Tamarack Lake, under sparsely wooded slopes of gray granite. The trail grows faint as it swings easily through this lightly wooded basin, but very soon it curves southeast beside the lovely lake at nearly 3.5 miles and 7740 feet. Tamarack is by far the prettiest of the lakes in this small basin. Contrary to what's on the topo, there are only confusing fragments of use trails from Tamarack to Ralston and Cagwin lakes.

Return to the Tamarack-Aloha junction, now at a little more than 3.5 miles total. To begin the loop part of this trip, turn left (west) toward Lake Aloha (otherwise, retrace your steps). Avoid a use trail that shortly comes in on the right. The trail, though hot and exposed, is flowery in season and ascends to a junction at 4.3 miles.

Go right (east-southeast), leaving the PCT and TYT and taking the lightly used trail to Triangle Lake, which climbs gradually to moderately on the hot, open south slope of Keiths Dome. Here there are a few flowers and a wealth of fabulous views, especially once the trail rounds the dome's southeast-trending ridge and reaches its high point: to Echo Lakes; to Tamarack and Ralston lakes; to crags and peaks in Desolation Wilderness; and, to the east, Lake Tahoe. After enjoying these spectacular views, round the northeast side of the ridge and descend into a lodgepole and red fir forest.

At a little over 5 miles reach the Triangle-Echo junction, on a saddle. From here, make an out-and-back leg to Triangle Lake: Turn left to follow a faint trail downhill and generally north through a damp, mixed-conifer forest, along meadows, over knobs, and then steeply down a little swale to an unmapped pond near Triangle Lake. From here, cross slabs to come out a little above the southwest shore of charming, secluded Triangle Lake at 5.5 miles and 8020 feet.

Return to the Triangle-Echo junction on the saddle. At nearly 6 miles total now, take the middle fork back to Echo Lakes, descending a rocky duff trail moderately to steeply, through red fir and lodgepole. The trail becomes very rocky as it emerges on an open slope and then reaches the Triangle-Tamarack junction with the PCT and TYT at 6.5 miles.

Turn left (east) here and retrace your steps to the trailhead at a little over 9.3 miles.

102 Bloodsucker Lake

Place	Total Distance	Elevation	Difficulty Level	Type
Trailhead		7040		
Bloodsucker Lake	4	7420	M	O&B

Best Time Late May–mid-October
Topos *Pyramid Peak 7.5'*; USDA/USFS *Desolation Wilderness*
Where to Stay
Mountain: Echo Chalet

Other: Kyburz Resort Motel, Strawberry Lodge

Towns and Agencies: El Dorado County Visitors Authority, Lake Tahoe Visitor Information, South Lake Tahoe Chamber of Commerce

HIGHLIGHTS Bloodsucker Lake is mighty pretty, and its resident population of leeches (bloodsuckers) makes it unusual and interesting.

Bloodsucker Lake

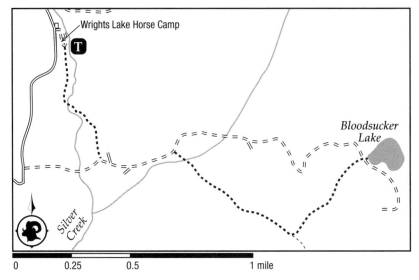

HOW TO GET TO THE TRAILHEAD About 8.2 miles west of Echo Summit (west of Strawberry and east of Kyburz), turn north on Forest Service Road 4 to Wrights Lake Recreation Area. Following signs, drive 7.6 miles on Forest Service Road 4, bypassing a junction with Forest Service Road 32, toward Wrights Lake. Find a spur road on the right into a large parking lot signed for Wrights Lake Horse Camp. Park here.

ON THE TRAIL From the parking lot, walk south into the equestrian camp, taking either side of the loop road the campsites branch from. At the far end, find the trailhead for the Bloodsucker Lake Trail. On a wide, sandy path, continue southeast into moderate lodgepole forest. At 0.3 mile cross Silver Creek. Horses have made the trail crossing very broad and muddy. When the water's high, this crossing can be troublesome, so look for logs. Shortly veer southeast away from Silver Creek and climb a moraine to meet a dirt road (not on the topo) at a little over 0.5 mile. Note this spot for the return.

Turn left (east) onto the road and avoid another road that shortly comes in from the left (northwest). Continue east toward the Crystal Range, visible in the distance. The going is sunstruck and dusty, and the route shortly passes another junction, where you should avoid a road that comes in from the right (south). Continue east; red firs and alders line the road here and provide a little shade. At a trail sign at nearly 0.6 mile, as the road curves northeast, turn right (east) off the road and onto a footpath. (The road eventually goes to Bloodsucker Lake, too, but is very dusty and sometimes very steep.)

Soon reach a very swampy section that may be wonderfully flowery but difficult in early season, and a little over 0.75 mile cross a multistranded tributary of Silver Creek. The trail, grown dusty again, abruptly climbs a moraine. Multiple tracks diverge and converge, and the going is increasingly unpleasant, dusty, and sunblasted. At the moraine's top at nearly 1.5 miles, reach a junction. Go left (northeast) and find that, after a level stretch, the trail climbs as the going becomes muddy and the surface poor—but the flowers around it are a sight to behold. At nearly 2 miles reach a road—another segment of the one you walked on earlier—and see the lake a few steps ahead.

Step across the road and down to the cool shore of lovely Bloodsucker Lake at 2 miles and 7420 feet. Blue Peak rises to the northeast, and other Crystal Range peaks are visible from here. In the water, look for a leech or two swimming by in an undulating fashion; they're about 2 to 3 inches long, about 0.25 inch wide, yellowish to grayish, flattened, and slightly tapered at either end. They're not native, and no one knows how they got here.

Return the way you came.

103 Grouse and Hemlock Lakes

Place	Total Distance	Elevation	Difficulty Level	Type
Trailhead		6940		
Grouse Lake	4.6	8140	M	O&B
Hemlock Lake	6	8380	S	O&B

Note   A permit is required for day use; they are available at a self-issue station at the trailhead.

Best Time   Early July–mid-October

Topos   *Pyramid Peak 7.5'*; USDA/USFS *Desolation Wilderness*

Where to Stay

Mountain: Echo Chalet

Other: Kyburz Resort Motel, Strawberry Lodge

Towns and Agencies: El Dorado County Visitors Authority, Lake Tahoe Visitor Information, South Lake Tahoe Chamber of Commerce

HIGHLIGHTS From beautiful Wrights Lake, ascend through a dramatic landscape to a chain of lovely little lakes, each with its own beauty and character.

HOW TO GET TO THE TRAILHEAD About 8.2 miles west of Echo Summit (west of Strawberry and east of Kyburz), turn north onto Forest Service Road 4 to Wrights Lake Recreation Area. Following signs, drive 7.6 miles on FSR 4, bypassing a junction with Forest Service Road 32, toward Wrights Lake. Continue past a spur road on the right signed for Wrights Lake Horse Camp, 0.1 mile farther to a loop road by an information station. Turn right (east) onto signed Forest Service Road 12N23. Go 0.7 mile, passing a campground entrance, all the way to the road's end at a small parking loop, with a restroom, at the north-north-east corner of Wrights Lake.

ON THE TRAIL Circumvent a locked gate on the left that bars cars beyond the parking loop. Head down the road and shortly find a large information sign just

Grouse, Hemlock, Twin, and Island Lakes

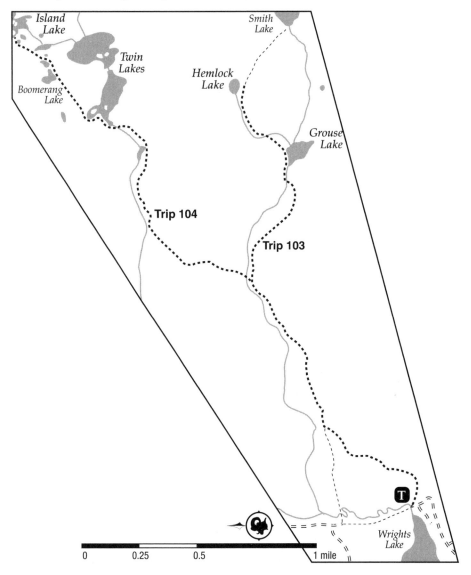

before a bridge. Your route hooks sharply to the right before the bridge. Head north-northeast through meadowy woods, curving around the lush meadow that borders the inlet, on a trail not shown on the 7.5′ topo. Cross several little streams while walking through the meadow, which is a flower garden in season. At nearly 0.3 mile reach a Y-junction. The left (west) branch is the Loop Trail around Wrights Lake.

Go right (east-northeast) to skirt granite slabs and climb, ignoring a use trail on the left. At about 0.5 mile, the trail levels out atop a small, dry ridge. Now dip into forest and then climb again, noticing a stream to the left. Climb a rocky ridge on loose zigzags, fording an unmapped stream at 0.75 mile. Continue up slabs, following ducks and coming abreast of Grouse Lake's outlet stream (on your left).

At a little under 1.25 miles enter Desolation Wilderness, and at 1.3 miles reach a junction: The left (north) trail goes to Twin Lakes (Trip 104). Turn right (east) for Grouse Lake, following more ducks up slabs full of potholes, keeping generally to the right side of the lovely granite bowl here, down which the outlet spills in picturesque cascades. Soon veer right, out of the bowl and into forest, and presently curve east-southeast in an open, slabby valley on a sandy trail. At a little more than 2 miles, at the head of the slabby valley, veer left (northeast) to climb steeply, briefly enjoy expansive views north and west, and then walk alongside the noisy outlet. At 2.25 miles ford the broad, multistranded outlet between cascades; there's a fine display of flowers here in season.

Reach beautiful Grouse Lake at a little more than 2.3 miles and 8140 feet. The trail traces Grouse's north shore over slabs and then veers away from the wonderland of meadows and streams around the lake's inlet to begin climbing the ridge separating Grouse and Hemlock lakes. The trail climbs steeply northeast on a rocky, often faint track before leveling out in open forest to ford the stream between Grouse and Hemlock lakes. The path then veers northeast to little Hemlock Lake at 3 miles and 8380 feet, which is set in handsome cliffs on the north and east and is shaded by mountain hemlocks on the south.

Retrace your steps.

104 Twin and Island Lakes

Place	Total Distance	Elevation	Difficulty Level	Type
Trailhead		6940		
Lower Twin Lake	5.5	7880	M	O&B
Island Lake	7	8140	S	O&B

Note   A permit is required for day use; they are available at a self-issue station at the trailhead.

Best Time   Late May–mid-October

Topos   *Pyramid Peak 7.5'*; USDA/USFS *Desolation Wilderness*

Where to Stay

Mountain: Echo Chalet

Other: Kyburz Resort Motel, Strawberry Lodge

Towns and Agencies: El Dorado County Visitors Authority, Lake Tahoe Visitor Information, South Lake Tahoe Chamber of Commerce

See map on page 286

HIGHLIGHTS Starting at Wrights Lake at the same trailhead as for Trip 103, climb through a spectacular landscape to two splendid lakes.

HOW TO GET TO THE TRAILHEAD About 8.2 miles west of Echo Summit (west of Strawberry and east of Kyburz), turn north on Forest Service Road 4 to Wrights

Island Lake

Lake Recreation Area. Following signs, drive 7.6 miles on FSR 4, bypassing a junction with Forest Service Road 32, toward Wrights Lake. Continue past a spur road on the right into a large parking lot signed for Wrights Lake Horse Camp 0.1 mile to a loop road by an information station. Turn right (east) onto signed Forest Service Road 12N23. Go 0.7 mile , passing a campground entrance, all the way the road's end at a small parking loop, with restroom facilities, at the north corner of Wrights Lake.

ON THE TRAIL Circumvent a locked gate on the left that bars travel beyond the parking loop. Head down the road and shortly find a large information sign just before a bridge. Your route hooks sharply to the right before the bridge. Head north-northeast through meadowy woods, curving around the lush meadow the borders the inlet, on a trail not shown on the 7.5′ topo. Cross several little streams while walking through the meadow, which is a flower garden in season. At nearly 0.3 mile reach a Y-junction. The left (west) branch is the Loop Trail around Wrights Lake.

Go right (east-northeast) to skirt granite slabs and climb, ignoring a use trail on the left. At about 0.5 mile, the trail levels out atop a small, dry ridge. Now dip into forest and then climb again, up a rocky ridge on loose zigzags, fording an unmapped stream at 0.75 mile. Continue up slabs, following ducks and coming abreast of Grouse Lake's outlet stream (on your left).

At a little under 1.25 miles enter Desolation Wilderness, and at 1.3 miles reach a junction: The right (east) trail goes to Grouse Lake (Trip 103). Turn left (north) toward Twin Lakes, fording Grouse Lake's outlet stream almost immediately. Begin a gradual ascent of slabs through a shallow bowl of mostly bare granite, heading northeast on the indistinct trail and soon crossing other strands of Grouse Lake's outlet in season.

Nearing 2 miles, top the ridge around the bowl at its lower, east end, about 0.25 mile east of a low knoll. Now descend north-northeast into forest and toward the showy, cascading outlet of Twin Lakes. Just before reaching the outlet, veer east-southeast on more slabs and into the next cirque to begin a long, climbing curve to the north. Blast marks in the slabs show how the route was built.

At last the trail, such as it is, levels out. Now curve into a peak-ringed cirque, passing a pond to the left (north). At a little more than 2.3 miles ford Twin Lakes' outlet on built-up stones before continuing deeper into the cirque. Reach dramatic, sparsely forested lower Twin Lake at 2.75 miles and 7880 feet. Across the lake, the cascading outlet of higher lakes makes a springtime spectacle.

Continuing, ford lower Twin Lake's outlet on a ruined dam that's more hindrance than help. Veer northeast on a very rocky trail along the north side of lower Twin Lake and over a ridgelet above tiny Boomerang Lake. The trail passes over the "strait" between Boomerang and a little pond and then follows a rocky track, presently skirting the north end of a long, narrow pond below Island Lake. After that, it's just a few steps to the shore of high, barren Island Lake at 3.5 miles and 8140 feet. The trail peters out a little before the lakeshore, so pick your way to the stony shore and get an eyeful.

Return the way you came.

State Route 89 Around Lake Tahoe

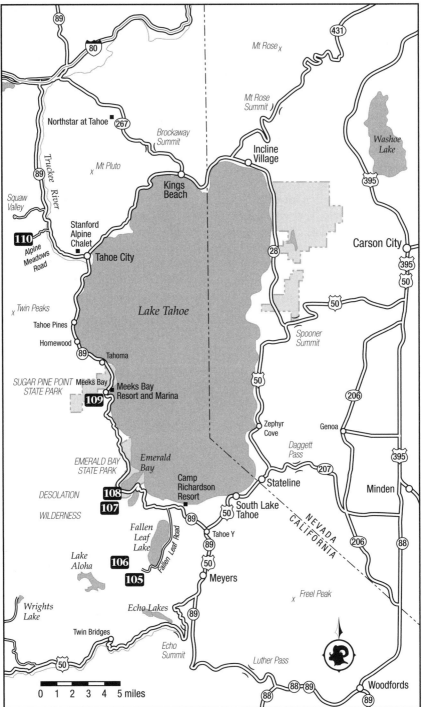

Note: Lodgings in the Norden and Soda Springs areas are shown on the map on p. 308.

CHAPTER 12

State Route 89 Around Lake Tahoe

From its junction with U.S. Highway 50 in South Lake Tahoe, State Route 89 curves west and then north around the California side of Lake Tahoe, past Tallac (pronounced tuh-LACK) Historic Site and the Lake Tahoe Visitor Center. Be sure to visit both. The highway soon begins swooping along cliffs overlooking Emerald Bay, past breathtaking viewpoints, and through woodsy hamlets. Unfortunately, Lake Tahoe is like Yosemite Valley in one respect: tranquil and sublimely beautiful early in the morning and in the evening, at midday it is hot, dusty, noisy, crowded, and choked with cars.

As with Yosemite Valley, the best way to enjoy Lake Tahoe at midday is to be somewhere else, such as on the wonderful trails high above the lake, mostly in Desolation Wilderness. All driving directions for these hikes start from "the Tahoe Y": It's the junction in the town of South Lake Tahoe where State Route 89 and U.S. Highway 50 meet. SR 89 heads around Lake Tahoe's west (California) side, and U.S. 50 rounds Lake Tahoe's east (Nevada) side. All the following trips are from 89 on the California side. I've intentionally kept driving distances between lodgings and trailheads in this section shorter than those allowed in other sections on account of the slow, heavy traffic on U.S. Highway 89 around Tahoe.

Recommended Maps

- *El Dorado National Forest.* U.S. Department of Agriculture and U.S. Forest Service.
- *Lake Tahoe Basin Management Unit.* U.S. Department of Agriculture and U.S. Forest Service.
- *Lake Tahoe* and *Desolation Wilderness.* Tom Harrison Maps.

Individual Lodgings

Name	Nearest Community	Type	Facilities	Price Range	Contact Information	Website and Email Address
Camp Richardson Resort	South Lake Tahoe	Other	Rooms, cabins	$–$$$	P.O. Box 9028 South Lake Tahoe, CA 96158 Phone: 800-544-1801 or 530-541-1801	www.camprichardson .com
Clair Tappaan Lodge	Norden	Mountain	Rooms, dormitories	$	P.O. Box 36 Norden, CA 95724 Phone: 800-679-6775 or 530-426-3632	www.sierraclub.org/ outings/lodges/ctl/ ctl@sierraclub.org
Ice Lakes Lodge	Soda Springs	Mountain	Rooms	$$	P.O. Box 1100 Soda Springs, CA 95728 Phone: 800-500-3871 or 530-426-3871	www.icelakeslodge.com reservations@royal gorge.com
Meeks Bay Resort and Marina	Tahoma	Mountain	Rooms, cabins, condos	$–$$$	7941 Emerald Bay Road Meeks Bay, CA 96142 Phone: 877-326-3357 or 530-525-6946	www.washoetribe.us/ meeksbayresort/index.asp
Northstar at Tahoe	Truckee	Other	Rooms, condos	$$$	P.O. Box 129 Truckee, CA 96160 Phone: 800-GO-NORTH	www.northstarattahoe.com
Rainbow Lodge Bed and Breakfast	Soda Springs	Other	Rooms	$$–$$$	P.O. Box 1100 Soda Springs, CA 95728 Phone: 800-500-3871 or 530-426-3871	www.royalgorge.com reservations@royal gorge.com
Stanford Alpine Chalet	Tahoe City	Mountain	Rooms	$–$$$	P.O. Box 6436 Tahoe City, CA 96145 Phone: 530-583-1550	www.stanfordalpine chalet.com www.stanfordalumni.org/ learningtravel/sierra/alpine chalet/.home.html chalet@stanford.edu
Summit House	Norden	Other	Rooms, condos	$$–$$$	10150 Ski Ranch Lane Truckee, CA 96162 Phone: 530-426-9323	www.summithouse.com summit@summithouse.com

Towns and Agencies

Name	Nearest Community	Type	Contact Information	Website and Email Address
Alpine Meadows	Tahoe City	Agency	P.O. Box 5279 Tahoe City, CA 96145 Phone: 800-949-3296 or 530-583-4232	http://skialpine.com info@skialpine.com
Castle Peak Vacation Rentals	Soda Springs	Agency	P.O. Box 979 Soda Springs, CA 95728 Phone: 888-253-5551 or 530-426-1226	www.castlepeak.com sue@castlepeak.com
Lake Tahoe Visitor Information (VirtualTahoe)	South Lake Tahoe	Agency	P.O. Box 7172 #173 Stateline, NV 89449 Phone: 800-210-3459, 800-371-2620, or 530-544-5050	www.virtualtahoe.com contactus@virtualtahoe.com
North Lake Tahoe Resort Association	Tahoe City	Chamber of Commerce/Visitors Bureau	P.O. Box 1757 Tahoe City, CA 96145 Phone: 888-434-1262 or 530-583-3494	www.puretahoenorth.com info@puretahoenorth.com kym@puretahoenorth.com
South Lake Tahoe Chamber of Commerce	South LakeTahoe	Chamber of Commerce	3066 Lake Tahoe Blvd. South Lake Tahoe, CA 96150 Phone: 530-541-5255	www.tahoeinfo.com sltcc@sierra.net
Squaw Valley	Squaw Valley	Agency	Phone: 800-403-0206	www.squaw.com
Truckee Donner Chamber of Commerce	Truckee, Donner Lake	Chamber of Commerce	10065 Donner Pass Road Truckee, CA 96161 Phone: 530-587-2757	www.truckee.com info@truckee.com

105 Grass Lake

Place	Total Distance	Elevation	Level	Type
Start		6560		
Grass Lake	4.5+	7420	M	O&B

Note A permit is required for day use; they are available at a self-issue station at the trailhead.

Best Time Late May–mid-October

Topos *Emerald Bay, Echo Lake* 7.5′; USDA/USFS *Desolation Wilderness*

Where to Stay

  Mountain: Meeks Bay Resort and Marina

  Other: Camp Richardson Resort

  Towns and Agencies: Lake Tahoe Visitor Information, South Lake Tahoe Chamber of Commerce

Grass, Gilmore, Half Moon, and Susie Lakes

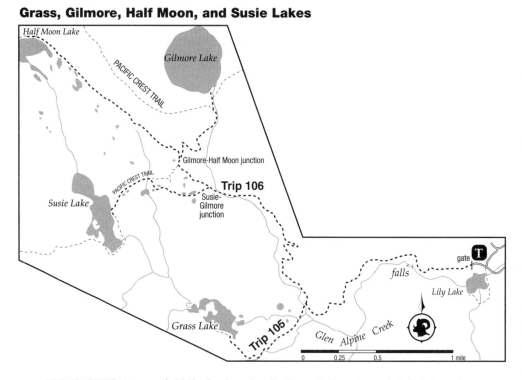

HIGHLIGHTS A peaceful hike leads to lovely Grass Lake, whose delightful setting invites visitors to linger.

HOW TO GET TO THE TRAILHEAD From the Tahoe Y, follow State Route 89 north along the lake to Fallen Leaf Road. Turn south onto Fallen Leaf Road and pass Fallen Leaf Lake and the turnoff to private Stanford High Sierra Camp, staying left where a spur road branches right over tumbling Glen Alpine Creek to the camp. The road, its condition growing worse by the yard, then climbs past attractive Glen Alpine Falls to the Glen Alpine Trailhead, where there are restrooms and parking at 5.6 miles next to Lily Lake.

ON THE TRAIL The unmarked trailhead is just beyond the restrooms at a locked gate across a very rocky old road. Head generally west on that road, where the first leg is a public right-of-way through private land. Be sure to stay on the main road as side roads dodge in and out.

At a little over 0.3 mile reach a viewpoint for a very handsome cascade on Glen Alpine Creek. Continuing, find that the road now rises, now is level, now is sunstruck, now is shady as it continues generally west past cabins, ponds, meadows, patches of forest, and patches of wildflowers. Nearing 1 mile reach the road's end and pick up the trail to Susie, Gilmore, and Grass lakes, which winds gradually up rocky knolls. Now dip into forest, pass the boundary of Desolation Wilderness, and reach a junction at a little more than 1.3 miles.

Take the left (southwest) fork, soon fording Gilmore Lake's and then Grass Lake's outlets. Come alongside a grassy pond and multiple, unmapped streamlets, making two more fords in short order. At an unmapped T-junction at a little more than 1.6 miles, go left, climbing moderately through chaparral and more rocky knolls, to reach multi-lobed, meadow-fringed Grass Lake at a little more than 2.25 miles and 7420 feet. If you continue beyond Grass Lake's first bay, you'll get an across-the-lake view of the wonderful cascades on one of its inlets, which happens to be higher Susie Lake's outlet (see Trip 106). Beyond the lake rise Jacks and Dicks peaks, and impressive cliffs bound the lake on its far side. This is a beautiful spot, and you'll want to spend some time here.

Retrace your steps.

106 Gilmore, Half Moon, or Susie Lake

Place	Total Distance	Elevation	Difficulty Level	Type
Start		6560		
Gilmore Lake only	8.6	8300	S	O&B
Half Moon Lake only	10	8040	S	O&B
Susie Lake only	8.5+	7800	S	O&B

Note   A permit is required for day use; they are available at a self-issue station at the trailhead.

Best Time   Early July to mid-October

Topos   *Emerald Bay, Echo Lake, Rockbound Valley 7.5'; USDA/USFS Desolation Wilderness*

See map on page 294

Where to Stay

Mountain: Meeks Bay Resort and Marina

Other: Camp Richardson Resort

Towns and Agencies: Lake Tahoe Visitor Information, South Lake Tahoe Chamber of Commerce

HIGHLIGHTS Long-vanished glaciers carved the drainage of Glen Alpine Creek and scattered many beautiful lakes throughout it. Trip 105 visited Grass Lake, one of the lower lakes. This trip visits your choice of three beauties higher in the drainage.

HOW TO GET TO THE TRAILHEAD From the Tahoe Y, follow State Route 89 north along the lake to Fallen Leaf Road. Turn south onto Fallen Leaf Road and pass Fallen Leaf Lake and the turnoff to private Stanford High Sierra Camp, staying where a spur road branches right over tumbling Glen Alpine Creek to the camp. The road, its condition growing worse by the yard, then climbs past attractive Glen Alpine Falls to the Glen Alpine Trailhead, where there are parking and restrooms at 5.6 miles next to Lily Lake.

ON THE TRAIL The unmarked trailhead is just beyond the restrooms at a locked gate across a very rocky old road. Head generally west on that road, where the first leg is a public right-of-way through private land. Be sure to stay on the main road as side roads dodge in and out.

The road goes up and down and in and out of shade as it continues generally west past cabins, ponds, meadows, patches of forest, and patches of wildflowers. Nearing 1 mile reach the road's end and pick up the trail to Susie, Gilmore, and Grass lakes. Reach a junction at a little more than 1.3 miles and go right (north). The trail winds now through forest, now over granite slabs, now up and around rocky outcrops, beneath a row of rust, gray, and brown peaks to the south and with an unmapped creek often nearby for company. At a little over 2.5 miles, ford the creek in forest, and then ford two seasonal trickles in the next 0.5 mile as the trail goes up a lightly forested gully.

Continuing, the trail is at first exposed, traversing over rusty rock above the cheery creek; then it enters a lodgepole and red fir forest, fords another creek, and shortly reaches what I call the Susie-Gilmore junction at 3.3 miles. The left (west) fork heads for Susie Lake and then Lake Aloha, and the right (west-northwest) fork goes Gilmore and Half Moon lakes and then Dicks Pass. (Note that later on, the right fork meets the Pacific Crest Trail, or PCT, and there is another opportunity to go to Susie Lake, but that route isn't covered in this trip.) Below are directions for visiting each of these three lakes individually. Which should you visit? Gilmore is the highest and seems the most peaceful of these lakes. Half Moon is the most remote and gets the fewest visitors. Susie is the lowest and has the most dramatic setting. Sturdy hikers can visit all three (a little over 14 miles), but doing that is beyond the limits of this book.

To go to Gilmore Lake or Half Moon Lake, go right at the Susie-Gilmore junction on a rocky and dusty trail through open forest, ascending while passing a talus slope on the right. Reddish Dicks Peak looms ahead. Soon, the gully to the left sprouts a lily-pad-dotted pond, while the Sierra Crest appears in the distance on the left. Near 3.6 miles meet the PCT: The left (southwest) branch heads to Susie Lake, and the right (northeast) branch heads to Half Moon and Gilmore lakes. Go right and almost immediately reach what I'll call the Gilmore-Half Moon junction, which may be unsigned.

To go to Gilmore Lake, go right (north) at the Gilmore-Half Moon junction and switchback up a hot, open slope with occasional shade from big old junipers; your effort is rewarded with expansive views that include Susie Lake. At the top, trade the views for a lodgepole forest, some pocket meadows, and, soon, the cascading outlet of Gilmore Lake. At about 4.25 miles reach another junction. Go right (north) to reach Gilmore Lake at 4.3 miles and 8300 feet. An apparent fork signals the edge of this big, beautiful lake, where use trails scoot off to the lakeshore. Retrace your steps to the trailhead.

To go to Half Moon Lake, turn left at the Gilmore-Half Moon junction. Soon the trail veers west-northwest toward Jacks and Dicks peaks on chaparral slopes on a trail that may be faint at times. Climb gradually, and from a rubbly shoulder there's a good view of dramatic Cracked Crag. Now descend into a damp forest of mountain hemlock, red fir, and lodgepole, meeting a tiny, unmapped creek that feeds pocket meadows and little tarns. Continue this ridge-and-forest pattern, gradually gaining elevation. Near 4.5 miles pass a large tarn on the left; it's one of Half Moon's outlying ponds. The trail, sometimes very faint, threads among pretty ponds to emerge on a grassy slope above a long, narrow lake that extends deep into a wonderfully rugged cirque bounded by Dicks and Jacks peaks. In season, the inlets bounding down this cirque form showy cascades. Descend to Half Moon Lake's shoreline at nearly 5 miles and 8040 feet. Return the way you came.

To go to Susie Lake, turn left at the Susie-Gilmore junction. Soon the trail dips through forest to pass several handsome ponds. Cross a seasonal stream feeding a meadow and pond on the left as the path climbs through moderate to dense lodgepole and red fir forest to reach a junction with the PCT at about 3.75 miles. Go left (west), through meadow and forest and then up a chaparral slope. Wind through an open forest, passing more ponds, and then pop over a tiny shoulder to a splendid sight: big, dramatic Susie Lake at a little more than 4.25 miles and 7800 feet, ringed by shattered, rusty rock and set under the Sierra Crest. Head for the lakeshore. Retrace your steps to the trailhead.

107 Granite, Velma, or Dicks Lake

Place	Total Distance	Elevation	Difficulty Level	Type
Start		6880		
Tahoe viewpoint	1+	7270	E	O&B
Granite Lake	2.5	7660	M	O&B
Upper Velma Lake	10	7940	S U	O&B
Middle Velma Lake	10	7900	S U	O&B
Dicks Lake	10	8420	S U	O&B
Cascade Falls	1.3	6800	E	O&B

Note   A permit is required for day use; they are available at a self-issue station at the trailhead.

Best Time   Late May–mid-October

Topos   *Emerald Bay, Rockbound Valley 7.5'*; USDA/USFS *Desolation Wilderness*

Where to Stay

Mountain: Meeks Bay Resort and Marina

Other: Camp Richardson Resort

Towns and Agencies: Lake Tahoe Visitor Information, South Lake Tahoe Chamber of Commerce

HIGHLIGHTS A dull first leg conceals the pleasures that await hikers farther on: a fabulous Emerald Bay-Tahoe viewpoint, lovely Granite Lake, and a chance to visit one of two higher lakes: alpine charmer Dicks Lake or islet-dotted Middle Velma Lake. An optional excursion to Cascade Falls rounds out the list of treats visitors can hike to from Bayview.

HOW TO GET TO THE TRAILHEAD From the Tahoe Y, drive 7.7 miles northwest on 89 to Bayview Campground. The turnoff is between Richardson's Resort and Meeks Bay. Turn south into the campground and drive through it about 0.2 mile to trailhead parking near its south end, which has restrooms.

ON THE TRAIL From the trailhead at the south end of the campground, walk about 45 feet south past the trailhead to a junction: The left (south) trail heads to Cascade Falls. Go right (southwest) for Granite Lake, zigzagging steeply up a dusty duff trail through spindly white firs.

At 0.5 mile enter Desolation Wilderness near an intermittent stream and soon reach a rocky viewpoint at a little more than 0.5 mile and about 7270 feet. Follow use trails to slightly different views, or scramble up onto the surrounding boulders. The scene here is simply magnificent, especially early in the morning before the midday haze settles in. The view is primarily east across Emerald Bay to Lake Tahoe and the Carson Range; this is a much more spectacular view of Emerald Bay than any from the highway. The next switchback reveals another superb view, this one including the head of Emerald Bay.

Granite, Velma, Dicks, and Eagles Lakes

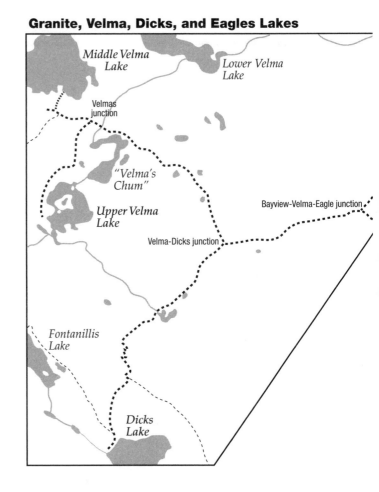

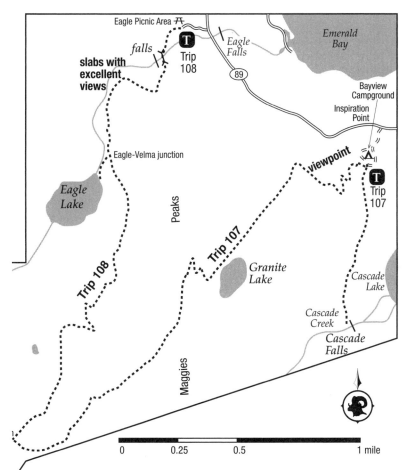

The grade eases as the path follows the alder-lined channel (not shown on the book's map) that is Granite Lake's seasonally flowing outlet, through a mixed conifer forest with a flowery understory. Nearing the lake, veer away from the outlet and into a bouldery chaparral area. The trail soon levels out above pretty, lodgepole-shaded Granite Lake at nearly 1.25 miles and 7660 feet, nestled in the cleavage of Maggies Peaks.

To continue, resume climbing steeply when leaving Granite Lake. Don't be misled onto use trails, particularly a large one leading south from the first big switchback above Granite Lake. The trail winds its way up the lightly wooded slope west of Granite Lake—the ridge between Maggies Peaks—on a series of rocky and sandy switchbacks. Views make the climb worth the trouble—increasingly excellent views over the South Lake Tahoe area, eventually including Lake Tahoe, Emerald Bay, Granite Lake, Cascade Lake, and Fallen Leaf Lake. The forest becomes thicker, the grade eases near the top of the climb, and the views are at their most expansive just before the trail rounds the ridgetop near 2.25 miles.

The other side of the ridge offers fine views west over Desolation Wilderness toward the Velma Lakes, and the path tops out at 8440 feet. Stroll through moderate to open forest, descending gradually to moderately, rounding some prominent knobs and ignoring a use trail that descends left to Azure Lake. Reenter moderate forest and, at a little more than 3 miles, on a small, viewless saddle, meet the trail coming up from Eagle Lake at the Bayview-Velma-Eagle junction. Go left (west-southwest) over a broad, sparsely wooded saddle from which there are rare glimpses of Azure Lake far below and even some over-the-shoulder views of Lake Tahoe.

At a little over 3.6 miles and 8220 feet, reach the Velma-Dicks junction: The left (southwest) fork heads to Dicks Lake, and the right (west-northwest) fork goes to the Velma Lakes. Choose between visiting Dicks Lake or one of the two Velma Lakes here. (Visiting all three of these lakes is beyond the limits of this book. However, sturdy hikers can make an estimated 5-plus-mile semiloop from this junction that passes Fontanillis Lake. This makes for a total hike of roughly 12.4 miles. The 5-mile semiloop estimate includes the out-and-back legs to the lakeshores.

To go to one of the Velma Lakes, turn right into a beautiful granite basin dotted with red fir and lodgepole. The sandy trail rolls along through wonderful mountain scenery that's highlighted every now and then by the sparkling waters of a seasonal pond. It's not long before you spot the big blue eye of one of the Velma Lakes "winking" at you far below. On the descent, twining down through lodgepole and granite, the trail grows faint as it traverses the shore of a lovely but unnamed lake just northeast of Upper Velma Lake, which I think of as "Velma's Chum." Splash across the outlet of Velma's Chum to pick up the trail on the other side. Shortly reach the Velmas junction with a spur trail to Upper Velma Lake at nearly 4.75 miles.

To go to Upper Velma Lake, turn left (southwest) at the Velmas junction and ford an unmapped creek. Proceed through damp, flowery forest and then over granite slabs. Use trails radiate lakeward from here to charming Upper Velma Lake at 5 miles and 7940 feet. The outlet of higher Fontanillis Lake makes a handsome, noisy cascade down the open slopes to the south-southwest. By the way, some maps show a spur trail between Upper Velma Lake and the trail to Dicks Lake, but it no longer exists as a maintained trail. Retrace your steps from here.

To go to Middle Velma Lake, go ahead (right) at the Velmas junction and shortly meet the junction with a trail to Fontanillis and Dicks lakes (incorrectly shown, or not shown at all, on most maps). Go ahead (right, west) about 300 feet to a great overlook of Middle Velma Lake (about 50 feet below) at nearly 5 miles and 7860 feet. Use up the rest of the 5 miles by picking a route down to Middle Velma Lake's shore. Retrace your steps from here.

To go to Dicks Lake, at the Velma-Dicks junction, turn left and follow the sometimes-faint trail through a wonderful, sparsely forested granite basin. Keep a sharp eye out for the track on this hard-rock terrain, keeping in mind that the correct route generally heads for prominent Dicks Peak to the south-southwest. Pass several pretty tarns and then an unnamed lakelet whose multistranded outlet the path presently fords at a low point on this leg. Cross a seasonal stream and begin ascending.

After a while, the route switchbacks moderately up the rocky slopes below Dicks Lake and reveals over-the-shoulder views of the Velma Lakes sparkling far below. Near the top, go right (southwest) at a junction for Dicks and Fontanillis lakes, pausing on the ridgetop at 8500 feet to take in a marvelous view over Desolation Wilderness and then descending a little to another junction at a little less than 5 miles. Go left (south), toddling downhill a little to lovely Dicks Lake at 5 miles and 8420 feet, cradled closely under Dicks Pass in half-wooded, half-talus slopes. Return the way you came.

Some publications call Cascade Falls "White Cloud Falls" for the clouds of white mist it throws up in season. If you'd like to visit these falls, back at the junction some 45 feet from the trailhead parking at Bayview, take the left fork south through open forest and then across chaparral slopes. You will soon enjoy excellent viewpoints of Cascade Falls above mostly private Cascade Lake, and then you can continue to Cascade Creek as it slithers over granite slabs just above seasonally showy Cascade Falls at 0.6 miles and 6800 feet (watch your footing!). Return the way you came.

108 Waterfall Below Eagle Lake and Eagle, Velma, or Dicks Lake

Place	Total Distance	Elevation	Difficulty Level	Type
Start		6580		
Waterfall	0.2	6660	E	O&B
Slabs with excellent views	0.6	6800	E	O&B
Eagle Lake	2	6880	E	O&B
Upper Velma Lake	10+	7940	S	O&B
Middle Velma Lake	10+	7900	S	O&B
Dicks Lake	10+	8420	S	O&B

Note	A permit is required for day use beyond the waterfall; they are available at a self-issue station at the trailhead.
Best Time	Late May–mid-October
Topos	*Emerald Bay, Rockbound Valley* 7.5'; USDA/USFS *Desolation Wilderness*

See map on page 298–299

Where to Stay

Mountain: Meeks Bay Resort and Marina

Other: Camp Richardson Resort

Towns and Agencies: Lake Tahoe Visitor Information, South Lake Tahoe Chamber of Commerce

HIGHLIGHTS The handsome little waterfall below Eagle Lake is a very popular destination, and beyond it is a fine viewpoint. Continue to attractive Eagle

Lake and then high into Desolation Wilderness to visit one of the many beautiful lakes there—the same higher lakes visited by Trip 107.

HOW TO GET TO THE TRAILHEAD From the Tahoe Y, drive northwest on SR 89 about 8.7 miles to the Eagle Falls Picnic Area/Trailhead between Meeks Bay and Inspiration Point. Turn west into the picnic area/parking lot with restroom facilities and parking. The trailhead is on the west end of the lot, which gets very crowded by midday.

ON THE TRAIL Go west from the trailhead on a broad, sandy trail that passes under a mixed conifer forest and then traverses chaparral. It presently begins to climb moderately to steeply on stone steps past junipers to a footbridge over a creek, overlooking a charming waterfall at less than 0.2 mile and 6660 feet. The officially named Eagle Falls are below the highway, but to countless visitors, *this* waterfall is "Eagle Falls." The fall dashes down a narrow, rocky valley that enhances its beauty but limits over-the-shoulder views back toward Emerald Bay.

To continue to Eagle Lake and beyond, cross the footbridge and almost immediately enter Desolation Wilderness. Pause to admire the steep, rocky cliffs hemming in this little valley before taking the rocky and sandy trail steeply upward on the creek's south bank. The grade eases near 0.3 mile and crosses an open area of juniper-dotted granite slabs, at 0.3 mile and 6800 feet, where there are excellent views east over Emerald Bay and Lake Tahoe. Leaving the sunny slabs, turn back into forest and reach the Eagle-Velma junction at 1 mile with the spur trail on the right (southwest) down to Eagle Lake. Going to Eagle Lake and then on to either the Velma Lakes or Dicks Lake will add 0.2 mile to the total trip.

To go to Eagle Lake, go right at the Eagle-Velma junction and dash 0.1 mile down the trail to the east shore of little Eagle Lake at about 1 mile and 6880 feet. Return to the main trail the way you came.

It's slightly over 10 miles total to visit either Dicks Lake or one of the Velma Lakes from here. To do so, go left at the Eagle-Velma junction (or right if you're returning from a visit to Eagle Lake) to climb a chaparral slope on a rocky and sandy trail, very steeply at first and then moderately. Enjoy views over Eagle Lake for a while on the climb, and then veer into forest, cross an unmapped stream, and zigzag moderately to steeply up a shady slope. Emerge briefly on sparsely wooded granite slabs and then continue switchbacking upward on a ridge, first on a sandy and rocky trail over the slabs, and then on a duff trail through forest.

At about 2.5 miles, swing around the nose of the ridge and into a beautiful granite basin. Descend a little, making a rolling, sandy traverse of the west side of the ridge, with views of a lily-pad-dotted lakelet deep in a boggy pocket. Next the trail winds uphill alongside an unmapped little stream, eventually crossing it. Beyond, the trail grows very faint, especially over a long, granite slab. The trail vanishes here, but there's nowhere else to go except south-southwest right up the slab, at the top of which hikers find the well-trod trail again. Pass to the south of a bouldery knoll to reach the Bayview-Velma-Eagle junction at a little over 3.25 miles.

Now on the same route as described for Trip 107, from the Bayview-Velma-Eagle junction, go left (west-southwest) over a broad, sparsely wooded saddle from which there are rare glimpses of Azure Lake far below and even some over-the-shoulder views of Lake Tahoe.

At 3.6 miles and 8220 feet, reach the Velma-Dicks junction: The left (southwest) fork heads to Dicks Lake, and the right (west-northwest) fork goes to the Velma Lakes. Choose between visiting Dicks Lake or one of the two Velma Lakes here. (Visiting all three of these lakes is beyond the limits of this book. However, sturdy hikers can make an estimated 5-plus-mile semiloop from this junction that passes Fontanillis Lake. This makes a total hike of roughly 12.75 miles. The 5-mile semiloop estimate includes the out-and-back legs to the lakeshores.)

To go to one of the Velma Lakes, turn right and follow a sandy trail that presently descends through lodgepole and granite. The trail grows faint as it traverses the shore of a lovely but unnamed lake just northeast of Upper Velma Lake, which I think of as "Velma's Chum." Splash across the outlet of Velma's Chum to pick up the trail on the other side. Shortly reach the Velmas junction with a spur trail to Upper Velma Lake at 4.75 miles.

To go to Upper Velma Lake, turn left (southwest) at the Velmas junction and ford an unmapped creek. Proceed through damp, flowery forest and then over granite slabs. Use trails radiate lakeward from here to charming Upper Velma Lake at 5 miles and 7940 feet. The outlet of higher Fontanillis Lake makes a handsome, noisy cascade down the open slopes to the south-southwest. By the way, some maps show a spur trail between Upper Velma Lake and the trail to Dicks Lake, but it no longer exists as a maintained trail. Retrace your steps from here.

To go to Middle Velma Lake, go ahead (right) at the Velmas junction and shortly meet the junction with a trail to Fontanillis and Dicks lakes. Go ahead (right, west) about 300 feet to a great overlook of Middle Velma Lake (about 50 feet below) at nearly 5 miles and 7860 feet. Pick a route down to Middle Velma Lake's shore. Retrace your steps from here.

To go to Dicks Lake, at the Velma-Dicks junction, turn left and follow the sometimes-faint trail through a granite basin. Keep a sharp eye out for the track on this hard-rock terrain, keeping in mind that the correct route generally heads for prominent Dicks Peak to the south-southwest. Pass several pretty tarns and then an unnamed lakelet whose multistranded outlet the path presently fords at a low point on this leg. Cross a seasonal stream and begin ascending.

After a while, the route switchbacks moderately up the rocky slopes below Dicks Lake. Near the top, go right (southwest) at a junction for Dicks and Fontanillis lakes. Descend a little to another junction at a little less than 5 miles. Go left (south), toddling downhill a little to lovely Dicks Lake at 5 miles and 8420 feet, cradled under Dicks Pass.

Return the way you came.

109 Meeks Creek Lakes

Place	Total Distance	Elevation	Difficulty Level	Type
Start		6235		
Lake Genevieve	8	7420	S	O&B
Crag Lake	8.5	7460	S	O&B
Shadow Lake	10	7660	S	O&B

Note   A permit is required for day use; they are available at a self-issue station at the trailhead.

Best Time   Late May–mid-October

Topos   *Homewood, Rockbound Valley 7.5'*; USDA/USFS *Desolation Wilderness*

Where to Stay

   Mountain: Meeks Bay Resort and Marina

   Other: Camp Richardson Resort

   Towns and Agencies: Alpine Meadows, Lake Tahoe Visitor Information, South Lake Tahoe Chamber of Commerce, Squaw Valley

HIGHLIGHTS This has to be the easiest long hike in this book, on the "moderate" side of "strenuous." After starting on a dirt road by a seasonally flower-filled meadow, a well-graded trail leads through forest to three charming lakes, each with its own ambience.

HOW TO GET TO THE TRAILHEAD From the Tahoe Y, drive 16.2 miles north on SR 89 to a very-hard-to-find trailhead on the west side of the highway at Log Cabin Road (the sign may be difficult to see) just north of a bridge over Meeks Creek. The trailhead is north of the resort-related road signs south of Meeks Bay Resort (e.g., HISTORIC RESORT AHEAD) and south of the resort's entrance. The trailhead is also opposite a large parking lot backed by a chain-link fence and on the east side of the highway; park here. A trailhead display stands about 100 feet west of the trailhead proper—difficult but not impossible to spot from the highway.

ON THE TRAIL The "trail" begins as a dirt road at a locked gate across that road just off SR 89. The gate bars the general public's vehicles from the road, but hikers may still meet vehicles on it. Beyond the gate, pass a big stump and head generally west on marked Forest Road 14N13. Follow the dusty road between a meadow on the left and a forested slope rising on the right; there is a wealth of wildflowers on display here in season. Presently, the meadow on the left gives way to forest. The road climbs very gradually as it lazily swings south. Near 1 mile glimpse another meadow off to the left, through the trees, and then, in a few more steps, reach a junction.

   Go right (west) on the dusty Tahoe-Yosemite Trail (TYT), climbing gradually to moderately, often through dense forest. Open areas offer few dramatic views except occasional over-the-shoulder views of Lake Tahoe. As the path approaches

Meeks Creek Lakes

a ridgeline, the forest thins and hikers traverse rocky outcrops. Rounding the ridge, the trail cuts through Meeks Creek's bracken- and alder-lined channel before reentering forest. At nearly 2 miles enter Desolation Wilderness; the trail, now duff, wanders levelly through moderate forest with a dense understory of bracken. Presently it swings through a sandy area dotted with sagebrush and mule ears and then climbs moderately to steeply on the rocky, switchbacking track. The trail levels out in damp forest and then crosses the creek on a footbridge at nearly 3 miles.

On the other side of Meeks Creek, the trail traverses below a ridge in dry forest and then climbs moderately and veers east around the head of a steep, west-trending gully. Emerge on a hot, chaparral-covered ridge nose, high above the east fork of Meeks Creek, and soon meet the creek again—it's a refreshing sight. At nearly 4 miles reach a junction. Go right (west) a few steps on the Lake Genevieve Trail to the lake at a little less than 4 miles and 7420 feet, prettier than any picture, especially as it's backed by the clifflike east slopes of Peak 7820.

Back on the TYT, climb a little to discover beautiful Crag Lake at nearly

4.25 miles and 7460 feet, the loveliest of these three lakes. For more solitude, press on, making a nearly level traverse a little above Crag Lake before climbing moderately toward Shadow Lake, crossing its outlet and spying Hidden Lake below, to the right. Bypassing a use trail to the right and steeply down to Hidden Lake, continue ahead to wind through gigantic boulders before reaching small Shadow Lake at almost 5 miles and 7660 feet. It's full of lily pads and surrounded by a forest of large, dead trees. Shadow Lake is a beaver pond; its rising waters have drowned the forest here. The beavers, which are not native to the Sierra, may be gone by the time you visit, but the pond remains. Shadow Lake is the most tranquil of the three lakes on this trip.

Return the way you came.

110 Five Lakes Basin

Place	Total Distance	Elevation	Difficulty Level	Type
Start		6560		
Largest, westernmost lake	4+	7500	M	O&B

Best Time   Late May–mid-October
Topos   *Tahoe City, Granite Chief* 7.5′
Where to Stay

   Mountain: Clair Tappaan Lodge, Meeks Bay Resort and Marina

   Other: Ice Lakes Lodge, Northstar at Tahoe, Rainbow Lodge Bed and Breakfast, Stanford Alpine Chalet, Summit House

   Towns and Agencies: Alpine Meadows, Castle Peak Vacation Rentals, Lake Tahoe Visitor Information, North Lake Tahoe Resort Association, Squaw Valley, Truckee Donner Chamber of Commerce

HIGHLIGHTS   This is a relatively easy hike to the attractive lakes of Granite Chief Wilderness's Five Lakes Basin. The maintained trail goes only to the largest, westernmost lake, but use trails dart off to the other, smaller lakes in the east part of the basin, inviting the adventurous to explore.

HOW TO GET TO THE TRAILHEAD   From the Tahoe Y, drive 30.9 miles north on SR 89, past the junction with State Route 28, to the turnoff west for Alpine Meadows Road and Alpine Meadows Ski Area. This turnoff is between the turnoff for Squaw Valley and the junction of SR 89 and SR 28 near Tahoe City. The trailhead, which may be unmarked on the road, is 2.1 more miles farther on Alpine Meadows Road, on the right, just opposite the much more obvious turnoff left onto Deer Park Road. Park on the shoulder, at 10.9 miles.

ON THE TRAIL   At the trailhead an information sign displays some warnings about Five Lakes Basin: it's day-use only. More troubling is the recommendation that

Five Lakes Basin

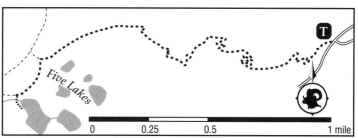

hikers should look out for unexploded ammunition used for avalanche control at adjacent Alpine Meadows Ski Area.

With one eye peeled for ammo and the other fixed on any children in the party, since they may think an unexploded shell is a toy, head west-southwest, climbing on long, nearly shadeless, dusty switchbacks through chaparral and under the occasional Jeffrey pine or white fir. The trail, lined with a handsome sprinkling of flowers in season, has more switchbacks than the topo shows. On the climb, the wooded hills up and down the canyon of the Truckee River come into view, as well as the bare knobs on Ward Peak above the ski area.

The grade eases as the track rounds a southwest-facing slope, and interesting pinnaclelike formations come into view uphill on the right. Cross a couple of runoff channels and negotiate another switchback or two on a gradual grade. Beyond, the trail swings briefly southwest toward some glaciated gray cliffs before crossing an outcrop of reddish rock. At 1 mile dip across a southeast-trending gully and then bypass a blocked-off use trail to the right.

Rounding an open ridge high above the gully now, ignore another use trail descending to the left and continue gradually up the main trail. Ahead rise interesting knobs, spires, cliffs, and outcrops in subtle shades of rust, gray, and orange—some are so dark and jagged they look volcanic while others are rounded and reminiscent of formations in Joshua Tree National Park in Southern California. A little past 1.3 miles pass a spring at the base of a dead tree before contouring around the head of the next gully, which is somewhat wetter and greener than the previous one. At somewhat over 1.5 miles, the path enters Granite Chief Wilderness. The trail soon levels out on a bench in the welcome shade of an open to moderate red fir forest, where the damper environment supports a lusher display of flowers than did the dry trail you just ascended.

Approaching 2 miles reach a junction. Go left (south-southwest) on the rocky and dusty trail, toward a forested hill and a bare, pyramidal little peak, and notice faint use trails darting off to the small lakes in the east part of this pretty little basin. Briefly trace the shore of the basin's westernmost, largest, and most trail-accessible lake and then reach a junction where a use trail branches left between huge firs. Take this use trail, cross the lake's alder-choked outlet, scramble over an outcrop, and find a view-filled spot on the west shore of the largest, westernmost lake in Five Lakes Basin, at a little more than 2 miles and 7500 feet. To the west, glimpse broad, brown Squaw Peak. The beautiful lakeside surroundings include fragrant red heather, sweetly singing birds, and shapely, droopy-topped mountain hemlocks. Return the way you came.

Interstate 80: Donner Summit Country

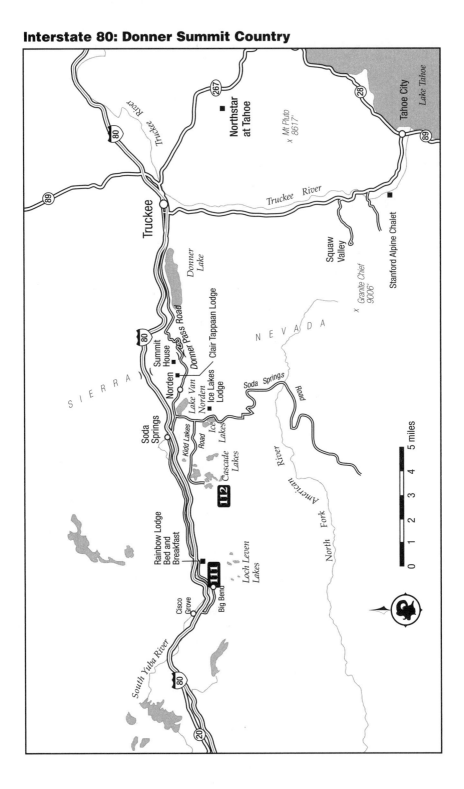

Lake Tahoe

Tahoe City

28

89

267

Northstar at Tahoe

x Mt Pluto 8617'

80

Truckee River

Truckee River

89

Squaw Valley

Stanford Alpine Chalet

x Granite Chief 9006'

Truckee

Donner Lake

NEVADA

80

Donner Pass Road

Summit House

Clair Tappaan Lodge

Norden

Lake Van Norden

Ice Lakes Lodge

Soda Springs

Soda Springs Road

SIERRA

Soda Springs

Kidd Lakes

Ice Lakes Road

Cascade Lakes

112

American River

North Fork

Rainbow Lodge Bed and Breakfast

Loch Leven Lakes

111

Cisco Grove

Big Bend

South Yuba River

80

20

0   1   2   3   4   5 miles

CHAPTER 13

Interstate 80: Donner Summit Country

Beyond the Alpine Meadows turnoff for Trip 110, State Route 89 continues north to Truckee to meet Interstate 80. I-80 roars in concrete, multilane, exhaust-fumed haste past Truckee and over Donner—a name that sends chills down the spine—Summit between Reno and Sacramento. The real Donner Pass and the site of the famous tragedy, Donner Lake, lie south of I-80 on old U.S. Highway 40.

Those interested in more about the Donner Party may want to visit Donner Lake and Donner Memorial State Park. A stop at the park's museum to learn more about the tragedy may keep you from asking, as a history-challenged friend of mine did, in jest, "Why didn't those Donners hang out in Reno till the weather got better and then take I-80?"

For hikers, there's good reason to linger here: A couple of outstanding hikes are just south of this incredibly busy road.

Recommended Maps

The following three maps are helpful when exploring this area:

- *Tahoe National Forest.* U.S. Department of Agriculture and U.S. Forest Service.
- *Lake Tahoe Basin Management Unit.* U.S. Department of Agriculture and U.S. Forest Service.
- *Lake Tahoe.* Tom Harrison Maps.

Individual Lodgings

Name	Nearest Community	Type	Facilities	Price Range	Contact Information	Website and Email Address
Clair Tappaan Lodge	Norden	Mountain	Rooms, dormitories	$	P.O. Box 36 Norden, CA 95724 Phone: 800-679-6775 or 530-426-3632	www.sierraclub.org/ outings/lodges/ctl/ ctl@sierraclub.org
Ice Lakes Lodge	Soda Springs	Mountain	Rooms	$$	P.O. Box 1100 Soda Springs, CA 95728 Phone: 800-500-3871 or 530-426-3871	www.icelakeslodge.com reservations@royalgorge. com
Northstar at Tahoe	Truckee	Other	Rooms, condos	$$$	P.O. Box 129 Truckee, CA 96160 Phone: 800-GO-NORTH	www.northstarattahoe. com
Rainbow Lodge Bed and Breakfast	Soda Springs	Other	Rooms	$$–$$$	P.O. Box 1100 Soda Springs, CA 95728 Phone: 800-500-3871 or 530-426-3871	www.royalgorge.com reservations@royalgorge. com
Stanford Alpine Chalet	Tahoe City	Mountain	Rooms	$–$$$	P.O. Box 6436 Tahoe City, CA 96145 Phone: 530-583-1550	www.stanfordalpine chalet.com www.stanfordalumni. org/learningtravel/sierra/ alpine-chalet/.home.html chalet@stanford.edu
Summit House	Norden	Other	Rooms, condos	$$–$$$	10150 Ski Ranch Lane Truckee, CA 96162 Phone: 530-426-9323	www.summithouse.com summit@summithouse. com

Towns and Agencies

Name	Nearest Community	Type	Contact Information	Website and Email Address
Alpine Meadows	Tahoe City	Agency	P.O. Box 5279 or 2600 Alpine Meadows Road Tahoe City, CA 96145 Phone: 800-949-3296 or 530-583-4232	http://skialpine.com info@skialpine.com
Castle Peak Vacation Rentals	Soda Springs	Agency	P.O. Box 979 Soda Springs, CA 95728 Phone: 888-253-5551 or 530-426-1226	www.castlepeak.com sue@castlepeak.com
Lake Tahoe Visitor Information (VirtualTahoe)	South Lake Tahoe	Agency	P.O. Box 7172 #173 Stateline, NV 89449 Phone: 800-210-3459, 800-371-2620, or 530-544-5050	www.virtualtahoe.com contactus@virtualtahoe.com
North Lake Tahoe Resort Association	Tahoe City	Chamber of Commerce/ Visitors Bureau	P.O. Box 1757 Tahoe City, CA 96145 Phone: 888-434-1262 or 530-583-3494	www.puretahoenorth.com info@puretahoenorth.com kym@puretahoenorth.com
Squaw Valley	Squaw Valley	Agency	Phone: 800-403-0206	www.squaw.com
Truckee Donner Chamber of Commerce	Truckee, Donner Lake	Chamber of Commerce	10065 Donner Pass Road Truckee, CA 96161 Phone: 530-587-2757	www.truckee.com info@truckee.com

111 Long Lake

Place	Total Distance	Elevation	Difficulty Level	Type
Start		6720		
Long Lake	1.3	6700	E U	O&B

Best Time   Late May–mid-October

Topos   *Soda Springs 7.5'*

Where to Stay

Mountain: Clair Tappaan Lodge

Other: Ice Lakes Lodge, Northstar at Tahoe, Rainbow Lodge Bed and Breakfast, Stanford Alpine Chalet, Summit House

Towns and Agencies: Alpine Meadows, Castle Peak Vacation Rentals, Lake Tahoe Visitor Information, North Lake Tahoe Resort Association, Squaw Valley, Truckee Donner Chamber of Commerce

HIGHLIGHTS Delightful Long Lake offers fine picnic spots and great scenery in exchange for a rough drive and a short but briefly trying hike.

HOW TO GET TO THE TRAILHEAD A high-clearance vehicle is desirable to reach this trailhead. Just 3.1 miles west of Donner Summit on I-80, get off at the Soda Springs exit and turn east on Donner Summit Road. Go 0.7 mile to Soda Springs Road; turn right and follow it 0.9 mile to Pahatsi Road. Turn right and follow it 3.9 miles to Devils Outlook Warming Hut; the road is unpaved, narrow, and rough beyond the buildings of Royal Gorge ski area. There is a large dirt parking area by Devils Outlook Warming Hut.

ON THE TRAIL After taking in the scenery—Devils Peak to the south-southwest is exceptionally striking—take off on foot south-southwest down a continuation of the road to a Y-junction in about 180 feet; take the left fork. The road is sparsely shaded and the going is sandy and rocky along a ridge with glimpses of upper Cascade Lake to the left and lower Cascade Lake to the right. At 0.25 mile reach the marked Palisades Creek Trailhead, and pause to enjoy the view of Cascade Lakes before heading very, very steeply down an old, blocked-off road toward the dam that separates upper and lower Cascade Lakes. Cross the dam to pick up a footpath in the shade of a patchy, moderate to dense lodgepole forest. In season, masses of red heather in bloom make the air incredibly sweet and fresh here. Pass between a low, rocky ridge to the left and seasonal tarns to the right, walking almost levelly, before making a very slight ascent between the ridge and a rocky outcrop. When beginning the descent, avoid a blocked-off use trail to the right.

Blue light sparkling ahead through the trees heralds your approach to Long Lake at 0.6 mile and 6700 feet. Numerous slabs along Long Lake's northeast shore offer excellent viewpoints overlooking this granite-cupped, bracken-fringed gem and its stern guardian, Devils Peak. Pick up and follow use trails along the lake's shore and down to the water's edge to fully experience this lovely lake.

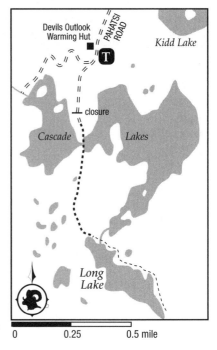

Long Lake

112 Loch Leven and Salmon Lakes

Place	Total Distance	Elevation	Difficulty Level	Type
Start		5740		
Lowest Loch Leven Lake	5.5	6780	M	O&B
Middle Loch Leven Lake	6.6	6780	S	O&B
High Loch Leven Lake	8.25	6860	S	O&B
Salmon Lake	7.3	6700	S	O&B
All four lakes	9.5+	6860	S	O&B

Best Time   Late May–mid-October

Topos   *Cisco Grove, Soda Springs 7.5'*

Where to Stay

Mountain: Clair Tappaan Lodge

Other: Ice Lakes Lodge, Northstar at Tahoe, Rainbow Lodge Bed and Breakfast, Stanford Alpine Chalet, Summit House

Towns and Agencies: Alpine Meadows, Castle Peak Vacation Rentals, Lake Tahoe Visitor Information, North Lake Tahoe Resort Association, Squaw Valley, Truckee Donner Chamber of Commerce

HIGHLIGHTS The beautiful Loch Leven Lakes are favorites of visitors to the Donner Summit area. Charming little Salmon Lake, just west of the Loch Leven Lakes, is nearly as pretty and sees far fewer visitors—quite a recommendation!

HOW TO GET TO THE TRAILHEAD Just 9.1 miles west of Donner Summit, get off I-80 at the Rainbow Road exit. Get oriented by driving to the Big Bend Visitor Center on Rainbow Road (sometimes called Hampshire Rocks Road; the way is well-signed). The visitor center, which has restrooms and water, is open daily in midsummer and on weekends only the rest of the year. From the visitor center, it is 0.1 mile northeast to the practical trailhead—at a gravel road on the east side of Rainbow Road—and 0.2 mile (0.1 mile beyond the trailhead) northeast to trailhead parking on the west side of Rainbow Road. Rainbow Lodge is 0.4 mile east of the trailhead parking. Restrooms and water are also available at nearby Big Bend Campground.

ON THE TRAIL From the practical trailhead, go southeast on that gravel road to reach the official, signed trailhead shortly. Leave the old road here and begin ascending a rocky, dusty, up-and-down, switchbacking foot trail that's very different from the one shown on the 7.5′ topo. The twisting trail heads first through moderate forest and then across open slabs with patches of flowers between

Loch Leven and Salmon Lakes

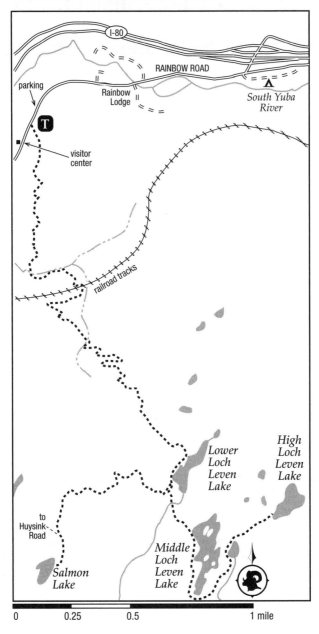

them. Around 0.6 mile, "steps" formed by slabs of rock lead steeply upward beside broad granite slabs that would otherwise demand friction-walking.

At a little more than 0.75 mile top out in forest on a duff trail and go south through terrain where the roar of nearby I-80 drowns out any birdsong. Approaching 1 mile, skirt an unmapped, lily-pad-speckled pond—probably seasonal—while climbing a little through outcrops on the pond's shore. Beyond the pond, descend an open slope and circle a pocket meadow bright with wildflowers. At a little more than 1 mile cross a tiny creek on a footbridge in an alder thicket. Climb away from the stream on a rocky trail that grows steeper as it nears some railroad tracks on the shelf above. At 1.3 miles, leave the forest and carefully cross the railroad tracks.

On the other side of the tracks, to the right of a green shed, reenter forest and begin a gradual to moderate ascent on long switchbacks, trending westward. Squish across seasonal seeps near the final set of rocky switchbacks. Finally, the grade eases on a forested bench as the trail curves generally southeast to emerge on a ridge from which there's a steep, rocky descent to the busiest lake, the lowest Loch Leven Lake at 2.75 miles and 6780 feet. Trace the lake's shore to its more open, south end, where there are, not only lots of visitors, but also a junction at nearly 3 miles: right (west) to Salmon Lake, and left (south) to the higher Loch Leven Lakes. Avoid a use trail that's also at this junction.

To go to the upper Loch Leven Lakes, take the middle fork south and down into a little gully and then up over a low ridge to Middle Loch Leven Lake at a little more than 3.3 miles and 6780 feet. This lake is far prettier and quieter than the first one. Continuing, follow the faint trail along the lake, with the help of blazes painted on trees and rocks. At the south end of the lake, find a junction. Go left to round the south end of the lake, and follow the faint, rocky trail past mostly unmapped tarns and over outlet streams. Ascend gradually except for a brief, very steep ascent up poor, rocky switchbacks atop which the track levels out again. A few more steps bring hikers to peaceful, beautiful High Loch Leven Lake at a little more than 4 miles and 6860 feet. It's the loveliest of these lakes. Its red-heather-fringed shores are the least visited of the three lakes, and there are many good spots from which to enjoy the scenery.

To go to Salmon Lake, take the right fork at the south end of the lowest Loch Leven Lake. Wind gradually up and over a ridge in patchy forest. Then dip briefly through a marshy spot and round the nose of the next ridge. Descend south-southwest moderately to steeply, winding through woods and open areas, and crossing a couple of seasonal channels. Reach a signed junction at 3.5 miles. Go ahead (south) to Salmon Lake, climbing a little over a low, rocky saddle. Descend moderately on a rocky track, level out in forest, and reach lodgepole- and granite-ringed Salmon Lake at 3.6 miles and 6700 feet. This pretty gem sees even fewer visitors than High Loch Leven Lake—enjoy!

Retrace your steps.

Top Picks

Best Overall

These hikes have superb combinations of scenery, views, lakes, flowers or fall color, and maybe even waterfalls.

5–7	10	13	41	55	64	67	70	71	95
104	106	107							

Best Wildflowers

Remember that wildflower displays are brief and seasonal and that the season's timing may vary from year to year. While most species peak in early season, some species, like gentians, may peak later.

4	5	10	11	13	15	18	23	38–39	43
67	87	92	94	95	96				

Best Waterfalls

Like wildflower displays, waterfalls are usually seasonal and short-lived; timing is everything. Hikes with stars (*) include at least one cascade that puts on a fair show throughout the hiking season, except in dry years.

4	25*	26	28*	36*	45	54	56	62
64*	66*	67*						

Most Lakes

All Sierra lakes are special; this category highlights hikes that visit lots of lakes—at least four beauties if you make the entire hike. The maximum number of lakes a hike visits is shown parenthetically.

3 (4)   6 (6)   7 (4–5) 8 (6)   13 (6–7) 37 (5)   55 (4)   70 (6)   112 (4)

Best Streamsides

For those who especially enjoy strolling along a stream, these hikes include lengthy streamside legs.

5	6	7	10	13	31	32	36	37	55
64	66	68	71	72	83	84	95		

Most Outstanding Views

Many hikes have fine views, but these hikes have one or more especially awe-inspiring, panoramic viewpoints.

1	22–24	30	43	46	48	49	51	52	63
64	66	78	79	93	107				

Interesting Ruins Along the Way

Seeing the ruins of old cabins and mining operations, and evidence of current operations, as these hikes do, is a special thrill for many hikers.

18	35	36	37	68	71	72	95	96

Giant Sequoias

If you're looking for giant sequoias, you'll find plenty on these hikes!

42	50	61

Best Fall Color

Like wildflower displays, fall color displays are seasonal and fleeting. Note that for Trips 30–34, 37, and 38, the best fall color display of the trip is along the drive to the trailhead.

9	10	15	31–36	39	55	60	66	68
82–84	109							

Best Meadows

Each of these hikes includes at least one big, beautiful, wet meadow. Like wildflower displays, the meadows you'll pass by or through on these hikes peak seasonally.

11	13	15	23	39	53	55	69	70	71
72	74	76	80	82	89	91	92	94	95
96	109								

Best Forests

For those who especially enjoy strolling among the trees, these hikes include lengthy forested legs.

9	12	17–23	25	40	42	45–48	50	55	60
61	74–80	84–86	88	91	98	103	109		

A Fine Destination with a Minimum of Effort

These hikes get you to a lovely destination, identified afterward, in less than 1 mile:

4:   First Falls

13: Viewpoint at Mono Pass-Morgan Pass junction

20: Emerald Lake

23: McCloud Lake

26: Devils Postpile or footbridge over San Joaquin

36: Falls at 0.6 mile

37: Blue Lake

51: Panoramic Point

53: Roaring River Falls

56: Rancheria Falls

61: California Tree

70: Greenstone Lake via ferry

90: Elephant Rock Lake

94: Frog Lake

101: Tamarack Lake via water-taxi

108: Waterfall at 0.2 mile

Hints for Staying in Lodgings

These hints are based on lessons I've learned the hard way. If you have other hints or other experiences, I'd like to hear from you. (You may contact me in care of Wilderness Press.)

- Remember that the experience of staying in true mountain lodgings and other lodgings of interest isn't necessarily a "House Beautiful" experience—it's more like "Mountains Beautiful, House Okay."

- Confirm before you book that the place has the facilities you want. Don't rely solely on web sites. Call or write for the latest brochure and study it before booking.

- Call a day or two before you leave home to confirm your reservation and any other arrangements of interest. If you expect to take your meals at the resort's restaurant, double-check before you leave home that the restaurant will be open while you are there and for all the meals you'll want to have there. If it won't meet your meal needs, ask about other restaurants in the area. If you plan to get groceries at the resort's store, double-check before you leave home to make sure that the store is open and well-stocked. If it will be closed, ask about other stores in the area or plan to bring your own groceries.

- Be patient. Leave your hurries as well as your worries at home. Time in the mountains—"mountain time"—moves more slowly than big-city time. For example, don't be upset if your meal doesn't arrive as promptly as it would at a big-city restaurant. Just tell yourself, "They're on mountain time." Also, since many lodgings are shoestring operations, they're chronically short-handed, which slows things down. So try to be on mountain time yourself!

- Take your sense of humor. When your visit rubs up against a resort's rougher edges, you'll be ready to laugh about it.

- Rustic cabins in the forest are apt to have the occasional mouse. If you want to stay where you're close to the deer and the bears, you can't help but be close to the mice, too. Safeguard your food by keeping everything except the canned food in the refrigerator or in a hard-sided cooler. Dispose of garbage promptly and properly.

- Don't get impatient if the hot water doesn't run hot right away. Let it run for awhile. Some places have to pipe the hot water quite a distance.

- Take it easy on the electricity. Many remote lodgings have to generate their own power, so leave your electricity-hungry widgets like hair dryers at home. A few lodgings save on generation by turning off the generator after a certain hour, say,

10 PM at night, and not turning it back on until, say, 6 AM in the morning. Be sure to bring flashlights!

■ Bring plenty of warm clothing. No matter how warm mountain days are, mountain nights can be very chilly. Don't forget slippers!

As every experienced traveler knows, even the best-run places can sometimes fall short. Carry the following with you to ease your stay: an all-purpose flat sink-stopper; a small sponge-and-scrubber pad; a can opener; a small bottle of biodegradable, all-purpose liquid soap like Camp Suds; rubber gloves for dishwashing and washing clothes; a travel clothesline; quarter-watt nightlights—one for each bedroom and for the bathroom—to help stave off nighttime disorientation in a strange place; working flashlights with extra bulbs and batteries, one for each person, to be kept at the bedside; a sewing kit; and a first-aid kit.

APPENDIX C

Backcountry Lodgings

This book doesn't include those lodgings reachable only by hikers and equestrians. Note that they are open only during the summer and that the exact dates vary from year to year, mostly depending on the previous winter's snowfall. After a very heavy winter, some camps may not open at all. Below is information about such lodgings in each of the national parks, in John Muir Wilderness, and in Giant Sequoia National Monument.

In Yosemite National Park

There are five High Sierra Camps in Yosemite wilderness: Glen Aulin, Merced Lake, Vogelsang, May Lake, and Sunrise. They are typically open from early July through early September. They range from 6.5 to 10 miles apart. Each camp has dormitory-style tent-cabins and a main building that includes a dining room, an office, a tiny store, and restrooms. Some have showers. The tent-cabins have steel-frame cots, mattresses, woolen blankets or comforters, and pillows. Linens aren't provided; those staying at such a lodge must bring a sheet sack as well as their own clothes, towels, toiletries, etc. Each night's stay includes dinner and breakfast in the dining room; sack lunches are available for an extra fee and can be ordered. Each camp also has an adjacent backpacker's campground, and backpackers can buy meals at the dining room as long as space is available. Stays at the five High Sierra Camps are initially booked by lottery: Apply at the end of a given year for a stay during the next season. After that, unreserved or canceled spaces are then available on a first-come, first-served basis. Ranger-guided trips that make a loop around these camps are also available; visitors dayhike between them. Book through the park's concessionaire, Delaware North, at www.yosemitepark.com/Accomodations_HighSierraCamps.aspx or call 559-253-5635 and ask for High Sierra Camps.

In Sequoia and Kings Canyon National Parks

Just outside the parks, in Giant Sequoia National Monument, find relatively luxurious Sequoia High Sierra Camp (www.sequoiahighsierracamp.com), also run by Delaware North. It's 1 or 11 miles by trail, depending on the trailhead. It has tent cabins and bungalows. The rates include three meals per day, which are prepared fresh daily. Guests need to carry in only their clothing and personal and dayhiking supplies.

Inside Sequoia National Park, find Bearpaw High Sierra Camp (also referred to as Bearpaw Meadow Lodge) along the first leg of the famed High Sierra Trail. It's 11.5 miles from the trailhead at Crescent Meadow, south of Giant Forest and is normally open June through September. There are six tent cabins and a lodge/dining room. Each cabin has twin beds with linens and towels; a third person can sleep on the floor but must bring a sleeping pad and bedding. The dining room serves breakfast and dinner (included in the lodge fee) only to guests, and guests can buy sack lunches. For more information, visit www.visitsequoia.com/1776.aspx or call 866-807-3598. Reservations are available beginning in January of the year you wish to book a stay. You must have a separate wilderness permit to hike into and stay at Bearpaw; contact the park at 559-565-3761 to reserve a permit, which must be picked up in person at Lodgepole Visitor Center. Unlike Yosemite's High Sierra Camps, Bearpaw does not offer meals to nonguests, but there is a tiny store where nonguests may find packaged snacks and other items.

In John Muir Wilderness

Historic Muir Trail Ranch is at Blayney Hot Springs, out of Florence Lake and along South Fork San Joaquin River and was "grandfathered" into the John Muir Wilderness. The ranch is typically open from June through September and offers log cabins, tent cabins, hot spring baths, horse corrals, and a lounge and dining room. Guests need to bring sleeping bags and towels. The ranch has horses, and equestrian activities are a specialty. Normally, stays are by the week only. Stays of less than a week are available from June through September. Visit www.muirtrailranch.com; email howdy@muirtrailranch.com; call 209-966-3195; or write Muir Trail Ranch at P.O. Box 176, Lakeshore, CA 93634 in summer or P.O. Box 700, Ahwahnee, CA 93601 in the off-season.

Travel in the Sierra

Travel in the Sierra is almost exclusively by car and is therefore determined by where the roads go. California's public transportation is woefully deficient. There's more on car travel below, but first, consider public transportation.

Public Transportation

The best area for public transportation is Yosemite National Park. There's a combined rail-bus option for getting to Yosemite Valley; call 800-321-8684 or see www.amtrakcalifornia.com/rail/go/amtrak/stations/u-z/yosemite-national-park/index.cfm. This option includes one-day trips from San Francisco with an open-air tram tour of the Valley. There's also a regional transportation system serving Yosemite from the west year-round and from the east when Tioga Pass is open. Visit www.yarts.com for information about the Yosemite Area Regional Transportation System (YARTS).

Within Yosemite Valley, there is a free shuttlebus system between major Valley points, including the Mirror Lake and John Muir trailheads (the latter for Vernal and Nevada falls). I like to begin my Valley visits by riding a shuttlebus all the way around its circuit to see the sights and get reoriented. Free shuttlebuses also run in the summer in the Wawona-Mariposa Grove area as well as in the Tuolumne Meadows area; see www.nps.gov/yose/planyourvisit/bus.htm. There are also concessionaire-operated bus tours to Glacier Point, Wawona and the Mariposa Grove, and Tuolumne Meadows. These operate in the summer and offer a one-way hiker option. For details, see www.nps.gov/yose/planyourvisit/tours.htm.

Within Sequoia National Park, there's a free shuttlebus system in the summer that connects Crescent Meadow on the south with Wuksachi on the north and points in between, with a transfer at Giant Forest Museum if necessary. For details, see www.nps.gov/seki/planyourvisit/publictransportation.htm or call 559-565-3341. In addition, the park plans a summertime, for-fee shuttlebus from the town of Visalia, through Three Rivers and up to Giant Forest Museum. Check the preceding website or call 559-713-4100 for details as this system develops.

There are several options for getting to Lake Tahoe: Check out the Tahoe Area Regional Transit (TART) at www.placer.ca.gov/Works/Transit/TART.aspx; call 530-550-1212 or 800-736-6365; or email tart@placer.ca.gov. Once at Lake Tahoe, TART operates a shuttlebus around "30 miles of Lake Tahoe shoreline." BlueGo also operates shuttle service in the Tahoe area, primarily in the towns of South Lake Tahoe and Stateline. Better suited to hikers is BlueGo's popular, summer Nifty Fifty Trolley service, combined with the Emerald Bay Trolley and the North Shore Emerald Bay Trolley for Tahoe's west shore. See www.bluego.org for more information about these options. Also for the west shore, check out the Tahoe Trolley at www.laketahoetransit.com. This site also provides links to the other transit options previously listed for the Tahoe area.

In the Mammoth Lakes area, there is a seasonal, mandatory, for-fee shuttlebus from Mammoth Mountain Ski/Mountain Bike area down to the Devils Postpile area, which serves all the area trailheads in this book. America the Beautiful Passes, Golden Passports, and National Park Passes are not accepted for the fee. The buses are not ADA-accessible; disabled visitors who can provide proof of their condition may drive their cars down. Be aware that the entire Devils Postpile area is only open seasonally, and opening and closing dates vary from year to year. Get more information at www. nps.gov/depo/planyourvisit/feesandreservations.htm or call 760-924-5500.

In this book, hikes in the Eastern Sierra are in either Inyo County or Mono County. Communities in Inyo and Mono counties are linked by the CREST Bus system, which further links these Eastern Sierra communities with Reno, Nevada, on the north and Ridgecrest, California, on the south. See inyo3d.org/Pages/county_depts/Transit.htm; call 760-872-1901 or 800-922-1930; write to P.O. Box 1357, Bishop, CA 93515; or email imtransit@schat.com. As of this writing, there is no formal system to get people from a CREST stop to a particular trailhead. However, the nearest ranger station usually maintains a list of people and services (if any) who can, for a fee, drive hikers to and from trailheads.

Private Transportation

For many visitors, only a car will offer the flexibility they need to enjoy their lodgings *and* their walks. Here are some suggestions for driving to and around the Sierra.

From the greater Los Angeles area, destinations on the east side and west side of the Sierra require roughly the same driving time. From the greater San Francisco and Sacramento areas, northern Sierra destinations are nearest, particularly those on the west sides of the major highways crossing the Sierra. From Reno, destinations on the east side of the northern Sierra are nearest.

Once in the Sierra, driving is generally slow because the roads are narrow, and they climb and wind. Take your time; don't expect to reach, much less maintain, freeway speeds! In spite of their worldwide fame, Sequoia and Kings Canyon and Yosemite national parks are served by very slow, windy two-lane roads. Also, allow a full day to change your base of operations, even if it's just, for example, from lodgings on one highway to lodgings on the next highway south.

Whether you rent a car or drive your own car, be sure the car is "trailhead-worthy." Under "trailhead-worthiness," I include a car's reliability, fuel economy, and attractiveness/vulnerability to thieves, vandals, and bears. Choose a modest-looking car to avoid tempting thieves and vandals, which do exist in the Sierra. A high-clearance car will be useful on those Sierra roads that get very rough. If a road becomes too bad but you know that the trailhead is close enough for you to walk to comfortably, then you can park and walk the rest of the way to the trailhead. Whatever car you take, be sure it's in good, safe condition before you hit the road, and take good care of it. Check and replenish its vital fluids, including the air in the tires, often. Always make sure to have plenty of gas before heading out. Gas may be unavailable in remote places (e.g., Yosemite Valley).

Never leave food in a car, if at all possible—it is an invitation to bears. A bear's sense of smell is 300 times more sensitive than yours, and bears have been known to tear a car apart to get half a candy bar. At some national park trailheads, there are large, steel, food-storage lockers where people can temporarily stash food and other fragrant items. Everyone at the trailhead shares the temporary use of these lockers; you may not put your own lock on them. If you must leave food in a car, wrap it well in odor-containing materials, put it in a cooler, and then cover the cooler with a blanket or tarp. In the Sierra, bears recognize food-storage containers like bags and coolers and will go after them.

Store everything left in the car out of sight—but not in the trunk, which is exceptionally easy to break into. Instead, carry everything of value with you in your daypack, and cover everything left in the car with blankets or lightweight, inexpensive tarps, to avoid tempting bears and thieves. No matter how hot it is, never leave the windows cracked open; you'd just be giving thieves and bears a head start. A cracked-open window also makes it easier for bears to smell any food in the car.

Never leave a pet in a car or tied up outside while you hike. The temperature inside a car can quickly rise to a lethal level. A tied-up pet is easy prey for bears, coyotes, and mountain lions.

Never hitchhike and never pick up a hitchhiker. Crimes involving hitchhikers do occur in the Sierra.

I strongly recommend joining a national auto club and signing up for its long-range emergency roadside service. You'll find its travel agency, maps, tour guides, emergency roadside service, and trip-planning advice invaluable. A membership will repay you handsomely in just one visit: with a wide selection of free, accurate, up-to-date road maps of California and the Sierra and with comprehensive tour guides for California. Whether you join one or not, arm yourself with road maps and tour guides.

Carry a cell phone on the road and also on the trail. The help you can summon with a cell phone, if a cell signal is available, may save a life. Too often there isn't a signal, but it's always worth a try.

How I Got the Data

I estimated hiking distances primarily by time, knowing that I hike an average of 2 miles per hour. I compared the distances I got by time with distance values supplied by the agencies in charge of the trails. When those distances were close, I felt satisfied with the distance I'd estimated by time. I usually rounded the distances off to the nearest quarter mile.

I got most driving distances from my car's odometer, which was consistent to within ±0.1 mile over routes I drove repeatedly. In those cases where I did not get usable odometer data, I used data from other reliable maps, principally the maps from the Automobile Club of Southern California.

I determined elevation from topos and with an altimeter. Where I had altimeter data, I looked for close correspondence between those values, topo values, and any values supplied by the agency in charge of the trail.

For the maps, I used relevant pieces of the USGS or Wilderness Press topos as a base. I left out the elevation contours because they are complicated and would have made these grayscale maps too busy. I added, deleted, or modified topo information that I knew had changed since the area had been scouted for my base map. My choices of conventions for trails, roads, boundaries, and so on, primarily reflect the capabilities of the software I used. A few trails do not appear at all on the topos or in usable form on any official agency map. For them, I approximated the route based on field notes and sketches and any other information I could find.

Trails change constantly. If, as you take these trips, you find significant differences between what's in this book and what's on the ground, differences that you think are not just the result of two different people looking at the same thing, please contact me in care of Wilderness Press at info@wildernesspress.com.

Index of Accommodations

Individual Lodging	Region	Chapter(s)
The Ahwahnee	Western Sierra	The Valleys of Yosemite National Park
Annett's Mono Village	Eastern Sierra	June Lake to Bridgeport
Base Camp Lodge	Northern Sierra	State Route 4
Bear Valley Lodge and Village Resort	Northern Sierra	State Route 4
Bishop Creek Lodge and Resort	Eastern Sierra	Lone Pine to Convict Lake
Camp Richardson Resort	Northern Sierra	State Route 89 Around Lake Tahoe
Caples Lake Resort	Northern Sierra	State Routes 88 and 89
Cardinal Village Resort	Eastern Sierra	Lone Pine to Convict Lake
Cedar Grove Lodge	Western Sierra	Sequoia and Kings Canyon National Parks
Clair Tappaan Lodge	Northern Sierra	State Route 89 Around Lake Tahoe Interstate 80
Convict Lake Resort	Eastern Sierra	Lone Pine to Convict Lake Mammoth Lakes June Lake to Bridgeport
Crystal Crag Lodge	Eastern Sierra	Lone Pine to Convict Lake Mammoth Lakes June Lake to Bridgeport
Curry Village	Western Sierra	The Valleys of Yosemite National Park
Dardanelle Resort	Northern Sierra	State Route 108
Doc and Al's Robinson Creek Resort	Eastern Sierra	June Lake to Bridgeport
Double Eagle Resort and Spa	Eastern Sierra	Lone Pine to Convict Lake Mammoth Lakes June Lake to Bridgeport State Route 120
Echo Chalet	Northern Sierra	U.S. Highway 50
Evergreen Lodge	Western Sierra	The Valleys of Yosemite National Park
Falcon's Nest Bed and Breakfast	Western Sierra	The Valleys of Yosemite National Park
Glacier Lodge	Eastern Sierra	Lone Pine to Convict Lake
Grant Grove Cabins	Western Sierra	Sequoia and Kings Canyon National Parks
Housekeeping Camp	Western Sierra	The Valleys of Yosemite National Park
Hunewill Guest Ranch	Eastern Sierra	June Lake to Bridgeport
Huntington Lake Resort	Western Sierra	Between the Parks
Ice Lakes Lodge	Northern Sierra	State Route 89 Around Lake Tahoe Interstate 80
John Muir Lodge	Western Sierra	Sequoia and Kings Canyon National Parks
Kennedy Meadows Resort and Pack Station	Northern Sierra	State Route 108
Kirkwood Ski and Summer Resort	Northern Sierra	State Routes 88 and 89
Kit Carson Lodge	Northern Sierra	State Routes 88 and 89
Kyburz Resort Motel	Northern Sierra	U.S. Highway 50

Individual Lodging	Region	Chapter(s)
Lake Alpine Lodge	Northern Sierra	State Route 4
Lakeshore Resort	Western Sierra	Between the Parks
Lakeview Cottages	Western Sierra	Between the Parks
Lundy Lake Resort	Eastern Sierra	June Lake to Bridgeport State Route 120
Mammoth Mountain Chalets	Eastern Sierra	Lone Pine to Convict Lake Mammoth Lakes June Lake to Bridgeport
Mammoth Mountain Inn	Eastern Sierra	Lone Pine to Convict Lake Mammoth Lakes June Lake to Bridgeport
McGee Creek Lodge	Eastern Sierra	Lone Pine to Convict Lake Mammoth Lakes June Lake to Bridgeport
Meeks Bay Resort and Marina	Northern Sierra	State Route 89 Around Lake Tahoe
Mono Hot Springs Resort	Western Sierra	Between the Parks
Mono Sierra Lodge	Eastern Sierra	Lone Pine to Convict Lake Mammoth Lakes June Lake to Bridgeport
Montecito Sequoia Lodge	Western Sierra	Sequoia and Kings Canyon National Parks
Northstar at Tahoe	Northern Sierra	State Route 89 Around Lake Tahoe Interstate 80
Parchers Resort	Eastern Sierra	Lone Pine to Convict Lake
Pinecrest Chalet	Northern Sierra	State Route 108
Pinecrest Lake Resort	Northern Sierra	State Route 108
Rainbow Lodge Bed and Breakfast	Northern Sierra	State Route 89 Around Lake Tahoe Interstate 80
Rainbow Tarns Bed and Breakfast	Eastern Sierra	Lone Pine to Convict Lake Mammoth Lakes
Red's Meadow Resort	Eastern Sierra	Mammoth Lakes
The Rivers Resort	Northern Sierra	State Route 108
Rock Creek Lakes Resort	Eastern Sierra	Lone Pine to Convict Lake Mammoth Lakes
Rock Creek Lodge	Eastern Sierra	Lone Pine to Convict Lake Mammoth Lakes
Sierra Gables Motel	Eastern Sierra	Lone Pine to Convict Lake June Lake to Bridgeport
Silver City Mountain Resort	Western Sierra	Sequoia and Kings Canyon National Parks
Silver Lake Resort	Eastern Sierra	Lone Pine to Convict Lake Mammoth Lakes June Lake to Bridgeport State Route 120
Sorensen's Resort	Northern Sierra	State Routes 88 and 89
Stanford Alpine Chalet	Northern Sierra	State Route 89 Around Lake Tahoe Interstate 80
Stony Creek Lodge	Western Sierra	Sequoia and Kings Canyon National Parks

Individual Lodging	Region	Chapter(s)
Strawberry Inn	Northern Sierra	State Route 108
Strawberry Lodge	Northern Sierra	U.S. Highway 50
Summit House	Northern Sierra	State Route 89 Around Lake Tahoe Interstate 80
Tamarack Lodge	Western Sierra	Between the Parks
Tamarack Lodge Bed and Breakfast	Northern Sierra	State Route 4
Tamarack Lodge and Resort	Eastern Sierra	Lone Pine to Convict Lake Mammoth Lakes June Lake to Bridgeport
Tioga Lodge	Eastern Sierra	Mammoth Lakes June Lake to Bridgeport State Route 120
Tioga Pass Resort	Eastern Sierra	June Lake to Bridgeport State Route 120
Tom's Place Resort	Eastern Sierra	Lone Pine to Convict Lake Mammoth Lakes
Tuolumne Meadows Lodge	Eastern Sierra	June Lake to Bridgeport State Route 120
Twin Lakes Resort	Eastern Sierra	June Lake to Bridgeport
Vermilion Valley Resort	Western Sierra	Between the Parks
Virginia Creek Settlement	Eastern Sierra	June Lake to Bridgeport
Virginia Lakes Resort	Eastern Sierra	June Lake to Bridgeport State Route 120
Wawona Hotel	Western Sierra	The Valleys of Yosemite National Park
Whispering Pines Resort	Eastern Sierra	Lone Pine to Convict Lake Mammoth Lakes June Lake to Bridgeport State Route 120
White Wolf Lodge	Northern Sierra	State Route 120
Wildyrie Lodge	Eastern Sierra	Lone Pine to Convict Lake Mammoth Lakes June Lake to Bridgeport
Woodfords Inn	Northern Sierra	State Routes 88 and 89
Woods Lodge	Eastern Sierra	Lone Pine to Convict Lake Mammoth Lakes June Lake to Bridgeport
Wuksachi Lodge	Western Sierra	Sequoia and Kings Canyon National Parks
Yosemite Lodge	Western Sierra	The Valleys of Yosemite National Park
Yosemite Peregrine Bed and Breakfast	Western Sierra	The Valleys of Yosemite National Park
Yosemite West High Sierra Bed and Breakfast	Western Sierra	The Valleys of Yosemite National Park

Index of Towns and Agencies

Town or Agency	Region	Chapter(s)
Alpine County Chamber of Commerce (represents Markleeville, Woodfords, etc.)	Northern Sierra	State Routes 88 and 89
Alpine Meadows	Northern Sierra	State Route 89 Around Lake Tahoe Interstate 80
Amador County Chamber of Commerce and Visitors Bureau	Western Sierra	State Routes 88 and 89
Bear Valley Vacation Rentals	Western Sierra	State Route 4
Big Pine Chamber of Commerce and Visitors Bureau	Eastern Sierra	Lone Pine to Convict Lake
Bishop Area Chamber of Commerce and Visitors Bureau	Eastern Sierra	Lone Pine to Convict Lake
Bridgeport Chamber of Commerce	Eastern Sierra	June Lake to Bridgeport State Route 108
Castle Peak Vacation Rentals	Northern Sierra	State Route 89 Around Lake Tahoe Interstate 80
El Dorado County Visitors Authority	Northern Sierra	U.S. Highway 50
Independence Chamber of Commerce	Eastern Sierra	Lone Pine to Convict Lake
June Lake Chamber of Commerce	Eastern Sierra	Lone Pine to Convict Lake Mammoth Lakes June Lake to Bridgeport State Route 120
K&K Property Management	Western Sierra	Between the Parks
Lake Tahoe Visitor Information (VirtualTahoe)	Northern Sierra	State Routes 88 and 89 U.S. Highway 50 State Route 89 Around Lake Tahoe Interstate 80
Lee Vining Chamber of Commerce	Eastern Sierra	Mammoth Lakes June Lake to Bridgeport State Route 120
Lone Pine Chamber of Commerce	Eastern Sierra	Lone Pine to Convict Lake
Mammoth Lakes Visitors Bureau	Eastern Sierra	Lone Pine to Convict Lake Mammoth Lakes June Lake to Bridgeport
Mariposa County Chamber of Commerce	Western Sierra	The Valleys of Yosemite National Park
North Lake Tahoe Resort Association	Northern Sierra	State Route 89 Around Lake Tahoe Interstate 80
National Park Service: Accommodations Outside and Between Sequoia and Kings Canyon Parks	Western Sierra	Sequoia and Kings Canyon National Parks
Recreation.gov	Western Sierra	Sequoia and Kings Canyon National Parks
The Redwoods	Western Sierra	The Valleys of Yosemite National Park
The Reservation Centre	Western Sierra	Sequoia and Kings Canyon National Parks

Town or Agency	Region	Chapter(s)
Sequoia Foothills Chamber of Commerce	Western Sierra	Sequoia and Kings Canyon National Parks
Shaver Lake Chamber of Commerce	Western Sierra	Between the Parks
South Lake Tahoe Chamber of Commerce	Northern Sierra	State Route 89 Around Lake Tahoe U.S. Highway 50 State Route 89 Around Lake Tahoe
Squaw Valley	Northern Sierra	State Route 89 Around Lake Tahoe Interstate 80
Truckee Donner Chamber of Commerce	Northern Sierra	State Route 89 Around Lake Tahoe Interstate 80
Tuolumne County Visitors Bureau	Western Sierra	State Route 108
Yosemite Lodging and Vacation Rentals	Western Sierra	The Valleys of Yosemite National Park
Yosemite Sierra Visitors Bureau	Western Sierra	The Valleys of Yosemite National Park
Yosemite West Condominiums	Western Sierra	The Valleys of Yosemite National Park
Yosemite's Four Seasons	Western Sierra	The Valleys of Yosemite National Park
Yosemite's Scenic Wonders	Western Sierra	The Valleys of Yosemite National Park

Index

Acknowledgments

Many, many thanks to Marshalle Wells-Genevieve for her hard work in updating the information on lodgings. Thanks to Ed Schwartz for his support. I am deeply indebted to the staff at Wilderness Press, particularly Laura Shauger and Roslyn Bullas, for their editorial skills and their patience, and Lisa Pletka for her fine layout. Great thanks to the many people who offered photos for this volume, even if we didn't in the end use them. Finally, I cannot thank enough my mentor and inspiration, Thomas Winnett, the founder of Wilderness Press.

About the Author

The backpacking bug hit Kathy Morey hard in the 1970s and hasn't let go yet. In 1990 she abandoned an aerospace career to write for Wilderness Press, authoring four hiking guides on Hawaii—*Hawaii Trails*, *Kauai Trails*, *Maui Trails*, and *Oahu Trails*—and *Guide to the John Muir Trail*, in addition to *Hot Showers, Soft Beds, & Dayhikes in the Sierra*. Kathy coauthored several previous editions of *Sierra North* and *Sierra South* and served as lead author for the most recent editions of both. She lives in Big Pine, California.